David Hume

Essays - Moral, Political, and Literary

Vol. II

David Hume

Essays - Moral, Political, and Literary
Vol. II

ISBN/EAN: 9783337073602

Printed in Europe, USA, Canada, Australia, Japan

Cover: Foto ©ninafisch / pixelio.de

More available books at **www.hansebooks.com**

ESSAYS

MORAL, POLITICAL, AND LITERARY

BY DAVID HUME

EDITED WITH PRELIMINARY DISSERTATIONS AND NOTES BY

T. H. GREEN   AND   T. H. GROSE

FELLOW AND TUTOR OF BALLIOL
COLLEGE, OXFORD

FELLOW AND TUTOR OF QUEEN'S
COLLEGE, OXFORD

IN TWO VOLUMES

VOL. II.

NEW IMPRESSION

LONGMANS, GREEN, AND CO.
39 PATERNOSTER ROW, LONDON
NEW YORK AND BOMBAY
1898

BIBLIOGRAPHICAL NOTE

First printed January 1873.
Reprinted September 1882; *January* 1889;
July 1898.

CONTENTS

THE SECOND VOLUME.

———

CONCERNING HUMAN UNDERSTANDING.

A DISSERTATION ON THE PASSIONS.

CONCERNING THE PRINCIPLES OF MORALS.

AN

ENQUIRY

CONCERNING

HUMAN

UNDERSTANDING.

B

AN ENQUIRY

CONCERNING HUMAN UNDERSTANDING.

SECT. I.—*Of the Different Species of Philosophy.*

MORAL philosophy, or the science of human nature, may be treated after two different manners; each of which has its peculiar merit, and may contribute to the entertainment, instruction, and reformation of mankind. The one considers man chiefly as born for action; and as influenced in his measures by taste and sentiment; pursuing one object, and avoiding another, according to the value which these objects seem to possess, and according to the light in which they present themselves. As virtue, of all objects, is allowed to be the most valuable, this species of philosophers paint her in the most amiable colours; borrowing all helps from poetry and eloquence, and treating their subject in an easy and obvious manner, and such as is best fitted to please the imagination, and engage the affections. They select the most striking observations and instances from common life; place opposite characters in a proper contrast; and alluring us into the paths of virtue by the views of glory and happiness, direct our steps in these paths by the soundest precepts and most illustrious examples. They make us *feel* the difference between vice and virtue; they excite and regulate our sentiments; and so they can but bend our hearts to the love of probity and true honour, they think, that they have fully attained the end of all their labours.

The other species of philosophers consider man in the light of a reasonable rather then an active being, and endeavour to form his understanding more than cultivate his manners. They regard human nature as a subject of speculation; and with a narrow scrutiny examine it, in order to find those principles, which regulate our understanding,

B 2

excite our sentiments, and make us approve or blame any particular object, action, or behaviour. They think it a reproach to all literature, that philosophy should not yet have fixed, beyond controversy, the foundation of morals, reasoning, and criticism : and should for ever talk of truth and falsehood, vice and virtue, beauty and deformity, without being able to determine the source of these distinctions. While they attempt this arduous task, they are deterred by no difficulties; but proceeding from particular instances to general principles, they still push on their enquiries to principles more general, and rest not satisfied till they arrive at those original principles, by which, in every science, all human curiosity must be bounded. Though their speculations seem abstract, and even unintelligible to common readers, they aim at the approbation of the learned and the wise; and think themselves sufficiently compensated for the labour of their whole lives, if they can discover some hidden truths, which may contribute to the instruction of posterity.

It is certain that the easy and obvious philosophy will always, with the generality of mankind, have the preference above the accurate and abstruse; and by many will be recommended, not only as more agreeable, but more useful than the other. It enters more into common life; moulds the heart and affections; and, by touching those principles which actuate men, reforms their conduct, and brings them nearer to that model of perfection which it describes. On the contrary, the abstruse philosophy, being founded on a turn of mind, which cannot enter into business and action, vanishes when the philosopher leaves the shade, and comes into open day; nor can its principles easily retain any influence over our conduct and behaviour. The feelings of our heart, the agitation of our passions, the vehemence of our affections, dissipate all its conclusions, and reduce the profound philosopher to a mere plebeian.

This also must be confessed, that the most durable, as well as justest fame, has been acquired by the easy philosophy, and that abstract reasoners seem hitherto to have enjoyed only a momentary reputation, from the caprice or ignorance of their own age, but have not been able to support their renown with more equitable posterity. It is easy for a profound philosopher to commit a mistake in his subtile reasonings; and one mistake is the necessary parent of another, while he pushes on his consequences, and is not deterred from embracing any conclusion, by its unusual appearance, or its contradiction to popular opinion.   But a philosopher, who purposes only to represent the common sense of mankind in more beautiful and more engaging colours, if by accident he falls into error, goes no farther; but renewing his appeal to common sense, and the natural sentiments of the mind, returns into the right path, and secures himself from any dangerous illusions.   The fame of Cicero flourishes at present; but that of Aristotle is utterly decayed.   La Bruyere passes the seas, and still maintains his reputation: But the glory of Malebranche is confined to his own nation, and to his own age.   And Addison, perhaps, will be read with pleasure, when Locke shall be entirely forgotten.[1]

The mere philosopher is a character, which is commonly but little acceptable in the world, as being supposed to contribute nothing either to the advantage or pleasure of society; while he lives remote from communication with mankind, and is wrapped up in principles and notions equally remote from their comprehension.   On the other hand, the mere ignorant is still more despised; nor is any thing deemed a surer sign of an illiberal genius in an age and nation where the sciences flourish, than to be entirely destitute of all relish for those noble entertainments.   The most perfect character is supposed to lie between those extremes; retaining an equal ability and taste for books, company, and business; preserving in conversation that discernment and delicacy which arise from polite letters; and in business, that probity and accuracy which are the natural result of a just philosophy.   In order to diffuse and cultivate so accomplished a character, nothing can be more useful than compositions of the easy style and manner, which draw not too much from life, require no deep application or retreat to be comprehended, and send back the student among mankind full of noble sentiments and wise precepts, applicable to every exigence of human life.   By means of such compositions, virtue becomes amiable, science agreeable, company instructive, and retirement entertaining.

[1] [Editions E and F add the note: This is not intended any way to detract from the Merit of Mr. *Locke*, who was really a great Philosopher, and a just and modest Reasoner. 'Tis only meant to shew the common Fate of such abstract Philosophy.]

Man is a reasonable being; and as such, receives from science his proper food and nourishment : But so narrow are the bounds of human understanding, that little satisfaction can be hoped for in this particular, either from the extent or security of his acquisitions. Man is a sociable, no less than a reasonable being : But neither can he always enjoy company agreeable and amusing, or preserve the proper relish for them. Man is also an active being; and from that disposition, as well as from the various necessities of human life, must submit to business and occupation : But the mind requires some relaxation, and cannot always support its bent to care and industry. It seems, then, that nature has pointed out a mixed kind of life as most suitable to human race, and secretly admonished them to allow none of these biasses to *draw* too much, so as to incapacitate them for other occupations and entertainments. Indulge your passion for science, says she, but let your science be human, and such as may have a direct reference to action and society. Abstruse thought and profound researches I prohibit, and will severely punish, by the pensive melancholy which they introduce, by the endless uncertainty in which they involve you, and by the cold reception which your pretended discoveries shall meet with, when communicated. Be a philosopher; but, amidst all your philosophy, be still a man.

Were the generality of mankind contented to prefer the easy philosophy to the abstract and profound, without throwing any blame or contempt on the latter, it might not be improper, perhaps, to comply with this general opinion, and allow every man to enjoy, without opposition, his own taste and sentiment. But as the matter is often carried farther, even to the absolute rejecting of all profound reasonings, or what is commonly called *metaphysics*, we shall now proceed to consider what can reasonably be pleaded in their behalf.

We may begin with observing, that one considerable advantage, which results from the accurate and abstract philosophy, is, its subserviency to the easy and humane: which, without the former, can never attain a sufficient degree of exactness in its sentiments, precepts, or reasonings. All polite letters are nothing but pictures of human life in various attitudes and situations; and inspire us with different sentiments, of praise or blame, admiration or ridicule, according to the qualities of the object, which they set before us. An artist must be better qualified to succeed in this undertaking, who, besides a delicate taste and a quick apprehension, possesses an accurate knowledge of the internal fabric, the operations of the understanding, the workings of the passions, and the various species of sentiment which discriminate vice and virtue. How painful soever this inward search or enquiry may appear, it becomes, in some measure, requisite to those, who would describe with success the obvious and outward appearances of life and manners. The anatomist presents to the eye the most hideous and disagreeable objects; but his science is useful to the painter in delineating even a VENUS or an HELEN. While the latter employs all the richest colours of his art, and gives his figures the most graceful and engaging airs; he must still carry his attention to the inward structure of the human body, the position of the muscles, the fabric of the bones, and the use and figure of every part or organ. Accuracy is, in every case, advantageous to beauty, and just reasoning to delicate sentiment. In vain would we exalt the one by depreciating the other.

Besides, we may observe, in every art or profession, even those which most concern life or action, that a spirit of accuracy, however acquired, carries all of them nearer their perfection, and renders them more subservient to the interests of society. And though a philosopher may live remote from business, the genius of philosophy, if carefully cultivated by several, must gradually diffuse itself throughout the whole society, and bestow a similar correctness on every art and calling. The politician will acquire greater foresight and subtility, in the subdividing and balancing of power; the lawyer more method and finer principles in his reasonings; and the general more regularity in his discipline, and more caution in his plans and operations. The stability of modern governments above the ancient, and the accuracy of modern philosophy, have improved, and probably will still improve, by similar gradations.

Were there no advantage to be reaped from these studies, beyond the gratification of an innocent curiosity, yet ought not even this to be despised: as being one accession to those few safe and harmless pleasures, which are bestowed on human race. The sweetest and most inoffensive path of life leads through the avenues of science and learning; and whoever can either remove any obstructions in this way, or open up any new prospect, ought so far to be esteemed a benefactor to mankind. And though these researches may appear painful and fatiguing, it is with some minds as with some bodies, which being endowed with vigorous and florid health, require severe exercise, and reap a pleasure from what, to the generality of mankind, may seem burdensome and laborious. Obscurity, indeed, is painful to the mind as well as to the eye; but to bring light from obscurity, by whatever labour, must needs be delightful and rejoicing.

But this obscurity in the profound and abstract philosophy, is objected to, not only as painful and fatiguing, but as the inevitable source of uncertainty and error. Here indeed lies the justest and most plausible objection against a considerable part of metaphysics, that they are not properly a science; but arise either from the fruitless efforts of human vanity, which would penetrate into subjects utterly inaccessible to the understanding, or from the craft of popular superstitions, which, being unable to defend themselves on fair ground, raise these intangling brambles to cover and protect their weakness. Chaced from the open country, these robbers fly into the forest, and lie in wait to break in upon every unguarded avenue of the mind, and overwhelm it with religious fears and prejudices. The stoutest antagonist, if he remit his watch a moment, is oppressed. And many, through cowardice and folly, open the gates to the enemies, and willingly receive them with reverence and submission, as their legal sovereigns.

But is this a sufficient reason, why philosophers should desist from such researches, and leave superstition still in possession of her retreat? Is it not proper to draw an opposite conclusion, and perceive the necessity of carrying the war into the most secret recesses of the enemy? In vain do we hope, that men, from frequent disappointment, will at last abandon such airy sciences, and discover the proper province of human reason. For, besides, that many persons find too sensible an interest in perpetually recalling such topics; besides this, I say, the motive of blind despair can never reasonably have place in the sciences; since, however unsuccessful former attempts may have proved, there is still room to hope, that the industry, good fortune, or improved sagacity of succeeding generations may reach discoveries unknown to former ages. Each adventurous genius will still leap at the arduous prize, and find himself stimulated, rather than discouraged, by the failures of his predecessors; while he hopes that the glory of atchieving so hard an adventure is reserved for him alone. The only method of freeing learning, at once, from these abstruse questions, is to enquire seriously into the nature of human understanding, and shew, from an exact analysis of its powers and capacity, that it is by no means fitted for such remote and abstruse subjects. We must submit to this fatigue, in order to live at ease ever after: And must cultivate true metaphysics with some care, in order to destroy the false and adulterate. Indolence, which, to some persons, affords a safeguard against this deceitful philosophy, is, with others, overbalanced by curiosity; and despair, which, at some moments, prevails, may give place afterwards to sanguine hopes and expectations. Accurate and just reasoning is the only catholic remedy, fitted for all persons and all dispositions; and is alone able to subvert that abstruse philosophy and metaphysical jargon, which, being mixed up with popular superstition, renders it in a manner impenetrable to careless reasoners, and gives it the air of science and wisdom.

Besides this advantage of rejecting, after deliberate enquiry, the most uncertain and disagreeable part of learning, there are many positive advantages, which result from an accurate scrutiny into the powers and faculties of human nature. It is remarkable concerning the operations of the mind, that, though most intimately present to us, yet, whenever they become the object of reflection, they seem involved in obscurity; nor can the eye readily find those lines and boundaries, which discriminate and distinguish them. The objects are too fine to remain long in the same aspect or situation; and must be apprehended in an instant, by a superior penetration, derived from nature, and improved by habit and reflection. It becomes, therefore, no inconsiderable part of science barely to know the different operations of the mind, to separate them from each other, to class them under their proper heads, and to correct all that seeming disorder, in which they lie involved, when made the object of reflection and enquiry. This task of ordering and distinguishing, which has no merit, when performed with regard to external bodies, the objects of our senses, rises in its value, when directed towards the operations of the mind, in proportion to the difficulty and labour, which we meet with in performing it. And if we can go no farther than this mental geography, or delineation of the distinct parts and powers of the mind, it is at least a satisfaction to go so far; and the more obvious this science may appear (and it is by no means obvious) the more contemptible still must the ignorance of it be esteemed, in all pretenders to learning and philosophy.

Nor can there remain any suspicion, that this science is uncertain and chimerical; unless we should entertain such a scepticism as is entirely subversive of all speculation, and even action. It cannot be doubted, that the mind is endowed with several powers and faculties, that these powers are distinct from each other, that what is really distinct to the immediate perception may be distinguished by reflection ; and consequently, that there is a truth and falsehood in all propositions on this subject, and a truth and falsehood, which lie not beyond the compass of human understanding. There are many obvious distinctions of this kind, such as those between the will and understanding, the imagination and passions, which fall within the comprehension of every human creature ; and the finer and more philosophical distinctions are no less real and certain, though more difficult to be comprehended. Some instances, especially late ones, of success in these enquiries, may give us a juster notion of the certainty and solidity of this branch of learning. And shall we esteem it worthy the labour of a philosopher to give us a true system of the planets, and adjust the position and order of those remote bodies ; while we affect to overlook those, who, with so much success, delineate the parts of the mind, in which we are so intimately concerned ?[1]

[1] [Editions E and F append the note:
That Faculty, by which we discern Truth and Falshood, and that by which we perceive Vice and Virtue had long been confounded with each other, and all Morality was supposed to be built on eternal and immutable Relations, which, to every intelligent Mind, were equally invariable as any Proposition concerning Quantity or Number. But a' late Philosopher has taught us, by the most convincing Arguments, that Morality is nothing in the abstract Nature of Things, but is entirely relative to the Sentiment or mental Taste of each particular Being ; in the same Manner as the Distinctions of sweet and bitter, hot and cold, arise from the particular feeling of each Sense or Organ. Moral Perceptions therefore, ought not to be class'd with the Operations of the Understanding, but with the Tastes or Sentiments.

It had been usual with Philosophers to divide all the Passions of the Mind into two Classes, the selfish and bene-

[Mr. Hutcheson.]

But may we not hope, that philosophy, if cultivated with care, and encouraged by the attention of the public, may carry its researches still farther, and discover, at least in some degree, the secret springs and principles, by which the human mind is actuated in its operations? Astronomers had long contented themselves with proving, from the phænomena, the true motions, order, and magnitude of the heavenly bodies: Till a philosopher, at last, arose, who seems, from the happiest reasoning, to have also determined the laws and forces, by which the revolutions of the planets are governed and directed. The like has been performed with regard to other parts of nature. And there is no reason to despair of equal success in our enquiries concerning the mental powers and œconomy, if prosecuted with equal capacity and caution. It is probable, that one operation and principle of the mind depends on another; which, again, may be resolved into one more general and universal: And how far these researches may possibly be carried, it will be difficult for us, before, or even after, a careful trial, exactly to determine. This is certain, that attempts of this kind are every day made even by those who philosophize the most negligently: And nothing can be more requisite than to enter upon the enterprize with thorough care and attention; that, if it lie within the compass of human understanding, it may at last be happily atchieved; if not, it may, however,

volent, which were suppos'd to stand in constant Opposition and Contrariety; nor was it thought that the latter could ever attain their proper Object but at the Expense of the former. Among the selfish Passions were rank'd Avarice, Ambition, Revenge: Among the benevolent, natural Affection, Friendship, Public spirit. Philosophers may now perceive the Impropriety of this Division. It has been prov'd, beyond all Controversy, that even the Passions, commonly esteem'd selfish, carry the Mind beyond Self, directly to the Object; that tho' the Satisfaction of these Passions gives us Enjoyment, yet the Prospect of this Enjoyment is not the Cause of the Passion, but on the contrary the Passion is antecedent to the Enjoyment, and without the former, the latter could never possibly exist; that the Case is precisely the same with the Passions, denominated benevolent, and consequently that a Man is no more interested when he seeks his own Glory than when the Happiness of his Friend is the Object of his Wishes; nor is he any more disinterested when he sacrifices his Ease and Quiet to public Good than when he labours for the Gratification of Avarice or Ambition. Here therefore is a considerable Adjustment in the Boundaries of the Passions, which had been confounded by the Negligence or Inaccuracy of former Philosophers. These two Instances may suffice to show us the Nature and Importance of this Species of Philosophy.]

[See Butler's Sermons.]

be rejected with some confidence and security. This last conclusion, surely, is not desirable; nor ought it to be embraced too rashly. For how much must we diminish from the beauty and value of this species of philosophy, upon such a supposition? Moralists have hitherto been accustomed, when they considered the vast multitude and diversity of those actions that excite our approbation or dislike, to search for some common principle, on which this variety of sentiments might depend. And though they have sometimes carried the matter too far, by their passion for some one general principle; it must, however, be confessed, that they are excusable in expecting to find some general principles, into which all the vices and virtues were justly to be resolved. The like has been the endeavour of critics, logicians, and even politicians: Nor have their attempts been wholly unsuccessful; though perhaps longer time, greater accuracy, and more ardent application may bring these sciences still nearer their perfection. To throw up at once all pretensions of this kind may justly be deemed more rash, precipitate, and dogmatical, than even the boldest and most affirmative philosophy, that has ever attempted to impose its crude dictates and principles on mankind.

What though these reasonings concerning human nature seem abstract, and of difficult comprehension? This affords no presumption of their falsehood. On the contrary, it seems impossible, that what has hitherto escaped so many wise and profound philosophers can be very obvious and easy. And whatever pains these researches may cost us, we may think ourselves sufficiently rewarded, not only in point of profit but of pleasure, if, by that means, we can make any addition to our stock of knowledge, in subjects of such unspeakable importance.

But as, after all, the abstractedness of these speculations is no recommendation, but rather a disadvantage to them, and as this difficulty may perhaps be surmounted by care and art, and the avoiding of all unnecessary detail, we have, in the following enquiry, attempted to throw some light upon subjects, from which uncertainty has hitherto deterred the wise, and obscurity the ignorant. Happy, if we can unite the boundaries of the different species of philosophy, by reconciling profound enquiry with clearness, and truth with novelty! And still more happy, if, reasoning in this easy manner, we can undermine the foundations of an abstruse philosophy, which seems to have hitherto served only as a shelter to superstition, and a cover to absurdity and error!

SECT. II. - *Of the Origin of Ideas.*

EVERY one will readily allow, that there is a considerable difference between the perceptions of the mind, when a man feels the pain of excessive heat, or the pleasure of moderate warmth, and when he afterwards recalls to his memory this sensation, or anticipates it by his imagination. These faculties may mimic or copy the perceptions of the senses; but they never can entirely reach the force and vivacity of the original sentiment. The utmost we say of them, even when they operate with greatest vigour, is, that they represent their object in so lively a manner, that we could *almost* say we feel or see it : But, except the mind be disordered by disease or madness, they never can arrive at such a pitch of vivacity, as to render these perceptions altogether undistinguishable. All the colours of poetry, however splendid, can never paint natural objects in such a manner as to make the description be taken for a real landskip. The most lively thought is still inferior to the dullest sensation.

We may observe a like distinction to run through all the other perceptions of the mind. A man in a fit of anger, is actuated in a very different manner from one who only thinks of that emotion. If you tell me, that any person is in love, I easily understand your meaning, and form a just conception of his situation ; but never can mistake that conception for the real disorders and agitations of the passion. When we reflect on our past sentiments and affections, our thought is a faithful mirror, and copies its objects truly ; but the colours which it employs are faint and dull, in comparison of those in which our original perceptions were clothed. It requires no nice discernment or metaphysical head to mark the distinction between them.

Here therefore we may divide all the perceptions of the mind into two classes or species, which are distinguished by their different degrees of force and vivacity. The less forcible and lively are commonly denominated THOUGHTS or IDEAS. The other species want a name in our language, and in most others; I suppose, because it was not requisite for any, but philosophical purposes, to rank them under a general term or appellation. Let us, therefore, use a little freedom, and call them IMPRESSIONS; employing that word in a sense somewhat different from the usual. By the term *impression*, then, I mean all our more lively perceptions, when we hear, or see, or feel, or love, or hate, or desire, or will. And impressions are distinguished from ideas, which are the less lively perceptions, of which we are conscious, when we reflect on any of those sensations or movements above mentioned.

Nothing, at first view, may seem more unbounded than the thought of man, which not only escapes all human power and authority, but is not even restrained within the limits of nature and reality. To form monsters, and join incongruous shapes and appearances, costs the imagination no more trouble than to conceive the most natural and familiar objects. And while the body is confined to one planet, along which it creeps with pain and difficulty; the thought can in an instant transport us into the most distant regions of the universe; or even beyond the universe, into the unbounded chaos, where nature is supposed to lie in total confusion. What never was seen, or heard of, may yet be conceived; nor is any thing beyond the power of thought, except what implies an absolute contradiction.

But though our thought seems to possess this unbounded liberty, we shall find, upon a nearer examination, that it is really confined within very narrow limits, and that all this creative power of the mind amounts to no more than the faculty of compounding, transposing, augmenting, or diminishing the materials afforded us by the senses and experience. When we think of a golden mountain, we only join two consistent ideas, *gold*, and *mountain*, with which we were formerly acquainted. A virtuous horse we can conceive; because, from our own feeling, we can conceive virtue; and this we may unite to the figure and shape of a horse, which is an animal familiar to us. In short, all the materials of thinking are derived either from our outward or inward sentiment: The mixture and composition of these belongs alone to the mind and will. Or, to express myself in philosophical language, all our ideas or more feeble perceptions are copies of our impressions or more lively ones.

To prove this, the two following arguments will, I hope, be sufficient. First, when we analyse our thoughts or ideas, however compounded or sublime, we always find, that they resolve themselves into such simple ideas as were copied from a precedent feeling or sentiment. Even those ideas, which, at first view, seem the most wide of this origin, are found, upon a nearer scrutiny, to be derived from it. The idea of God, as meaning an infinitely intelligent, wise, and good Being, arises from reflecting on the operations of our own mind, and augmenting, without limit, those qualities of goodness and wisdom. We may prosecute this enquiry to what length we please; where we shall always find, that every idea which we examine is copied from a similar impression. Those who would assert, that this position is not universally true nor without exception, have only one, and that an easy method of refuting it; by producing that idea, which, in their opinion, is not derived from this source. It will then be incumbent on us, if we would maintain our doctrine, to produce the impression or lively perception, which corresponds to it.

Secondly. If it happen, from a defect of the organ, that a man is not susceptible of any species of sensation, we always find, that he is as little susceptible of the correspondent ideas. A blind man can form no notion of colours; a deaf man of sounds. Restore either of them that sense, in which he is deficient; by opening this new inlet for his sensations, you also open an inlet for the ideas; and he finds no difficulty in conceiving these objects. The case is the same, if the object, proper for exciting any sensation, has never been applied to the organ. A LAPLANDER or NEGROE has no notion of the relish of wine. And though there are few or no instances of a like deficiency in the mind, where a person has never felt or is wholly incapable of a sentiment or passion, that belongs to his species; yet we find the same observation to take place in a less degree. A man of mild manners can form no idea of inveterate revenge or cruelty; nor can a selfish heart easily conceive the heights of friendship and generosity. It is readily allowed, that other beings may possess many senses of which we can have no conception; because the ideas of them have never been introduced to us, in the only manner, by which an idea can have access to the mind, to wit, by the actual feeling and sensation.

There is, however, one contradictory phænomenon, which may prove, that it is not absolutely impossible for ideas to arise, independent of their correspondent impressions. I believe it will readily be allowed, that the several distinct ideas of colour, which enter by the eye, or those of sound, which are conveyed by the ear, are really different from each other; though, at the same time, resembling. Now if this be true of different colours, it must be no less so of the different shades of the same colour; and each shade produces a distinct idea, independent of the rest. For if this should be denied, it is possible, by the continual gradation of shades, to run a colour insensibly into what is most remote from it; and if you will not allow any of the means to be different, you cannot, without absurdity, deny the extremes to be the same. Suppose, therefore, a person to have enjoyed his sight for thirty years, and to have become perfectly acquainted with colours of all kinds, except one particular shade of blue, for instance, which it never has been his fortune to meet with. Let all the different shades of that colour, except that single one, be placed before him, descending gradually from the deepest to the lightest; it is plain, that he will perceive a blank, where that shade is wanting, and will be sensible, that there is a greater distance in that place between the contiguous colours than in any other. Now I ask, whether it be possible for him, from his own imagination, to supply this deficiency, and raise up to himself the idea of that particular shade, though it had never been conveyed to him by his senses? I believe there are few but will be of opinion that he can: And this may serve as a proof, that the simple ideas are not always, in every instance, derived from the correspondent impressions; though this instance is so singular, that it is scarcely worth our observing, and does not merit, that for it alone we should alter our general maxim.

Here, therefore, is a proposition, which not only seems, in itself, simple and intelligible; but, if a proper use were made of it, might render every dispute equally intelligible, and banish all that jargon, which has so long taken possession of metaphysical reasonings, and drawn disgrace upon them. All ideas, especially abstract ones, are naturally faint and obscure: The mind has but a slender hold of them: They are apt to be confounded with other resembling ideas; and when we have often employed any term, though without a distinct meaning, we are apt to imagine it has a determinate idea, annexed to it. On the contrary, all impressions, that is, all sensations, either outward or inward, are strong and vivid : The limits between them are more exactly determined : Nor is it easy to fall into any error or mistake with regard to them. When we entertain, therefore, any suspicion, that a philosophical term is employed without any meaning or idea (as is but too frequent), we need but enquire, *from what impression is that supposed idea derived ?* And if it be impossible to assign any, this will serve to confirm our suspicion. By bringing ideas into so clear a light, we may reasonably hope to remove all dispute, which may arise, concerning their nature and reality.[1]

SECT. III.—*Of the [2]Association of Ideas.*

IT is evident, that there is a principle of connexion between the different thoughts or ideas of the mind, and that, in their appearance to the memory or imagination, they introduce each other with a certain degree of method and regularity. In our more serious thinking or discourse, this is so observable, that any particular thought, which breaks in upon the regular tract or chain of ideas, is immediately remarked and rejected. And even in our wildest and most wandering reveries, nay in our very dreams, we shall find,

[1] It is probable that no more was meant by those, who denied innate ideas, than that all ideas were copies of our impressions; though it must be confessed, that the terms, which they employed, were not chosen with such caution, nor so exactly defined, as to prevent all mistakes about their doctrine. For what is meant by *innate*? If innate be equivalent to natural, then all the perceptions and ideas of the mind must be allowed to be innate or natural, in whatever sense we take the latter word, whether in opposition to what is uncommon, artificial, or miraculous. If by innate be meant, cotemporary to our birth, the dispute seems to be frivolous; nor is it worth while to enquire at what time thinking begins, whether before, at, or after our birth. Again, the word *idea*, seems to be commonly taken in a very loose sense, by *Locke* and others; as standing for any of our perceptions,

our sensations and passions, as well as thoughts. Now in this sense, I should desire to know, what can be meant by asserting, that self-love, or resentment of injuries, or the passion between the sexes is not innate?

But admitting these terms, *impressions* and *ideas*, in the sense above explained, and understanding by *innate*, what is original or copied from no precedent perception, then may we assert, that all our impressions are innate, and our ideas not innate.

To be ingenuous, I must own it to be my opinion, that Mr. LOCKE was betrayed into this question by the schoolmen, who, making use of undefined terms, draw out their disputes to a tedious length, without ever touching the point in question. A like ambiguity and circumlocution seem to run through all that great philosopher's reasonings on this as well as most other subjects.

[2] [Connexion: Editions E and F.

if we reflect, that the imagination ran not altogether at adventures, but that there was still a connexion upheld among the different ideas, which succeeded each other. Were the loosest and freest conversation to be transcribed, there would immediately be observed something, which connected it in all its transitions. Or where this is wanting, the person, who broke the thread of discourse, might still inform you, that there had secretly revolved in his mind a succession of thought, which had gradually led him from the subject of conversation. Among different languages, even where we cannot suspect the least connexion or communication, it is found, that the words, expressive of ideas, the most compounded, do yet nearly correspond to each other : A certain proof, that the simple ideas, comprehended in the compound ones, were bound together by some universal principle, which had an equal influence on all mankind.

Though it be too obvious to escape observation, that different ideas are connected together ; I do not find, that any philosopher has attempted to enumerate or class all the principles of association ; a subject, however, that seems worthy of curiosity. To me, there appear to be only three principles of connexion among ideas, namely, *Resemblance, Contiguity* in time or place, and *Cause* or *Effect*.

That these principles serve to connect ideas will not, I believe, be much doubted. A picture naturally leads our thoughts to the original : [1] The mention of one apartment in a building naturally introduces an enquiry or discourse concerning the others : [2] And if we think of a wound, we can scarcely forbear reflecting on the pain which follows it.[3] But that this enumeration is compleat, and that there are no other principles of association, except these, may be difficult to prove to the satisfaction of the reader, or even to a man's own satisfaction. All we can do, in such cases, is to run over several instances, and examine carefully the principle, which binds the different thoughts to each other, never stopping till we render the principle as general as possible.[4] The more instances we examine, and the more care we em-

---

[1] Resemblance.
[2] Contiguity.
[3] Cause and Effect.
[4] For instance, Contrast or Contrariety is also a connexion among Ideas : But it may, perhaps, be considered as a mixture of *Causation* and *Resemblance*. Where two objects are contrary, the one destroys the other ; that is, the cause of its annihilation, and the idea of the annihilation of an object, implies the idea of its former existence.

OF THE ASSOCIATION OF IDEAS. 19

ploy, the more assurance shall we acquire, that the enumeration, which we form from the whole, is compleat and entire.[1]

[1] [In Editions E to Q the Essay continues: Instead of entering into a detail of this kind, which would lead into many useless subtilties, we shall consider some of the effects of this connexion upon the passions and imagination; where we may open a field of speculation more entertaining, and perhaps more instructive, than the other.

As man is a reasonable being, and is continually in pursuit of happiness, which he hopes to attain by the gratification of some passion or affection, he seldom acts or speaks or thinks without a purpose and intention. He has still some object in view; and however improper the means may sometimes be, which he chuses for the attainment of his end, he never loses view of an end, nor will he so much as throw away his thoughts or reflections, where he hopes not to reap any satisfaction from them.

In all compositions of genius, therefore, 'tis requisite that the writer have some plan or object; and tho' he may be hurried from this plan by the vehemence of thought, as in an ode, or drop it carelessly, as in an epistle or essay, there must appear some aim or intention in his first setting out, if not in the composition of the whole work. A production without a design would resemble more the raving of a madman, than the sober efforts of genius and learning.

As this rule admits of no exception, it follows, that in narrative compositions, the events or actions, which the writer relates, must be connected together, by some bond or tye: They must be related to each other in the imagination, and form a kind of *Unity*, which may bring them under one plan or view, and which may be the object or end of the writer in his first undertaking.

This connecting principle among the several events, which form the subject of a poem or history, may be very different, according to the different designs of the poet or historian. Ovid has formed his plan upon the connecting principle of resemblance. Every fabulous transformation, produced by the miraculous power of the gods, falls within the compass of his work. There needs but this one circumstance in any event to bring it under his original plan or intention.

An annalist or historian who should undertake to write the history of Europe during any century, would be influenced by the connexion of contiguity in time and place. All events, which happen in that portion of space, and period of time, are comprehended in his design, tho' in other respects different and unconnected. They have still a species of unity, amidst all their diversity.

But the most usual species of connexion among the different events, which enter into any narrative composition, is that of cause and effect: while the historian traces the series of actions according to their natural order, remounts to their secret springs and principles, and delineates their most remote consequences. He chuses for his subject a certain portion of that great chain of events, which compose the history of mankind: Each link in this chain he endeavours to touch in his narration. Sometimes unavoidable ignorance renders all his attempts fruitless: Sometimes, he supplies by conjecture what is wanting in knowledge: And always, he is sensible, that the more unbroken the chain is, which he presents to his readers, the more perfect is his production. He sees, that the knowledge of causes is not only the most satisfactory; this relation or connexion being the strongest of all others; but also the most instructive; since it is by this knowledge alone, we are enabled to controul events, and govern futurity.

Here therefore we may attain some notion of that *Unity of Action*, about which all critics, after ARISTOTLE, have talked so much: Perhaps, to little purpose, while they directed not their taste or sentiment by the accuracy of philosophy. It appears, that in all productions, as well as in the epic and tragic, there is a certain unity required, and that, on no occasion, can our thoughts be allowed to run at adventures, if we would produce a work, which will give any lasting entertainment to mankind. It appears also, that even a biographer, who should write the life of ACHILLES, would connect the events, by shewing their mutual dependence and relation, as much as a poet, who should make the

SECT. IV.—*Sceptical Doubts concerning the Operations of the Understanding.*

PART I.

ALL the objects of human reason or enquiry may naturally be divided into two kinds, to wit, *Relations of Ideas*, and *Matters of Fact.* Of the first kind are the sciences of Geometry, Algebra, and Arithmetic; and in short, every affirmation, which is either intuitively or demonstratively certain. *That the square of the hypothenuse is equal to the square of the two sides*, is a proposition, which expresses a

anger of that hero, the subject of his narration.[1] Not only in any limited portion of life, a man's actions have a dependence on each other, but also during the whole period of his duration, from the cradle to the grave; nor is it possible to strike off one link, however minute, in this regular chain, without affecting the whole series of events, which follow. The unity of action, therefore, which is to be found in biography or history, differs from that of epic poetry, not in kind, but in degree. In epic poetry, the connexion among the events is more close and sensible: The narration is not carried on thro' such a length of time: And the actors hasten to some remarkable period, which satisfies the curiosity of the reader. This conduct of the epic poet depends on that particular situation of the *Imagination* and of the *Passions*, which is supposed in that production. The imagination, both of writer and reader, is more enlivened, and the passions more enflamed than in history, biography, or any species of narration, which confine themselves to strict truth and reality. Let us consider the effect of these two circumstances, an enlivened imagination and enflamed passions, circumstances, which belong to poetry, especially the epic kind, above any other species of composition: and let us examine the reason why they require a stricter and closer unity in the fable.

First. All poetry, being a species

of painting, approaches us nearer to the objects than any other species of narration, throws a stronger light upon them, and delineates more distinctly those minute circumstances, which, tho' to the historian they seem superfluous, serve mightily to enliven the imagery, and gratify the fancy. If it be not necessary, as in the *Iliad*, to inform us each time the hero buckles his shoes, and ties his garters, it will be requisite, perhaps, to enter into a greater detail than in the HENRIADE; where the events are run over with such rapidity, that we scarce have leisure to become acquainted with the scene or action. Were a poet, therefore, to comprehend in his subject any great compass of time or series of events, and trace up the death of HECTOR to its remote causes, in the rape of HELEN, or the judgment of PARIS, he must draw out his poem to an immeasurable length, in order to fill this large canvas with just painting and imagery. The reader's imagination, enflamed with such a series of poetical descriptions, and his passions, agitated by a continual sympathy with the actors, must flag long before the period of the narration, and must sink into lassitude and disgust, from the repeated violence of the same movements.

Secondly. That an epic poet must not trace the causes to any great distance, will farther appear, if we consider another reason, which is drawn from a property of the passions still more re-

---

[1] Contrary to ARISTOTLE, Μῦθος δ' ἐστὶν εἷς, οὐχ ὥσπερ τινὲς οἴονται, ἐὰν περὶ ἕνα ᾖ. πολλὰ γὰρ καὶ ἄπειρα τῷ γένει συμβαίνει, ἐξ ὧν ἐνίων οὐδέν ἐστιν ἕν. οὕτω δὲ καὶ πράξεις ἑνὸς πολλαί εἰσιν, ἐξ ὧν μία οὐδεμία γίνεται πρᾶξις, &c. Κεφ. ή. 1450Α.

relation between these figures. *That three times five is equal to the half of thirty*, expresses a relation between these numbers. Propositions of this kind are discoverable by the

markable and singular. 'Tis evident, that in a just composition, all the affections, excited by the different events, described and represented, add mutual force to each other; and that while the heroes are all engaged in one common scene, and each action is strongly connected with the whole, the concern is continually awake, and the passions make an easy transition from one object to another. The strong connection of the events, as it facilitates the passage of the thought or imagination from one to another, facilitates also the transfusion of the passions, and preserves the affections still in the same channel and direction. Our sympathy and concern for EVE prepares the way for a like sympathy with ADAM: The affection is preserved almost entire in the transition; and the mind seizes immediately the new object as strongly related to that which formerly engaged its attention. But were the poet to make a total digression from his subject, and introduce a new actor, nowise connected with the personages, the imagination, feeling a breach in the transition, would enter coldly into the new scene, would kindle by slow degrees; and in returning to the main subject of the poem, would pass, as it were, upon foreign ground, and have its concern to excite anew, in order to take party with the principal actors. The same inconvenience follows in a less degree, where the poet traces his events to too great a distance, and binds together actions, which tho' not entirely disjoined, have not so strong a connexion as is requisite to forward the transition of the passions. Hence arises the artifice of the oblique narration, employed in the

Odyssey and *Æneid*; where the hero is introduced, at first, near the period of his designs, and afterwards shows us, as it were in perspective, the more distant events and causes. By this means, the reader's curiosity is immediately excited: The events follow with rapidity, and in a very close connexion: And the concern is preserved alive, and, by means of the near relation of the objects, continually increases, from the beginning to the end of the narration.

The same rule takes place in dramatic poetry; nor is it ever permitted, in a regular composition, to introduce an actor, who has no connexion, or but a small one, with the principal personages of the fable. The spectator's concern must not be diverted by any scenes, disjoined and separated from the rest. This breaks the course of the passions, and prevents that communication of the several emotions, by which one scene adds force to another, and transfuses the pity and terror, which it excites, upon each succeeding scene, 'till the whole produces that rapidity of movement, which is peculiar to the theatre. How must it extinguish this warmth of affection to be entertained, on a sudden, with a new action and new personages, no wise related to the former; to find so sensible a breach or vacuity in the course of the passions, by means of this breach in the connexion of ideas; and instead of carrying the sympathy of one scene into the following, to be obliged every moment, to excite a new concern, and take party in a new scene of action?

'To return to the comparison of history and epic poetry, we may conclude, from the foregoing reasonings, that as

――― ――― ―――

[1] [Editions E to N insert the following paragraph:— But tho' this rule of unity of action be common to dramatic and epic poetry; we may still observe a difference betwixt them, which may, perhaps, deserve our attention. In both these species of composition, 'tis requisite the action be one and simple, in order to preserve the concern or sympathy entire and undiverted: but in epic or narrative poetry, this rule is

also establish'd upon another foundation, viz. the necessity, that is incumbent on every writer, to form some plan or design, before he enter on any discourse or narration, and to comprehend his subject in some general aspect or united view, which may be the constant object of his attention. As the author is entirely lost in dramatic compositions, and the spectator supposes himself to be really present at the actions mere operation of thought, without dependence on what is any where existent in the universe. Though there never were a circle or triangle in nature, the truths, demonstrated by EUCLID, would for ever retain their certainty and evidence.

Matters of fact, which are the second objects of human reason, are not ascertained in the same manner; nor is our

---

a certain unity is requisite in all productions, it cannot be wanting to history more than to any other; that in history, the connexion among the several events, which unites them into one body, is the relation of cause and effect, the same which takes place in epic poetry; and that in the latter composition, this connexion is only required to be closer and more sensible, on account of the lively imagination and strong passions, which must be touched by the poet in his narration. The PELOPONNESIAN war is a proper subject for history, the siege of ATHENS for an epic poem, and the death of ALCIBIADES for a tragedy.

As the difference, therefore, between history and epic poetry consists only in the degrees of connexion, which bind together those several events, of which their subject is composed, it will be difficult, if not impossible, by words, to determine exactly the bounds which separate them from each other. That is a matter of taste more than of reasoning; and perhaps, this unity may often be discovered in a subject, where, at first view, and from an abstract consideration, we should least expect to find it.

'Tis evident, that HOMER, in the course of his narration, exceeds the first proposition of his subject; and that the anger of ACHILLES, which caused the death of HECTOR, is not the same with that which produced so many ills to the GREEKS. But the strong connexion between these two movements, the quick transition from one to another, the contrast between the effects of concord and discord among the princes, and the natural curiosity which we have to see ACHILLES in action, after such long repose; all these causes carry on the reader, and produce a sufficient unity in the subject.

It may be objected to MILTON, that he has traced up his causes to too great a distance, and that the rebellion of the angels produces the fall of man by a train of events, which is both very long and very casual. Not to mention that the creation of the world, which he has related at length, is no more the cause of that catastrophe, than of the battle of PHARSALIA, or any other

---

represented; this *reason* has no place with regard to the stage; but any dialogue or conversation may be introduc'd, which, without improbability, might have pass'd in that determinate portion of space, represented by the theatre. Hence in all our ENGLISH comedies, even those of CONGREVE, the unity of action is never strictly observ'd; but the poet thinks it sufficient, if his personages be any way related to each other, by blood, or by living in the same family; and he afterwards introduces them in particular scenes, where they display their humors and characters, without much forwarding the main action. The double plots of TERENCE are licenses of the same kind; but in a lesser degree. And tho' this conduct be not perfectly regular, it is not wholly unsuitable to the nature of comedy, where the movements and passions are not rais'd to such a height as in tragedy; at the same time, that the fiction or representation palliates, in some degree, such licenses. In a narrative poem, the first proposition or design confines the author to one subject; and any digressions of this nature would, at first view, be rejected as absurd and monstrous. Neither BOCCACE, LA FONTAINE, nor any author of that kind, tho' pleasantry be their chief object, have ever indulg'd them.]

‡ Contrast or contrariety is a connexion among ideas, which may, perhaps, be considered as a mixture of causation and resemblance. Where two objects are contrary, the one destroys the other, i. e. is the cause of its annihilation, and the idea of the annihilation of an object implies the idea of its former existence.

evidence of their truth, however great, of a like nature with the foregoing. The contrary of every matter of fact is still possible; because it can never imply a contradiction, and is conceived by the mind with the same facility and distinctness, as if ever so conformable to reality. *That the sun will not rise to-morrow* is no less intelligible a proposition, and implies no more contradiction, than the affirmation, *that it will rise.* We should in vain, therefore, attempt to demonstrate its falsehood. Were it demonstratively false, it would imply a contradiction, and could never be distinctly conceived by the mind.

It may, therefore, be a subject worthy of curiosity, to enquire what is the nature of that evidence, which assures us of any real existence and matter of fact, beyond the present testimony of our senses, or the records of our memory. This part of philosophy, it is observable, has been little cultivated, either by the ancients or moderns; and therefore our doubts and errors, in the prosecution of so important an enquiry, may be the more excusable; while we march through such difficult paths, without any guide or direction. They may even prove useful, by exciting curiosity, and destroying that implicit faith and security, which is the bane of

event, that has ever happened. But if we consider, on the other hand, that all these events, the rebellion of the angels, the creation of the world, and the fall of man, *resemble* each other, in being miraculous and out of the common course of nature; that they are supposed to be *contiguous* in time; and that being detached from all other events, and being the only original facts, which revelation discovers, they strike the eye at once, and naturally recall each other to the thought or imagination: If we consider all these circumstances, I say, we shall find, that these parts of the action have a sufficient unity to make them be comprehended in one fable or narration. To which we may add, that the rebellion of the angels and the fall of man have a peculiar resemblance, as being counterparts to each other, and presenting to the reader the same moral, of obedience to our Creator.

These loose hints I have thrown together, in order to excite the curiosity of philosophers, and beget a suspicion at least, if not a full persuasion, that this subject is very copious, and that many operations of the human mind depend on the connexion or association of ideas, which is here explained. Particularly, the sympathy between the passions and imagination will, perhaps, appear remarkable; while we observe that the affections, excited by one object, pass easily to another connected with it; but transfuse themselves with difficulty, or not at all, along different objects, which have no manner of connexion together. By introducing, into any composition, personages and actions, foreign to each other, an injudicious author loses that communication of emotions, by which alone he can interest the heart, and raise the passions to their proper height and period. The full explication of this principle and all its consequences would lead us into reasonings too profound and too copious for this enquiry. 'Tis sufficient, at present, to have established this conclusion, that the three connecting principles of all ideas are the relations of *Resemblance, Contiguity, and Causation.*

all reasoning and free enquiry. The discovery of defects in the common philosophy, if any such there be, will not, I presume, be a discouragement, but rather an incitement, as is usual, to attempt something more full and satisfactory, than has yet been proposed to the public.

All reasonings concerning matter of fact seem to be founded on the relation of *Cause and Effect*. By means of that relation alone we can go beyond the evidence of our memory and senses. If you were to ask a man, why he believes any matter of fact, which is absent; for instance, that his friend is in the country, or in FRANCE; he would give you a reason; and this reason would be some other fact; as a letter received from him, or the knowledge of his former resolutions and promises. A man, finding a watch or any other machine in a desart island, would conclude, that there had once been men in that island. All our reasonings concerning fact are of the same nature. And here it is constantly supposed, that there is a connexion between the present fact and that which is inferred from it. Were there nothing to bind them together, the inference would be entirely precarious. The hearing of an articulate voice and rational discourse in the dark assures us of the presence of some person: Why? because these are the effects of the human make and fabric, and closely connected with it. If we anatomize all the other reasonings of this nature, we shall find, that they are founded on the relation of cause and effect, and that this relation is either near or remote, direct or collateral. Heat and light are collateral effects of fire, and the one effect may justly be inferred from the other.

If we would satisfy ourselves, therefore, concerning the nature of that evidence, which assures us of matters of fact, we must enquire how we arrive at the knowledge of cause and effect.

I shall venture to affirm, as a general proposition, which admits of no exception, that the knowledge of this relation is not, in any instance, attained by reasonings *à priori*; but arises entirely from experience, when we find, that any particular objects are constantly conjoined with each other. Let an object be presented to a man of ever so strong natural reason and abilities; if that object be entirely new to him, he will not be able, by the most accurate examination of its sensible qualities, to discover any of its causes or effects. Adam, though his rational faculties be supposed, at the very first, entirely perfect, could not have inferred from the fluidity, and transparency of water, that it would suffocate him, or from the light and warmth of fire, that it would consume him. No object ever discovers, by the qualities which appear to the senses, either the causes which produced it, or the effects which will arise from it; nor can our reason, unassisted by experience, ever draw any inference concerning real existence and matter of fact.

This proposition, *that causes and effects are discoverable, not by reason, but by experience*, will readily be admitted with regard to such objects, as we remember to have once been altogether unknown to us; since we must be conscious of the utter inability, which we then lay under, of foretelling, what would arise from them. Present two smooth pieces of marble to a man, who has no tincture of natural philosophy; he will never discover, that they will adhere together, in such a manner as to require great force to separate them in a direct line, while they make so small a resistance to a lateral pressure. Such events, as bear little analogy to the common course of nature, are also readily confessed to be known only by experience; nor does any man imagine that the explosion of gunpowder, or the attraction of a loadstone, could ever be discovered by arguments *à priori*. In like manner, when an effect is supposed to depend upon an intricate machinery or secret structure of parts, we make no difficulty in attributing all our knowledge of it to experience. Who will assert, that he can give the ultimate reason, why milk or bread is proper nourishment for a man, not for a lion or a tyger?

But the same truth may not appear, at first sight, to have the same evidence with regard to events, which have become familiar to us from our first appearance in the world, which bear a close analogy to the whole course of nature, and which are supposed to depend on the simple qualities of objects, without any secret structure of parts. We are apt to imagine, that we could discover these effects by the mere operation of our reason, without experience. We fancy, that were we brought, on a sudden, into this world, we could at first have inferred, that one Billiard-ball would communicate motion to another upon impulse; and that we needed not to have waited for the event, in order to pronounce with certainty concerning it. Such is the influence of custom, that, where it is strongest, it not only covers our natural ignorance, but even conceals itself, and seems not to take place, merely because it is found in the highest degree.

But to convince us, that all the laws of nature, and all the operations of bodies without exception, are known only by experience, the following reflections may, perhaps, suffice. Were any object presented to us, and were we required to pronounce concerning the effect, which will result from it, without consulting past observation; after what manner, I beseech you, must the mind proceed in this operation? It must invent or imagine some event, which it ascribes to the object as its effect; and it is plain that this invention must be entirely arbitrary. The mind can never possibly find the effect in the supposed cause, by the most accurate scrutiny and examination. For the effect is totally different from the cause, and consequently can never be discovered in it. Motion in the second Billiard-ball is a quite distinct event from motion in the first; nor is there any thing in the one to suggest the smallest hint of the other. A stone or piece of metal raised into the air, and left without any support, immediately falls: But to consider the matter *à priori*, is there any thing we discover in this situation, which can beget the idea of a downward, rather than an upward, or any other motion, in the stone or metal?

And as the first imagination or invention of a particular effect, in all natural operations, is arbitrary, where we consult not experience; so must we also esteem the supposed tye or connection between the cause and effect, which binds them together, and renders it impossible, that any other effect could result from the operation of that cause. When I see, for instance, a Billiard-ball moving in a straight line towards another; even suppose motion in the second ball should by accident be suggested to me, as the result of their contact or impulse; may I not conceive, that a hundred different events might as well follow from that cause? May not both these balls remain at absolute rest? May not the first ball return in a straight line, or leap off from the second in any line or direction? All the suppositions are consistent and conceivable. Why then should we give the preference to one, which is no more consistent or conceivable than the rest? All our reasonings *à priori* will never be able to shew us any foundation for this preference.

In a word, then, every effect is a distinct event from its cause. It could not, therefore, be discovered in the cause, and the first invention or conception of it, *à priori*, must be entirely arbitrary. And even after it is suggested, the conjunction of it with the cause must appear equally arbitrary ; since there are always many other effects, which, to reason, must seem fully as consistent and natural. In vain, therefore, should we pretend to determine any single event, or infer any cause or effect, without the assistance of observation and experience.

Hence we may discover the reason, why no philosopher, who is rational and modest, has ever pretended to assign the ultimate cause of any natural operation, or to show distinctly the action of that power, which produces any single effect in the universe. It is confessed, that the utmost effort of human reason is, to reduce the principles, productive of natural phaenomena, to a greater simplicity, and to resolve the many particular effects into a few general causes, by means of reasonings from analogy, experience, and observation. But as to the causes of these general causes, we should in vain attempt their discovery ; nor shall we ever be able to satisfy ourselves, by any particular explication of them. These ultimate springs and principles are totally shut up from human curiosity and enquiry. Elasticity, gravity, cohesion of parts, communication of motion by impulse ; these are probably the ultimate causes and principles which we shall ever discover in nature : and we may esteem ourselves sufficiently happy, if, by accurate enquiry and reasoning, we can trace up the particular phaenomena to, or near to, these general principles. The most perfect philosophy of the natural kind only staves off our ignorance a little longer : As perhaps the most perfect philosophy of the moral or metaphysical kind serves only to discover larger portions of it. Thus the observation of human blindness and weakness is the result of all philosophy, and meets us, at every turn, in spite of our endeavours to elude or avoid it.

Nor is geometry, when taken into the assistance of natural philosophy, even able to remedy this defect, or lead us into the knowledge of ultimate causes, by all that accuracy of reasoning, for which it is so justly celebrated. Every part of mixed mathematics proceeds upon the supposition, that certain laws are established by nature in her operations; and abstract reasonings are employed, either to assist experience in the discovery of these laws, or to determine their influence in particular instances, where it depends upon any precise degree of distance and quantity. Thus, it is a law of motion, discovered by experience, that the moment or force of any body in motion is in the compound ratio or proportion of its solid contents and its velocity; and consequently, that a small force may remove the greatest obstacle or raise the greatest weight, if, by any contrivance or machinery, we can encrease the velocity of that force, so as to make it an overmatch for its antagonist. Geometry assists us in the application of this law, by giving us the just dimensions of all the parts and figures, which can enter into any species of machine; but still the discovery of the law itself is owing merely to experience, and all the abstract reasonings in the world could never lead us one step towards the knowledge of it. When we reason *à priori*, and consider merely any object or cause, as it appears to the mind, independent of all observation, it never could suggest to us the notion of any distinct object, such as its effect; much less, shew us the inseparable and inviolable connection between them. A man must be very sagacious, who could discover by reasoning, that crystal is the effect of heat, and ice of cold, without being previously acquainted with the operation of these qualities.

PART II.

But we have not, yet, attained any tolerable satisfaction with regard to the question first proposed. Each solution still gives rise to a new question as difficult as the foregoing, and leads us on to farther enquiries. When it is asked, *What is the nature of all our reasonings concerning matter of fact?* the proper answer seems to be, that they are founded on the relation of cause and effect. When again it is asked, *What is the foundation of all our reasonings and conclusions concerning that relation?* it may be replied in one word, EXPERIENCE. But if we still carry on our sifting humour, and ask, *What is the foundation of all conclusions from experience?* this implies a new question, which may be of more difficult solution and explication. Philosophers, that give themselves airs of superior wisdom and sufficiency, have a hard task, when they encounter persons of inquisitive dispositions, who push them from every corner, to which they retreat, and who are sure at last to bring them to some dangerous dilemma. The best expedient to prevent this confusion, is to be modest in our pretensions; and even to discover the difficulty ourselves before it is objected to us. By this means, we may make a kind of merit of our very ignorance.

I shall content myself, in this section, with an easy task, and shall pretend only to give a negative answer to the question here proposed. I say then, that, even after we have experience of the operations of cause and effect, our conclusions from that experience are *not* founded on reasoning, or any process of the understanding. This answer we must endeavour, both to explain and to defend.

It must certainly be allowed, that nature has kept us at a great distance from all her secrets, and has afforded us only the knowledge of a few superficial qualities of objects; while she conceals from us those powers and principles, on which the influence of these objects entirely depends. Our senses inform us of the colour, weight, and consistence of bread; but neither sense nor reason can ever inform us of those qualities, which fit it for the nourishment and support of a human body. Sight or feeling conveys an idea of the actual motion of bodies; but as to that wonderful force or power, which would carry on a moving body for ever in a continued change of place, and which bodies never lose but by communicating it to others; of this we cannot form the most distant conception. But notwithstanding this ignorance of natural powers[1] and principles, we always presume, when we see like sensible qualities, that they have like secret powers, and expect, that effects, similar to those which we have experienced, will follow from them. If a body of like colour and consistence with that bread, which we have formerly eat, be presented to us, we make no scruple of repeating the experiment, and foresee, with certainty, like nourishment and support. Now this is a process of the mind or thought, of which I would willingly know the foundation. It is

[1] The word, Power, is here used in a loose and popular sense. The more accurate explication of it would give additional evidence to this argument. See Sec. 7. This note was added in Ed. F.

allowed on all hands, that there is no known connexion between the sensible qualities and the secret powers; and consequently, that the mind is not led to form such a conclusion concerning their constant and regular conjunction, by any thing which it knows of their nature. As to past *Experience*, it can be allowed to give *direct* and *certain* information of those precise objects only, and that precise period of time, which fell under its cognizance : But why this experience should be extended to future times, and to other objects, which for aught we know, may be only in appearance similar; this is the main question on which I would insist. The bread, which I formerly eat, nourished me ; that is, a body of such sensible qualities, was, at that time, endued with such secret powers : But does it follow, that other bread must also nourish me at another time, and that like sensible qualities must always be attended with like secret powers? The consequence seems nowise necessary. At least, it must be acknowledged, that there is here a consequence drawn by the mind; that there is a certain step taken; a process of thought, and an inference, which wants to be explained. These two propositions are far from being the same, *I have found that such an object has always been attended with such an effect*, and *I foresee, that other objects, which are, in appearance, similar, will be attended with similar effects*. I shall allow, if you please, that the one proposition may justly be inferred from the other : I know in fact, that it always is inferred. But if you insist, that the inference is made by a chain of reasoning, I desire you to produce that reasoning. The connexion between these propositions is not intuitive. There is required a medium, which may enable the mind to draw such an inference, if indeed it be drawn by reasoning and argument. What that medium is, I must confess, passes my comprehension ; and it is incumbent on those to produce it, who assert, that it really exists, and is the origin of all our conclusions concerning matter of fact.

This negative argument must certainly, in process of time, become altogether convincing, if many penetrating and able philosophers shall turn their enquiries this way ; and no one be ever able to discover any connecting proposition or intermediate step, which supports the understanding in this conclusion. But as the question is yet new, every reader may not trust so far to his own penetration, as to conclude, because an argument escapes his enquiry, that therefore it does not really exist. For this reason it may be requisite to venture upon a more difficult task; and enumerating all the branches of human knowledge, endeavour to shew, that none of them can afford such an argument.

All reasonings may be divided into two kinds, namely demonstrative reasoning, or that concerning relations of ideas, and moral[1] reasoning, or that concerning matter of fact and existence. That there are no demonstrative arguments in the case, seems evident; since it implies no contradiction, that the course of nature may change, and that an object, seemingly like those which we have experienced, may be attended with different or contrary effects. May I not clearly and distinctly conceive, that a body, falling from the clouds, and which, in all other respects, resembles snow, has yet the taste of salt or feeling of fire? Is there any more intelligible proposition than to affirm, that all the trees will flourish in DECEMBER and JANUARY, and decay in MAY and JUNE? Now whatever is intelligible, and can be distinctly conceived, implies no contradiction, and can never be proved false by any demonstrative argument or abstract reasoning à priori.

If we be, therefore, engaged by arguments to put trust in past experience, and make it the standard of our future judgment, these arguments must be probable only, or such as regard matter of fact and real existence, according to the division above mentioned. But that there is no argument of this kind, must appear, if our explication of that species of reasoning be admitted as solid and satisfactory. We have said, that all arguments concerning existence are founded on the relation of cause and effect; that our knowledge of that relation is derived entirely from experience; and that all our experimental conclusions proceed upon the supposition, that the future will be conformable to the past. To endeavour, therefore, the proof of this last supposition by probable arguments, or arguments regarding existence, must be evidently going in a circle, and taking that for granted, which is the very point in question.

In reality, all arguments from experience are founded on the similarity, which we discover among natural objects, and by which we are induced to expect effects similar to those, which we have found to follow from such objects. And

---

[1] [Moral or probable: Editions E and F.]

though none but a fool or madman will ever pretend to dispute the authority of experience, or to reject that great guide of human life; it may surely be allowed a philosopher to have so much curiosity at least, as to examine the principle of human nature, which gives this mighty authority to experience, and makes us draw advantage from that similarity, which nature has placed among different objects. From causes, which appear *similar*, we expect similar effects. This is the sum of all our experimental conclusions. Now it seems evident, that, if this conclusion were formed by reason, it would be as perfect at first, and upon one instance, as after ever so long a course of experience. But the case is far otherwise. Nothing so like as eggs; yet no one, on account of this appearing similarity, expects the same taste and relish in all of them. It is only after a long course of uniform experiments in any kind, that we attain a firm reliance and security with regard to a particular event. Now where is that process of reasoning, which, from one instance, draws a conclusion, so different from that which it infers from a hundred instances, that are nowise different from that single one? This question I propose as much for the sake of information, as with an intention of raising difficulties. I cannot find, I cannot imagine any such reasoning. But I keep my mind still open to instruction, if any one will vouchsafe to bestow it on me.

Should it be said, that, from a number of uniform experiments, we *infer* a connection between the sensible qualities and the secret powers; this, I must confess, seems the same difficulty, couched in different terms. The question still recurs, on what process of argument this *inference* is founded? Where is the medium, the interposing ideas, which join propositions so very wide of each other? It is confessed, that the colour, consistence, and other sensible qualities of bread appear not, of themselves, to have any connexion with the secret powers of nourishment and support. For otherwise we could infer these secret powers from the first appearance of these sensible qualities, without the aid of experience; contrary to the sentiment of all philosophers, and contrary to plain matter of fact. Here then is our natural state of ignorance with regard to the powers and influence of all objects. How is this remedied by experience? It only shews us a number of uniform effects, resulting from certain objects, and teaches us, that those particular objects, at that particular time, were endowed with such powers and forces. When a new object, endowed with similar sensible qualities, is produced, we expect similar powers and forces, and look for a like effect. From a body of like colour and consistence with bread, we expect like nourishment and support. But this surely is a step or progress of the mind, which wants to be explained. When a man says, *I have found, in all past instances, such sensible qualities conjoined with such secret powers:* And when he says, *similar sensible qualities will always be conjoined with similar secret powers;* he is not guilty of a tautology, nor are these propositions in any respect the same. You say that the one proposition is an inference from the other. But you must confess that the inference is not intuitive; neither is it demonstrative: Of what nature is it then? To say it is experimental, is begging the question. For all inferences from experience suppose, as their foundation, that the future will resemble the past, and that similar powers will be conjoined with similar sensible qualities. If there be any suspicion, that the course of nature may change, and that the past may be no rule for the future, all experience becomes useless, and can give rise to no inference or conclusion. It is impossible, therefore, that any arguments from experience can prove this resemblance of the past to the future: since all these arguments are founded on the supposition of that resemblance. Let the course of things be allowed hitherto ever so regular; that alone, without some new argument or inference, proves not, that, for the future, it will continue so. In vain do you pretend to have learned the nature of bodies from your past experience. Their secret nature, and consequently, all their effects and influence, may change, without any change in their sensible qualities. This happens sometimes, and with regard to some objects: Why may it not happen always, and with regard to all objects? What logic, what process of argument secures you against this supposition? My practice, you say, refutes my doubts. But you mistake the purport of my question. As an agent, I am quite satisfied in the point; but as a philosopher, who has some share of curiosity, I will not say scepticism, I want to learn the foundation of this inference. No reading, no enquiry has yet been able to remove my difficulty, or give me satisfaction in a matter of such importance. Can I do better

than propose the difficulty to the public, even though, perhaps, I have small hopes of obtaining a solution? We shall
at least, by this means, be sensible of our ignorance, if we do
not augment our knowledge.

I must confess, that a man is guilty of unpardonable arrogance, who concludes, because an argument has escaped his
own investigation, that therefore it does not really exist. I
must also confess, that, though all the learned, for several
ages, should have employed themselves in fruitless search
upon any subject, it may still, perhaps, be rash to conclude
positively, that the subject must, therefore, pass all human
comprehension. Even though we examine all the sources of
our knowledge, and conclude them unfit for such a subject,
there may still remain a suspicion, that the enumeration is
not compleat, or the examination not accurate. But with
regard to the present subject, there are some considerations,
which seem to remove all this accusation of arrogance or
suspicion of mistake.

It is certain, that the most ignorant and stupid peasants,
nay infants, nay even brute beasts, improve by experience,
and learn the qualities of natural objects, by observing the
effects, which result from them. When a child has felt the
sensation of pain from touching the flame of a candle, he will
be careful not to put his hand near any candle; but will
expect a similar effect from a cause, which is similar in its
sensible qualities and appearance. If you assert, therefore,
that the understanding of the child is led into this conclusion
by any process of argument or ratiocination, I may justly
require you to produce that argument; nor have you any
pretence to refuse so equitable a demand. You cannot say,
that the argument is abstruse, and may possibly escape your
enquiry; since you confess, that it is obvious to the capacity
of a mere infant. If you hesitate, therefore, a moment, or
if, after reflection, you produce any intricate or profound
argument, you, in a manner, give up the question, and confess, that it is not reasoning which engages us to suppose the
past resembling the future, and to expect similar effects from
causes, which are, to appearance, similar. This is the proposition which I intended to enforce in the present section.
If I be right, I pretend not to have made any mighty discovery. And if I be wrong, I must acknowledge myself to
be indeed a very backward scholar; since I cannot now dis-

cover an argument, which, it seems, was perfectly familiar to me, long before I was out of my cradle.

Sect. V.—*Sceptical Solution of these Doubts.*

PART I

THE passion for philosophy, like that for religion, seems liable to this inconvenience, that, though it aims at the correction of our manners, and extirpation of our vices, it may only serve, by imprudent management, to foster a predominant inclination, and push the mind, with more determined resolution, towards that side, which already *draws* too much, by the biass and propensity of the natural temper. It is certain, that, while we aspire to the magnanimous firmness of the philosophic sage, and endeavour to confine our pleasures altogether within our own minds, we may, at last, render our philosophy like that of EPICTETUS, and other *Stoics*, only a more refined system of selfishness, and reason ourselves out of all virtue, as well as social enjoyment. While we study with attention the vanity of human life, and turn all our thoughts towards the empty and transitory nature of riches and honours, we are, perhaps, all the while, flattering our natural indolence, which, hating the bustle of the world, and drudgery of business, seeks a pretence of reason, to give itself a full and uncontrouled indulgence. There is, however, one species of philosophy, which seems little liable to this inconvenience, and that because it strikes in with no disorderly passion of the human mind, nor can mingle itself with any natural affection or propensity; and that is the ACADEMIC or SCEPTICAL philosophy. The academics always talk of doubt and suspense of judgment, of danger in hasty determinations, of confining to very narrow bounds the enquiries of the understanding, and of renouncing all speculations which lie not within the limits of common life and practice. Nothing, therefore, can be more contrary than such a philosophy to the supine indolence of the mind, its rash arrogance, its lofty pretensions, and its superstitious credulity. Every passion is mortified by it, except the love of truth: and that passion never is, nor can be carried to too high a degree. It is surprising, therefore,

D 2

that this philosophy, which, in almost every instance, must be harmless and innocent, should be the subject of so much groundless reproach and obloquy. But, perhaps, the very circumstance, which renders it so innocent, is what chiefly exposes it to the public hatred and resentment. By flattering no irregular passion, it gains few partizans: By opposing so many vices and follies, it raises to itself abundance of enemies, who stigmatize it as libertine, profane, and irreligious.

Nor need we fear, that this philosophy, while it endeavours to limit our enquiries to common life, should ever undermine the reasonings of common life, and carry its doubts so far as to destroy all action, as well as speculation. Nature will always maintain her rights, and prevail in the end over any abstract reasoning whatsoever. Though we should conclude, for instance, as in the foregoing section, that, in all reasonings from experience, there is a step taken by the mind, which is not supported by any argument or process of the understanding, there is no danger, that these reasonings, on which almost all knowledge depends, will ever be affected by such a discovery. If the mind be not engaged by argument to make this step, it must be induced by some other principle of equal weight and authority; and that principle will preserve its influence as long as human nature remains the same. What that principle is, may well be worth the pains of enquiry.

Suppose a person, though endowed with the strongest faculties of reason and reflection, to be brought on a sudden into this world; he would, indeed, immediately observe a continual succession of objects, and one event following another; but he would not be able to discover any thing farther. He would not, at first, by any reasoning, be able to reach the idea of cause and effect; since the particular powers, by which all natural operations are performed, never appear to the senses; nor is it reasonable to conclude, merely because one event, in one instance, precedes another, that therefore the one is the cause, the other the effect. Their conjunction may be arbitrary and casual. There may be no reason to infer the existence of one from the appearance of the other. And in a word, such a person, without more experience, could never employ his conjecture or reasoning concerning any matter of fact, or be assured of any thing beyond what was immediately present to his memory and senses.

Suppose again, that he has acquired more experience, and has lived so long in the world as to have observed similar objects or events to be constantly conjoined together; what is the consequence of this experience? He immediately infers the existence of one object from the appearance of the other. Yet he has not, by all his experience, acquired any idea or knowledge of the secret power, by which the one object produces the other; nor is it, by any process of reasoning, he is engaged to draw this inference. But still he finds himself determined to draw it: And though he should be convinced, that his understanding has no part in the operation, he would nevertheless continue in the same course of thinking. There is some other principle, which determines him to form such a conclusion.

This principle is CUSTOM or HABIT. For wherever the repetition of any particular act or operation produces a propensity to renew the same act or operation, without being impelled by any reasoning or process of the understanding; we always say, that this propensity is the effect of *Custom*. By employing that word, we pretend not to have given the ultimate reason of such a propensity. We only point out a principle of human nature, which is universally acknowledged, and which is well known by its effects. Perhaps, we can push our enquiries no farther, or pretend to give the cause of this cause; but must rest contented with it as the ultimate principle, which we can assign, of all our conclusions from experience. It is sufficient satisfaction, that we can go so far; without repining at the narrowness of our faculties, because they will carry us no farther. And it is certain we here advance a very intelligible proposition at least, if not a true one, when we assert, that, after the constant conjunction of two objects, heat and flame, for instance, weight and solidity, we are determined by custom alone to expect the one from the appearance of the other. This hypothesis seems even the only one, which explains the difficulty, why we draw, from a thousand instances, an inference, which we are not able to draw from one instance, that is, in no respect, different from them. Reason is incapable of any such variation. The conclusions, which it draws from considering one circle, are the same which it would form upon surveying all the circles in the universe. But no man, having seen only one body move after being impelled by another, could infer, that every other body will move after a like impulse. All inferences from experience, therefore, are effects of custom, not of reasoning.[1]

[1] Nothing is more usual than for writers, even on *moral, political*, or *physical* subjects, to distinguish between *reason* and *experience*, and to suppose, that these species of argumentation are entirely different from each other. The former are taken for the mere result of our intellectual faculties, which, by considering *à priori* the nature of things, and examining the effects, that must follow from their operation, establish particular principles of science and philosophy. The latter are supposed to be derived entirely from sense and observation, by which we learn what has actually resulted from the operation of particular objects, and are thence able to infer, what will, for the future, result from them. Thus, for instance, the limitations and restraints of civil government, and a legal constitution, may be defended, either from *reason*, which reflecting on the great frailty and corruption of human nature, teaches, that no man can safely be trusted with unlimited authority; or from *experience* and history, which inform us of the enormous abuses, that ambition, in every age and country, has been found to make of so imprudent a confidence.

The same distinction between reason and experience is maintained in all our deliberations concerning the conduct of life; while the experienced statesman, general, physician, or merchant is trusted and followed; and the unpractised novice, with whatever natural talents endowed, neglected and despised. Though it be allowed, that reason may form very plausible conjectures with regard to the consequences of such a particular conduct in such particular circumstances; it is still supposed imperfect, without the assistance of experience, which is alone able to give stability and certainty to the maxims, derived from study and reflection.

But notwithstanding that this distinction be thus universally received, both in the active and speculative scenes of life, I shall not scruple to pronounce, that it is, at bottom, erroneous, at least superficial.

If we examine those arguments which, in any of the sciences above-mentioned, are supposed to be the mere effects of reasoning and reflection, they will be found to terminate, at last, in some general principle or conclusion, for which we can assign no reason but observation and experience. The only difference between them and those maxims, which are vulgarly esteemed the result of pure experience, is, that the former cannot be established without some process of thought, and some reflection on what we have observed, in order to distinguish its circumstances, and trace its consequences: Whereas in the latter, the experienced event is exactly and fully similar to that which we infer as the result of any particular situation. The history of a TIBERIUS or a NERO makes us dread a like tyranny, were our monarchs freed from the restraints of laws and senates: But the observation of any fraud or cruelty in private life is sufficient, with the aid of a little thought, to give us the same apprehension; while it serves as an instance of the general corruption of human nature, and shews us the danger which we must incur by reposing an entire confidence in mankind. In both cases, it is experience which is ultimately the foundation of our inference and conclusion.

There is no man so young and unexperienced, as not to have formed, from observation, many general and just maxims concerning human affairs and the conduct of life; but it must be confessed, that, when a man comes to put these in practice, he will be extremely liable to error, till time and farther experience both enlarge these maxims, and teach him their proper use and application. In every situation or incident, there are many particular and seemingly minute circumstances, which the man of greatest talents is, at first, apt to overlook, though on them the justness of his conclusions, and consequently the prudence of his conduct, entirely depend. Not to mention, that, to a young beginner, the general observations and maxims occur not always on the proper occasions, nor can be immediately applied with due calmness

Custom, then, is the great guide of human life. It is that principle alone, which renders our experience useful to us, and makes us expect, for the future, a similar train of events with those which have appeared in the past. Without the influence of custom, we should be entirely ignorant of every matter of fact, beyond what is immediately present to the memory and senses. We should never know how to adjust means to ends, or to employ our natural powers in the production of any effect. There would be an end at once of all action, as well as of the chief part of speculation.

But here it may be proper to remark, that though our conclusions from experience carry us beyond our memory and senses, and assure us of matters of fact, which happened in the most distant places and most remote ages; yet some fact must always be present to the senses or memory, from which we may first proceed in drawing these conclusions. A man, who should find in a desert country the remains of pompous buildings, would conclude, that the country had, in ancient times, been cultivated by civilized inhabitants: but did nothing of this nature occur to him, he could never form such an inference. We learn the events of former ages from history; but then we must peruse the volumes, in which this instruction is contained, and thence carry up our inferences from one testimony to another, till we arrive at the eye-witnesses and spectators of these distant events. In a word, if we proceed not upon some fact, present to the memory or senses, our reasonings would be merely hypothetical; and however the particular links might be connected with each other, the whole chain of inferences would have nothing to support it, nor could we ever, by its means, arrive at the knowledge of any real existence. If I ask, why you believe any particular matter of fact, which you relate, you must tell me some reason; and this reason will be some other fact, connected with it. But as you cannot proceed after this manner, *in infinitum*, you must at last terminate in some fact, which is present to your memory or senses; or must allow that your belief is entirely without foundation.

What then is the conclusion of the whole matter? A

and distinction. The truth is, an unexperienced reasoner could be no reasoner at all, were he absolutely inexperienced; and when we assign a character to any one, we mean it only in a comparative sense, and suppose him possessed of experience, in a smaller and more imperfect degree.

simple one; though, it must be confessed, pretty remote from the common theories of philosophy. All belief of matter of fact or real existence is derived merely from some object, present to the memory or senses, and a customary conjunction between that and some other object. Or in other words; having found, in many instances, that any two kinds of objects, flame and heat, snow and cold, have always been conjoined together; if flame or snow be presented anew to the senses, the mind is carried by custom to expect heat or cold, and to *believe*, that such a quality does exist, and will discover itself upon a nearer approach. This belief is the necessary result of placing the mind in such circumstances. It is an operation of the soul, when we are so situated, as unavoidable as to feel the passion of love, when we receive benefits : or hatred, when we meet with injuries. All these operations are a species of natural instincts, which no reasoning or process of the thought and understanding is able, either to produce, or to prevent.

At this point, it would be very allowable for us to stop our philosophical researches. In most questions, we can never make a single step farther; and in all questions, we must terminate here at last, after our most restless and curious enquiries. But still our curiosity will be pardonable, perhaps commendable, if it carry us on to still farther researches, and make us examine more accurately the nature of this *belief*, and of the *customary conjunction*, whence it is derived. By this means we may meet with some explications and analogies, that will give satisfaction; at least to such as love the abstract sciences, and can be entertained with speculations, which, however accurate, may still retain a degree of doubt and uncertainty. As to readers of a different taste; the remaining part of this section is not calculated for them, and the following enquiries may well be understood, though it be neglected.

PART II.

Nothing is more free than the imagination of man; and though it cannot exceed that original stock of ideas, furnished by the internal and external senses, it has unlimited power of mixing, compounding, separating, and dividing these ideas, in all the varieties of fiction and vision. It can feign a train of events, with all the appearance of reality, ascribe to them a particular time and place, conceive them as existent, and paint them out to itself with every circumstance, that belongs to any historical fact, which it believes with the greatest certainty. Wherein, therefore, consists the difference between such a fiction and belief? It lies not merely in any peculiar idea, which is annexed to such a conception as commands our assent, and which is wanting to every known fiction. For as the mind has authority over all its ideas, it could voluntarily annex this particular idea to any fiction, and consequently be able to believe whatever it pleases; contrary to what we find by daily experience. We can, in our conception, join the head of a man to the body of a horse; but it is not in our power to believe, that such an animal has ever really existed.

It follows, therefore, that the difference between *fiction* and *belief* lies in some sentiment or feeling, which is annexed to the latter, not to the former, and which depends not on the will, nor can be commanded at pleasure. It must be excited by nature, like all other sentiments; and must arise from the particular situation, in which the mind is placed at any particular juncture. Whenever any object is presented to the memory or senses, it immediately, by the force of custom, carries the imagination to conceive that object, which is usually conjoined to it; and this conception is attended with a feeling or sentiment, different from the loose reveries of the fancy. In this consists the whole nature of belief. For as there is no matter of fact which we believe so firmly, that we cannot conceive the contrary, there would be no difference between the conception assented to, and that which is rejected, were it not for some sentiment, which distinguishes the one from the other. If I see a billiard-ball moving towards another, on a smooth table, I can easily conceive it to stop upon contact. This conception implies no contradiction; but still it feels very differently from that conception, by which I represent to myself the impulse, and the communication of motion from one ball to another.

Were we to attempt a *definition* of this sentiment, we should, perhaps, find it a very difficult, if not an impossible task; in the same manner as if we should endeavour to define the feeling of cold or passion of anger, to a creature who never had any experience of these sentiments. BELIEF is the true and proper name of this feeling; and no one is ever at a loss to know the meaning of that term; because every man is every moment conscious of the sentiment represented by it.   It may not, however, be improper to attempt a *description* of this sentiment; in hopes we may, by that means, arrive at some analogies, which may afford a more perfect explication of it.   I say then, that belief is nothing but a more vivid, lively, forcible, firm, steady conception of an object, than what the imagination alone is ever able to attain. This variety of terms, which may seem so unphilosophical, is intended only to express that act of the mind, which renders realities, or what is taken for such, more present to us than fictions, causes them to weigh more in the thought, and gives them a superior influence on the passions and the imagination.   Provided we agree about the thing, it is needless to dispute about the terms.   The imagination has the command over all its ideas, and can join and mix and vary them, in all the ways possible.   It may conceive fictitious objects with all the circumstances of place and time.   It may set them, in a manner, before our eyes, in their true colours, just as they might have existed.   But as it is impossible, that this faculty of imagination can ever, of itself, reach belief, it is evident, that belief consists not in the peculiar nature or order of ideas, but in the *manner* of their conception, and in their *feeling* to the mind.   I confess, that it is impossible perfectly to explain this feeling or manner of conception.   We may make use of words, which express something near it.   But its true and proper name, as we observed before, is *belief*; which is a term, that every one sufficiently understands in common life.   And in philosophy, we can go no farther than assert, that *belief* is something felt by the mind, which distinguishes the ideas of the judgment from the fictions of the imagination.   It gives them more weight and influence; makes them appear of greater importance: inforces them in the mind: and renders them the governing principle of our actions.   I hear at present, for instance, a person's voice, with whom I am acquainted: and the sound comes as from the next room.   This impression of my senses immediately conveys my thought to the person, together with all the surrounding objects.   I paint them out to myself as existing at present, with the same qualities and relations, of which I formerly knew them possessed.   These ideas take faster hold of my mind, than ideas of an enchanted castle.

They are very different to the feeling, and have a much greater influence of every kind, either to give pleasure or pain, joy or sorrow.

Let us, then, take in the whole compass of this doctrine, and allow, that the sentiment of belief is nothing but a conception more intense and steady than what attends the mere fictions of the imagination, and that this *manner* of conception arises from a customary conjunction of the object with something present to the memory or senses : I believe that it will not be difficult, upon these suppositions, to find other operations of the mind analogous to it, and to trace up these phænomena to principles still more general.

We have already observed, that nature has established connexions among particular ideas, and that no sooner one idea occurs to our thoughts than it introduces its correlative, and carries our attention towards it, by a gentle and insensible movement. These principles of connexion or association we have reduced to three, namely, *Resemblance, Contiguity,* and *Causation* ; which are the only bonds, that unite our thoughts together, and beget that regular train of reflection or discourse, which, in a greater or less degree, takes place among all mankind. Now here arises a question, on which the solution of the present difficulty will depend. Does it happen, in all these relations, that, when one of the objects is presented to the senses or memory, the mind is not only carried to the conception of the correlative, but reaches a steadier and stronger conception of it than what otherwise it would have been able to attain? This seems to be the case with that belief, which arises from the relation of cause and effect. And if the case be the same with the other relations or principles of association, this may be established as a general law, which takes place in all the operations of the mind.

We may, therefore, observe, as the first experiment to our present purpose, that, upon the appearance of the picture of an absent friend, our idea of him is evidently enlivened by the *resemblance*, and that every passion, which that idea occasions, whether of joy or sorrow, acquires new force and vigour. In producing this effect, there concur both a relation and a present impression. Where the picture bears him no resemblance, at least was not intended for him, it never so much as conveys our thought to him : And where it is absent, as well as the person; though the mind may pass from the thought of the one to that of the other; it feels its idea to be rather weakened than enlivened by that transition. We take a pleasure in viewing the picture of a friend, when it is set before us; but when it is removed, rather chuse to consider him directly, than by reflection in an image, which is equally distant and obscure.

The ceremonies of the ROMAN CATHOLIC religion may be considered as instances of the same nature. The devotees of that [1] superstition usually plead in excuse for the mummeries, with which they are upbraided, that they feel the good effect of those external motions, and postures, and actions, in enlivening their devotion and quickening their fervour, which otherwise would decay, if directed entirely to distant and immaterial objects. We shadow out the objects of our faith, say they, in sensible types and images, and render them more present to us by the immediate presence of these types, than it is possible for us to do, merely by an intellectual view and contemplation. Sensible objects have always a greater influence on the fancy than any other; and this influence they readily convey to those ideas, to which they are related, and which they resemble. I shall only infer from these practices, and this reasoning, that the effect of resemblance in enlivening the ideas is very common : and as in every case a resemblance and a present impression must concur, we are abundantly supplied with experiments to prove the reality of the foregoing principle.

We may add force to these experiments by others of a different kind, in considering the effects of *contiguity* as well as of *resemblance*. It is certain, that distance diminishes the force of every idea, and that, upon our approach to any object; though it does not discover itself to our senses; it operates upon the mind with an influence, which imitates an immediate impression. The thinking on any object readily transports the mind to what is contiguous; but it is only the actual presence of an object, that transports it with a superior vivacity. When I am a few miles from home, whatever relates to it touches me more nearly than when I am two hundred leagues distant; though even at that distance the reflecting on any thing in the neighbourhood of my friends or family naturally produces an idea of them. But as in

[1] [That strange superstition: Editions E and F.]

this latter case, both the objects of the mind are ideas; notwithstanding there is an easy transition between them; that transition alone is not able to give a superior vivacity to any of the ideas, for want of some immediate impression.[1]

No one can doubt but causation has the same influence as the other two relations of resemblance and contiguity. Superstitious people are fond of the reliques of saints and holy men, for the same reason, that they seek after types or images, in order to enliven their devotion, and give them a more intimate and strong conception of those exemplary lives, which they desire to imitate. Now it is evident, that one of the best reliques, which a devotee could procure, would be the handywork of a saint; and if his cloaths and furniture are ever to be considered in this light, it is because they were once at his disposal, and were moved and affected by him; in which respect they are to be considered as imperfect effects, and as connected with him by a shorter chain of consequences than any of those, by which we learn the reality of his existence.

Suppose, that the son of a friend, who had been long dead or absent, were presented to us; it is evident, that this object would instantly revive its correlative idea, and recal to our thoughts all past intimacies and familiarities, in more lively colours than they would otherwise have appeared to us. This is another phænomenon, which seems to prove the principle above-mentioned.

We may observe, that, in these phænomena, the belief of the correlative object is always presupposed; without which the relation could have no effect. The influence of the picture supposes, that we *believe* our friend to have once existed. Contiguity to home can never excite our ideas of home, unless we *believe* that it really exists. Now I assert, that this belief, where it reaches beyond the memory or

[1] 'Naturane nobis, inquit, datum dicam, an errore quodam, ut, cum ea loca videamus, in quibus memoria dignos viros accepimus multum esse versatos, magis moveamur, quam siquando eorum ipsorum aut facta audiamus aut scriptum aliquod legamus? Velut ego nunc moveor. Venit enim mihi PLATONIS in mentem, quem accepimus primum hic disputare solitum: Cujus etiam illi hortuli propinqui non memoriam solum mihi afferunt, sed ipsum videntur in conspectu meo hic ponere. Hic SPEUSIPPUS, hic XENOCRATES, hic ejus auditor POLEMO; cujus ipsa illa sessio fuit, quam videamus. Equidem etiam curiam nostram HOSTILIAM dico, non hanc novam, quae mihi minor esse videtur postquam est major, solebam intueus, SCIPIONEM, CATONEM, LÆLIUM, nostrum vero in primis avum cogitare. Tanta vis admonitionis est in locis; ut non sine causa ex his memoriae deducta sit disciplina.' CICERO *de Finibus*. Lib. v. 2.

senses, is of a similar nature, and arises from similar causes, with the transition of thought and vivacity of conception here explained. When I throw a piece of dry wood into a fire, my mind is immediately carried to conceive, that it augments, not extinguishes the flame. This transition of thought from the cause to the effect proceeds not from reason. It derives its origin altogether from custom and experience. And as it first begins from an object, present to the senses, it renders the idea or conception of flame more strong and lively than any loose, floating reverie of the imagination. That idea arises immediately. The thought moves instantly towards it, and conveys to it all that force of conception, which is derived from the impression present to the senses. When a sword is levelled at my breast, does not the idea of wound and pain strike me more strongly, than when a glass of wine is presented to me, even though by accident this idea should occur after the appearance of the latter object? But what is there in this whole matter to cause such a strong conception, except only a present object and a customary transition to the idea of another object, which we have been accustomed to conjoin with the former? This is the whole operation of the mind, in all our conclusions concerning matter of fact and existence; and it is a satisfaction to find some analogies, by which it may be explained. The transition from a present object does in all cases give strength and solidity to the related idea.

Here, then, is a kind of pre-established harmony between the course of nature and the succession of our ideas; and though the powers and forces, by which the former is governed, be wholly unknown to us; yet our thoughts and conceptions have still, we find, gone on in the same train with the other works of nature. Custom is that principle, by which this correspondence has been effected; so necessary to the subsistence of our species, and the regulation of our conduct, in every circumstance and occurrence of human life. Had not the presence of an object instantly excited the idea of those objects, commonly conjoined with it, all our knowledge must have been limited to the narrow sphere of our memory and senses; and we should never have been able to adjust means to ends, or employ our natural powers, either to the producing of good, or avoiding of evil. Those, who delight in the discovery and contemplation of *final causes,* have here ample subject to employ their wonder and admiration.

I shall add, for a further confirmation of the foregoing theory, that, as this operation of the mind, by which we infer like effects from like causes, and *vice versa*, is so essential to the subsistence of all human creatures, it is not probable, that it could be trusted to the fallacious deductions of our reason, which is slow in its operations; appears not, in any degree, during the first years of infancy; and at best is, in every age and period of human life, extremely liable to error and mistake. It is more conformable to the ordinary wisdom of nature to secure so necessary an act of the mind, by some instinct or mechanical tendency, which may be infallible in its operations, may discover itself at the first appearance of life and thought, and may be independent of all the laboured deductions of the understanding. As nature has taught us the use of our limbs, without giving us the knowledge of the muscles and nerves, by which they are actuated; so has she implanted in us an instinct, which carries forward the thought in a correspondent course to that which she has established among external objects: though we are ignorant of those powers and forces, on which this regular course and succession of objects totally depends.

Section VI.— *Of Probability.*[1]

Though there be no such thing as *Chance* in the world; our ignorance of the real cause of any event has the same influence on the understanding, and begets a like species of belief or opinion.

There is certainly a probability, which arises from a superiority of chances on any side; and according as this superiority encreases, and surpasses the opposite chances, the probability receives a proportionable encrease, and begets still a higher degree of belief or assent to that side, in which we discover the superiority. If a dye were marked with one figure or number of spots on four sides, and with another

[1] Mr. Locke divides all arguments into demonstrative and probable. In this view, we must say, that it is only probable all men must die, or that the sun will rise to-morrow. But to conform our language more to common use, we ought to divide arguments into demonstrations, proofs, and probabilities. By proofs meaning such arguments from experience as leave no room for doubt or opposition.

figure or number of spots on the two remaining sides, it
would be more probable, that the former would turn up than
the latter ; though, if it had a thousand sides marked in the
same manner, and only one side different, the probability
would be much higher, and our belief or expectation of the
event more steady and secure. This process of the thought
or reasoning may seem trivial and obvious ; but to those who
consider it more narrowly, it may, perhaps, afford matter for
curious speculation.

It seems evident, that, when the mind looks forward to
discover the event, which may result from the throw of such
a dye, it considers the turning up of each particular side as
alike probable ; and this is the very nature of chance, to
render all the particular events, comprehended in it, entirely
equal. But finding a greater number of sides concur in the
one event than in the other, the mind is carried more frequently to that event, and meets it oftener, in revolving the
various possibilities or chances, on which the ultimate result
depends. This concurrence of several views in one particular
event begets immediately, by an inextricable contrivance of
nature, the sentiment of belief, and gives that event the
advantage over its antagonist, which is supported by a smaller
number of views, and recurs less frequently to the mind. If
we allow, that belief is nothing but a firmer and stronger
conception of an object than what attends the mere fictions
of the imagination, this operation may, perhaps, in some
measure be accounted for. The concurrence of these several
views or glimpses imprints the idea more strongly on the
imagination ; gives it superior force and vigour ; renders its
influence on the passions and affections more sensible ; and
in a word, begets that reliance or security, which constitutes
the nature of belief and opinion.

The case is the same with the probability of causes, as
with that of chance. There are some causes, which are entirely uniform and constant in producing a particular effect ;
and no instance has ever yet been found of any failure or
irregularity in their operation. Fire has always burned, and
water suffocated every human creature : The production of
motion by impulse and gravity is an universal law, which has
hitherto admitted of no exception. But there are other
causes, which have been found more irregular and uncertain ;
nor has rhubarb always proved a purge, or opium a soporific
to every one, who has taken these medicines. It is true,

when any cause fails of producing its usual effect, philosophers ascribe not this to any irregularity in nature; but suppose, that some secret causes, in the particular structure of parts, have prevented the operation. Our reasonings, however, and conclusions concerning the event are the same as if this principle had no place. Being determined by custom to transfer the past to the future, in all our inferences; where the past has been entirely regular and uniform, we expect the event with the greatest assurance, and leave no room for any contrary supposition. But where different effects have been found to follow from causes, which are to *appearance* exactly similar, all these various effects must occur to the mind in transferring the past to the future, and enter into our consideration, when we determine the probability of the event. Though we give the preference to that which has been found most usual, and believe that this effect will exist, we must not overlook the other effects, but must assign to each of them a particular weight and authority, in proportion as we have found it to be more or less frequent. It is more probable, in almost every country of Europe, that there will be frost sometime in JANUARY, than that the weather will continue open throughout that whole month; though this probability varies according to the different climates, and approaches to a certainty in the more northern kingdoms. Here then it seems evident, that, when we transfer the past to the future, in order to determine the effect, which will result from any cause, we transfer all the different events, in the same proportion as they have appeared in the past, and conceive one to have existed a hundred times, for instance, another ten times, and another once. As a great number of views do here concur in one event, they fortify and confirm it to the imagination, beget that sentiment which we call *belief*, and give its object the preference above the contrary event, which is not supported by an equal number of experiments, and recurs not so frequently to the thought in transferring the past to the future. Let any one try to account for this operation of the mind upon any of the received systems of philosophy, and he will be sensible of the difficulty. For my part, I shall think it sufficient, if the present hints excite the curiosity of philosophers, and make them sensible how defective all common theories are in treating of such curious and such sublime subjects.

SECT. VII.—*Of the Idea[1] of Necessary Connexion.*

PART I.

THE great advantage of the mathematical sciences above the moral consists in this, that the ideas of the former, being sensible, are always clear and determinate, the smallest distinction between them is immediately perceptible, and the same terms are still expressive of the same ideas, without ambiguity or variation. An oval is never mistaken for a circle, nor an hyperbola for an ellipsis. The isosceles and scalenum are distinguished by boundaries more exact than vice and virtue, right and wrong. If any term be defined in geometry, the mind readily, of itself, substitutes, on all occasions, the definition for the term defined: Or even when no definition is employed, the object itself may be presented to the senses, and by that means be steadily and clearly apprehended. But the finer sentiments of the mind, the operations of the understanding, the various agitations of the passions, though really in themselves distinct, easily escape us, when surveyed by reflection; nor is it in our power to recal the original object, as often as we have occasion to contemplate it. Ambiguity, by this means, is gradually introduced into our reasonings: Similar objects are readily taken to be the same: And the conclusion becomes at last very wide of the premises.

One may safely, however, affirm, that, if we consider these sciences in a proper light, their advantages and disadvantages nearly compensate each other, and reduce both of them to a state of equality. If the mind, with greater facility, retains the ideas of geometry clear and determinate, it must carry on a much longer and more intricate chain of reasoning, and compare ideas much wider of each other, in order to reach the abstruser truths of that science. And if moral ideas are apt, without extreme care, to fall into obscurity and confusion, the inferences are always much shorter in these disquisitions, and the intermediate steps, which lead to the conclusion, much fewer than in the sciences which treat of quantity and number. In reality, there is scarcely a proposition in EUCLID so simple, as not to consist

[1] [Of Power or, &c.: Editions E and F.]

of more parts, than are to be found in any moral reasoning
which runs not into chimera and conceit. Where we trace
the principles of the human mind through a few steps, we
may be very well satisfied with our progress; considering
how soon nature throws a bar to all our enquiries concerning causes, and reduces us to an acknowledgment of our
ignorance. The chief obstacle, therefore, to our improvement in the moral or metaphysical sciences is the obscurity
of the ideas, and ambiguity of the terms. The principal
difficulty in the mathematics is the length of inferences and
compass of thought, requisite to the forming of any conclusion.
And, perhaps, our progress in natural philosophy is chiefly
retarded by the want of proper experiments and phænomena,
which are often discovered by chance, and cannot always be
found, when requisite, even by the most diligent and prudent
enquiry. As moral philosophy seems hitherto to have received less improvement than either geometry or physics,
we may conclude, that, if there be any difference in this respect among these sciences, the difficulties, which obstruct
the progress of the former, require superior care and capacity
to be surmounted.

There are no ideas, which occur in metaphysics, more
obscure and uncertain, than those of *power, force, energy,* or
necessary connexion, of which it is every moment necessary
for us to treat in all our disquisitions. We shall, therefore,
endeavour, in this section, to fix, if possible, the precise
meaning of these terms, and thereby remove some part of
that obscurity, which is so much complained of in this species
of philosophy.

It seems a proposition, which will not admit of much dispute, that all our ideas are nothing but copies of our impressions, or, in other words, that it is impossible for us to
think of any thing, which we have not antecedently *felt,*
either by our external or internal senses. I have endeavoured [1] to explain and prove this proposition, and have
expressed my hopes, that, by a proper application of it, men
may reach a greater clearness and precision in philosophical
reasonings, than what they have hitherto been able to attain.
Complex ideas may, perhaps, be well known by definition,
which is nothing but an enumeration of those parts or
simple ideas, that compose them. But when we have pushed

[1] Section II. Of the Origin of Ideas.

up definitions to the most simple ideas, and find still some ambiguity and obscurity; what resource are we then possessed of? By what invention can we throw light upon these ideas, and render them altogether precise and determinate to our intellectual view? Produce the impressions or original sentiments, from which the ideas are copied. These impressions are all strong and sensible. They admit not of ambiguity. They are not only placed in a full light themselves, but may throw light on their correspondent ideas, which lie in obscurity. And by this means, we may, perhaps, attain a new microscope or species of optics, by which, in the moral sciences, the most minute, and most simple ideas may be so enlarged as to fall readily under our apprehension, and be equally known with the grossest and most sensible ideas, that can be the object of our enquiry.

To be fully acquainted, therefore, with the idea of power or necessary connexion, let us examine its impression; and in order to find the impression with greater certainty, let us search for it in all the sources, from which it may possibly be derived.

When we look about us towards external objects, and consider the operation of causes, we are never able, in a single instance, to discover any power or necessary connexion; any quality, which binds the effect to the cause, and renders the one an infallible consequence of the other. We only find, that the one does actually, in fact, follow the other. The impulse of one billiard-ball is attended with motion in the second. This is the whole that appears to the *outward* senses. The mind feels no sentiment or *inward* impression from this succession of objects: Consequently, there is not, in any single, particular instance of cause and effect, any thing which can suggest the idea of power or necessary connexion.

From the first appearance of an object, we never can conjecture what effect will result from it. But were the power or energy of any cause discoverable by the mind, we could foresee the effect, even without experience; and might, at first, pronounce with certainty concerning it, by the mere dint of thought and reasoning.

In reality, there is no part of matter, that does ever, by its sensible qualities, discover any power or energy, or give us ground to imagine, that it could produce any thing, or be followed by any other object, which we could denominate its effect. Solidity, extension, motion; these qualities are all complete in themselves, and never point out any other event which may result from them. The scenes of the universe are continually shifting, and one object follows another in an uninterrupted succession; but the power or force, which actuates the whole machine, is entirely concealed from us, and never discovers itself in any of the sensible qualities of body. We know, that, in fact, heat is a constant attendant of flame; but what is the connexion between them, we have no room so much as to conjecture or imagine. It is impossible, therefore, that the idea of power can be derived from the contemplation of bodies, in single instances of their operation; because no bodies ever discover any power, which can be the original of this idea.[1]

Since, therefore, external objects as they appear to the senses, give us no idea of power or necessary connexion, by their operation in particular instances, let us see, whether this idea be derived from reflection on the operations of our own minds, and be copied from any internal impression. It may be said, that we are every moment conscious of internal power; while we feel, that, by the simple command of our will, we can move the organs of our body, or direct the faculties of our mind. An act of volition produces motion in our limbs, or raises a new idea in our imagination. This influence of the will we know by consciousness. Hence we acquire the idea of power or energy; and are certain, that we ourselves and all other intelligent beings are possessed of power.[2] This idea, then, is an idea of reflection, since it arises from reflecting on the operations of our own mind, and on the command which is exercised by will, both over the organs of the body and faculties of the [3]soul.

We shall proceed to examine this pretension;[4] and first with regard to the influence of volition over the organs of

[1] Mr. Locke, in his chapter of power says, that, finding from experience, that there are several new productions in matter, and concluding that there must somewhere be a power capable of producing them, we arrive at last by this reasoning at the idea of power. But no reasoning can ever give us a new, original simple idea; as this philo-

sopher himself confesses. This, therefore, can never be the origin of that idea.

[2] [Editions E and F add: However this may be, the Operations and mutual Influence of Bodies are, perhaps, sufficient to prove, that they also are possess'd of it.]

[3] [Of the Mind: Editions E to Q.]

[4] [Editions E and F read: We shall

the body. This influence, we may observe, is a fact, which, like all other natural events, can be known only by experience, and can never be foreseen from any apparent energy or power in the cause, which connects it with the effect, and renders the one an infallible consequence of the other. The motion of our body follows upon the command of our will. Of this we are every moment conscious. But the means, by which this is effected; the energy, by which the will performs so extraordinary an operation; of this we are so far from being immediately conscious, that it must for ever escape our most diligent enquiry.

For *first*; is there any principle in all nature more mysterious than the union of soul with body; by which a supposed spiritual substance acquires such an influence over a material one, that the most refined thought is able to actuate the grossest matter? Were we empowered, by a secret wish, to remove mountains, or control the planets in their orbit; this extensive authority would not be more extraordinary, nor more beyond our comprehension. But if by consciousness we perceived any power or energy in the will, we must know this power; we must know its connexion with the effect; we must know the secret union of soul and body, and the nature of both these substances; by which the one is able to operate, in so many instances, upon the other.

Secondly, We are not able to move all the organs of the body with a like authority: though we cannot assign any reason besides experience, for so remarkable a difference between one and the other. Why has the will an influence over the tongue and fingers, not over the heart or liver? This question would never embarrass us, were we conscious of a power in the former case, not in the latter. We should then perceive, independent of experience, why the authority of will over the organs of the body is circumscribed within such particular limits. Being in that case fully acquainted with the power or force, by which it operates, we should also know, why its influence reaches precisely to such boundaries, and no farther.

proceed to examine this Pretension, and shall endeavour to avoid, as far as we are able, all Jargon and Confusion, in treating of such subtile and such pro-

found Subjects.

I assert, then,' in the *first* Place, that the Influence of Volition over the Organs of the Body, is a Fact, &c.]

' [Ed. omits ' in the first Place.]

A man, suddenly struck with a palsy in the leg or arm, or who had newly lost those members, frequently endeavours, at first, to move them, and employ them in their usual offices. Here he is as much conscious of power to command such limbs, as a man in perfect health is conscious of power to actuate any member which remains in its natural state and condition. But consciousness never deceives. Consequently, neither in the one case nor in the other, are we ever conscious of any power. We learn the influence of our will from experience alone. And experience only teaches us, how one event constantly follows another; without instructing us in the secret connexion, which binds them together, and renders them inseparable.

Thirdly, We learn from anatomy, that the immediate object of power in voluntary motion, is not the member itself which is moved, but certain muscles, and nerves, and animal spirits, and, perhaps, something still more minute and more unknown, through which the motion is successively propagated, ere it reach the member itself whose motion is the immediate object of volition. Can there be a more certain proof, that the power, by which this whole operation is performed, so far from being directly and fully known by an inward sentiment or consciousness, is, to the last degree, mysterious and unintelligible? Here the mind wills a certain event: Immediately another event, unknown to ourselves, and totally different from the one intended, is produced: This event produces another, equally unknown: Till at last, through a long succession, the desired event is produced. But if the original power were felt, it must be known: Were it known, its effect must also be known; since all power is relative to its effect. And *vice versa*, if the effect be not known, the power cannot be known nor felt. How indeed can we be conscious of a power to move our limbs, when we have no such power; but only that to move certain animal spirits, which, though they produce at last the motion of our limbs, yet operate in such a manner as is wholly beyond our comprehension?

We may, therefore, conclude from the whole, I hope, without any temerity, though with assurance; that our idea of power is not copied from any sentiment or consciousness of power within ourselves, when we give rise to animal motion, or apply our limbs to their proper use and office.

That their motion follows the command of the will is a matter of common experience, like other natural events: But the power or energy by which this is effected, like that in other natural events, is unknown and inconceivable.[1]

Shall we then assert, that we are conscious of a power or energy in our own minds, when, by an act or command of our will, we raise up a new idea, fix the mind to the contemplation of it, turn it on all sides, and at last dismiss it for some other idea, when we think that we have surveyed it with sufficient accuracy? I believe the same arguments will prove, that even this command of the will gives us no real idea of force or energy.

First, It must be allowed, that, when we know a power, we know that very circumstance in the cause, by which it is enabled to produce the effect: For these are supposed to be synonimous. We must, therefore, know both the cause and effect, and the relation between them. But do we pretend to be acquainted with the nature of the human soul and the nature of an idea, or the aptitude of the one to produce the other? This is a real creation; a production of something out of nothing: Which implies a power so great, that it may seem, at first sight, beyond the reach of any being, less than infinite. At least it must be owned, that such a power is not felt, nor known, nor even conceivable by the mind. We only feel the event, namely, the existence of an idea, consequent to a command of the will: But the manner, in which this operation is performed; the power, by which it is produced; is entirely beyond our comprehension.

Secondly, The command of the mind over itself is limited, as well as its command over the body; and these limits are

[1] It may be pretended, that the resistance which we meet with in bodies, obliging us frequently to exert our force, and call up all our power, this gives us the idea of force and power. It is this *nisus* or strong endeavour, of which we are conscious, that is the original impression from which this idea is copied. But, first, we attribute power to a vast number of objects, where we never can suppose this resistance or exertion of force to take place; to the Supreme Being, who never meets with any resistance; to the mind in its command over its ideas and limbs, in common thinking and motion, where the effect follows immediately upon the will, without any exertion or summoning up of force; to inanimate matter, which is not capable of this sentiment. *Secondly*, This sentiment of an endeavour to overcome resistance has no known connexion with any event: What follows it, we know by experience; but could not know it *à priori*. It must, however, be confessed, that the animal *nisus*, which we experience, though it can afford no accurate precise idea of power, enters very much into that vulgar, inaccurate idea, which is formed of it. [The last sentence is not in Editions E and F.]

not known by reason, or any acquaintance with the nature of cause and effect; but only by experience and observation, as in all other natural events and in the operation of external objects. Our authority over our sentiments and passions is much weaker than that over our ideas; and even the latter authority is circumscribed within very narrow boundaries. Will any one pretend to assign the ultimate reason of these boundaries, or show why the power is deficient in one case and not in another.

Thirdly. This self-command is very different at different times. A man in health possesses more of it, than one languishing with sickness. We are more master of our thoughts in the morning than in the evening: Fasting, than after a full meal. Can we give any reason for these variations, except experience? Where then is the power, of which we pretend to be conscious? Is there not here, either in a spiritual or material substance, or both, some secret mechanism or structure of parts, upon which the effect depends, and which, being entirely unknown to us, renders the power or energy of the will equally unknown and incomprehensible?

Volition is surely an act of the mind, with which we are sufficiently acquainted. Reflect upon it. Consider it on all sides. Do you find anything in it like this creative power, by which it raises from nothing a new idea, and with a kind of FIAT, imitates the omnipotence of its Maker, if I may be allowed so to speak, who called forth into existence all the various scenes of nature? So far from being conscious of this energy in the will, it requires as certain experience, as that of which we are possessed, to convince us, that such extraordinary effects do ever result from a simple act of volition.

The generality of mankind never find any difficulty in accounting for the more common and familiar operations of nature; such as the descent of heavy bodies, the growth of plants, the generation of animals, or the nourishment of bodies by food: But suppose, that, in all these cases, they perceive the very force or energy of the cause, by which it is connected with its effect, and is for ever infallible in its operation. They acquire, by long habit, such a turn of mind, that, upon the appearance of the cause, they immediately expect with assurance its usual attendant, and hardly conceive it possible, that any other event could result from it.

It is only on the discovery of extraordinary phænomena, such as earthquakes, pestilence, and prodigies of any kind, that they find themselves at a loss to assign a proper cause, and to explain the manner, in which the effect is produced by it. It is usual for men, in such difficulties, to have recourse to some invisible intelligent principle,[1] as the immediate cause of that event, which surprises them, and which, they think, cannot be accounted for from the common powers of nature. But philosophers, who carry their scrutiny a little farther, immediately perceive, that, even in the most familiar events, the energy of the cause is as unintelligible as in the most unusual, and that we only learn by experience the frequent CONJUNCTION of objects, without being ever able to comprehend any thing like CONNEXION between them. Here then, many philosophers think themselves obliged by reason to have recourse, on all occasions, to the same principle, which the vulgar never appeal to but in cases, that appear miraculous and supernatural. They acknowledge mind and intelligence to be, not only the ultimate and original cause of all things, but the immediate and sole cause of every event, which appears in nature. They pretend, that those objects, which are commonly denominated *causes*, are in reality nothing but *occasions*; and that the true and direct principle of every effect is not any power or force in nature, but a volition of the Supreme Being, who wills, that such particular objects should, for ever, be conjoined with each other. Instead of saying, that one billiard-ball moves another, by a force, which it has derived from the author of nature; it is the Deity himself, they say, who, by a particular volition, moves the second ball, being determined to this operation by the impulse of the first ball: in consequence of those general laws, which he has laid down to himself in the government of the universe. But philosophers advancing still in their enquiries, discover, that, as we are totally ignorant of the power, on which depends the mutual operation of bodies, we are no less ignorant of that power, on which depends the operation of mind on body, or of body on mind; nor are we able, either from our senses or consciousness, to assign the ultimate principle in one case, more than in the other. The same ignorance, therefore, reduces them to the

---

[1] Θεὸς ἀπὸ μηχανῆς. [El. E reads: *Qua si Deus ex machina.* F adds the reference: Cic. de Nat. Deorum.]

same conclusion. They assert, that the Deity is the immediate cause of the union between soul and body; and that
they are not the organs of sense, which, being agitated by
external objects, produce sensations in the mind; but that
it is a particular volition of our omnipotent Maker, which
excites such a sensation, in consequence of such a motion in
the organ. In like manner, it is not any energy in the will,
that produces local motion in our members: It is God himself, who is pleased to second our will, in itself impotent,
and to command that motion, which we erroneously attribute
to our own power and efficacy. Nor do philosophers stop at
this conclusion. They sometimes extend the same inference
to the mind itself, in its internal operations. Our mental
vision or conception of ideas is nothing but a revelation made
to us by our Maker. When we voluntarily turn our thoughts
to any object, and raise up its image in the fancy; it is not
the will which creates that idea: It is the universal Creator,
who discovers it to the mind, and renders it present to us.

Thus, according to these philosophers, every thing is full
of God. Not content with the principle, that nothing exists
but by his will, that nothing possesses any power but by his
concession: They rob nature, and all created beings, of every
power, in order to render their dependence on the Deity still
more sensible and immediate. They consider not, that, by
this theory, they diminish, instead of magnifying, the grandeur of those attributes, which they affect so much to celebrate. It argues surely more power in the Deity to delegate
a certain degree of power to inferior creatures, than to produce every thing by his own immediate volition. It argues
more wisdom to contrive at first the fabric of the world with
such perfect foresight, that, of itself, and by its proper
operation, it may serve all the purposes of providence, than
if the great Creator were obliged every moment to adjust its
parts, and animate by his breath all the wheels of that stu-
pendous machine.

But if we would have a more philosophical confutation of
this theory, perhaps the two following reflections may
suffice.

First, It seems to me, that this theory of the universal
energy and operation of the Supreme Being, is too bold ever
to carry conviction with it to a man, sufficiently apprized of
the weakness of human reason, and the narrow limits, to

which it is confined in all its operations. Though the chain of arguments, which conduct to it, were ever so logical, there must arise a strong suspicion, if not an absolute assurance, that it has carried us quite beyond the reach of our faculties, when it leads to conclusions so extraordinary, and so remote from common life and experience. We are got into fairy land, long ere we have reached the last steps of our theory; and *there* we have no reason to trust our common method of argument, or to think that our usual analogies and probabilities have any authority. Our line is too short to fathom such immense abysses. And however we may flatter ourselves, that we are guided, in every step which we take, by a kind of verisimilitude and experience; we may be assured, that this fancied experience has no authority, when we thus apply it to subjects, that lie entirely out of the sphere of experience. But on this we shall have occasion to touch afterwards.[1]

Secondly, I cannot perceive any force in the arguments, on which this theory is founded. We are ignorant, it is true, of the manner in which bodies operate on each other : Their force or energy is entirely incomprehensible : But are we not equally ignorant of the manner or force by which a mind, even the supreme mind, operates either on itself or on body? Whence, I beseech you, do we acquire any idea of it? We have no sentiment or consciousness of this power in ourselves. We have no idea of the Supreme Being but what we learn from reflection on our own faculties. Were our ignorance, therefore, a good reason for rejecting any thing, we should be led into that principle of denying all energy in the Supreme Being as much as in the grossest matter. We surely comprehend as little the operations of one as of the other. Is it more difficult to conceive, that motion may arise from impulse, than that it may arise from volition? All we know is our profound ignorance in both cases.[2]

---

[1] Section XII.

[2] I need not examine at length the *vis inertiæ* which is so much talked of in the new philosophy, and which is ascribed to matter. We find by experience, that a body at rest or in motion continues for ever in its present state, till put from it by some new cause : And that a body impelled takes as much motion from the impelling body as it acquires itself. These are facts. When we call this a *vis inertiæ*, we only mark these facts, without pretending to have any idea of the inert power : in the same manner as, when we talk of gravity, we mean certain effects without comprehending that active power. It was never the meaning of Sir Isaac Newton[1] to rob second causes of all force or energy; though some of his followers

---

[1] [Matter : Edition E and F.]

But to hasten to a conclusion of this argument, which is already drawn out to too great a length: We have sought in vain for an idea of power or necessary connexion, in all the sources from which we could suppose it to be derived. It appears, that, in single instances of the operation of bodies, we never can, by our utmost scrutiny, discover any thing but one event following another; without being able to comprehend any force or power, by which the cause operates, or any connexion between it and its supposed effect. The same difficulty occurs in contemplating the operations of mind on body; where we observe the motion of the latter to follow upon the volition of the former; but are not able to observe or conceive the tye, which binds together the motion and volition, or the energy by which the mind produces this effect. The authority of the will over its own faculties and ideas is not a whit more comprehensible: So that, upon the whole, there appears not, throughout all nature, any one instance of connexion, which is conceivable by us. All events seem entirely loose and separate. One event follows another; but we never can observe any tye between them. They seem *conjoined*, but never *connected*. And as we can have no idea of any thing, which never appeared to our outward sense or inward sentiment, the necessary conclusion *seems* to be, that we have no idea of connexion or power at all, and that these words are absolutely without any meaning, when employed either in philosophical reasonings, or common life.

But there still remains one method of avoiding this conclusion, and one source which we have not yet examined. When any natural object or event is presented, it is impossible for us, by any sagacity or penetration, to discover, or even conjecture, without experience, what event will result

---

have endeavoured to establish that theory upon his authority. On the contrary, that great philosopher had recourse to an etherial active fluid to explain his universal attraction: though he was so cautious and modest as to allow, that it was a mere hypothesis, not to be insisted on, without more experiments. I must confess, that there is something in the fate of opinions a little extraordinary. Des Cartes insinuated that doctrine of the universal and sole efficacy of the Deity, without insisting on it. Malebranche and other Cartesians made it the foundation of all their philosophy. It had, however, no authority in England. Locke, Clarke, and Cudworth, never so much as take notice of it, but supposed all along, that matter has a real, though subordinate and derived power. By what means has it become so prevalent among our modern metaphysicians?

from it, or to carry our foresight beyond that object, which is immediately present to the memory and senses. Even after one instance or experiment, where we have observed a particular event to follow upon another, we are not entitled to form a general rule, or foretel what will happen in like cases; it being justly esteemed an unpardonable temerity to judge of the whole course of nature from one single experiment, however accurate or certain. But when one particular species of event has always, in all instances, been conjoined with another, we make no longer any scruple of foretelling one upon the appearance of the other, and of employing that reasoning, which can alone assure us of any matter of fact or existence. We then call the one object, *Cause*; the other, *Effect*. We suppose, that there is some connection between them; some power in the one, by which it infallibly produces the other, and operates with the greatest certainty and strongest necessity.

It appears, then, that this idea of a necessary connexion among events arises from a number of similar instances, which occur, of the constant conjunction of these events; nor can that idea ever be suggested by any one of these instances, surveyed in all possible lights and positions. But there is nothing in a number of instances, different from every single instance, which is supposed to be exactly similar; except only, that after a repetition of similar instances, the mind is carried by habit, upon the appearance of one event, to expect its usual attendant, and to believe, that it will exist. This connexion, therefore, which we *feel* in the mind, this customary transition of the imagination from one object to its usual attendant, is the sentiment or impression, from which we form the idea of power or necessary connexion. Nothing farther is in the case. Contemplate the subject on all sides; you will never find any other origin of that idea. This is the sole difference between one instance, from which we can never receive the idea of connexion, and a number of similar instances, by which it is suggested. The first time a man saw the communication of motion by impulse, as by the shock of two billiard-balls, he could not pronounce that the one event was *connected*: but only that it was *conjoined* with the other. After he had observed several instances of this nature, he then pronounces them to be *connected*. What alteration has happened to give rise to this new idea of *con-*

nexion? Nothing but that he now *feels* these events to be *connected* in his imagination, and can readily foretel the existence of one from the appearance of the other. When we say, therefore, that one object is connected with another, we mean only, that they have acquired a connexion in our thought, and give rise to this inference, by which they become proofs of each other's existence: A conclusion, which is somewhat extraordinary; but which seems founded on sufficient evidence. Nor will its evidence be weakened by any general diffidence of the understanding, or sceptical suspicion concerning every conclusion, which is new and extraordinary. No conclusions can be more agreeable to scepticism than such as make discoveries concerning the weakness and narrow limits of human reason and capacity.

And what stronger instance can be produced of the surprising ignorance and weakness of the understanding, than the present? For surely, if there be any relation among objects, which it imports to us to know perfectly, it is that of cause and effect. On this are founded all our reasonings concerning matter of fact or existence. By means of it alone we attain any assurance concerning objects, which are removed from the present testimony of our memory and senses. The only immediate utility of all sciences, is to teach us, how to control and regulate future events by their causes. Our thoughts and enquiries are, therefore, every moment, employed about this relation: Yet so imperfect are the ideas which we form concerning it, that it is impossible to give any just definition of cause, except what is drawn from something extraneous and foreign to it. Similar objects are always conjoined with similar. Of this we have experience. Suitably to this experience, therefore, we may define a cause to be *an object, followed by another, and where all the objects, similar to the first, are followed by objects similar to the second.* ¹Or, in other words, *where, if the first object had not been, the second never had existed.* The appearance of a cause always conveys the mind, by a customary transition, to the idea of the effect. Of this also we have experience. We may, therefore, suitably to this experience, form another definition of cause; and call it, *an object followed by another, and whose appearance always conveys the thought to that other.* But though both these definitions be drawn from circumstances foreign to the

¹ [This sentence was added in Edition K.]

cause, we cannot remedy this inconvenience, or attain any more perfect definition, which may point out that circumstance in the cause, which gives it a connexion with its effect. We have no idea of this connexion; nor even any distinct notion what it is we desire to know, when we endeavour at a conception of it. We say, for instance, that the vibration of this string is the cause of this particular sound. But what do we mean by that affirmation? We either mean, *that this vibration is followed by this sound, and that all similar vibrations have been followed by similar sounds : Or, that this vibration is followed by this sound, and that upon the appearance of one, the mind anticipates the senses, and forms immediately an idea of the other.* We may consider the relation of cause and effect in either of these two lights; but beyond these, we have no idea of it.[1]

To recapitulate, therefore, the reasonings of this section : Every idea is copied from some preceding impression or sentiment; and where we cannot find any impression, we may be certain that there is no idea. In all single instances of the operation of bodies or minds, there is nothing that pro-

---

[1] According to these explications and definitions, the idea of *power* is relative as much as that of *cause*; and both have a reference to an effect, or some other event constantly conjoined with the former. When we consider the *unknown* circumstance of an object, by which the degree or quantity of its effect is fixed and determined, we call that its power : And accordingly, it is allowed by all philosophers, that the effect is the measure of the power. But if they had any idea of power, as it is in itself, why could not they measure it in itself? The dispute whether the force of a body in motion be as its velocity, or the square of its velocity; this dispute, I say, needed not be decided by comparing its effects in equal or unequal times; but by a direct mensuration and comparison.

As to the frequent use of the words, Force, Power, Energy, &c. which every where occur in common conversation, as well as in philosophy; that is no proof, that we are acquainted, in any instance, with the connecting principle between cause and effect, or can account ultimately for the production of one thing by another. These words, as commonly used, have very loose meanings annexed to them; and their ideas are very uncertain and confused. No animal can put external bodies in motion without the sentiment of a *nisus* or endeavour; and every animal has a sentiment or feeling from the stroke or blow of an external object, that is in motion. These sensations, which are merely animal, and from which we can *à priori* draw no inference, we are apt to transfer to inanimate objects, and to suppose, that they have some such feelings, whenever they transfer or receive motion. With regard to energies, which are exerted, without our annexing to them any idea of communicated motion, we consider only the constant experienced conjunction of the events; and as we *feel* a customary connexion between the ideas, we transfer that feeling to the objects; as nothing is more usual than to apply to external bodies every internal sensation, which they occasion.

[This note was added in Ed. F: which, however, rea's in place of the second paragraph :

A *Cause* is different from a *Sign*; as it implies Precedency and Contiguity in Time and Place, as well as constant Conjunction. A Sign is nothing but a correlative Effect from the same Cause.]

duces any impression, nor consequently can suggest any idea, of power or necessary connexion. But when many uniform instances appear, and the same object is always followed by the same event; we then begin to entertain the notion of cause and connexion. We then *feel* a new sentiment or impression, to wit, a customary connexion in the thought or imagination between one object and its usual attendant; and this sentiment is the original of that idea which we seek for. For as this idea arises from a number of similar instances, and not from any single instance; it must arise from that circumstance, in which the number of instances differ from every individual instance. But this customary connexion or transition of the imagination is the only circumstance, in which they differ. In every other particular they are alike. The first instance which we saw of motion, communicated by the shock of two billiard-balls (to return to this obvious illustration) is exactly similar to any instance that may, at present, occur to us; except only, that we could not, at first, *infer* one event from the other; which we are enabled to do at present, after so long a course of uniform experience. I know not, whether the reader will readily apprehend this reasoning. I am afraid, that, should I multiply words about it, or throw it into a greater variety of lights, it would only become more obscure and intricate. In all abstract reasonings, there is one point of view, which, if we can happily hit, we shall go farther towards illustrating the subject, than by all the eloquence and copious expression in the world. This point of view we should endeavour to reach, and reserve the flowers of rhetoric for subjects which are more adapted to them.

SECTION VIII.—*Of Liberty and Necessity.*

PART I.

IT might reasonably be expected, in questions, which have been canvassed and disputed with great eagerness, since the first origin of science and philosophy, that the meaning of all the terms, at least, should have been agreed upon among the disputants; and our enquiries, in the course of two thousand years, been able to pass from words to the true and real subject of the controversy. For how easy may it seem to give exact definitions of the terms employed in reasoning, and make these definitions, not the mere sound of words, the object of future scrutiny and examination? But if we consider the matter more narrowly, we shall be apt to draw a quite opposite conclusion. From this circumstance alone, that a controversy has been long kept on foot, and remains still undecided, we may presume, that there is some ambiguity in the expression, and that the disputants affix different ideas to the terms employed in the controversy. For as the faculties of the mind are supposed to be naturally alike in every individual; otherwise nothing could be more fruitless than to reason or dispute together; it were impossible, if men affix the same ideas to their terms, that they could so long form different opinions of the same subject; especially when they communicate their views, and each party turn themselves on all sides, in search of arguments, which may give them the victory over their antagonists. It is true; if men attempt the discussion of questions, which lie entirely beyond the reach of human capacity, such as those concerning the origin of worlds, or the œconomy of the intellectual system or region of spirits, they may long beat the air in their fruitless contests, and never arrive at any determinate conclusion. But if the question regard any subject of common life and experience; nothing, one would think, could preserve the dispute so long undecided, but some ambiguous expressions, which keep the antagonists still at a distance, and hinder them from grappling with each other.

This has been the case in the long disputed question concerning liberty and necessity; and to so remarkable a degree, that, if I be not much mistaken, we shall find, that all mankind, both learned and ignorant, have always been of the same opinion with regard to this subject, and that a few intelligible definitions would immediately have put an end to the whole controversy. I own, that this dispute has been so much canvassed on all hands, and has led philosophers into such a labyrinth of obscure sophistry, that it is no wonder, if a sensible reader indulge his ease so far as to turn a deaf ear to the proposal of such a question, from which he can expect neither instruction nor entertainment. But the state of the argument here proposed may, perhaps, serve to renew his attention; as it has more novelty, promises at least some decision of the controversy, and will not much disturb his ease by any intricate or obscure reasoning.

I hope, therefore, to make it appear, that all men have ever agreed in the doctrine both of necessity and of liberty, according to any reasonable sense, which can be put on these terms; and that the whole controversy has hitherto turned merely upon words. We shall begin with examining the doctrine of necessity.

It is universally allowed, that matter, in all its operations, is actuated by a necessary force, and that every natural effect is so precisely determined by the energy of its cause, that no other effect, in such particular circumstances, could possibly have resulted from it. The degree and direction of every motion is, by the laws of nature, prescribed with such exactness, that a living creature may as soon arise from the shock of two bodies, as motion, in any other degree or direction than what is actually produced by it. Would we, therefore, form a just and precise idea of *necessity*, we must consider whence that idea arises, when we apply it to the operation of bodies.

It seems evident, that, if all the scenes of nature were continually shifted in such a manner, that no two events bore any resemblance to each other, but every object was entirely new, without any similitude to whatever had been seen before, we should never, in that case, have attained the least idea of necessity, or of a connexion among these objects. We might say, upon such a supposition, that one object or event has followed another; not that one was produced by the other. The relation of cause and effect must be utterly unknown to mankind. Inference and reasoning concerning the operations of nature would, from that moment, be at an end; and the memory and senses remain the only canals, by which the knowledge of any real existence could possibly have access to the mind. Our idea, therefore, of necessity and causation arises entirely from the uniformity, observable in the operations of nature; where similar objects are constantly conjoined together, and the mind is determined by custom to infer the one from the appearance of the other. These two circumstances form the whole of that necessity, which we ascribe to matter. Beyond the constant *conjunction* of similar objects, and the consequent *inference* from one to the other, we have no notion of any necessity, or connexion.

If it appear, therefore, that all mankind have ever allowed, without any doubt or hesitation, that these two circumstances

F 2

take place in the voluntary actions of men, and in the operations of mind ; it must follow, that all mankind have ever
agreed in the doctrine of necessity, and that they have
hitherto disputed, merely for not understanding each other.

As to the first circumstance, the constant and regular conjunction of similar events ; we may possibly satisfy ourselves
by the following considerations. It is universally acknowledged, that there is a great uniformity among the actions
of men, in all nations and ages, and that human nature remains still the same, in its principles and operations. The
same motives always produce the same actions: The same
events follow from the same causes. Ambition, avarice, self-
love, vanity, friendship, generosity, public spirit; these passions, mixed in various degrees, and distributed through
society, have been, from the beginning of the world, and still
are, the source of all the actions and enterprizes, which have
ever been observed among mankind. Would you know the
sentiments, inclinations, and course of life of the GREEKS
and ROMANS? Study well the temper and actions of the
FRENCH and ENGLISH: You cannot be much mistaken in
transferring to the former *most* of the observations, which
you have made with regard to the latter. Mankind are so
much the same, in all times and places, that history informs
us of nothing new or strange in this particular. Its chief
use is only to discover the constant and universal principles
of human nature, by shewing men in all varieties of circumstances and situations, and furnishing us with materials,
from which we may form our observations, and become acquainted with the regular springs of human action and
behaviour. These records of wars, intrigues, factions, and
revolutions, are so many collections of experiments, by which
the politician or moral philosopher fixes the principles of his
science ; in the same manner as the physician or natural
philosopher becomes acquainted with the nature of plants,
minerals, and other external objects, by the experiments, which
he forms concerning them. Nor are the earth, water, and
other elements, examined by ARISTOTLE, and HIPPOCRATES,
more like to those, which at present lie under our observation, than the men, described by POLYBIUS and TACITUS, are
to those, who now govern the world.

Should a traveller, returning from a far country, bring us
an account of men, wholly different from any, with whom we

were ever acquainted; men, who were entirely divested of avarice, ambition, or revenge; who knew no pleasure but friendship, generosity, and public spirit; we should immediately, from these circumstances, detect the falsehood, and prove him a liar, with the same certainty as if he had stuffed his narration with stories of centaurs and dragons, miracles and prodigies. And if we would explode any forgery in history, we cannot make use of a more convincing argument, than to prove, that the actions, ascribed to any person, are directly contrary to the course of nature, and that no human motives, in such circumstances, could ever induce him to such a conduct. The veracity of QUINTUS CURTIUS is as much to be suspected, when he describes the supernatural courage of ALEXANDER, by which he was hurried on singly to attack multitudes, as when he describes his supernatural force and activity, by which he was able to resist them. So readily and universally do we acknowledge a uniformity in human motives and actions as well as in the operations of body.

Hence likewise the benefit of that experience, acquired by long life and a variety of business and company, in order to instruct us in the principles of human nature, and regulate our future conduct, as well as speculation. By means of this guide, we mount up to the knowledge of men's inclinations and motives, from their actions, expressions, and even gestures; and again, descend to the interpretation of their actions from our knowledge of their motives and inclinations. The general observations, treasured up by a course of experience, give us the clue of human nature, and teach us to unravel all its intricacies. Pretexts and appearances no longer deceive us. Public declarations pass for the specious colouring of a cause. And though virtue and honour be allowed their proper weight and authority, that perfect disinterestedness, so often pretended to, is never expected in multitudes and parties; seldom in their leaders; and scarcely even in individuals of any rank or station. But were there no uniformity in human actions, and were every experiment, which we could form of this kind, irregular and anomalous, it were impossible to collect any general observations concerning mankind; and no experience, however accurately digested by reflection, would ever serve to any purpose. Why is the aged husbandman more skilful in his calling than the young beginner, but because there is a certain uniformity in

the operation of the sun, rain, and earth, towards the production of vegetables ; and experience teaches the old prac-
titioner the rules, by which this operation is governed and
directed ?

We must not, however, expect, that this uniformity of
human actions should be carried to such a length, as that all
men, in the same circumstances, will always act precisely in
the same manner, without making any allowance for the
diversity of characters, prejudices, and opinions. Such a
uniformity in every particular, is found in no part of nature.
On the contrary, from observing the variety of conduct in
different men, we are enabled to form a greater variety of
maxims, which still suppose a degree of uniformity and
regularity.

Are the manners of men different in different ages and
countries? We learn thence the great force of custom and
education, which mould the human mind from its infancy,
and form it into a fixed and established character. Is the
behaviour and conduct of the one sex very unlike that of the
other? It is thence we become acquainted with the different
characters, which nature has impressed upon the sexes, and
which she preserves with constancy and regularity. Are the
actions of the same person much diversified in the different
periods of his life, from infancy to old age? This affords
room for many general observations concerning the gradual
change of our sentiments and inclinations, and the different
maxims, which prevail in the different ages of human creatures. Even the characters, which are peculiar to each
individual, have a uniformity in their influence; otherwise
our acquaintance with the persons and our observation of
their conduct, could never teach us their dispositions, or serve
to direct our behaviour with regard to them.

I grant it possible to find some actions, which seem to have
no regular connexion with any known motives, and are exceptions to all the measures of conduct, which have ever
been established for the government of men. But if we would
willingly know, what judgment should be formed of such irregular and extraordinary actions ; we may consider the sentiments, commonly entertained with regard to those irregular
events, which appear in the course of nature, and the
operations of external objects. All causes are not conjoined
to their usual effects, with like uniformity. An artificer, who

handles only dead matter, may be disappointed of his aim, as well as the politician, who directs the conduct of sensible and intelligent agents.

The vulgar, who take things according to their first appearance, attribute the uncertainty of events to such an uncertainty in the causes as makes the latter often fail of their usual influence; though they meet with no impediment in their operation. But philosophers, observing, that, almost in every part of nature, there is contained a vast variety of springs and principles, which are hid, by reason of their minuteness or remoteness, find, that it is at least possible the contrariety of events may not proceed from any contingency in the cause, but from the secret operation of contrary causes. This possibility is converted into certainty by farther observation; when they remark, that, upon an exact scrutiny, a contrariety of effects always betrays a contrariety of causes, and proceeds from their mutual opposition. A peasant can give no better reason for the stopping of any clock or watch than to say that it does not commonly go right: But an artist easily perceives, that the same force in the spring or pendulum has always the same influence on the wheels; but fails of its usual effect, perhaps by reason of a grain of dust, which puts a stop to the whole movement. From the observation of several parallel instances, philosophers form a maxim, that the connexion between all causes and effects is equally necessary, and that its seeming uncertainty in some instances proceeds from the secret opposition of contrary causes.

Thus for instance, in the human body, when the usual symptoms of health or sickness disappoint our expectation; when medicines operate not with their wonted powers; when irregular events follow from any particular cause; the philosopher and physician are not surprized at the matter, nor are ever tempted to deny, in general, the necessity and uniformity of those principles, by which the animal œconomy is conducted. They know, that a human body is a mighty complicated machine: That many secret powers lurk in it, which are altogether beyond our comprehension: That to us it must often appear very uncertain in its operations: And that therefore the irregular events, which outwardly discover themselves, can be no proof, that the laws of nature are not observed with the greatest regularity in its internal operations and government.

The philosopher, if he be consistent, must apply the same reasoning to the actions and volitions of intelligent agents. The most irregular and unexpected resolutions of men may frequently be accounted for by those, who know every particular circumstance of their character and situation. A person of an obliging disposition gives a peevish answer. But he has the toothake, or has not dined. A stupid fellow discovers an uncommon alacrity in his carriage: But he has met with a sudden piece of good fortune. Or even when an action, as sometimes happens, cannot be particularly accounted for, either by the person himself or by others; we know, in general, that the characters of men are, to a certain degree, inconstant and irregular. This is, in a manner, the constant character of human nature; though it be applicable, in a more particular manner, to some persons, who have no fixed rule for their conduct, but proceed in a continued course of caprice and inconstancy. The internal principles and motives may operate in a uniform manner, notwithstanding these seeming irregularities; in the same manner as the winds, rain, clouds, and other variations of the weather are supposed to be governed by steady principles; though not easily discoverable by human sagacity and enquiry.

Thus it appears, not only that the conjunction between motives and voluntary actions is as regular and uniform, as that between the cause and effect in any part of nature; but also that this regular conjunction has been universally acknowledged among mankind, and has never been the subject of dispute, either in philosophy or common life. Now, as it is from past experience, that we draw all inferences concerning the future, and as we conclude, that objects will always be conjoined together, which we find to have always been conjoined; it may seem superfluous to prove, that this experienced uniformity in human actions is a[1] source, whence we draw *inferences* concerning them. But in order to throw the argument into a greater variety of lights, we shall also insist, though briefly, on this latter topic.

The mutual dependence of men is so great, in all societies, that scarce any human action is entirely compleat in itself, or is performed without some reference to the actions of others, which are requisite to make it answer fully the inten-

[1] [The source of all the *inferences*, which we form concerning them.—Editions E to P.]

tion of the agent. The poorest artificer, who labours alone, expects at least the protection of the magistrate, to ensure him the enjoyment of the fruits of his labour. He also expects, that, when he carries his goods to market, and offers them at a reasonable price, he shall find purchasers; and shall be able, by the money he acquires, to engage others to supply him with those commodities, which are requisite for his subsistence. In proportion as men extend their dealings, and render their intercourse with others more complicated, they always comprehend, in their schemes of life, a greater variety of voluntary actions, which they expect, from the proper motives, to co-operate with their own. In all these conclusions, they take their measures from past experience, in the same manner as in their reasonings concerning external objects; and firmly believe, that men, as well as all the elements, are to continue, in their operations, the same, that they have ever found them. A manufacturer reckons upon the labour of his servants, for the execution of any work, as much as upon the tools, which he employs, and would be equally surprized, were his expectations disappointed. In short, this experimental inference and reasoning concerning the actions of others enters so much into human life, that no man, while awake, is ever a moment without employing it. Have we not reason, therefore, to affirm, that all mankind have always agreed in the doctrine of necessity, according to the foregoing definition and explication of it?

Nor have philosophers ever entertained a different opinion from the people in this particular. For not to mention, that almost every action of their life supposes that opinion; there are even few of the speculative parts of learning, to which it is not essential. What would become of *history*, had we not a dependence on the veracity of the historian, according to the experience, which we have had of mankind? How could *politics* be a science, if laws and forms of government had not a uniform influence upon society? Where would be the foundation of *morals*, if particular characters had no certain or determinate power to produce particular sentiments, and if these sentiments had no constant operation on actions? And with what pretence could we employ our *criticism* upon any poet or polite author, if we could not pronounce the conduct and sentiments of his actors, either natural or unnatural, to such characters, and in such circumstances? It seems almost impossible, therefore, to engage, either in science or action of any kind, without acknowledging the doctrine of necessity, and this *inference* from motives to voluntary actions; from characters to conduct.

And indeed, when we consider how aptly *natural* and *moral* evidence link together, and form only one chain of argument, we shall make no scruple to allow, that they are of the same nature, and derived from the same principles. A prisoner, who has neither money nor interest, discovers the impossibility of his escape, as well when he considers the obstinacy of the gaoler, as the walls and bars, with which he is surrounded; and, in all attempts for his freedom, chuses rather to work upon the stone and iron of the one, than upon the inflexible nature of the other. The same prisoner, when conducted to the scaffold, foresees his death as certainly from the constancy and fidelity of his guards, as from the operation of the ax or wheel. His mind runs along a certain train of ideas: The refusal of the soldiers to consent to his escape; the action of the executioner; the separation of the head and body; bleeding, convulsive motions, and death. Here is a connected chain of natural causes and voluntary actions; but the mind feels no difference between them, in passing from one link to another: Nor is it less certain of the future event than if it were connected with the objects present to the memory or senses, by a train of causes, cemented together by what we are pleased to call a *physical* necessity. The same experienced union has the same effect on the mind, whether the united objects be motives, volition, and actions; or figure and motion. We may change the names of things; but their nature and their operation on the understanding never change.

[1] Were a man, whom I know to be honest and opulent, and with whom I live in intimate friendship, to come into my house, where I am surrounded with my servants, I rest assured, that he is not to stab me before he leaves it, in order to rob me of my silver standish; and I no more suspect this event, than the falling of the house itself which is new, and solidly built and founded. *But he may have been seized with a sudden and unknown frenzy.* So may a sudden earthquake arise, and shake and tumble my house about my ears. I shall therefore change the suppositions. I shall say, that

[1] [This paragraph was added in Edition R.]

I know with certainty, that he is not to put his hand into the fire, and hold it there, till it be consumed: And this event, I think I can foretell with the same assurance, as that, if he throw himself out at the window, and meet with no obstruction, he will not remain a moment suspended in the air. No suspicion of an unknown frenzy can give the least possibility to the former event, which is so contrary to all the known principles of human nature. A man who at noon leaves his purse full of gold on the pavement at Charing-Cross, may as well expect that it will fly away like a feather, as that he will find it untouched an hour after. Above one half of human reasonings contain inferences of a similar nature, attended with more or less degrees of certainty, proportioned to our experience of the usual conduct of mankind in such particular situations.

I have frequently considered, what could possibly be the reason, why all mankind, though they have ever, without hesitation, acknowledged the doctrine of necessity, in their whole practice and reasoning, have yet discovered such a reluctance to acknowledge it in words, and have rather shewn a propensity, in all ages, to profess the contrary opinion. The matter, I think, may be accounted for, after the following manner. If we examine the operations of body, and the production of effects from their causes, we shall find, that all our faculties can never carry us farther in our knowledge of this relation, than barely to observe, that particular objects are *constantly conjoined* together, and that the mind is carried, by a *customary transition*, from the appearance of one to the belief of the other. But though this conclusion concerning human ignorance be the result of the strictest scrutiny of this subject, men still entertain a strong propensity to believe, that they penetrate farther into the powers of nature, and perceive something like a necessary connexion between the cause and the effect. When again they turn their reflections towards the operations of their own minds, and *feel* no such connexion of the motive and the action; they are thence apt to suppose, that there is a difference between the effects, which result from material force, and those which arise from thought and intelligence. But being once convinced, that we know nothing farther of causation of any kind, than merely the *constant conjunction* of objects, and the consequent *inference* of the mind from one to another and finding, that these two circumstances are universally allowed to have place in voluntary actions; we may be more easily led to own the same necessity common to all causes. And though this reasoning may contradict the systems of many philosophers, in ascribing necessity to the determinations of the will, we shall find, upon reflection, that they dissent from it in words only, not in their real sentiment. Necessity, according to the sense, in which it is here taken, has never yet been rejected, nor can ever, I think, be rejected by any philosopher. It may only, perhaps, be pretended, that the mind can perceive, in the operations of matter, some farther connexion between the cause and effect; and a connexion that has not place in the voluntary actions of intelligent beings. Now whether it be so or not, can only appear upon examination; and it is incumbent on these philosophers to make good their assertion, by defining or describing that necessity, and pointing it out to us in the operations of material causes.

It would seem, indeed, that men begin at the wrong end of this question concerning liberty and necessity, when they enter upon it by examining the faculties of the soul, the influence of the understanding, and the operations of the will. Let them first discuss a more simple question, namely, the operations of body and of brute unintelligent matter; and try whether they can there form any idea of causation and necessity, except that of a constant conjunction of objects, and subsequent inference of the mind from one to another. If these circumstances form, in reality, the whole of that necessity, which we conceive in matter, and if these circumstances be also universally acknowledged to take place in the operations of the mind, the dispute is at an end; at least, must be owned to be thenceforth merely verbal. But as long as we will rashly suppose, that we have some farther idea of necessity and causation in the operations of external objects: at the same time, that we can find nothing farther, in the voluntary actions of the mind; there is no possibility of bringing the question to any determinate issue, while we proceed upon so erroneous a supposition. The only method of undeceiving us, is, to mount up higher; to examine the narrow extent of science when applied to material causes; and to convince ourselves, that all we know of them, is, the constant conjunction and inference above mentioned. We may, perhaps, find, that it is with difficulty we are induced to fix such narrow limits to human understanding : But we can afterwards find no difficulty when we come to apply this doctrine to the actions of the will. For as it is evident, that these have a regular conjunction with motives and circumstances and characters, and as we always draw inferences from one to the other, we must be obliged to acknowledge in words, that necessity, which we have already avowed, in every deliberation of our lives, and in every step of our conduct and behaviour.[1]

But to proceed in this reconciling project with regard to the question of liberty and necessity ; the most contentious question, of metaphysics, the most contentious science ; it will not require many words to prove, that all mankind have ever agreed in the doctrine of liberty as well as in that of necessity, and that the whole dispute, in this respect also, has been hitherto merely verbal. For what is meant by liberty, when applied to voluntary actions ? We cannot surely mean, that actions have so little connexion with motives, inclinations, and circumstances, that one does not

---

[1] The prevalence of the doctrine of liberty may be accounted for, from another cause, viz. a false sensation or seeming experience which we have, or may have, of liberty or indifference, in many of our actions. The necessity of any action, whether of matter or of mind, is not, properly speaking, a quality in the agent, but in any thinking or intelligent being, who may consider the action ; and it consists chiefly in the determination of his thoughts to infer the existence of that action from some preceding objects ; as liberty, when opposed to necessity, is nothing but the want of that determination, and a certain looseness or indifference, which we feel, in passing, or not passing, from the idea of one object to that of any succeeding one. Now we may observe, that, though, in *reflecting* on human actions, we seldom feel such a looseness or indifference, but are commonly able to infer them with considerable certainty from their motives, and from the dispositions of the agent ; yet it frequently happens, that, in *performing* the actions themselves, we are sensible of something like it : And as all resembling objects are readily taken for each other, this has been employed as a demonstrative and even intuitive proof of human liberty. We feel, that our actions are subject to our will, on most occasions ; and imagine we feel, that the will itself is subject to nothing, because, when by a denial of it we are provoked to try, we feel, that it moves easily every way, and produces an image of itself, (or a *Velleity*, as it is called in the schools) even on that side, on which it did not settle. This image, or faint motion, we persuade ourselves, could, at that time, have been compleated into the thing itself ; because, should that be denied, we find, upon a second trial, that, at present, it can. We consider not, that the fantastical desire of shewing liberty, is here the motive of our actions. And it seems certain, that, however we may imagine we feel a liberty within ourselves, a spectator can commonly infer our actions from our motives and character ; and even where he cannot, he concludes in general, that he might, were he perfectly acquainted with every circumstance of our situation and temper, and the most secret springs of our complexion and disposition. Now this is the very essence of necessity, according to the foregoing doctrine.

follow with a certain degree of uniformity from the other, and that one affords no inference by which we can conclude the existence of the other. For these are plain and acknowledged matters of fact. By liberty, then, we can only mean *a power of acting or not acting, according to the determinations of the will*; that is, if we chuse to remain at rest, we may; if we chuse to move, we also may. Now this hypothetical liberty is universally allowed to belong to every one, who is not a prisoner and in chains. Here then is no subject of dispute.

Whatever definition we may give of liberty, we should be careful to observe two requisite circumstances; *first*, that it be consistent with plain matter of fact; *secondly*, that it be consistent with itself. If we observe these circumstances, and render our definition intelligible, I am persuaded that all mankind will be found of one opinion with regard to it.

It is universally allowed, that nothing exists without a cause of its existence, and that chance, when strictly examined, is a mere negative word, and means not any real power, which has any where, a being in nature. But it is pretended, that some causes are necessary, some not necessary. Here then is the advantage of definitions. Let any one *define* a cause, without comprehending, as a part of the definition, a *necessary connexion* with its effect; and let him shew distinctly the origin of the idea, expressed by the definition; and I shall readily give up the whole controversy. But if the foregoing explication of the matter be received, this must be absolutely impracticable. Had not objects a regular conjunction with each other, we should never have entertained any notion of cause and effect; and this regular conjunction produces that inference of the understanding, which is the only connexion, that we can have any comprehension of. Whoever attempts a definition of cause, exclusive of these circumstances, will be obliged, either to employ unintelligible terms, or such as are synonimous to the term, which he endeavours to define.[1] And if the definition above

---

[1] Thus, if a cause be defined, *that which produces any thing*; it is easy to observe, that *producing* is synonimous to *causing*. In like manner, if a cause be defined, *that by which anything exists*; this is liable to the same objection. For what is meant by these words, *by which*? Had it been said, that a cause is *that after which anything constantly exists*; we should have understood the terms. For this is, indeed, all we know of the matter. And this constancy forms the very essence of necessity, nor have we any other idea of it.

mentioned be admitted; liberty, when opposed to necessity, not to constraint, is the same thing with chance; which is universally allowed to have no existence.

PART II.

There is no method of reasoning more common, and yet none more blameable, than, in philosophical disputes, to endeavour the refutation of any hypothesis, by a pretence of its dangerous consequences to religion and morality. When any opinion leads to absurdities, it is certainly false; but it is not certain that an opinion is false, because it is of dangerous consequence. Such topics, therefore, ought entirely to be forborne; as serving nothing to the discovery of truth, but only to make the person of an antagonist odious. This I observe in general, without pretending to draw any advantage from it. I frankly submit to an examination of this kind, and shall venture to affirm, that the doctrines, both of necessity and of liberty, as above explained, are not only consistent with [1] morality, but are absolutely essential to its support.

Necessity may be defined two ways, conformably to the two definitions of *cause*, of which it makes an essential part. It consists either in the constant conjunction of like objects, or in the inference of the understanding from one object to another. Now necessity, in both these senses, (which, indeed, are, at bottom, the same) has universally, though tacitly, in the schools, in the pulpit, and in common life, been allowed to belong to the will of man; and no one has ever pretended to deny, that we can draw inferences concerning human actions, and that those inferences are founded on the experienced union of like actions, with like motives, inclinations, and circumstances. The only particular, in which any one can differ, is, that either, perhaps, he will refuse to give the name of necessity to this property of human actions: But as long as the meaning is understood, I hope the word can do no harm: Or that he will maintain it possible to discover something farther in the operations of matter. But this, it must be acknowledged, can be of no consequence to morality or religion, whatever it may be to natural philosophy or metaphysics. We may here be mistaken in asserting, that

[1] [Morality and religion: Editions E to Q.]

there is no idea of any other necessity or connexion in the actions of body : But surely we ascribe nothing to the actions of the mind, but what every one does, and must readily allow of. We change no circumstance in the received orthodox system with regard to the will, but only in that with regard to material objects and causes. Nothing therefore can be more innocent, at least, than this doctrine.

All laws being founded on rewards and punishments, it is supposed as a fundamental principle, that these motives have a regular and uniform influence on the mind, and both produce the good and prevent the evil actions. We may give to this influence what name we please ; but, as it is usually conjoined with the action, it must be esteemed a *cause*, and be looked upon as an instance of that necessity, which we would here establish.

The only proper object of hatred or vengeance, is a person or creature, endowed with thought and consciousness ; and when any criminal or injurious actions excite that passion, it is only by their relation to the person, or connexion with him. Actions are, by their very nature, temporary and perishing ; and where they proceed not from some *cause* in the character and disposition of the person who performed them, they can neither redound to his honour, if good ; nor infamy, if evil. The actions themselves may be blameable ; they may be contrary to all the rules of morality and religion : But the person is not answerable for them ; and as they proceeded from nothing in him, that is durable and constant, and leave nothing of that nature behind them, it is impossible he can, upon their account, become the object of punishment or vengeance. According to the principle, therefore, which denies necessity, and consequently causes, a man is as pure and untainted, after having committed the most horrid crime, as at the first moment of his birth, nor is his character any wise concerned in his actions ; since they are not derived from it, and the wickedness of the one can never be used as a proof of the depravity of the other.

Men are not blamed for such actions, as they perform ignorantly and casually, whatever may be the consequences. Why? but because the principles of these actions are only momentary, and terminate in them alone. Men are less blamed for such actions as they perform hastily and unpremeditately, than for such as proceed from deliberation. For what reason? but because a hasty temper, though a constant cause or principle in the mind, operates only by intervals, and infects not the whole character. Again, repentance wipes off every crime, if attended with a reformation of life and manners. How is this to be accounted for? but by asserting, that actions render a person criminal, merely as they are proofs of criminal principles in the mind; and when, by an alteration of these principles, they cease to be just proofs, they likewise cease to be criminal. But, except upon the doctrine of necessity, they never were just proofs, and consequently never were criminal.

It will be equally easy to prove, and from the same arguments, that *liberty*, according to that definition above mentioned, in which all men agree, is also essential to morality, and that no human actions, where it is wanting, are susceptible of any moral qualities, or can be the objects either of approbation or dislike. For as actions are objects of our moral sentiment, so far only as they are indications of the internal character, passions, and affections; it is impossible that they can give rise either to praise or blame, where they proceed not from these principles, but are derived altogether from external violence.

I pretend not to have obviated or removed all objections to this theory, with regard to necessity and liberty. I can foresee other objections, derived from topics, which have not here been treated of. It may be said, for instance, that, if voluntary actions be subjected to the same laws of necessity with the operations of matter, there is a continued chain of necessary causes, pre-ordained and pre-determined, reaching from the original cause of all, to every single volition of every human creature. No contingency any where in the universe; no indifference; no liberty. While we act, we are, at the same time, acted upon. The ultimate Author of all our volitions is the Creator of the world, who first bestowed motion on this immense machine, and placed all beings in that particular position, whence every subsequent event, by an inevitable necessity, must result. Human actions, therefore, either can have no moral turpitude at all, as proceeding from so good a cause; or if they have any turpitude, they must involve our Creator in the same guilt, while he is acknowledged to be their ultimate cause and author. For as a man, who fired a mine, is answerable for all the consequences, whether the train he employed be long or short; so wherever a continued chain of necessary causes is fixed, that Being, either finite or infinite, who produces the first, is likewise the author of all the rest, and must both bear the blame and acquire the praise, which belong to them. Our clear and unalterable ideas of morality establish this rule, upon unquestionable reasons, when we examine the consequences of any human action; and these reasons must still have greater force, when applied to the volitions and intentions of a Being, infinitely wise and powerful. Ignorance or impotence may be pleaded for so limited a creature as man; but those imperfections have no place in our Creator. He foresaw, he ordained, he intended all those actions of men, which we so rashly pronounce criminal. And we must therefore conclude, either that they are not criminal, or that the Deity, not man, is accountable for them. But as either of these positions is absurd and impious, it follows, that the doctrine, from which they are deduced, cannot possibly be true, as being liable to all the same objections. An absurd consequence, if necessary, proves the original doctrine to be absurd; in the same manner as criminal actions render criminal the original cause, if the connexion between them be necessary and inevitable.

This objection consists of two parts, which we shall examine separately; First, that, if human actions can be traced up, by a necessary chain, to the Deity, they can never be criminal; on account of the infinite perfection of that Being, from whom they are derived, and who can intend nothing but what is altogether good and laudable. Or, Secondly, if they be criminal, we must retract the attribute of perfection, which we ascribe to the Deity, and must acknowledge him to be the ultimate author of guilt and moral turpitude in all his creatures.

The answer to the first objection seems obvious and convincing. There are many philosophers, who, after an exact scrutiny of all the phænomena of nature, conclude, that the WHOLE, considered as one system, is, in every period of its existence, ordered with perfect benevolence; and that the utmost possible happiness will, in the end, result to all created beings, without any mixture of positive or absolute ill and misery. Every physical ill, say they, makes an essential part of this benevolent system, and could not possibly be removed, even by the Deity himself, considered as a wise agent, without giving entrance to greater ill, or excluding greater good, which will result from it. From this theory, some philosophers, and the ancient *Stoics* among the rest, derived a topic of consolation under all afflictions, while they taught their pupils, that those ills, under which they laboured, were, in reality, goods to the universe; and that to an enlarged view, which could comprehend the whole system of nature, every event became an object of joy and exultation. But though this topic be specious and sublime, it was soon found in practice weak and ineffectual. You would surely more irritate, than appease a man, lying under the racking pains of the gout, by preaching up to him the rectitude of those general laws, which produced the malignant humours in his body, and led them through the proper canals, to the sinews and nerves, where they now excite such acute torments. These enlarged views may, for a moment, please the imagination of a speculative man, who is placed in ease and security; but neither can they dwell with constancy on his mind, even though undisturbed by the emotions of pain or passion; much less can they maintain their ground, when attacked by such powerful antagonists. The affections take a narrower and more natural survey of their object; and by an œconomy, more suitable to the infirmity of human minds, regard alone the beings around us, and are actuated by such events as appear good or ill to the private system.

The case is the same with *moral* as with *physical* ill. It cannot reasonably be supposed, that those remote considerations, which are found of so little efficacy with regard to one, will have a more powerful influence with regard to the other. The mind of man is so formed by nature, that, upon the appearance of certain characters, dispositions, and actions, it immediately feels the sentiment of approbation or blame; nor are there any emotions more essential to its frame and constitution. The characters, which engage our approbation, are chiefly such as contribute to the peace and security of human society; as the characters, which excite blame, are chiefly such as tend to public detriment and disturbance: Whence it may reasonably be presumed, that the moral sentiments arise, either mediately or immediately, from a reflection on these opposite interests. What though philosophical meditations establish a different opinion or conjecture; that every thing is right with regard to the WHOLE, and that the qualities, which disturb society, are, in the main, as beneficial, and are as suitable to the primary intention of nature, as those which more directly promote its happiness and welfare? Are such remote and uncertain speculations able to counterbalance the sentiments, which arise from the natural and immediate view of the objects? A man who is robbed of a considerable sum; does he find his vexation for the loss any wise diminished by these sublime reflections? Why then should his moral resentment against the crime be supposed incompatible with them? Or why should not the acknowledgment of a real distinction between vice and virtue be reconcileable to all speculative systems of philosophy, as well as that of a real distinction between personal beauty and deformity? Both these distinctions are founded in the natural sentiments of the human mind: And these sentiments are not to be controuled or altered by any philosophical theory or speculation whatsoever.

The *second* objection admits not of so easy and satisfactory an answer; nor is it possible to explain distinctly, how the Deity can be the mediate cause of all the actions of men, without being the author of sin and moral turpitude. These are mysteries, which mere natural and unassisted reason is very unfit to handle; and whatever system she embraces, she must find herself involved in inextricable difficulties, and even contradictions, at every step which she takes with regard to such subjects. To reconcile the indifference and contingency of human actions with prescience; or to defend absolute decrees, and yet free the Deity from being the author of sin, has been found hitherto to exceed all the power of philosophy. Happy, if she be thence sensible of her temerity, when she pries into these sublime mysteries; and leaving a scene so full of obscurities and perplexities, return, with suitable modesty, to her true and proper province, the examination of common life; where she will find difficulties enow to employ her enquiries, without launching into so boundless an ocean of doubt, uncertainty, and contradiction!

ALL our reasonings concerning matter of fact are founded on a species of ANALOGY, which leads us to expect from any cause the same events, which we have observed to result from similar causes. Where the causes are entirely similar, the analogy is perfect, and the inference, drawn from it, is regarded as certain and conclusive : Nor does any man ever entertain a doubt, where he sees a piece of iron, that it will have weight and cohesion of parts ; as in all other instances, which have ever fallen under his observation. But where the objects have not so exact a similarity, the analogy is less perfect, and the inference is less conclusive ; though still it has some force, in proportion to the degree of similarity and resemblance. The anatomical observations, formed upon one animal, are, by this species of reasoning, extended to all animals : and it is certain, that when the circulation of the blood, for instance, is clearly proved to have place in one creature, as a frog, or fish, it forms a strong presumption, that the same principle has place in all. These analogical observations may be carried farther, even to this science, of which we are now treating : and any theory, by which we explain the operations of the understanding, or the origin and connexion of the passions in man, will acquire additional authority, if we find, that the same theory is requisite to explain the same phænomena in all other animals. We shall make trial of this, with regard to the hypothesis, by which, we have, in the foregoing discourse, endeavoured to account for all experimental reasonings ; and it is hoped, that this new point of view will serve to confirm all our former observations.

First. It seems evident, that animals, as well as men, learn many things from experience, and infer, that the same events will always follow from the same causes. By this principle they become acquainted with the more obvious properties of external objects, and gradually, from their birth, treasure up a knowledge of the nature of fire, water, earth, stones, heights, depths, &c. and of the effects, which result from their operation. The ignorance and inexperience of the young are here plainly distinguishable from the cunning and sagacity of the old, who have learned, by long observation, to avoid what hurt them, and to pursue what gave ease or pleasure. A horse, that has been accustomed to the field, becomes acquainted with the proper height, which he can leap, and will never attempt what exceeds his force and ability. An old greyhound will trust the more fatiguing part of the chase to the younger, and will place himself so as to meet the hare in her doubles; nor are the conjectures, which he forms on this occasion, founded in any thing but his observation and experience.

This is still more evident from the effects of discipline and education on animals, who, by the proper application of rewards and punishments, may be taught any course of action, the most contrary to their natural instincts and propensities. Is it not experience, which renders a dog apprehensive of pain, when you menace him, or lift up the whip to beat him? Is it not even experience, which makes him answer to his name, and infer, from such an arbitrary sound, that you mean him rather than any of his fellows, and intend to call him, when you pronounce it in a certain manner, and with a certain tone and accent?

In all these cases, we may observe, that the animal infers some fact beyond what immediately strikes his senses; and that this inference is altogether founded on past experience, while the creature expects from the present object the same consequences, which it has always found in its observation to result from similar objects.

Secondly, It is impossible, that this inference of the animal can be founded on any process of argument or reasoning, by which he concludes, that like events must follow like objects, and that the course of nature will always be regular in its operations. For if there be in reality any arguments of this nature, they surely lie too abstruse for the observation of such imperfect understandings; since it may well employ the utmost care and attention of a philosophic genius to discover and observe them. Animals, therefore, are not guided in these inferences by reasoning: Neither are children: Neither are the generality of mankind, in their ordinary actions and conclusions: Neither are philosophers themselves, who, in all the active parts of life, are, in the main, the same with the vulgar, and are governed by the same maxims. Nature must have provided some other principle, of more ready, and more general use and application; nor can an operation of such immense consequence in life, as that of inferring effects from causes, be trusted to the uncertain process of reasoning and argumentation. Were this doubtful with regard to men, it seems to admit of no question with regard to the brute creation; and the conclusion being once firmly established in the one, we have a strong presumption, from all the rules of analogy, that it ought to be universally admitted, without any exception or reserve. It is custom alone, which engages animals, from every object, that strikes their senses, to infer its usual attendant, and carries their imagination, from the appearance of the one, to conceive the other, in that particular manner, which we denominate *belief*. No other explication can be given of this operation, in all the higher, as well as lower classes of sensitive beings, which fall under our notice and observation.[1]

[1] Since all reasonings concerning facts or causes is derived merely from custom, it may be asked how it happens, that men so much surpass animals in reasoning, and one man so much surpasses another? Has not the same custom the same influence on all?

We shall here endeavour briefly to explain the great difference in human understandings: After which the reason of the difference between men and animals will easily be comprehended.

1. When we have lived any time, and have been accustomed to the uniformity of nature, we acquire a general habit, by which we always transfer the known to the unknown, and conceive the latter to resemble the former. By means of this general habitual principle, we regard even one experiment as the foundation of reasoning, and expect a similar event with some degree of certainty, where the experiment has been made accurately, and free from all foreign circumstances. It is therefore considered as a matter of great importance to observe the consequences of things; and as one man may very much surpass another in attention and memory and observation, this will make a very great difference in their reasoning.

2. Where there is a complication of causes to produce any effect, one mind may be much larger than another, and better able to comprehend the whole system of objects, and to infer justly their consequences.

3. One man is able to carry on a chain of consequences to a greater length than another.

4. Few men can think long without running into a confusion of ideas, and mistaking one for another; and there are various degrees of this infirmity.

5. The circumstance, on which the effect depends, is frequently involved in other circumstances, which are foreign and extrinsic. The separation of it often requires great attention, accuracy, and subtilty.

6. The forming of general maxims from particular observation is a very nice operation; and nothing is more usual, from haste or a narrowness of mind, which sees not on all sides, than to commit mistakes in this particular.

7. When we reason from analogies, the man, who has the greater experience or the greater promptitude of suggesting analogies, will be the better reasoner.

8. Byasses from prejudice, education, passion, party, &c. hang more upon one mind than another.

9. After we have acquired a confidence in human testimony, books and conversation enlarge much more the sphere of one man's experience and thought than those of another.

It would be easy to discover many other circumstances that make a difference in the understandings of men.[2]

[2] [This note was added in Edition F.]

But though animals learn many parts of their knowledge from observation, there are also many parts of it, which they derive from the original hand of nature; which much exceed the share of capacity they possess on ordinary occasions; and in which they improve, little or nothing, by the longest practice and experience. These we denominate INSTINCTS, and are so apt to admire, as something very extraordinary, and inexplicable by all the disquisitions of human understanding. But our wonder will, perhaps, cease or diminish; when we consider, that the experimental reasoning itself, which we possess in common with beasts, and on which the whole conduct of life depends, is nothing but a species of instinct or mechanical power, that acts in us unknown to ourselves; and in its chief operations, is not directed by any such relations or comparisons of ideas, as are the proper objects of our intellectual faculties. Though the instinct be different, yet still it is an instinct, which teaches a man to avoid the fire; as much as that, which teaches a bird, with such exactness, the art of incubation, and the whole œconomy and order of its nursery.

SECTION X.—*Of Miracles.*[1]

PART I.

THERE is, in Dr. TILLOTSON's writings, an argument against the *real presence*, which is as concise, and elegant, and strong as any argument can possibly be supposed against a doctrine, so little worthy of a serious refutation. It is acknowledged on all hands, says that learned prelate, that the authority, either of the scripture or of tradition, is founded merely in the testimony of the apostles, who were eye-witnesses to those miracles of our Saviour, by which he proved his divine mission. Our evidence, then, for the truth of the *Christian* religion is less than the evidence for the truth of our senses; because, even in the first authors of our religion, it was no greater; and it is evident it must diminish in passing from them to their disciples; nor can any one rest such confidence in their testimony, as in the immediate object of his senses. But a weaker evidence can never destroy a stronger; and therefore, were the doctrine of the real presence ever so

[1] [For the history of this Section see 'History of the Editions,' Vol iii. p. 50. Ed.]

clearly revealed in scripture, it were directly contrary to the rules of just reasoning to give our assent to it. It contradicts sense, though both the scripture and tradition, on which it is supposed to be built, carry not such evidence with them as sense; when they are considered merely as external evidences, and are not brought home to every one's breast, by the immediate operation of the Holy Spirit.

Nothing is so convenient as a decisive argument of this kind, which must at least *silence* the most arrogant bigotry and superstition, and free us from their impertinent solicitations. I flatter myself, that I have discovered an argument of a like nature, which, if just, will, with the wise and learned, be an everlasting check to all kinds of superstitious delusion, and consequently, will be useful as long as the world endures. For so long, I presume, will the accounts of miracles and prodigies be found in all history, sacred and profane.[1]

Though experience be our only guide in reasoning concerning matters of fact; it must be acknowledged, that this guide is not altogether infallible, but in some cases is apt to lead us into errors. One, who in our climate, should expect better weather in any week of JUNE than in one of DECEMBER, would reason justly, and conformably to experience; but it is certain, that he may happen, in the event, to find himself mistaken. However, we may observe, that, in such a case, he would have no cause to complain of experience; because it commonly informs us beforehand of the uncertainty, by that contrariety of events, which we may learn from a diligent observation. All effects follow not with like certainty from their supposed causes. Some events are found, in all countries and all ages, to have been constantly conjoined together: Others are found to have been more variable, and sometimes to disappoint our expectations; so that, in our reasonings concerning matter of fact, there are all imaginable degrees of assurance, from the highest certainty to the lowest species of moral evidence.

A wise man, therefore, proportions his belief to the evidence. In such conclusions as are founded on an infallible experience, he expects the event with the last degree of assurance, and regards his past experience as a full *proof* of the future existence of that event. In other cases, he proceeds with more caution: He weighs the opposite experi-

[1] [In all prophane history: Editions E and F.]

ments : He considers which side is supported by the greater number of experiments : To that side he inclines, with doubt and hesitation ; and when at last he fixes his judgment, the evidence exceeds not what we properly call *probability*. All probability, then, supposes an opposition of experiments and observations, where the one side is found to overbalance the other, and to produce a degree of evidence, proportioned to the superiority. A hundred instances or experiments on one side, and fifty on another, afford a doubtful expectation of any event ; though a hundred uniform experiments, with only one that is contradictory, reasonably beget a pretty strong degree of assurance. In all cases, we must balance the opposite experiments, where they are opposite, and deduct the smaller number from the greater, in order to know the exact force of the superior evidence.

To apply these principles to a particular instance ; we may observe, that there is no species of reasoning more common, more useful, and even necessary to human life, than that which is derived from the testimony of men, and the reports of eye-witnesses and spectators. This species of reasoning, perhaps, one may deny to be founded on the relation of cause and effect. I shall not dispute about a word. It will be sufficient to observe, that our assurance in any argument of this kind is derived from no other principle than our observation of the veracity of human testimony, and of the usual conformity of facts to the reports of witnesses. It being a general maxim, that no objects have any discoverable connexion together, and that all the inferences, which we can draw from one to another, are founded merely on our experience of their constant and regular conjunction ; it is evident, that we ought not to make an exception to this maxim in favour of human testimony, whose connexion with any event seems, in itself, as little necessary as any other.[1] Were not the memory tenacious to a certain degree ; had not men commonly an inclination to truth and a principle of probity ; were they not sensible to shame, when detected in a falsehood : Were not these, I say, discovered by *experience* to be qualities, inherent in human nature, we should never repose the least confidence in human testimony. A man delirious,

---

[1] [Editions E to K substitute : Did not Men's Imagination naturally follow their Memory.]

or noted for falsehood and villany, has no manner of authority with us.

And as the evidence, derived from witnesses and human testimony, is founded on past experience, so it varies with the experience, and is regarded either as a *proof* or a *probability*, according as the conjunction between any particular kind of report and any kind of object has been found to be constant or variable. There are a number of circumstances to be taken into consideration in all judgments of this kind; and the ultimate standard, by which we determine all disputes, that may arise concerning them, is always derived from experience and observation. Where this experience is not entirely uniform on any side, it is attended with an unavoidable contrariety in our judgments, and with the same opposition and mutual destruction of argument as in every other kind of evidence. We frequently hesitate concerning the reports of others. We balance the opposite circumstances, which cause any doubt or uncertainty; and when we discover a superiority on any side, we incline to it; but still with a diminution of assurance, in proportion to the force of its antagonist.

This contrariety of evidence, in the present case, may be derived from several different causes; from the opposition of contrary testimony; from the character or number of the witnesses; from the manner of their delivering their testimony; or from the union of all these circumstances. We entertain a suspicion concerning any matter of fact, when the witnesses contradict each other; when they are but few, or of a doubtful character; when they have an interest in what they affirm; when they deliver their testimony with hesitation, or on the contrary, with too violent asseverations. There are many other particulars of the same kind, which may diminish or destroy the force of any argument, derived from human testimony.

Suppose, for instance, that the fact, which the testimony endeavours to establish, partakes of the extraordinary and the marvellous; in that case, the evidence, resulting from the testimony, admits of a diminution, greater or less, in proportion as the fact is more or less unusual. The reason, why we place any credit in witnesses and historians, is not derived from any *connexion*, which we perceive *à priori*, between testimony and reality, but because we are accustomed to find a conformity between them. But when the fact attested is such a one as has seldom fallen under our observation, here is a contest of two opposite experiences ; of which the one destroys the other, as far as its force goes, and the superior can only operate on the mind by the force, which remains. The very same principle of experience, which gives us a certain degree of assurance in the testimony of witnesses, gives us also, in this case, another degree of assurance against the fact, which they endeavour to establish ; from which contradiction there necessarily arises a counterpoise, and mutual destruction of belief and authority.

[1] *I should not believe such a story were it told me by* CATO ; was a proverbial saying in ROME, even during the lifetime of that philosophical patriot.[2] The incredibility of a fact, it was allowed, might invalidate so great an authority.

[3] The INDIAN prince, who refused to believe the first relations concerning the effects of frost, reasoned justly ; and it naturally required very strong testimony to engage his assent to facts, that arose from a state of nature, with which he was unacquainted, and which bore so little analogy to those events, of which he had had constant and uniform experience. Though they were not contrary to his experience, they were not conformable to it.[4]

But in order to encrease the probability against the testi-

---

[1] [This paragraph was added in Edition K.]

[2] PLUTARCH, in vita Catonis Min. 19.

[3] [This paragraph was added in Edition F.]

[4] No INDIAN, it is evident, could have experience that water did not freeze in cold climates. This is placing nature in a situation quite unknown to him ; and it is impossible for him to tell *à priori* what will result from it. It is making a new experiment, the consequence of which is always uncertain. One may sometimes conjecture from analogy what will follow ; but still this is but conjecture. And it must be confessed, that, in the present case of freezing, the event follows contrary to the rules of analogy, and is such as a rational INDIAN would not look for. The operations of cold upon water are not gradual, according to the degrees of cold ; but whenever it comes to the freezing point, the water passes in a moment, from the utmost liquidity to perfect hardness. Such an event, therefore, may be denominated *extraordinary*, and requires a pretty strong testimony, to render it credible to people in a warm climate : But still it is not *miraculous*, nor contrary to uniform experience of the course of nature in cases where all the circumstances are the same. The inhabitants of SUMATRA have always seen water fluid in their own climate, and the freezing of their rivers ought to be deemed a prodigy : But they never saw water in MUSCOVY during the winter ; and therefore they cannot reasonably be positive what would there be the consequence.[5]

[5] [This note first appears in the last page of Edition F, with the preface : The distance of the Author from the Press is the Cause, why the following Passage arriv'd not in time to be inserted in its proper Place.]

.nony of witnesses, let us suppose, that the fact, which they affirm, instead of being only marvellous, is really miraculous; and suppose also, that the testimony, considered apart and in itself, amounts to an entire proof; in that case, there is proof against proof, of which the strongest must prevail, but still with a diminution of its force, in proportion to that of its antagonist.

A miracle is a violation of the laws of nature; and as a firm and unalterable experience has established these laws, the proof against a miracle, from the very nature of the fact, is as entire as any argument from experience can possibly be imagined. Why is it more than probable, that all men must die; that lead cannot, of itself, remain suspended in the air; that fire consumes wood, and is extinguished by water; unless it be, that these events are found agreeable to the laws of nature, and there is required a violation of these laws, or in other words, a miracle to prevent them? Nothing is esteemed a miracle, if it ever happen in the common course of nature. It is no miracle that a man, seemingly in good health, should die on a sudden: because such a kind of death, though more unusual than any other, has yet been frequently observed to happen. But it is a miracle, that a dead man should come to life; because that has never been observed, in any age or country. There must, therefore, be a uniform experience against every miraculous event, otherwise the event would not merit that appellation. And as an uniform experience amounts to a proof, there is here a direct and full *proof*, from the nature of the fact, against the existence of any miracle; nor can such a proof be destroyed, or the miracle rendered credible, but by an opposite proof, which is superior.[1]

[1] Sometimes an event may not, *in itself*, *seem* to be contrary to the laws of nature, and yet, if it were real, it might, by reason of some circumstances, be denominated a miracle; because, in *fact*, it is contrary to these laws. Thus if a person, claiming a divine authority, should command a sick person to be well, a healthful man to fall down dead, the clouds to pour rain, the winds to blow, in short, should order many natural events, which immediately follow upon his command: these might justly be esteemed miracles, because they are really, in this case, contrary to the laws of nature. For if any suspicion remain, that the event and command concurred by accident, there is no miracle and no transgression of the laws of nature. If this suspicion be removed, there is evidently a miracle, and a transgression of these laws; because nothing can be more contrary to nature than that the voice or command of a man should have such an influence. A miracle may be accurately defined, *a transgression of a law of nature by a particular volition of the Deity, or by the interposition of some invisible agent*. A miracle may either be discoverable

The plain consequence is (and it is a general maxim worthy of our attention), 'That no testimony is sufficient to establish 'a miracle, unless the testimony be of such a kind, that its 'falsehood would be more miraculous, than the fact, which it 'endeavours to establish: And even in that case there is a 'mutual destruction of arguments, and the superior only 'gives us an assurance suitable to that degree of force, which 'remains, after deducting the inferior.' When any one tells me, that he saw a dead man restored to life, I immediately consider with myself, whether it be more probable, that this person should either deceive or be deceived, or that the fact, which he relates, should really have happened. I weigh the one miracle against the other; and according to the superiority, which I discover, I pronounce my decision, and always reject the greater miracle. If the falsehood of his testimony would be more miraculous, than the event which he relates; then, and not till then, can he pretend to command my belief or opinion.

PART II.

In the foregoing reasoning we have supposed, that the testimony, upon which a miracle is founded, may possibly amount to an entire proof, and that the falsehood of that testimony would be a real prodigy: But it is easy to shew, that we have been a great deal too liberal in our concession, and that there never was a miraculous event[1] established on so full an evidence.

For *first*, there is not to be found in all history, any miracle attested by a sufficient number of men, of such unquestioned good-sense, education, and learning, as to secure us against all delusion in themselves; of such undoubted integrity, as to place them beyond all suspicion of any design to deceive others; of such credit and reputation in the eyes of mankind, as to have a great deal to lose in case of their being detected in any falsehood; and at the same time, attesting facts, performed in such a public manner, and in so celebrated a part of the world, as to render the detection unavoidable:

by men or not. This alters not its nature and essence. The raising of a house or ship into the air is a visible miracle. The raising of a feather, when the wind wants ever so little of a force requisite for that purpose, is as real a miracle, though not so sensible with regard to us.

[1] [In any History: Editions E and F.]

All which circumstances are requisite to give us a full assurance in the testimony of men.

Secondly. We may observe in human nature a principle, which, if strictly examined, will be found to diminish extremely the assurance, which we might, from human testimony, have, in any kind of prodigy. The maxim, by which we commonly conduct ourselves in our reasonings, is, that the objects, of which we have no experience, resemble those, of which we have; that what we have found to be most usual is always most probable; and that where there is an opposition of arguments, we ought to give the preference to such as are founded on the greatest number of past observations. But though, in proceeding by this rule, we readily reject any fact which is unusual and incredible in an ordinary degree; yet in advancing farther, the mind observes not always the same rule; but when anything is affirmed utterly absurd and miraculous, it rather the more readily admits of such a fact, upon account of that very circumstance, which ought to destroy all its authority. The passion of *surprize* and *wonder*, arising from miracles, being an agreeable emotion, gives a sensible tendency towards the belief of those events, from which it is derived. And this goes so far, that even those who cannot enjoy this pleasure immediately, nor can believe those miraculous events, of which they are informed, yet love to partake of the satisfaction at second-hand or by rebound, and place a pride and delight in exciting the admiration of others.

With what greediness are the miraculous accounts of travellers received, their descriptions of sea and land monsters, their relations of wonderful adventures, strange men, and uncouth manners? But if the spirit of religion join itself to the love of wonder, there is an end of common sense; and human testimony, in these circumstances, loses all pretensions to authority. A religionist may be an enthusiast, and imagine he sees what has no reality: He may know his narrative to be false, and yet persevere in it, with the best intentions in the world, for the sake of promoting so holy a cause: Or even where this delusion has not place, vanity, excited by so strong a temptation, operates on him more powerfully than on the rest of mankind in any other circumstances; and self-interest with equal force. His auditors may not have, and commonly have not, sufficient judgment to canvass his evidence : What judgment they have, they renounce by principle, in these sublime and mysterious subjects: Or if they were ever so willing to employ it, passion and a heated imagination disturb the regularity of its operations. Their credulity encreases his impudence : And his impudence overpowers their credulity.

Eloquence, when at its highest pitch, leaves little room for reason or reflection ; but addressing itself entirely to the fancy or the affections, captivates the willing hearers, and subdues their understanding. Happily, this pitch it seldom attains. But what a TULLY or a DEMOSTHENES could scarcely effect over a ROMAN or ATHENIAN audience, every *Capuchin*, every itinerant or stationary teacher can perform over the generality of mankind, and in a higher degree, by touching such gross and vulgar passions.

[1] The many instances of forged miracles, and prophecies, and supernatural events, which, in all ages, have either been detected by contrary evidence, or which detect themselves by their absurdity, prove sufficiently the strong propensity of mankind to the extraordinary and the marvellous, and ought reasonably to beget a suspicion against all relations of this kind. This is our natural way of thinking, even with regard to the most common and most credible events. For instance: There is no kind of report, which rises so easily, and spreads so quickly, especially in country places and provincial towns, as those concerning marriages ; insomuch that two young persons of equal condition never see each other twice, but the whole neighbourhood immediately join them together. The pleasure of telling a piece of news so interesting, of propagating it, and of being the first reporters of it, spreads the intelligence. And this is so well known, that no man of sense gives attention to these reports, till he find them confirmed by some greater evidence. Do not the same passions, and others still stronger, incline the generality of mankind to believe and report, with the greatest vehemence and assurance, all religious miracles?

Thirdly. It forms a strong presumption against all supernatural and miraculous relations, that they are observed chiefly to abound among ignorant and barbarous nations ; or if a civilized people has ever given admission to any of them,

---

[1] [This paragraph was printed as a note in Editions E to P.]

that people will be found to have received them from ignorant and barbarous ancestors, who transmitted them with that inviolable sanction and authority, which always attend received opinions. When we peruse the first histories of all nations, we are apt to imagine ourselves transported into some new world; where the whole frame of nature is disjointed, and every element performs its operations in a different manner, from what it does at present. Battles, revolutions, pestilence, famine, and death, are never the effect of those natural causes, which we experience. Prodigies, omens, oracles, judgments, quite obscure the few natural events, that are intermingled with them. But as the former grow thinner every page, in proportion as we advance nearer the enlightened ages, we soon learn, that there is nothing mysterious or supernatural in the case, but that all proceeds from the usual propensity of mankind towards the marvellous, and that, though this inclination may at intervals receive a check from sense and learning, it can never be thoroughly extirpated from human nature.

It is strange, a judicious reader is apt to say, upon the perusal of these wonderful historians, *that such prodigious events never happen in our days.* But it is nothing strange, I hope, that men should lie in all ages. You must surely have seen instances enow of that frailty. You have yourself heard many such marvellous relations started, which, being treated with scorn by all the wise and judicious, have at last been abandoned even by the vulgar. Be assured, that those renowned lies, which have spread and flourished to such a monstrous height, arose from like beginnings; but being sown in a more proper soil, shot up at last into prodigies almost equal to those which they relate.

It was a wise policy in that [1] false prophet, ALEXANDER, who, though now forgotten, was once so famous, to lay the first scene of his impostures in PAPHLAGONIA, where, as LUCIAN tells us, the people were extremely ignorant and stupid, and ready to swallow even the grossest delusion. People at a distance, who are weak enough to think the matter at all worth enquiry, have no opportunity of receiving better information. The stories come magnified to them by a hundred circumstances. Fools are industrious in propagating the imposture; while the wise and learned are contented, in

---

[1] [Cunning impostor: Editions E to P.]

general, to deride its absurdity, without informing themselves of the particular facts, by which it may be distinctly refuted.   And thus the impostor above-mentioned was enabled to proceed, from his ignorant PAPHLAGONIANS, to the enlisting of votaries, even among the GRECIAN philosophers, and men of the most eminent rank and distinction in ROME: Nay, could engage the attention of the sage emperor MARCUS AURELIUS; so far as to make him trust the success of a military expedition to his delusive prophecies.

The advantages are so great, of starting an imposture among an ignorant people, that, even though the delusion should be too gross to impose on the generality of them (*which, though seldom, is sometimes the case*) it has a much better chance for succeeding in remote countries, than if the first scene has been laid in a city renowned for arts and knowledge.   The most ignorant and barbarous of these barbarians carry the report abroad.   None of their countrymen have a large correspondence, or sufficient credit and authority to contradict and beat down the delusion.   Men's inclination to the marvellous has full opportunity to display itself. And thus a story, which is universally exploded in the place where it was first started, shall pass for certain at a thousand miles distance.   But had ALEXANDER fixed his residence at ATHENS, the philosophers of that renowned mart of learning had immediately spread, throughout the whole ROMAN empire, their sense of the matter; which, being supported by so great authority, and displayed by all the force of reason and eloquence, had entirely opened the eyes of mankind.   It is true; LUCIAN, passing by chance through PAPHLAGONIA, had an opportunity of performing this good office.   But, though much to be wished, it does not always happen, that every ALEXANDER meets with a LUCIAN, ready to expose and detect his impostures.[1]

I may add as a *fourth* reason, which diminishes the authority of prodigies, that there is no testimony for any, even

---

[1] [Editions E to P append the following note: It may here, perhaps, be objected, that I proceed rashly, and form my notions of ALEXANDER merely from the account given of him by LUCIAN, a professed enemy.   It were, indeed, to be wished, that some of the accounts published by his followers and accomplices had remained.   The opposition and contrast between the character and conduct of the same man, as drawn by friend or enemy, is as strong, even in common life, much more in these religious matters, as that betwixt any two men in the world, betwixt ALEXANDER and St. PAUL, for instance.   See a letter to GILBERT WEST, Esq; on the conversion and apostleship of St. PAUL.]

those which have not been expressly detected, that is not opposed by an infinite number of witnesses; so that not only the miracle destroys the credit of testimony, but the testimony destroys itself. To make this the better understood, let us consider, that, in matters of religion, whatever is different is contrary; and that it is impossible the religions of ancient ROME, of TURKEY, of SIAM, and of CHINA should, all of them, be established on any solid foundation. Every miracle, therefore, pretended to have been wrought in any of these religions (and all of them abound in miracles), as its direct scope is to establish the particular system to which it is attributed; so has it the same force, though more indirectly, to overthrow every other system. In destroying a rival system, it likewise destroys the credit of those miracles, on which that system was established; so that all the prodigies of different religions are to be regarded as contrary facts, and the evidences of these prodigies, whether weak or strong, as opposite to each other. According to this method of reasoning, when we believe any miracle of MAHOMET or his successors, we have for our warrant the testimony of a few barbarous ARABIANS : And on the other hand, we are to regard the authority of TITUS LIVIUS, PLUTARCH, TACITUS, and, in short, of all the authors and witnesses, GRECIAN, CHINESE, and ROMAN CATHOLIC, who have related any miracle in their particular religion; I say, we are to regard their testimony in the same light as if they had mentioned that MAHOMETAN miracle, and had in express terms contradicted it, with the same certainty as they have for the miracle they relate. This argument may appear over subtile and refined; but is not in reality different from the reasoning of a judge, who supposes, that the credit of two witnesses, maintaining a crime against any one, is destroyed by the testimony of two others, who affirm him to have been two hundred leagues distant, at the same instant when the crime is said to have been committed.

One of the best attested miracles in all profane history, is that which TACITUS reports of VESPASIAN, who cured a blind man in ALEXANDRIA, by means of his spittle, and a lame man by the mere touch of his foot; in obedience to a vision of the god SERAPIS, who had enjoined them to have recourse to the Emperor, for these miraculous cures. The story may be seen in that fine historian;[1] where every circumstance seems to add weight to the testimony, and might be displayed at large with all the force of argument and eloquence, if any one were now concerned to enforce the evidence of that exploded and idolatrous superstition. The gravity, solidity, age, and probity of so great an emperor, who, through the whole course of his life, conversed in a familiar manner with his friends and courtiers, and never affected those extraordinary airs of divinity assumed by ALEXANDER and DEMETRIUS. The historian, a cotemporary writer, noted for candour and veracity, and withal, the greatest and most penetrating genius, perhaps, of all antiquity; and so free from any tendency to credulity, that he even lies under the contrary imputation, of atheism and profaneness: The persons, from whose authority he related the miracle, of established character for judgment and veracity, as we may well presume; eye-witnesses of the fact, and confirming their testimony, after the FLAVIAN family was despoiled of the empire, and could no longer give any reward, as the price of a lie. *Utrumque, qui interfuere, nunc quoque memorant, post quam nullum mendacio pretium.* To which if we add the public nature of the facts, as related, it will appear, that no evidence can well be supposed stronger for so gross and so palpable a falsehood.

There is also a memorable story related by Cardinal DE RETZ, which may well deserve our consideration. When that intriguing politician fled into SPAIN, to avoid the persecution of his enemies, he passed through SARAGOSSA, the capital of ARRAGON, where he was shewn, in the cathedral, a man, who had served[2] seven years as a door-keeper, and was well known to every body in town, that had ever paid his devotions at that church. He had been seen, for so long a time, wanting a leg; but recovered that limb by the rubbing of holy oil upon the stump;[3] and the cardinal assures us that he saw him with two legs. This miracle was vouched by all the canons of the church; and the whole company in town were appealed to for a confirmation of the fact; whom the cardinal found, by their zealous devotion, to be thorough

[1] Hist. lib. v. cap. 8. SUETONIUS gives nearly the same account *in vita Vesp.* 7. [The reference to Suetonius was added in the Errata to Ed. F.]
[2] [20. Editions E to N.]

[3] [Editions E and F substitute: And when the Cardinal examin'd it, he found it to be a true natural Leg, like the other.]

believers of the miracle. Here the relater was also cotemporary to the supposed prodigy, of an incredulous and libertine character, as well as of great genius; the miracle of so *singular* a nature as could scarcely admit of a counterfeit, and the witnesses very numerous, and all of them, in a manner, spectators of the fact, to which they gave their testimony. And what adds mightily to the force of the evidence, and may double our surprize on this occasion, is, that the cardinal himself, who relates the story, seems not to give any credit to it, and consequently cannot be suspected of any concurrence in the holy fraud. He considered justly, that it was not requisite, in order to reject a fact of this nature, to be able accurately to disprove the testimony, and to trace its falsehood, through all the circumstances of knavery and credulity which produced it. He knew, that, as this was commonly altogether impossible at any small distance of time and place; so was it extremely difficult, even where one was immediately present, by reason of the bigotry, ignorance, cunning, and roguery of a great part of mankind. He therefore concluded, like a just reasoner, that such an evidence carried falsehood upon the very face of it, and that a miracle supported by any human testimony, was more properly a subject of derision than of argument.

There surely never was a greater number of miracles ascribed to one person, than those, which were lately said to have been wrought in FRANCE upon the tomb of Abbé PARIS, the famous JANSENIST, with whose sanctity the people were so long deluded. The curing of the sick, giving hearing to the deaf, and sight to the blind, were every where talked of as the usual effects of that holy sepulchre. But what is more extraordinary; many of the miracles were immediately proved upon the spot, before judges of unquestioned integrity, attested by witnesses of credit and distinction, in a learned age, and on the most eminent theatre that is now in the world. Nor is this all: A relation of them was published and dispersed every where; nor were the *Jesuits*, though a learned body, supported by the civil magistrate, and determined enemies to those opinions, in whose favour the miracles were said to have been wrought, ever able distinctly to refute or detect them.[1] Where shall we find such a number of cir-

---

[1] This book was writ by Mons. Montgeron, counsellor or judge of the parliament of Paris, a man of figure and character, who was also a martyr to the

SECT.
X.

cumstances, agreeing to the corroboration of one fact? And what have we to oppose to such a cloud of witnesses, but

cause, and is now said to be somewhere in a dungeon on account of his book.

There is another book in three volumes (called *Recueil des Miracles de l'Abbé* PARIS) giving an account of many of these miracles, and accompanied with prefatory discourses, which are very well written. There runs, however, through the whole of these a ridiculous comparison between the miracles of our Saviour and those of the Abbé; wherein it is asserted, that the evidence for the latter is equal to that for the former: As if the testimony of men could ever be put in the balance with that of God himself, who conducted the pen of the inspired writers. If these writers, indeed, were to be considered merely as human testimony, the FRENCH author is very moderate in his comparison: since he might, with some appearance of reason, pretend, that the JANSENIST miracles much surpass the other in evidence and authority. The following circumstances are drawn from authentic papers, inserted in the above-mentioned book.

Many of the miracles of Abbé PARIS were proved immediately by witnesses before the officiality or bishop's court at PARIS, under the eye of cardinal NOAILLES, whose character for integrity and capacity was never contested even by his enemies.

His [1] successor in the archbishopric was an enemy to the JANSENISTS, and for that reason promoted to the see by the court. Yet 22 rectors or *curés* of PARIS, with infinite earnestness, press him to examine those miracles, which they assert to be known to the whole world, and undisputably certain: But he wisely forbore.

The MOLINIST party had tried to discredit these miracles in one instance, that of Mademoiselle le FRANC. But, besides that their proceedings were in many respects the most irregular in the world, particularly in citing only a few of the JANSENIST witnesses, whom they tampered with: Besides this, I say, they soon found themselves overwhelmed by a cloud of new witnesses, one hundred and twenty in number, most of them persons of credit and substance in PARIS, who gave oath for the miracle.

This was accompanied with a solemn and earnest appeal to the parliament. But the parliament were forbidden by authority to meddle in the affair. It was at last observed, that where men are heated by zeal and enthusiasm, there is no degree of human testimony so strong as may not be procured for the greatest absurdity: And those who will be so silly as to examine the affair by that medium, and seek particular flaws in the testimony, are almost sure to be confounded. It must be a miserable imposture, indeed, that does not prevail in that contest.

All who have been in FRANCE about that time have heard of the reputation of Mons. HERAULT, the *lieutenant de Police*, whose vigilance, penetration, activity, and extensive intelligence have been much talked of. This magistrate, who by the nature of his office is almost absolute, was invested with full powers, on purpose to suppress or discredit these miracles; and he frequently seized immediately, and examined the witnesses and subjects of them: But never could reach any thing satisfactory against them.

In the case of Mademoiselle THIBAUT he sent the famous DE SYLVA to examine her: whose evidence is very curious. The physician declares, that it was impossible she could have been so ill as was proved by witnesses; because it was impossible she could, in so short a time, have recovered so perfectly as he found her. He reasoned, like a man of sense, from natural causes; but the opposite party told him, that the whole was a miracle, and that his evidence was the very best proof of it.

The MOLINISTS were in a sad dilemma. They durst not assert the absolute insufficiency of human evidence, to prove a miracle. They were obliged to say, that these miracles were wrought by witchcraft and the devil. But they were told, that this was the resource of the JEWS of old.

No JANSENIST was ever embarrassed to account for the cessation of the miracles, when the church-yard was shut up by the king's edict. It was the touch of the tomb, which produced

[1] [M. de Ventimille.— ED.]

the absolute impossibility or miraculous nature of the events, which they relate? And this surely, in the eyes of all reasonable people, will alone be regarded as a sufficient refutation.

Is the consequence just, because some human testimony has the utmost force and authority in some cases, when it relates the battle of PHILIPPI or PHARSALIA for instance; that therefore all kinds of testimony must, in all cases, have equal force and authority? Suppose that the CÆSAREAN and POMPEIAN factions had, each of them, claimed the victory in these battles, and that the historians of each party had uniformly ascribed the advantage to their own side; how could mankind, at this distance, have been able

these extraordinary effects; and when no one could approach the tomb, no effects could be expected. God, indeed, could have thrown down the walls in a moment: but he is master of his own graces and works, and it belongs not to us to account for them. He did not throw down the walls of every city like those of JERICHO, on the sounding of the rams' horns, nor break up the prison of every apostle, like that of St. PAUL.

No less a man, than the Duc de CHATILLON, a duke and peer of FRANCE, of the highest rank and family, gives evidence of a miraculous cure, performed upon a servant of his, who had lived several years in his house with a visible and palpable infirmity.

I shall conclude with observing, that no clergy are more celebrated for strictness of life and manners than the secular clergy of FRANCE, particularly the rectors or curés of PARIS, who bear testimony to these impostures.

The learning, genius, and probity of the gentlemen, and the austerity of the nuns of PORT-ROYAL, have been much celebrated all over EUROPE. Yet they all give evidence for a miracle, wrought on the niece of the famous PASCAL, whose sanctity of life, as well as extraordinary capacity, is well known.[1] The famous RACINE gives an account of this miracle in his famous history of PORT-ROYAL, and fortifies it with all the proofs, which a multitude of nuns, priests, physicians, and men of the

world, all of them of undoubted credit, could bestow upon it. Several men of letters, particularly the bishop of TOURNAY, thought this miracle so certain, as to employ it in the refutation of atheists and free-thinkers. The queen-regent of FRANCE, who was extremely prejudiced against the PORT-ROYAL, sent her own physician to examine the miracle, who returned an absolute convert. In short, the supernatural cure was so uncontestable, that it saved, for a time, that famous monastery from the ruin with which it was threatened by the JESUITS. Had it been a cheat, it had certainly been detected by such sagacious and powerful antagonists, and must have hastened the ruin of the contrivers. Our divines, who can build up a formidable castle from such despicable materials; what a prodigious fabric could they have reared from these and many other circumstances, which I have not mentioned! How often would the great names of PASCAL, RACINE, ARNAUD, NICOLE, have resounded in our ears? But if they be wise, they had better adopt the miracle, as being more worth, a thousand times, than all the rest of their collection. Besides, it may serve very much to their purpose. For that miracle was really performed by the touch of an authentic holy prickle of the holy thorn, which composed the holy crown, which, &c. [This note was added in Ed. F.]

---

[1] [Edition F adds: Tho' he also was a Believer, in that and in many other Miracles, which he had less opportunity of being inform'd of. See his Life. Here Ed. F stops.]

to determine between them? The contrariety is equally strong between the miracles related by HERODOTUS or PLUTARCH, and those delivered by MARIANA, BEDE, or any monkish historian.

The wise lend a very academic faith to every report which favours the passion of the reporter; whether it magnifies his country, his family, or himself, or in any other way strikes in with his natural inclinations and propensities. But what greater temptation than to appear a missionary, a prophet, an ambassador from heaven? Who would not encounter many dangers and difficulties, in order to attain so sublime a character? Or if, by the help of vanity and a heated imagination, a man has first made a convert of himself, and entered seriously into the delusion; who ever scruples to make use of pious frauds, in support of so holy and meritorious a cause?

The smallest spark may here kindle into the greatest flame; because the materials are always prepared for it. The *avidum genus auricularum*,[1] the gazing populace, receive greedily, without examination, whatever sooths superstition, and promotes wonder.

How many stories of this nature, have, in all ages, been detected and exploded in their infancy? How many more have been celebrated for a time, and have afterwards sunk into neglect and oblivion? Where such reports, therefore, fly about, the solution of the phænomenon is obvious; and we judge in conformity to regular experience and observation, when we account for it by the known and natural principles of credulity and delusion. And shall we, rather than have a recourse to so natural a solution, allow of a miraculous violation of the most established laws of nature?

I need not mention the difficulty of detecting a falsehood in any private or even public history, at the place, where it is said to happen; much more when the scene is removed to ever so small a distance. Even a court of judicature, with all the authority, accuracy, and judgment, which they can employ, find themselves often at a loss to distinguish between truth and falsehood in the most recent actions. But the matter never comes to any issue, if trusted to the common method of altercation and debate and flying rumours;

---

[1] Lucret. iv. 594.— [This reference was added in Ed. F; and the mistranslation was inserted in the text in Ed. M.]

especially when men's passions have taken part on either side.

In the infancy of new religions, the wise and learned commonly esteem the matter too inconsiderable to deserve their attention or regard. And when afterwards they would willingly detect the cheat, in order to undeceive the deluded multitude, the season is now past, and the records and witnesses, which might clear up the matter, have perished beyond recovery.

No means of detection remain, but those which must be drawn from the very testimony itself of the reporters: And these, though always sufficient with the judicious and knowing, are commonly too fine to fall under the comprehension of the vulgar.

Upon the whole, then, it appears, that no testimony for any kind of miracle [1] has ever amounted to a probability, much less to a proof; and that, even supposing it amounted to a proof, it would be opposed by another proof; derived from the very nature of the fact, which it would endeavour to establish. It is experience only, which gives authority to human testimony; and it is the same experience, which assures us of the laws of nature. When, therefore, these two kinds of experience are contrary, we have nothing to do but substract the one from the other, and embrace an opinion, either on one side or the other, with that assurance which arises from the remainder. But according to the principle here explained, this substraction, with regard to all popular religions, amounts to an entire annihilation: and therefore we may establish it as a maxim, that no human testimony can have such force as to prove a miracle, and make it a just foundation for any such system of religion.

[2] I beg the limitations here made may be remarked, when I say, that a miracle can never be proved, so as to be the foundation of a system of religion. For I own, that otherwise, there may possibly be miracles, or violations of the usual course of nature, of such a kind as to admit of proof from human testimony; though, perhaps, it will be impossible to find any such in all the records of history. Thus, suppose, all authors, in all languages, agree, that, from the first of

[1] [Can ever possibly amount to: Editions E and F.]

[2] [This and the three following para- graphs are given as a note in Editions E to P.]

January 1600, there was a total darkness over the whole earth for eight days: Suppose that the tradition of this extraordinary event is still strong and lively among the people: That all travellers, who return from foreign countries, bring us accounts of the same tradition, without the least variation or contradiction: It is evident, that our present philosophers, instead of doubting the fact, ought to receive it as certain, and ought to search for the causes whence it might be derived. [1] The decay, corruption, and dissolution of nature, is an event rendered probable by so many analogies, that any phænomenon, which seems to have a tendency towards that catastrophe, comes within the reach of human testimony, if that testimony be very extensive and uniform.

But suppose, that all the historians who treat of England, should agree, that, on the first of January 1600, Queen Elizabeth died; that both before and after her death she was seen by her physicians and the whole court, as is usual with persons of her rank; that her successor was acknowledged and proclaimed by the parliament; and that, after being interred a month, she again appeared, resumed the throne, and governed England for three years: I must confess that I should be surprized at the occurrence of so many odd circumstances, but should not have the least inclination to believe so miraculous an event. I should not doubt of her pretended death, and of those other public circumstances that followed it: I should only assert it to have been pretended, and that it neither was, nor possibly could be real. You would in vain object to me the difficulty, and almost impossibility of deceiving the world in an affair of such consequence; the wisdom [2] and solid judgment of that renowned queen; with the little or no advantage which she could reap from so poor an artifice: All this might astonish me; but I would still reply, that the knavery and folly of men are such common phænomena, that I should rather believe the most extraordinary events to arise from their concurrence, than admit of so signal a violation of the laws of nature.

But should this miracle be ascribed to any new system of religion; men, in all ages, have been so much imposed on by ridiculous stories of that kind, that this very circumstance would be a full proof of a cheat, and sufficient, with all men of sense, not only to make them reject the fact, but reject it without farther examination. Though the Being to whom the miracle is ascribed, be, in this case, Almighty, it does not, upon that account, become a whit more probable; since it is impossible for us to know the attributes or actions of such a Being, otherwise than from the experience which we have of his productions, in the usual course of nature. This still reduces us to past observation, and obliges us to compare the instances of the violation of truth in the testimony of men, with those of the violation of the laws of nature by miracles, in order to judge which of them is most likely and probable. As the violations of truth are more common in the testimony concerning religious miracles, than in that concerning any other matter of fact; this must diminish very much the authority of the former testimony, and make us form a general resolution, never to lend any attention to it, with whatever specious pretence it may be covered.

[1] Lord BACON seems to have embraced the same principles of reasoning. ' We ought,' says he, ' to make a collection or particular history of all monsters and prodigious births or productions, and in a word of every thing new, rare, and extraordinary in nature. But this must be done with the most severe scrutiny, lest we depart from truth. Above all, every relation must be considered as suspicious, which depends in any degree upon religion, as the prodigies of LIVY: And no less so, every thing that is to be found in the writers of natural magic or alchimy, or such authors, who seem, all of them, to have an unconquerable appetite for falsehood and fable.' [2]

I am the better pleased with the method of reasoning here delivered, as I think it may serve to confound those dangerous friends or disguised enemies to the *Christian Religion*, who have undertaken to defend it by the principles of human reason. Our most holy religion is founded on *Faith*, not on reason; and it is a sure method of exposing it to put it to such a trial as it is, by no means, fitted to endure. To make this more evident, let us examine those miracles, related in scripture; and not to lose ourselves in too wide

---

[1] [This paragraph, which is not found in Editions E and F, is also put in the note in Editions K to P. It is quoted in Latin in Editions K to Q.]
[2] Nov. Org. lib. ii. aph. 29.

a field, let us confine ourselves to such as we find in the *Pentateuch*, which we shall examine, according to the principles of those pretended Christians, not as the word or testimony of God himself, but as the production of a mere human writer and historian. Here then we are first to consider a book, presented to us by a barbarous and ignorant people, written in an age when they were still more barbarous, and in all probability long after the facts which it relates, corroborated by no concurring testimony, and resembling those fabulous accounts, which every nation gives of its origin. Upon reading this book, we find it full of prodigies and miracles. It gives an account of a state of the world and of human nature entirely different from the present: Of our fall from that state: Of the age of man, extended to near a thousand years: Of the destruction of the world by a deluge: Of the arbitrary choice of one people, as the favourites of heaven: and that people the countrymen of the author: Of their deliverance from bondage by prodigies the most astonishing imaginable: I desire any one to lay his hand upon his heart, and after a serious consideration declare, whether he thinks that the falsehood of such a book, supported by such a testimony, would be more extraordinary and miraculous than all the miracles it relates: which is, however, necessary to make it be received, according to the measures of probability above established.

What we have said of miracles may be applied, without any variation, to prophecies; and indeed, all prophecies are real miracles, and as such only, can be admitted as proofs of any revelation. If it did not exceed the capacity of human nature to foretel future events, it would be absurd to employ any prophecy as an argument for a divine mission or authority from heaven. So that, upon the whole, we may conclude, that the *Christian Religion* not only was at first attended with miracles, but even at this day cannot be believed by any reasonable person without one. Mere reason is insufficient to convince us of its veracity: And whoever is moved by *Faith* to assent to it, is conscious of a continued miracle in his own person, which subverts all the principles of his understanding, and gives him a determination to believe what is most contrary to custom and experience.

SECTION XI.   *Of a Particular Providence and of a Future State.*[1]

I WAS lately engaged in conversation with a friend who loves sceptical paradoxes; where, though he advanced many principles, of which I can by no means approve, yet as they seem to be curious, and to bear some relation to the chain of reasoning carried on throughout this enquiry, I shall here copy them from my memory as accurately as I can, in order to submit them to the judgment of the reader.

Our conversation began with my admiring the singular good fortune of philosophy, which, as it requires entire liberty above all other privileges, and chiefly flourishes from the free opposition of sentiments and argumentation, received its first birth in an age and country of freedom and toleration, and was never cramped, even in its most extravagant principles, by any creeds, confessions, or penal statutes. For, except the banishment of PROTAGORAS, and the death of SOCRATES, which last event proceeded partly from other motives, there are scarcely any instances to be met with, in ancient history, of this bigotted jealousy, with which the present age is so much infested. EPICURUS lived at ATHENS to an advanced age, in peace and tranquillity: EPICUREANS[2] were even admitted to receive the sacerdotal character, and to officiate at the altar, in the most sacred rites of the established religion: And the public encouragement[3] of pensions and salaries was afforded equally, by the wisest of all the ROMAN emperors,[4] to the professors of every sect of philosophy. How requisite such kind of treatment was to philosophy, in her early youth, will easily be conceived, if we reflect, that, even at present, when she may be supposed more hardy and robust, she bears with much difficulty the inclemency of the seasons, and those harsh winds of calumny and persecution, which blow upon her.

You admire, says my friend, as the singular good fortune of philosophy, what seems to result from the natural course of things, and to be unavoidable in every age and nation. This pertinacious bigotry, of which you complain, as so fatal

---

[1] [Of the Practical Consequences of Natural Religion: Ed. E.]

[2] Luciani *πνοι. ἤ Λαπιθαι.* 9.

[3] Luciani *ευνοῦχος.* 3.

[4] Id. & Dio.

to philosophy, is really her offspring, who, after allying with superstition, separates himself entirely from the interest of his parent, and becomes her most inveterate enemy and persecutor. Speculative dogmas of religion, the present occasions of such furious dispute, could not possibly be conceived or admitted in the early ages of the world; when mankind, being wholly illiterate, formed an idea of religion more suitable to their weak apprehension, and composed their sacred tenets of such tales chiefly as were the objects of traditional belief, more than of argument or disputation. After the first alarm, therefore, was over, which arose from the new paradoxes and principles of the philosophers; these teachers seem ever after, during the ages of antiquity, to have lived in great harmony with the established superstition, and to have made a fair partition of mankind between them; the former claiming all the learned and wise, the latter possessing all the vulgar and illiterate.

It seems then, say I, that you leave politics entirely out of the question, and never suppose, that a wise magistrate can justly be jealous of certain tenets of philosophy, such as those of EPICURUS, which, denying a divine existence, and consequently a providence and a future state, seem to loosen, in a great measure, the ties of morality, and may be supposed, for that reason, pernicious to the peace of civil society.

I know, replied he, that in fact these persecutions never, in any age, proceeded from calm reason, or from experience of the pernicious consequences of philosophy; but arose entirely from passion and prejudice. But what if I should advance farther, and assert, that, if EPICURUS had been accused before the people, by any of the *sycophants* or informers of those days, he could easily have defended his cause, and proved his principles of philosophy to be as salutary as those of his adversaries, who endeavoured, with such zeal, to expose him to the public hatred and jealousy.

I wish, said I, you would try your eloquence upon so extraordinary a topic, and make a speech for EPICURUS, which might satisfy, not the mob of ATHENS, if you will allow that ancient and polite city to have contained any mob, but the more philosophical part of his audience, such as might be supposed capable of comprehending his arguments.

The matter would not be difficult, upon such conditions, replied he: And if you please, I shall suppose myself

Epicurus for a moment, and make you stand for the Athenian people, and shall deliver you such an harangue as will fill all the urn with white beans, and leave not a black one to gratify the malice of my adversaries.

Very well: Pray proceed upon these suppositions.

I come hither, O ye Athenians, to justify in your assembly what I maintained in my school, and I find myself impeached by furious antagonists, instead of reasoning with calm and dispassionate enquirers. Your deliberations, which of right should be directed to questions of public good, and the interest of the commonwealth, are diverted to the disquisitions of speculative philosophy; and these magnificent, but perhaps fruitless enquiries, take place of your more familiar but more useful occupations. But so far as in me lies, I will prevent this abuse. We shall not here dispute concerning the origin and government of worlds. We shall only enquire how far such questions concern the public interest. And if I can persuade you, that they are entirely indifferent to the peace of society and security of government, I hope that you will presently send us back to our schools, there to examine, at leisure, the question, the most sublime, but, at the same time, the most speculative of all philosophy.

The religious philosophers, not satisfied with the tradition of your forefathers, and doctrine of your priests (in which I willingly acquiesce), indulge a rash curiosity, in trying how far they can establish religion upon the principles of reason; and they thereby excite, instead of satisfying, the doubts, which naturally arise from a diligent and scrutinous enquiry. They paint, in the most magnificent colours, the order, beauty, and wise arrangement of the universe; and then ask, if such a glorious display of intelligence could proceed from the fortuitous concourse of atoms, or if chance could produce what the greatest genius can never sufficiently admire. I shall not examine the justness of this argument. I shall allow it to be as solid as my antagonists and accusers can desire. It is sufficient, if I can prove, from this very reasoning, that the question is entirely speculative, and that, when, in my philosophical disquisitions, I deny a providence and a future state, I undermine not the foundations of society, but advance principles, which they themselves, upon their own topics, if they argue consistently, must allow to be solid and satisfactory.

You then, who are my accusers, have acknowledged, that the chief or sole argument for a divine existence (which I never questioned) is derived from the order of nature; where there appear such marks of intelligence and design, that you think it extravagant to assign for its cause, either chance, or the blind and unguided force of matter. You allow, that this is an argument drawn from effects to causes. From the order of the work, you infer, that there must have been project and forethought in the workman. If you cannot make out this point, you allow, that your conclusion fails; and you pretend not to establish the conclusion in a greater latitude than the phænomena of nature will justify. These are your concessions. I desire you to mark the consequences.

When we infer any particular cause from an effect, we must proportion the one to the other, and can never be allowed to ascribe to the cause any qualities, but what are exactly sufficient to produce the effect. A body of ten ounces raised in any scale may serve as a proof, that the counter-balancing weight exceeds ten ounces; but can never afford a reason that it exceeds a hundred. If the cause, assigned for any effect, be not sufficient to produce it, we must either reject that cause, or add to it such qualities as will give it a just proportion to the effect. But if we ascribe to it farther qualities, or affirm it capable of producing other effects, we can only indulge the licence of conjecture, and arbitrarily suppose the existence of qualities and energies, without reason or authority.

The same rule holds, whether the cause assigned be brute unconscious matter, or a rational intelligent being. If the cause be known only by the effect, we never ought to ascribe to it any qualities, beyond what are precisely requisite to produce the effect: Nor can we, by any rules of just reasoning, return back from the cause, and infer other effects from it, beyond those by which alone it is known to us. No one, merely from the sight of one of ZEUXIS's pictures, could know, that he was also a statuary or architect, and was an artist no less skilful in stone and marble than in colours. The talents and taste, displayed in the particular work before us; these we may safely conclude the workman to be possessed of. The cause must be proportioned to the effect; and if we exactly and precisely proportion it, we shall never find in it any qualities, that point farther, or afford an inference concerning any other design or performance. Such qualities must be somewhat beyond what is merely requisite for producing the effect, which we examine.

Allowing, therefore, the gods to be the authors of the existence or order of the universe; it follows, that they possess that precise degree of power, intelligence, and benevolence, which appears in their workmanship; but nothing farther can ever be proved, except we call in the assistance of exaggeration and flattery to supply the defects of argument and reasoning. So far as the traces of any attributes, at present, appear, so far may we conclude these attributes to exist. The supposition of farther attributes is mere hypothesis; much more the supposition, that, in distant regions of space or periods of time, there has been, or will be, a more magnificent display of these attributes, and a scheme of administration more suitable to such imaginary virtues. We can never be allowed to mount up from the universe, the effect, to Jupiter, the cause; and then descend downwards, to infer any new effect from that cause; as if the present effects alone were not entirely worthy of the glorious attributes, which we ascribe to that deity. The knowledge of the cause being derived solely from the effect, they must be exactly adjusted to each other; and the one can never refer to any thing farther, or be the foundation of any new inference and conclusion.

You find certain phaenomena in nature. You seek a cause or author. You imagine that you have found him. You afterwards become so enamoured of this offspring of your brain, that you imagine it impossible, but he must produce something greater and more perfect than the present scene of things, which is so full of ill and disorder. You forget, that this superlative intelligence and benevolence are entirely imaginary, or, at least, without any foundation in reason; and that you have no ground to ascribe to him any qualities, but what you see he has actually exerted and displayed in his productions. Let your gods, therefore, O philosophers, be suited to the present appearances of nature: And presume not to alter these appearances by arbitrary suppositions, in order to suit them to the attributes, which you so fondly ascribe to your deities.

When priests and poets, supported by your authority, O ATHENIANS, talk of a golden or silver age, which preceded the present state of vice and misery, I hear them with attention and with reverence. But when philosophers, who pretend to neglect authority, and to cultivate reason, hold the same discourse, I pay them not, I own, the same obsequious submission and pious deference. I ask; who carried them into the celestial regions, who admitted them into the councils of the gods, who opened to them the book of fate, that they thus rashly affirm, that their deities have executed, or will execute, any purpose beyond what has actually appeared? If they tell me, that they have mounted [1] on the steps or by the gradual ascent of reason, and by drawing inferences from effects to causes, I still insist, that they have aided the [2] ascent of reason by the wings of imagination; otherwise they could not thus change their manner of inference, and argue from causes to effects; presuming, that a more perfect production than the present world would be more suitable to such perfect beings as the gods, and forgetting that they have no reason to ascribe to these celestial beings any perfection or any attribute, but what can be found in the present world.

Hence all the fruitless industry to account for the ill appearances of nature, and save the honour of the gods; while we must acknowledge the reality of that evil and disorder, with which the world so much abounds. The obstinate and intractable qualities of matter, we are told, or the observance of general laws, or some such reason, is the sole cause, which controlled the power and benevolence of JUPITER, and obliged him to create mankind and every sensible creature so imperfect and so unhappy. These attributes, then, are, it seems, beforehand, taken for granted, in their greatest latitude. And upon that supposition, I own, that such conjectures may, perhaps, be admitted as plausible solutions of the ill phaenomena. But still I ask; Why take these attributes for granted, or why ascribe to the cause any qualities but what actually appear in the effect? Why torture your brain to justify the course of nature upon suppositions, which, for aught you know, may be entirely imaginary, and of which there are to be found no traces in the course of nature?

The religious hypothesis, therefore, must be considered only as a particular method of accounting for the visible

---

[1] [On the Steps or Scale of Reason: Ed. E.]   [2] [Scale: Ed. E.]

phaenomena of the universe: But no just reasoner will ever presume to infer from it any single fact, and alter or add to the phaenomena, in any single particular. If you think, that the appearances of things prove such causes, it is allowable for you to draw an inference concerning the existence of these causes. In such complicated and sublime subjects, every one should be indulged in the liberty of conjecture and argument. But here you ought to rest. If you come backward, and arguing from your inferred causes, conclude, that any other fact has existed, or will exist, in the course of nature, which may serve as a fuller display of particular attributes; I must admonish you, that you have departed from the method of reasoning, attached to the present subject, and have certainly added something to the attributes of the cause, beyond what appears in the effect; otherwise you could never, with tolerable sense or propriety, add any thing to the effect, in order to render it more worthy of the cause.

Where, then, is the odiousness of that doctrine, which I teach in my school, or rather, which I examine in my gardens? Or what do you find in this whole question, wherein the security of good morals, or the peace and order of society is in the least concerned?

I deny a providence, you say, and supreme governour of the world, who guides the course of events, and punishes the vicious with infamy and disappointment, and rewards the virtuous with honour and success, in all their undertakings. But surely, I deny not the course itself of events, which lies open to every one's enquiry and examination. I acknowledge, that, in the present order of things, virtue is attended with more peace of mind than vice, and meets with a more favourable reception from the world. I am sensible, that, according to the past experience of mankind, friendship is the chief joy of human life, and moderation the only source of tranquillity and happiness. I never balance between the virtuous and the vicious course of life; but am sensible, that, to a well disposed mind, every advantage is on the side of the former. And what can you say more, allowing all your suppositions and reasonings? You tell me, indeed, that this disposition of things proceeds from intelligence and design. But whatever it proceeds from, the disposition itself, on which depends our happiness or misery, and consequently our conduct and deportment in life, is still the same. It is still open for me, as well as you, to regulate my behaviour, by my experience of past events. And if you affirm, that, while a divine providence is allowed, and a supreme distributive justice in the universe, I ought to expect some more particular reward of the good, and punishment of the bad, beyond the ordinary course of events; I here find the same fallacy, which I have before endeavoured to detect. You persist in imagining, that, if we grant that divine existence, for which you so earnestly contend, you may safely infer consequences from it, and add something to the experienced order of nature, by arguing from the attributes which you ascribe to your gods. You seem not to remember, that all your reasonings on this subject can only be drawn from effects to causes; and that every argument, deduced from causes to effects, must of necessity be a gross sophism; since it is impossible for you to know any thing of the cause, but what you have antecedently, not inferred, but discovered to the full, in the effect.

But what must a philosopher think of those vain reasoners, who, instead of regarding the present scene of things as the sole object of their contemplation, so far reverse the whole course of nature, as to render this life merely a passage to something farther; a porch, which leads to a greater, and vastly different building; a prologue, which serves only to introduce the piece, and give it more grace and propriety? Whence, do you think, can such philosophers derive their idea of the gods? From their own conceit and imagination surely. For if they derived it from the present phænomena, it would never point to anything farther, but must be exactly adjusted to them. That the divinity may *possibly* be endowed with attributes, which we have never seen exerted; may be governed by principles of action, which we cannot discover to be satisfied: All this will freely be allowed. But still this is mere *possibility* and hypothesis. We can never have reason to *infer* any attributes, or any principles of action in him, but so far as we know them to have been exerted and satisfied.

Are there any marks of a distributive justice in the world? If you answer in the affirmative, I conclude, that, since justice here exerts itself, it is satisfied. If you reply in the negative, I conclude, that you have then no reason to ascribe justice, in our sense of it, to the gods. If you hold a medium between affirmation and negation, by saying, that the justice of the gods, at present, exerts itself in part, but not in its full extent; I answer, that you have no reason to give it any particular extent, but only as far as you see it, *at present*, exert itself.

Thus I bring the dispute, O ATHENIANS, to a short issue with my antagonists. The course of nature lies open to my contemplation as well as to theirs. The experienced train of events is the great standard, by which we all regulate our conduct. Nothing else can be appealed to in the field, or in the senate. Nothing else ought ever to be heard of in the school, or in the closet. In vain would our limited understanding break through these boundaries, which are too narrow for our fond imagination. While we argue from the course of nature, and infer a particular intelligent cause, which first bestowed, and still preserves order in the universe, we embrace a principle, which is both uncertain and useless. It is uncertain; because the subject lies entirely beyond the reach of human experience. It is useless; because our knowledge of this cause being derived entirely from the course of nature, we can never, according to the rules of just reasoning, return back from the cause with any new inference, or making additions to the common and experienced course of nature, establish any new principles of conduct and behaviour.

I observe (said I, finding he had finished his harangue) that you neglect not the artifice of the demagogues of old; and as you were pleased to make me stand for the people, you insinuate yourself into my favour by embracing those principles, to which, you know, I have always expressed a particular attachment. But allowing you to make experience (as indeed I think you ought) the only standard of our judgment concerning this, and all other questions of fact; I doubt not but, from the very same experience, to which you appeal, it may be possible to refute this reasoning, which you have put into the mouth of EPICURUS. If you saw, for instance, a half-finished building, surrounded with heaps of brick and stone and mortar, and all the instruments of masonry: could you not *infer* from the effect, that it was a work of design and contrivance? And could you not return again, from this inferred cause, to infer new additions to the effect, and conclude, that the building would soon be finished, and receive all the further improvements, which art could bestow upon it? If you saw upon the sea-shore the print of one human foot, you would conclude, that a man had passed that way, and that he had also left the traces of the other foot, though effaced by the rolling of the sands or inundation of the waters. Why then do you refuse to admit the same method of reasoning with regard to the order of nature? Consider the world and the present life only as an imperfect building, from which you can infer a superior intelligence; and arguing from that superior intelligence, which can leave nothing imperfect; why may you not infer a more finished scheme or plan, which will receive its completion in some distant point of space or time? Are not these methods of reasoning exactly similar? And under what pretence can you embrace the one, while you reject the other?

The infinite difference of the subjects, replied he, is a sufficient foundation for this difference in my conclusions. In works of *human* art and contrivance, it is allowable to advance from the effect to the cause, and returning back from the cause, to form new inferences concerning the effect, and examine the alterations, which it has probably undergone, or may still undergo. But what is the foundation of this method of reasoning? Plainly this; that man is a being, whom we know by experience, whose motives and designs we are acquainted with, and whose projects and inclinations have a certain connexion and coherence, according to the laws which nature has established for the government of such a creature. When, therefore, we find, that any work has proceeded from the skill and industry of man; as we are otherwise acquainted with the nature of the animal, we can draw a hundred inferences concerning what may be expected from him; and these inferences will all be founded in experience and observation. But did we know man only from the single work or production which we examine, it were impossible for us to argue in this manner; because our knowledge of all the qualities, which we ascribe to him, being in that case derived from the production, it is impossible they could point to any thing farther, or be the foundation of any new inference. The print of a foot in the sand can only prove, when considered alone, that there was some figure

OF A PROVIDENCE AND FUTURE STATE.

adapted to it, by which it was produced: But the print of a human foot proves likewise, from our other experience, that there was probably another foot, which also left its impression, though effaced by time or other accidents. Here we mount from the effect to the cause; and descending again from the cause, infer alterations in the effect; but this is not a continuation of the same simple chain of reasoning. We comprehend in this case a hundred other experiences and observations, concerning the *usual* figure and members of that species of animal, without which this method of argument must be considered as fallacious and sophistical.

The case is not the same with our reasonings from the works of nature. The Deity is known to us only by his productions, and is a single being in the universe, not comprehended under any species or genus, from whose experienced attributes or qualities, we can, by analogy, infer any attribute or quality in him. As the universe shews wisdom and goodness, we infer wisdom and goodness. As it shews a particular degree of these perfections, we infer a particular degree of them, precisely adapted to the effect which we examine. But farther attributes or farther degrees of the same attributes, we can never be authorised to infer or suppose, by any rules of just reasoning. Now, without some such licence of supposition, it is impossible for us to argue from the cause, or infer any alteration in the effect, beyond what has immediately fallen under our observation. Greater good produced by this Being must still prove a greater degree of goodness: A more impartial distribution of rewards and punishments must proceed from a greater regard to justice and equity. Every supposed addition to the works of nature makes an addition to the attributes of the Author of nature; and consequently, being entirely unsupported by any reason or argument, can never be admitted but as mere conjecture and hypothesis.[1]

The great source of our mistake in this subject, and of

---

[1] In general, it may, I think, be established as a maxim, that where any cause is known only by its particular effects, it must be impossible to infer any new effects from that cause; since the qualities, which are requisite to produce these new effects along with the former, must either be different, or superior, or of more extensive operation, than those which simply produced the effect, whence alone the cause is supposed to be known to us. We can never, therefore, have any reason to suppose the existence of these qualities. To say, that the new effects proceed only from a continuation of the same

----

[2] [Editions E and F print in the text as far as 'qualities,' and throw the rest into a note.]

the unbounded licence of conjecture, which we indulge, is, that we tacitly consider ourselves, as in the place of the Supreme Being, and conclude, that he will, on every occasion, observe the same conduct, which we ourselves, in his situation, would have embraced as reasonable and eligible. But, besides that the ordinary course of nature may convince us, that almost everything is regulated by principles and maxims very different from ours; besides this, I say, it must evidently appear contrary to all rules of analogy to reason, from the intentions and projects of men, to those of a Being so different, and so much superior. In human nature, there is a certain experienced coherence of designs and inclinations; so that when, from any fact, we have discovered one intention of any man, it may often be reasonable, from experience, to infer another, and draw a long chain of conclusions concerning his past or future conduct. But this method of reasoning can never have place with regard to a Being, so remote and incomprehensible, who bears much less analogy to any other being in the universe than the sun to a waxen taper, and who discovers himself only by some faint traces or outlines, beyond which we have no authority to ascribe to him any attribute or perfection. What we imagine to be a superior perfection, may really be a defect. Or were it ever so much a perfection, the ascribing of it to the Supreme Being, where it appears not to have been really exerted, to the full, in his works, savours more of flattery and panegyric, than of just reasoning and sound philosophy. All the philosophy, therefore, in the world, and all the religion, which is nothing but a species of philosophy, will never be able to carry us beyond the usual course of experience, or give us measures of conduct and behaviour different from those which are furnished by reflections on common life. No new fact can ever be inferred from the religious hypothesis; no event foreseen or foretold; no reward or punishment expected or dreaded, beyond what is already known by

energy, which is already known from the first effects, will not remove the difficulty. For even granting this to be the case (which can seldom be supposed), the very continuation and exertion of a like energy (for it is impossible it can be absolutely the same), I say, this exertion of a like energy, in a different period of space and time, is a very arbitrary supposition, and what there cannot possibly be any traces of in the effects, from which all our knowledge of the cause is originally derived. Let the *inferred* cause be exactly proportioned (as it should be) to the known effect; and it is impossible that it can possess any qualities, from which new or different effects can be *inferred*.

practice and observation. So that my apology for Epicurus will still appear solid and satisfactory ; nor have the political interests of society any connexion with the philosophical disputes concerning metaphysics and religion.

There is still one circumstance, replied I, which you seem to have overlooked. Though I should allow your premises, I must deny your conclusion. You conclude, that religious doctrines and reasonings *can* have no influence on life, because they *ought* to have no influence ; never considering, that men reason not in the same manner as you do, but draw many consequences from the belief of a divine Existence, and suppose that the Deity would inflict punishments on vice, and bestow rewards on virtue, beyond what appear in the ordinary course of nature. Whether this reasoning of theirs be just or not, is no matter. Its influence on their life and conduct must still be the same. And, those, who attempt to disabuse them of such prejudices, may, for aught I know, be good reasoners, but I cannot allow them to be good citizens and politicians ; since they free men from one restraint upon their passions, and make the infringement of the laws of society, in one respect, more easy and secure.

After all, I may, perhaps, agree to your general conclusion in favour of liberty, though upon different premises from those, on which you endeavour to found it. I think, that the state ought to tolerate every principle of philosophy ; nor is there an instance, that any government has suffered in its political interests by such indulgence. There is no enthusiasm among philosophers ; their doctrines are not very alluring to the people ; and no restraint can be put upon their reasonings, but what must be of dangerous consequence to the sciences, and even to the state, by paving the way for persecution and oppression in points, where the generality of mankind are more deeply interested and concerned.

But there occurs to me (continued I) with regard to your main topic, a difficulty, which I shall just propose to you, without insisting on it ; lest it lead into reasonings of too nice and delicate a nature. In a word, I much doubt whether it be possible for a cause to be known only by its effect (as you have all along supposed) or to be of so singular and particular a nature as to have no parallel and no similarity with any other cause or object, that has ever fallen under our observation. It is only when two *species* of objects are found to be constantly conjoined, that we can infer the one from the other; and were an effect presented, which was entirely singular, and could not be comprehended under any known *species*, I do not see, that we could form any conjecture or inference at all concerning its cause. If experience and observation and analogy be, indeed, the only guides which we can reasonably follow in inferences of this nature; both the effect and cause must bear a similarity and resemblance to other effects and causes, which we know, and which we have found, in many instances, to be conjoined with each other. I leave it to your own reflection to pursue the consequences of this principle. I shall just observe, that, as the antagonists of EPICURUS always suppose the universe, an effect quite singular and unparalleled, to be the proof of a Deity, a cause no less singular and unparalleled; your reasonings, upon that supposition, seem, at least, to merit our attention. There is, I own, some difficulty, how we can ever return from the cause to the effect, and, reasoning from our ideas of the former, infer any alteration on the latter, or any addition to it.

SECTION XII.—*Of the Academical or Sceptical Philosophy.*

PART I.

THERE is not a greater number of philosophical reasonings, displayed upon any subject, than those, which prove the existence of a Deity, and refute the fallacies of *Atheists*; and yet the most religious philosophers still dispute whether any man can be so blinded as to be a speculative atheist. How shall we reconcile these contradictions? The knights-errant, who wandered about to clear the world of dragons and giants, never entertained the least doubt with regard to the existence of these monsters.

The *Sceptic* is another enemy of religion, who naturally provokes the indignation of all divines and graver philosophers; though it is certain, that no man ever met with any such absurd creature, or conversed with a man, who had no opinion or principle concerning any subject, either of action or speculation. This begets a very natural question; What is meant by a sceptic? And how far it is possible to push these philosophical principles of doubt and uncertainty?

There is a species of scepticism, *antecedent* to all study and philosophy, which is much inculcated by DES CARTES and others, as a sovereign preservative against error and precipitate judgment. It recommends an universal doubt, not only of all our former opinions and principles, but also of our very faculties; of whose veracity, say they, we must assure ourselves, by a chain of reasoning, deduced from some original principle, which cannot possibly be fallacious or deceitful. But neither is there any such original principle, which has a prerogative above others, that are self-evident and convincing: Or if there were, could we advance a step beyond it, but by the use of those very faculties, of which we are supposed to be already diffident. The CARTESIAN doubt, therefore, were it ever possible to be attended by any human creature (as it plainly is not) would be entirely incurable; and no reasoning could ever bring us to a state of assurance and conviction upon any subject.

It must, however, be confessed, that this species of scepticism, when more moderate, may be understood in a very reasonable sense, and is a necessary preparative to the study of philosophy, by preserving a proper impartiality in our judgments, and weaning our mind from all those prejudices, which we may have imbibed from education or rash opinion. To begin with clear and self-evident principles, to advance by timorous and sure steps, to review frequently our conclusions, and examine accurately all their consequences; though by these means we shall make both a slow and a short progress in our systems: are the only methods, by which we can ever hope to reach truth, and attain a proper stability and certainty in our determinations.

There is another species of scepticism, *consequent* to science and enquiry, when men are supposed to have discovered, either the absolute fallaciousness of their mental faculties, or their unfitness to reach any fixed determination in all those curious subjects of speculation, about which they are commonly employed. Even our very senses are brought into dispute, by a certain species of philosophers; and the maxims of common life are subjected to the same doubt as the most profound principles or conclusions of metaphysics and theology. As these paradoxical tenets (if they may be called tenets) are to be met with in some philosophers, and the refutation of them in several, they naturally excite our curiosity, and make us enquire into the arguments, on which they may be founded.

I need not insist upon the more trite topics, employed by the sceptics in all ages, against the evidence of *sense*; such as those which are derived from the imperfection and fallaciousness of our organs, on numberless occasions; the crooked appearance of an oar in water; the various aspects of objects, according to their different distances; the double images which arise from the pressing one eye; with many other appearances of a like nature. These sceptical topics, indeed, are only sufficient to prove, that the senses alone are not implicitly to be depended on; but that we must correct their evidence by reason, and by considerations, derived from the nature of the medium, the distance of the object, and the disposition of the organ, in order to render them, within their sphere, the proper *criteria* of truth and falsehood. There are other more profound arguments against the senses, which admit not of so easy a solution.

It seems evident, that men are carried, by a natural instinct or prepossession, to repose faith in their senses; and that, without any reasoning, or even almost before the use of reason, we always suppose an external universe, which depends not on our perception, but would exist, though we and every sensible creature were absent or annihilated. Even the animal creation are governed by a like opinion, and preserve this belief of external objects, in all their thoughts, designs, and actions.

It seems also evident, that, when men follow this blind and powerful instinct of nature, they always suppose the very images, presented by the senses, to be the external objects, and never entertain any suspicion, that the one are nothing but representations of the other. This very table, which we see white, and which we feel hard, is believed to exist, independent of our perception, and to be something external to our mind, which perceives it. Our presence bestows not being on it: Our absence does not annihilate it. It preserves its existence uniform and entire, independent of the situation of intelligent beings, who perceive or contemplate it.

But this universal and primary opinion of all men is soon destroyed by the slightest philosophy, which teaches us, that nothing can ever be present to the mind but an image or perception, and that the senses are only the inlets, through which these images are conveyed, without being able to produce any immediate intercourse between the mind and the object. The table, which we see, seems to diminish, as we remove farther from it : But the real table, which exists independent of us, suffers no alteration : It was, therefore, nothing but its image, which was present to the mind. These are the obvious dictates of reason ; and no man, who reflects, ever doubted, that the existences, which we consider, when we say, *this house* and *that tree*, are nothing but perceptions in the mind, and fleeting copies or representations of other existences, which remain uniform and independent.

So far, then, are we necessitated by reasoning to contradict or depart from the primary instincts of nature, and to embrace a new system with regard to the evidence of our senses. But here philosophy finds herself extremely embarrassed, when she would justify this new system, and obviate the cavils and objections of the sceptics. She can no longer plead the infallible and irresistible instinct of nature : For that led us to a quite different system, which is acknowledged fallible and even erroneous. And to justify this pretended philosophical system, by a chain of clear and convincing argument, or even any appearance of argument, exceeds the power of all human capacity.

By what argument can it be proved, that the perceptions of the mind must be caused by external objects, entirely different from them, though resembling them (if that be possible) and could not arise either from the energy of the mind itself, or from the suggestion of some invisible and unknown spirit, or from some other cause still more unknown to us? It is acknowledged, that, in fact, many of these perceptions arise not from any thing external, as in dreams, madness, and other diseases. And nothing can be more inexplicable than the manner, in which body should so operate upon mind as ever to convey an image of itself to a substance, supposed of so different, and even contrary a nature.

It is a question of fact, whether the perceptions of the senses be produced by external objects, resembling them : How shall this question be determined? By experience surely ; as all other questions of a like nature. But here experience is, and must be entirely silent. The mind has never any thing present to it but the perceptions, and cannot possibly reach any experience of their connexion with objects. The supposition of such a connexion is, therefore, without any foundation in reasoning.

To have recourse to the veracity of the supreme Being, in order to prove the veracity of our senses, is surely making a very unexpected circuit. If his veracity were at all concerned in this matter, our senses would be entirely infallible; because it is not possible that he can ever deceive. Not to mention, that, if the external world be once called in question, we shall be at a loss to find arguments, by which we may prove the existence of that Being or any of his attributes.

This is a topic, therefore, in which the profounder and more philosophical sceptics will always triumph, when they endeavour to introduce an universal doubt into all subjects of human knowledge and enquiry. Do you follow the instincts and propensities of nature, may they say, in assenting to the veracity of sense? But these lead you to believe, that the very perception or sensible image is the external object. Do you disclaim this principle, in order to embrace a more rational opinion, that the perceptions are only representations of something external? You here depart from your natural propensities and more obvious sentiments; and yet are not able to satisfy your reason, which can never find any convincing argument from experience to prove, that the perceptions are connected with any external objects.

There is another sceptical topic of a like nature, derived from the most profound philosophy; which might merit our attention, were it requisite to dive so deep, in order to discover arguments and reasonings, which can so little serve to any serious purpose. It is universally allowed by modern enquirers, that all the sensible qualities of objects, such as hard, soft, hot, cold, white, black, &c., are merely secondary, and exist not in the objects themselves, but are perceptions of the mind, without any external archetype or model, which they represent. If this be allowed, with regard to secondary qualities, it must also follow, with regard to the supposed primary qualities of extension and solidity; nor can the latter be any more entitled to that denomination than the former. The idea of extension is entirely acquired from the senses of sight and feeling; and if all the qualities, perceived by the senses, be in the mind, not in the object, the same conclusion must reach the idea of extension, which is wholly dependent on the sensible ideas or the ideas of secondary qualities. Nothing can save us from this conclusion, but the asserting, that the ideas of those primary qualities are attained by *Abstraction*; an opinion, which, if we examine it accurately, we shall find to be unintelligible, and even absurd. An extension, that is neither tangible nor visible, cannot possibly be conceived: And a tangible or visible extension, which is neither hard nor soft, black nor white, is equally beyond the reach of human conception. Let any man try to conceive a triangle in general, which is neither *Isoceles* nor *Scalenum*, nor has any particular length or proportion of sides; and he will soon perceive the absurdity of all the scholastic notions with regard to abstraction and general ideas.[1]

Thus the first philosophical objection to the evidence of sense or to the opinion of external existence consists in this, that such an opinion, if rested on natural instinct, is contrary to reason, and if referred to reason, is contrary to natural instinct, and at the same time carries no rational evidence with it, to convince an impartial enquirer. The second objection goes farther, and represents this opinion as contrary to reason: at least, if it be a principle of reason, that all sensible qualities are in the mind, not in the object. [2] Bereave matter of all its intelligible qualities, both primary and secondary, you in a manner annihilate it, and leave only a certain unknown, inexplicable *something*, as the cause of our perceptions; a notion so imperfect, that no sceptic will think it worth while to contend against it.

PART II.

It may seem a very extravagant attempt of the sceptics to destroy *reason* by argument and ratiocination; yet is this the grand scope of all their enquiries and disputes. They en-

---

[1] This argument is drawn from Dr. BERKELEY; and indeed most of the writings of that very ingenious author form the best lessons of scepticism, which are to be found either among the ancient or modern philosophers, BAYLE not excepted. He professes, however, in his title-page (and undoubtedly with great truth) to have composed his book against the sceptics as well as against the atheists and free thinkers. But that all his arguments, though otherwise intended, are, in reality, merely sceptical, appears from this, *that they admit of no answer and produce no conviction.* Their only effect is to cause that momentary amazement and irresolution and confusion, which is the result of scepticism.

[2] [This sentence was added in Ed R.]

deavour to find objections, both to our abstract reasonings, and to those which regard matter of fact and existence.

The chief objection against all *abstract* reasonings is derived from the ideas of space and time; ideas, which, in common life and to a careless view, are very clear and intelligible, but when they pass through the scrutiny of the profound sciences (and they are the chief object of these sciences) afford principles, which seem full of absurdity and contradiction. No priestly *dogmas*, invented on purpose to tame and subdue the rebellious reason of mankind, ever shocked common sense more than the doctrine of the infinite divisibility of extension, with its consequences; as they are pompously displayed by all geometricians and metaphysicians, with a kind of triumph and exultation. A real quantity, infinitely less than any finite quantity, containing quantities infinitely less than itself, and so on *in infinitum*; this is an edifice so bold and prodigious, that it is too weighty for any pretended demonstration to support, because it shocks the clearest and most natural principles of human reason.[1] But what renders the matter more extraordinary, is, that these seemingly absurd opinions are supported by a chain of reasoning, the clearest and most natural; nor is it possible for us to allow the premises without admitting the consequences. Nothing can be more convincing and satisfactory than all the conclusions concerning the properties of circles and triangles; and yet, when these are once received, how can we deny, that the angle of contact between a circle and its tangent is infinitely less than any rectilineal angle, that as you may encrease the diameter of the circle *in infinitum*, this angle of contact becomes still less, even *in infinitum*, and that the angle of contact between other curves and their tangents may be infinitely less than those between any circle and its tangent, and so on, *in infinitum?* The demonstration of these principles seems as unexceptionable as that which proves the three angles of a triangle to be equal to two right

---

[1] Whatever disputes there may be about mathematical points, we must allow that there are physical points; that is, parts of extension, which cannot be divided or lessened, either by the eye or imagination. These images, then, which are present to the fancy or senses, are absolutely indivisible, and consequently must be allowed by mathematicians to be infinitely less than any real part of extension; and yet nothing appears more certain to reason, than that an infinite number of them composes an infinite extension. How much more an infinite number of those infinitely small parts of extension, which are still supposed infinitely divisible?

ones, though the latter opinion be natural and easy, and the former big with contradiction and absurdity. Reason here seems to be thrown into a kind of amazement and suspence, which, without the suggestions of any sceptic, gives her a diffidence of herself, and of the ground on which she treads. She sees a full light, which illuminates certain places; but that light borders upon the most profound darkness. And between these she is so dazzled and confounded, that she scarcely can pronounce with certainty and assurance concerning any one object.

The absurdity of these bold determinations of the abstract sciences seems to become, if possible, still more palpable with regard to time than extension. An infinite number of real parts of time, passing in succession, and exhausted one after another, appears so evident a contradiction, that no man, one should think, whose judgment is not corrupted, instead of being improved, by the sciences, would ever be able to admit of it.

Yet still reason must remain restless, and unquiet, even with regard to that scepticism, to which she is driven by these seeming absurdities and contradictions. How any clear, distinct idea can contain circumstances, contradictory to itself, or to any other clear, distinct idea, is absolutely incomprehensible; and is, perhaps, as absurd as any proposition, which can be formed. So that nothing can be more sceptical, or more full of doubt and hesitation, than this scepticism itself, which arises from some of the paradoxical conclusions of geometry or the science of quantity.[1]

---

[1] It seems to me not impossible to avoid these absurdities and contradictions, if it be admitted, that there is no such thing as abstract or general ideas, properly speaking; but that all general ideas are, in reality, particular ones, attached to a general term, which recalls, upon occasion, other particular ones, that resemble, in certain circumstances, the idea, present to the mind. Thus when the term Horse, is pronounced, we immediately figure to ourselves the idea of a black or a white animal, of a particular size or figure: But as that term is also usually applied to animals of other colours, figures and sizes, these ideas, though not actually present to the imagination, are easily recalled; and our reasoning and conclusion proceed in the same way, as if they were actually present. If this be admitted (as seems reasonable) it follows that all the ideas of quantity, upon which mathematicians reason, are nothing but particular, and such as are suggested by the senses and imagination, and consequently, cannot be infinitely divisible.[1] It is sufficient

---

[1] [Editions E and F insert: In general, we may pronounce, that the Ideas of *greater, less, or equal*, which are the chief Objects of Geometry, are far from being so exact or determinate as to be the Foundation of such extraordinary Inferences. Ask a Mathematician what he means, when he pronounces two

K

　　The sceptical objections to *moral* evidence, or to the reasonings concerning matter of fact, are either *popular* or *philosophical*. The popular objections are derived from the natural weakness of human understanding; the contradictory opinions, which have been entertained in different ages and nations; the variations of our judgment in sickness and health, youth and old age, prosperity and adversity; the perpetual contradiction of each particular man's opinions and sentiments; with many other topics of that kind. It is needless to insist farther on this head. These objections are but weak. For as, in common life, we reason every moment concerning fact and existence, and cannot possibly subsist, without continually employing this species of argument, any popular objections, derived from thence, must be insufficient to destroy that evidence. The great subverter of *Pyrrhonism* or the excessive principles of scepticism, is action, and employment, and the occupations of common life. These principles may flourish and triumph in the schools; where it is, indeed, difficult, if not impossible, to refute them. But as soon as they leave the shade, and by the presence of the real objects, which actuate our passions and sentiments, are put in opposition to the more powerful principles of our nature, they vanish like smoke, and leave the most determined sceptic in the same condition as other mortals.

　　The sceptic, therefore, had better keep within his proper sphere, and display those *philosophical* objections, which arise from more profound researches. Here he seems to have ample matter of triumph; while he justly insists, that all our evidence for any matter of fact, which lies beyond the testimony of sense or memory, is derived entirely from the relation of cause and effect; that we have no other idea of this relation than that of two objects, which have been frequently *conjoined* together; that we have no argument to convince us, that objects, which have, in our experience, been

to have dropped this hint at present, without prosecuting it any farther. It certainly concerns all lovers of science not to expose themselves to the ridicule and contempt of the ignorant by their conclusions; and this seems the readiest solution of these difficulties.

Quantities to be equal, and he must say, that the Idea of *Equality* is one of those, which cannot be defined, and that 'tis sufficient to present two equal Quantities before any one, in order to suggest it. Now this is an Appeal to the general Appearances of Objects to the Imagination or Senses, and consequently can never afford Conclusions so directly contrary to these Faculties.

frequently conjoined, will likewise, in other instances, be conjoined in the same manner; and that nothing leads us to this inference but custom or a certain instinct of our nature; which it is indeed difficult to resist, but which, like other instincts, may be fallacious and deceitful. While the sceptic insists upon these topics, he shews his force, or rather, indeed, his own and our weakness; and seems, for the time at least, to destroy all assurance and conviction. These arguments might be displayed at greater length, if any durable good or benefit to society could ever be expected to result from them.

For here is the chief and most confounding objection to *excessive* scepticism, that no durable good can ever result from it; while it remains in its full force and vigour. We need only ask such a sceptic, *What his meaning is? And what he proposes by all these curious researches?* He is immediately at a loss, and knows not what to answer. A COPERNICAN or PTOLEMAIC, who supports each his different system of astronomy, may hope to produce a conviction, which will remain constant and durable, with his audience. A STOIC or EPICUREAN displays principles, which may not only be durable, but which have an effect on conduct and behaviour. But a PYRRHONIAN cannot expect, that his philosophy will have any constant influence on the mind: Or if it had, that its influence would be beneficial to society. On the contrary, he must acknowledge, if he will acknowledge any thing, that all human life must perish, were his principles universally and steadily to prevail. All discourse, all action would immediately cease; and men remain in a total lethargy, till the necessities of nature, unsatisfied, put an end to their miserable existence. It is true; so fatal an event is very little to be dreaded. Nature is always too strong for principle. And though a PYRRHONIAN may throw himself or others into a momentary amazement and confusion by his profound reasonings; the first and most trivial event in life will put to flight all his doubts and scruples, and leave him the same, in every point of action and speculation, with the philosophers of every other sect, or with those who never concerned themselves in any philosophical researches. When he awakes from his dream, he will be the first to join in the laugh against himself, and to confess, that all his objections are mere amusement, and can have no other tendency than to show the whimsical condition of mankind, who must act and reason and believe; though they are not able, by their most diligent enquiry, to satisfy themselves concerning the foundation of these operations, or to remove the objections, which may be raised against them.

PART III.

There is, indeed, a more *mitigated* scepticism or *academical* philosophy, which may be both durable and useful, and which may, in part, be the result of this PYRRHONISM, or *excessive* scepticism, when its undistinguished doubts are, in some measure, corrected by common sense and reflection. The greater part of mankind are naturally apt to be affirmative and dogmatical in their opinions; and while they see objects only on one side, and have no idea of any counterpoising argument, they throw themselves precipitately into the principles, to which they are inclined; nor have they any indulgence for those who entertain opposite sentiments. To hesitate or balance perplexes their understanding, checks their passion, and suspends their action. They are, therefore, impatient till they escape from a state, which to them is so uneasy; and they think, that they can never remove themselves far enough from it, by the violence of their affirmations and obstinacy of their belief. But could such dogmatical reasoners become sensible of the strange infirmities of human understanding, even in its most perfect state, and when most accurate and cautious in its determinations; such a reflection would naturally inspire them with more modesty and reserve, and diminish their fond opinion of themselves, and their prejudice against antagonists. The illiterate may reflect on the disposition of the learned, who, amidst all the advantages of study and reflection, are commonly still diffident in their determinations: And if any of the learned be inclined, from their natural temper, to haughtiness and obstinacy, a small tincture of PYRRHONISM might abate their pride, by showing them, that the few advantages, which they may have attained over their fellows, are but inconsiderable, if compared with the universal perplexity and confusion, which is inherent in human nature. In general, there is a degree of doubt, and caution, and modesty, which, in all kinds of scrutiny and decision, ought for ever to accompany a just reasoner.

Another species of *mitigated* scepticism, which may be of advantage to mankind, and which may be the natural result of the PYRRHONIAN doubt and scruples, is the limitation of our enquiries to such subjects as are best adapted to the narrow capacity of human understanding. The *imagination* of man is naturally sublime, delighted with whatever is remote and extraordinary, and running, without controul, into the most distant parts of space and time in order to avoid the objects, which custom has rendered too familiar to it. A correct *Judgment* observes a contrary method, and avoiding all distant and high enquiries, confines itself to common life, and to such subjects as fall under daily practice and experience; leaving the more sublime topics to the embellishment of poets and orators, or to the arts of priests and politicians. To bring us to so salutary a determination, nothing can be more serviceable, than to be once thoroughly convinced of the force of the PYRRHONIAN doubt, and of the impossibility, that any thing, but the strong power of natural instinct, could free us from it. Those who have a propensity to philosophy, will still continue their researches; because they reflect, that, besides the immediate pleasure, attending such an occupation, philosophical decisions are nothing but the reflections of common life, methodized and corrected. But they will never be tempted to go beyond common life, so long as they consider the imperfection of those faculties which they employ, their narrow reach, and their inaccurate operations. While we cannot give a satisfactory reason, why we believe, after a thousand experiments, that a stone will fall, or fire burn; can we ever satisfy ourselves concerning any determination, which we may form, with regard to the origin of worlds, and the situation of nature, from, and to eternity?

This narrow limitation, indeed, of our enquiries, is, in every respect, so reasonable, that it suffices to make the slightest examination into the natural powers of the human mind, and to compare them with their objects, in order to recommend it to us. We shall then find what are the proper subjects of science and enquiry.

It seems to me, that the only objects of the abstract sciences or of demonstration are quantity and number, and that all attempts to extend this more perfect species of knowledge beyond these bounds are mere sophistry and illusion. As the component parts of quantity and number are entirely similar, their relations become intricate and involved; and nothing can be more curious, as well as useful, than to trace, by a variety of mediums, their equality or inequality, through their different appearances. But as all other ideas are clearly distinct and different from each other, we can never advance farther, by our utmost scrutiny, than to observe this diversity, and, by an obvious reflection, pronounce one thing not to be another. Or if there be any difficulty in these decisions, it proceeds entirely from the undeterminate meaning of words, which is corrected by juster definitions. That *the square of the hypothenuse is equal to the squares of the other two sides*, cannot be known, let the terms be ever so exactly defined, without a train of reasoning and enquiry. But to convince us of this proposition, *that where there is no property, there can be no injustice*, it is only necessary to define the terms, and explain injustice to be a violation of property. This proposition is, indeed, nothing but a more imperfect definition. It is the same case with all those pretended syllogistical reasonings, which may be found in every other branch of learning, except the sciences of quantity and number; and these may safely, I think, be pronounced the only proper objects of knowledge and demonstration.

All other enquiries of men regard only matter of fact and existence; and these are evidently incapable of demonstration. Whatever *is* may *not be*. No negation of a fact can involve a contradiction. The non-existence of any being, without exception, is as clear and distinct an idea as its existence. The proposition, which affirms it not to be, [1] however false, is no less conceivable and intelligible, than that which affirms it to be. The case is different with the sciences, properly so called. Every proposition, which is not true, is there confused and unintelligible. That the cube root of 64 is equal to the half of 10, is a false proposition, and can never be distinctly conceived. But that CÆSAR, or the angel GABRIEL, or any being never existed, may be a false proposition, but still is perfectly conceivable, and implies no contradiction.

The existence, therefore, of any being can only be proved by arguments from its cause or its effect; and these arguments are founded entirely on experience. If we reason à *priori*, any thing may appear able to produce any thing. The falling of a pebble may, for aught we know, extinguish the sun; or the wish of a man controul the planets in their orbits. It is only experience, which teaches us the nature and bounds of cause and effect, and enables us to infer the existence of one object from that of another.[1] Such is the foundation of moral reasoning, which forms the greater part of human knowledge, and is the source of all human action and behaviour.

Moral reasonings are either concerning particular or general facts. All deliberations in life regard the former; as also all disquisitions in history, chronology, geography, and astronomy.

The sciences, which treat of general facts, are politics, natural philosophy, physic, chymistry, &c. where the qualities, causes and effects of a whole species of objects are enquired into.

Divinity or Theology, as it proves the existence of a Deity, and the immortality of souls, is composed partly of reasonings concerning particular, partly concerning general facts. It has a foundation in *reason*, so far as it is supported by experience. But its best and most solid foundation is *faith* and divine revelation.

Morals and criticism are not so properly objects of the understanding as of taste and sentiment. Beauty, whether moral or natural, is felt, more properly than perceived. Or if we reason concerning it, and endeavour to fix its standard, we regard a new fact, to wit, the general taste of mankind, or some such fact, which may be the object of reasoning and enquiry.

When we run over libraries, persuaded of these principles, what havoc must we make? If we take in our hand any volume; of divinity or school metaphysics, for instance: let us ask, *Does it contain any abstract reasoning concerning quantity or number?* No. *Does it contain any experimental reasoning concerning matter of fact and existence?* No. Commit it then to the flames: For it can contain nothing but sophistry and illusion.

---

[1] That impious maxim of the ancient philosophy, *Ex nihilo, nihil fit*, by which the creation of matter was excluded, ceases to be a maxim, according to this philosophy. Not only the will of the supreme Being may create matter; but, for aught we know *à priori*, the will of any other being might create it, or any other cause, that the most whimsical imagination can assign.

A

DISSERTATION

ON THE

PASSIONS.

A DISSERTATION ON THE PASSIONS.

1. SOME objects produce immediately an agreeable sensation, by the original structure of our organs, and are thence denominated GOOD; as others, from their immediate disagreeable sensation, acquire the appellation of EVIL. Thus moderate warmth is agreeable and good; excessive heat painful and evil.

Some objects again, by being naturally conformable or contrary to passion, excite an agreeable or painful sensation; and are thence called *Good* or *Evil*. The punishment of an adversary, by gratifying revenge, is good; the sickness of a companion, by affecting friendship, is evil.

2. All good or evil, whence-ever it arises, produces various passions and affections, according to the light in which it is surveyed.

When good is certain or very probable, it produces JOY: When evil is in the same situation, there arises GRIEF or SORROW.

When either good or evil is uncertain, it gives rise to FEAR or HOPE, according to the degree of uncertainty on one side or the other.

DESIRE arises from good considered simply; and AVERSION, from evil. The WILL exerts itself, when either the presence of the good or absence of the evil may be attained by any action of the mind or body.

3. None of these passions seem to contain any thing curious or remarkable, except *Hope* and *Fear*, which, being derived from the probability of any good or evil, are mixed passions, that merit our attention.

Probability arises from an opposition of contrary chances or causes, by which the mind is not allowed to fix on either side; but is incessantly tossed from one to another, and is determined, one moment, to consider an object as existent, and another moment as the contrary. The imagination or understanding, call it which you please, fluctuates between the opposite views; and though perhaps it may be oftener turned to one side than the other, it is impossible for it, by reason of the opposition of causes or chances, to rest on either. The *pro* and *con* of the question alternately prevail; and the mind, surveying the objects in their opposite causes, finds such a contrariety as destroys all certainty or established opinion.

Suppose, then, that the object, concerning which we are doubtful, produces either desire or aversion; it is evident, that, according as the mind turns itself to one side or the other, it must feel a momentary impression of joy or sorrow. An object, whose existence we desire, gives satisfaction, when we think of those causes, which produce it; and for the same reason, excites grief or uneasiness from the opposite consideration. So that, as the understanding, in probable questions, is divided between the contrary points of view, the heart must in the same manner be divided between opposite emotions.

Now, if we consider the human mind, we shall observe, that, with regard to the passions, it is not like a wind instrument of music, which, in running over all the notes, immediately loses the sound when the breath ceases; but rather resembles a string-instrument, where, after each stroke, the vibrations still retain some sound, which gradually and insensibly decays. The imagination is extremely quick and agile; but the passions, in comparison, are slow and restive: For which reason, when any object is presented, which affords a variety of views to the one and emotions to the other; though the fancy may change its views with great celerity; each stroke will not produce a clear and distinct note of passion, but the one passion will always be mixed and confounded with the other. According as the probability inclines to good or evil, the passion of grief or joy predominates in the composition; and these passions being intermingled by means of the contrary views of the imagination, produce by the union the passions of hope or fear.

4. As this theory seems to carry its own evidence along with it, we shall be more concise in our proofs.

The passions of fear and hope may arise, when the chances are equal on both sides, and no superiority can be discovered in one above the other. Nay, in this situation the passions are rather the strongest, as the mind has then the least foundation to rest upon, and is tost with the greatest uncertainty. Throw in a superior degree of probability to the side of grief, you immediately see that passion diffuse itself over the composition, and tincture it into fear. Encrease the probability, and by that means the grief; the fear prevails still more and more, 'till at last it runs insensibly, as the joy continually diminishes, into pure grief. After you have brought it to this situation, diminish the grief, by a contrary operation to that, which encreased it, to wit, by diminishing the probability on the melancholy side; and you will see the passion clear every moment, 'till it changes insensibly into hope; which again runs, by slow degrees, into joy, as you encrease that part of the composition, by the encrease of the probability. Are not these as plain proofs, that the passions of fear and hope are mixtures of grief and joy, as in optics it is a proof, that a coloured ray of the sun, passing through a prism, is a composition of two others, when, as you diminish or encrease the quantity of either, you find it prevail proportionably, more or less, in the composition?

5. Probability is of two kinds; either when the object is itself uncertain, and to be determined by chance: or when, though the object be already certain, yet it is uncertain to our judgment, which finds a number of proofs or presumptions on each side of the question. Both these kinds of probability cause fear and hope; which must proceed from that property, in which they agree; namely, the uncertainty and fluctuation which they bestow on the passion, by that contrariety of views, which is common to both.

6. It is a probable good or evil, which commonly causes hope or fear; because probability, producing an inconstant and wavering survey of an object, occasions naturally a like mixture and uncertainty of passion. But we may observe, that, wherever, from other causes, this mixture can be produced, the passions of fear and hope will arise, even though there be no probability.

An evil, conceived as barely *possible*, sometimes produces fear; especially if the evil be very great. A man cannot think on excessive pain and torture without trembling, if he runs the least risque of suffering them. The smallness of the probability is compensated by the greatness of the evil.

But even *impossible* evils cause fear; as when we tremble on the brink of a precipice, though we know ourselves to be in perfect security, and have it in our choice, whether we will advance a step farther. The immediate presence of the evil influences the imagination and produces a species of belief; but being opposed by the reflection on our security, that belief is immediately retracted, and causes the same kind of passion, as when, from a contrariety of chances, contrary passions are produced.

Evils, which are *certain*, have sometimes the same effect as the possible or impossible. A man, in a strong prison, without the least means of escape, trembles at the thoughts of the rack, to which he is sentenced. The evil is here fixed in itself; but the mind has not courage to fix upon it; and this fluctuation gives rise to a passion of a similar appearance with fear.

7. But it is not only where good or evil is uncertain as to its *existence*, but also as to its *kind*, that fear or hope arises. If any one were told that one of his sons is suddenly killed; the passion, occasioned by this event, would not settle into grief, 'till he got certain information which of his sons he had lost. Though each side of the question produces here the same passion; that passion cannot settle, but receives from the imagination, which is unfixed, a tremulous unsteady motion, resembling the mixture and contention of grief and joy.

8. Thus all kinds of uncertainty have a strong connexion with fear, even though they do not cause any opposition of passions, by the opposite views, which they present to us. Should I leave a friend in any malady, I should feel more anxiety upon his account, than if he were present: though perhaps I am not only incapable of giving him assistance, but likewise of judging concerning the event of his sickness. There are a thousand little circumstances of his situation and condition, which I desire to know; and the knowledge of them would prevent that fluctuation and uncertainty, so nearly allied to fear. Horace [1] has remarked this phænomenon.

*Ut assidens implumibus pullis avis
Serpentium allapsus timet,
Magis relictis; non, ut adsit, auxili
Latura plus præsentibus.*

A virgin on her bridal-night goes to bed full of fears and

---

[1] [In the Treatise, Vol. ii. p. 222, the ....um.' Hume's quotations from Latin quotation reads 'pullus' and 'serpet... are frequently incorrect. — Ed.]

apprehensions, though she expects nothing but pleasure. The confusion of wishes and joys, the newness and greatness of the unknown event, so embarrass the mind, that it knows not in what image or passion to fix itself.

9. Concerning the mixture of affections, we may remark, in general, that when contrary passions arise from objects nowise connected together, they take place alternately. Thus when a man is afflicted for the loss of a law-suit, and joyful for the birth of a son, the mind, running from the agreeable to the calamitous object ; with whatever celerity it may perform this motion, can scarcely temper the one affection with the other, and remain between them in a state of indifference.

It more easily attains that calm situation, when the *same* event is of a mixed nature, and contains something adverse and something prosperous in its different circumstances. For in that case, both the passions, mingling with each other by means of the relation, often become mutually destructive, and leave the mind in perfect tranquillity.

But suppose, that the object is not a compound of good and evil, but is considered as probable or improbable in any degree ; in that case, the contrary passions will both of them be present at once in the soul, and instead of balancing and tempering each other, will subsist together, and by their union produce a third impression or affection, such as hope or fear.

The influence of the relations of ideas (which we shall explain more fully afterwards) is plainly seen in this affair. In contrary passions, if the objects be *totally different*, the passions are like two opposite liquors in different bottles, which have no influence on each other. If the objects be intimately *connected*, the passions are like an *alcali* and an *acid*, which, being mingled, destroy each other. If the relation be more imperfect, and consist in the *contradictory* views of the *same* object, the passions are like oil and vinegar, which, however mingled, never perfectly unite and incorporate.

The effect of a mixture of passions, when one of them is predominant, and swallows up the other, shall be explained afterwards.

SECT. II.

1. Besides those passions above-mentioned, which arise from a direct pursuit of good and aversion to evil, there are others which are of a more complicated nature, and imply more than one view or consideration. Thus *Pride* is a certain satisfaction in ourselves, on account of some accomplishment or possession, which we enjoy: *Humility*, on the other hand, is a dissatisfaction with ourselves, on account of some defect or infirmity.

Love or *Friendship* is a complacency in another, on account of his accomplishments or services: *Hatred*, the contrary.

2. In these two sets of passion, there is an obvious distinction to be made between the *object* of the passion and its *cause*. The object of pride and humility is self: The cause of the passion is some excellence in the former case; some fault, in the latter. The object of love and hatred is some other person: The causes, in like manner, are either excellencies or faults.

With regard to all these passions, the causes are what excite the emotion; the object is what the mind directs its view to when the emotion is excited. Our merit, for instance, raises pride; and it is essential to pride to turn our view on ourselves with complacency and satisfaction.

Now, as the causes of these passions are very numerous and various, though their object be uniform and simple; it may be a subject of curiosity to consider, what that circumstance is, in which all these various causes agree; or in other words, what is the real efficient cause of the passion. We shall begin with pride and humility.

3. In order to explain the causes of these passions, we must reflect on certain principles, which, though they have a mighty influence on every operation, both of the understanding and passions, are not commonly much insisted on by philosophers. The first of these is the *association* of ideas, or that principle, by which we make an easy transition from one idea to another. However uncertain and changeable our thoughts may be, they are not entirely without rule and method in their changes. They usually pass with regularity, from one object, to what resembles it, is contiguous to

it, or produced by it.[1] When one idea is present to the imagination, any other, united by these relations, naturally follows it, and enters with more facility, by means of that introduction.

The *second* property, which I shall observe in the human mind, is a like association of impressions or emotions. All *resembling* impressions are connected together; and no sooner one arises, than the rest naturally follow. Grief and disappointment give rise to anger, anger to envy, envy to malice, and malice to grief again. In like manner, our temper, when elevated with joy, naturally throws itself into love, generosity, courage, pride, and other resembling affections.

In the *third* place, it is observable of these two kinds of association, that they very much assist and forward each other, and that the transition is more easily made, where they both concur in the same object. Thus, a man, who, by an injury received from another, is very much discomposed and ruffled in his temper, is apt to find a hundred subjects of hatred, discontent, impatience, fear, and other uneasy passions; especially, if he can discover these subjects in or near the person, who was the object of his first emotion. These principles, which forward the transition of ideas, here concur with those which operate on the passions; and both, uniting in one action, bestow on the mind a double impulse.

Upon this occasion I may cite a passage from an elegant writer, who expresses himself in the following manner:[2] ' As the fancy delights in every thing, that is great, strange, ' or beautiful, and is still the more pleased the more it finds ' of these perfections in the *same* object, so it is capable of ' receiving new satisfaction by the assistance of another ' sense. Thus, any continual sound, as the music of birds, ' or a fall of waters, awakens every moment the mind of the ' beholder, and makes him more attentive to the several ' beauties of the place, that lie before him. Thus, if there ' arises a fragrancy of smells or perfumes, they heighten the ' pleasure of the imagination, and make even the colours and ' verdure of the landscape appear more agreeable; for the ' ideas of both senses recommend each other, and are ' pleasanter together than where they enter the mind separately: As the different colours of a picture, when they ' are well disposed, set off one another, and receive an addi-

[1] See Enquiry concerning Human Understanding. Sect. III, Of the Association of Ideas, p. 17.

[2] ADDISON. Spectator, No. 412.

' tional beauty from the advantage of the situation.' In these phænomena, we may remark the association both of impressions and ideas: as well as the mutual assistance these associations lend to each other.

4. It seems to me, that both these species of relations have place in producing *Pride* or *Humility*, and are the real, efficient causes of the passion.

With regard to the first relation, that of ideas, there can be no question. Whatever we are proud of must, in some manner, belong to us. It is always *our* knowledge, *our* sense, beauty, possessions, family, on which we value ourselves. Self, which is the *object* of the passion, must still be related to that quality or circumstance, which *causes* the passion. There must be a connexion between them; an easy transition of the imagination; or a facility of the conception in passing from one to the other. Where this connexion is wanting, no object can either excite pride or humility; and the more you weaken the connexion, the more you weaken the passion.

5. The only subject of enquiry is, whether there be a like relation of impressions or sentiments, wherever pride or humility is felt; whether the circumstance, which causes the passion, previously excites a sentiment similar to the passion; and whether there be an easy transfusion of the one into the other.

The feeling or sentiment of pride is agreeable; of humility, painful. An agreeable sensation is, therefore, related to the former; a painful, to the latter. And if we find, after examination, that every object, which produces pride, produces also a separate pleasure; and every object, which causes humility, excites in like manner a separate uneasiness: we must allow, in that case, that the present theory is fully proved and ascertained. The double relation of ideas and sentiments will be acknowledged incontestable.

6. To begin with personal merit and demerit, the most obvious causes of these passions; it would be entirely foreign to our present purpose to examine the foundation of moral distinctions. It is sufficient to observe, that the foregoing theory concerning the origin of the passions may be defended on any hypothesis. The most probable system, which has been advanced to explain the difference between vice and virtue, is, that either from a primary constitution of nature, or from a sense of public or private interest, certain charac-

ters, upon the very view and contemplation, produce uneasiness; and others, in like manner, excite pleasure. The uneasiness and satisfaction, produced in the spectator, are essential to vice and virtue. To approve of a character, is to feel a delight upon its appearance. To disapprove of it, is to be sensible of an uneasiness. The pain and pleasure, therefore, being, in a manner, the primary source of blame or praise, must also be the causes of all their effects; and consequently, the causes of pride and humility, which are the unavoidable attendants of that distinction.

But supposing this theory of morals should not be received; it is still evident that pain and pleasure, if not the sources of moral distinctions, are at least inseparable from them. A generous and noble character affords a satisfaction even in the survey; and when presented to us, though only in a poem or fable, never fails to charm and delight us. On the other hand, cruelty and treachery displease from their very nature; nor is it possible ever to reconcile us to these qualities, either in ourselves or others. Virtue, therefore, produces always a pleasure distinct from the pride or self-satisfaction which attends it: Vice, an uneasiness separate from the humility or remorse.

But a high or low conceit of ourselves arises not from those qualities alone of the mind, which, according to common systems of ethics, have been defined parts of moral duty; but from any other, which have a connexion with pleasure or uneasiness. Nothing flatters our vanity more than the talent of pleasing by our wit, good-humour, or any other accomplishment; and nothing gives us a more sensible mortification, than a disappointment in any attempt of that kind. No one has ever been able to tell precisely, what *wit* is, and to shew why such a system of thought must be received under that denomination, and such another rejected. It is by taste alone we can decide concerning it; nor are we possessed of any other standard, by which we can form a judgment of this nature. Now what is this *taste*, from which true and false wit in a manner receive their being, and without which no thought can have a title to either of these denominations? It is plainly nothing but a sensation of pleasure from true wit, and of disgust from false, without our being able to tell the reasons of that satisfaction or uneasiness. The power of exciting these opposite sensations is, therefore, the very es-

sence of true or false wit ; and consequently, the cause of that
vanity or mortification, which arises from one or the other.

7. Beauty of all kinds gives us a peculiar delight and
satisfaction ; as deformity produces pain, upon whatever
subject it may be placed, and whether surveyed in an animate or inanimate object. If the beauty or deformity belong
to our own face, shape, or person, this pleasure or uneasiness
is converted into pride or humility ; as having in this case
all the circumstances requisite to produce a perfect transition, according to the present theory.

It would seem, that the very essence of beauty consists in
its power of producing pleasure. All its effects, therefore,
must proceed from this circumstance : And if beauty is so
universally the subject of vanity, it is only from its being the
cause of pleasure.

Concerning all other bodily accomplishments, we may
observe in general, that whatever in ourselves is either useful,
beautiful, or surprizing, is an object of pride ; and the contrary
of humility. These qualities agree in producing a separate
pleasure ; and agree in nothing else.

We are vain of the surprizing adventures which we have met
with, the escapes which we have made, the dangers to which
we have been exposed ; as well as of our surprizing feats of
vigour and activity. Hence the origin of vulgar lying ;
where men, without any interest, and merely out of vanity,
heap up a number of extraordinary events, which are either
the fictions of their brain ; or, if true, have no connexion
with themselves. Their fruitful invention supplies them
with a variety of adventures ; and where that talent is wanting, they appropriate such as belong to others, in order to
gratify their vanity : For between that passion, and the
sentiment of pleasure, there is always a close connexion.

8. But though pride and humility have the qualities of
our mind and body, that is, of self, for their natural and
more immediate causes ; we find by experience, that many
other objects produce these affections. We found vanity
upon houses, gardens, equipage, and other external objects ;
as well as upon personal merit and accomplishments. This
happens when external objects acquire any particular relation to ourselves, and are associated or connected with us.
A beautiful fish in the ocean, a well-proportioned animal in
a forest, and indeed, any thing, which neither belongs nor is
related to us, has no manner of influence on our vanity :

whatever extraordinary qualities it may be endowed with, and whatever degree of surprize and admiration it may naturally occasion. It must be someway associated with us, in order to touch our pride. Its idea must hang, in a manner, upon that of ourselves; and the transition from one to the other must be easy and natural.

Men are vain of the beauty either of *their* country, or *their* county, or even of *their* parish. Here the idea of beauty plainly produces a pleasure. This pleasure is related to pride. The object or cause of this pleasure is, by the supposition, related to self, the object of pride. By this double relation of sentiments and ideas, a transition is made from one to the other.

Men are also vain of the happy temperature of the climate, in which they are born; of the fertility of their native soil; of the goodness of the wines, fruits, or victuals, produced by it; of the softness or force of their language, with other particulars of that kind. These objects have plainly a reference to the pleasures of sense, and are originally considered as agreeable to the feeling, taste or hearing. How could they become causes of pride, except by means of that transition above explained?

There are some, who discover a vanity of an opposite kind, and affect to depreciate their own country, in comparison of those, to which they have travelled. These persons find, when they are at home, and surrounded with their countrymen, that the strong relation between them and their own nation is shared with so many, that it is in a manner lost to them; whereas, that distant relation to a foreign country, which is formed by their having seen it, and lived in it, is augmented by their considering how few have done the same. For this reason, they always admire the beauty, utility, and rarity of what they met with abroad, above what they find at home.

Since we can be vain of a country, climate or any inanimate object, which bears a relation to us: it is no wonder we should be vain of the qualities of those, who are connected with us by blood or friendship. Accordingly we find, that any qualities which, when belonging to ourselves, produce pride, produce also, in a less degree, the same affection, when discovered in persons, related to us. The beauty, address, merit, credit, and honours of their kindred are carefully displayed by the proud, and are considerable sources of their vanity.

As we are proud of riches in ourselves, we desire, in order to gratify our vanity, that every one who has any connexion with us, should likewise be possessed of them, and are ashamed of such as are mean or poor among our friends and relations. Our forefathers being regarded as our nearest relations ; every one naturally affects to be of a good family, and to be descended from a long succession of rich and honourable ancestors.

Those, who boast of the antiquity of their families, are glad when they can join this circumstance, that their ancestors, for many generations, have been uninterrupted proprietors of the *same* portion of land, and that their family has never changed its possessions, or been transplanted into any other county or province. It is an additional subject of vanity, when they can boast, that these possessions have been transmitted through a descent, composed entirely of males, and that the honours and fortune have never passed through any female. Let us endeavour to explain these phaenomena from the foregoing theory.

When any one values himself on the antiquity of his family, the subjects of his vanity are not merely the extent of time and number of ancestors (for in that respect all mankind are alike), but these circumstances, joined to the riches and credit of his ancestors, which are supposed to reflect a lustre on himself, upon account of his connexion with them. Since therefore the passion depends on the connexion, whatever strengthens the connexion must also encrease the passion, and whatever weakens the connexion must diminish the passion. But it is evident, that the sameness of the possessions must strengthen the relation of ideas, arising from blood and kindred, and convey the fancy with greater facility from one generation to another; from the remotest ancestors to their posterity, who are both their heirs and their descendants. By this facility, the sentiment is transmitted more entire, and excites a greater degree of pride and vanity.

The case is the same with the transmission of the honours and fortune, through a succession of males, without their passing through any female. It is an obvious quality of human nature, that the imagination naturally turns to whatever is important and considerable; and where two objects are presented, a small and a great, it usually leaves the former, and dwells entirely on the latter. This is the reason, why children commonly bear their father's name, and are esteemed to be of a nobler or meaner birth, according to *his* family. And though the mother should be possessed of superior qualities to the father, as often happens, the *general rule* prevails, notwithstanding the exception, according to the doctrine, which shall be explained afterwards. Nay, even when a superiority of any kind is so great, or when any other reasons have such an effect, as to make the children rather represent the mother's family than the father's, the general rule still retains an efficacy, sufficient to weaken the relation, and make a kind of breach in the line of ancestors. The imagination runs not along them with the same facility, nor is able to transfer the honour and credit of the ancestors to their posterity of the same name and family so readily, as when the transition is conformable to the general rule, and passes through the male line, from father to son, or from brother to brother.

9. But *property*, as it gives the fullest power and authority over any object, is the relation, which has the greatest influence on these passions.[1]

Every thing, belonging to a vain man, is the best that is any where to be found. His houses, equipage, furniture, cloaths, horses, hounds, excel all others in his conceit; and it is easy to observe, that, from the least advantage in any of these he draws a new subject of pride and vanity. His wine, if you will believe him, has a finer flavour than any other; his cookery is more exquisite; his table more orderly; his servants more expert; the air, in which he lives, more healthful; the soil, which he cultivates, more fertile; his fruits ripen earlier, and to greater perfection: Such a thing is remarkable for its novelty; such another for its antiquity:

---

[1] That property is a species of relation, which produces a connexion between the person and the object is evident: The imagination passes naturally and easily from the consideration of a field to that of the person to whom it belongs. It may only be asked, how this relation is resolvable into any of those three, *viz. causation, contiguity,* and *resemblance,* which we have affirmed to be the only connecting principles among ideas. To be the proprietor of any thing is to be the sole person, who, by the laws of society, has a right to dispose of it, and to enjoy the benefit of it. This right has at least a tendency to procure the person the use of it; and in fact does commonly procure him that advantage. For rights which had no influence, and never took place, would be no rights at all. Now a person who disposes of an object, and reaps benefit from it, both produces, or may produce effects on it, and is affected by it. Property therefore is a species of causation. It is a person's power of producing alterations on the object, and it supposes that his condition is improved and altered by it. It is indeed the relation the most interesting of any, and occurs the most frequently to the mind. *This is also observed in Ess.*

N

This is the workmanship of a famous artist; that belonged once to such a prince or great man. All objects, in a word, which are useful, beautiful, or surprizing, or are related to such, may, by means of property, give rise to this passion. These all agree in giving pleasure. This alone is common to them; and therefore must be the quality, that produces the passion, which is their common effect. As every new instance is a new argument, and as the instances are here without number; it would seem, that this theory is sufficiently confirmed by experience.

Riches imply the power of acquiring whatever is agreeable: and as they comprehend many particular objects of vanity, necessarily become one of the chief causes of that passion.

10. Our opinions of all kinds are strongly affected by society and sympathy, and it is almost impossible for us to support any principle or sentiment, against the universal consent of every one, with whom we have any friendship or correspondence. But of all our opinions, those, which we form in our own favour; however lofty or presuming; are, at bottom, the frailest, and the most easily shaken by the contradiction and opposition of others. Our great concern, in this case, makes us soon alarmed, and keeps our passions upon the watch: Our consciousness of partiality still makes us dread a mistake: And the very difficulty of judging concerning an object, which is never set at a due distance from us, nor is seen in a proper point of view, makes us hearken anxiously to the opinions of others, who are better qualified to form just opinions concerning us. Hence that strong love of fame, with which all mankind are possessed. It is in order to fix and confirm their favourable opinion of themselves, not from any original passion, that they seek the applauses of others. And when a man desires to be praised, it is for the same reason, that a beauty is pleased with surveying herself in a favourable looking-glass, and seeing the reflection of her own charms.

Though it be difficult, in all points of speculation, to distinguish a cause, which encreases an effect, from one, which solely produces it; yet in the present case the phaenomena seem pretty strong and satisfactory in confirmation of the foregoing principle.

We receive a much greater satisfaction from the approbation of those whom we ourselves esteem and approve of, than of those whom we contemn and despise.

When esteem is obtained after a long and intimate acquaintance, it gratifies our vanity in a peculiar manner.

The suffrage of those, who are shy and backward in giving praise, is attended with an additional relish and enjoyment, if we can obtain it in our favour.

Where a great man is delicate in his choice of favourites, every one courts with greater earnestness his countenance and protection.

Praise never gives us much pleasure, unless it concur with our own opinion, and extol us for those qualities, in which we chiefly excel.

These phaenomena seem to prove, that the favourable suffrages of the world are regarded only as authorities, or as confirmations of our own opinion. And if the opinions of others have more influence in this subject than in any other, it is easily accounted for from the nature of the subject.

11. Thus few objects, however related to us, and whatever pleasure they produce, are able to excite a great degree of pride or self-satisfaction; unless they be also obvious to others, and engage the approbation of the spectators. What disposition of mind so desirable as the peaceful, resigned, contented; which readily submits to all the dispensations of providence, and preserves a constant serenity amidst the greatest misfortunes and disappointments? Yet this disposition, though acknowledged to be a virtue or excellence, is seldom the foundation of great vanity or self-applause; having no brilliancy or exterior lustre, and rather cheering the heart, than animating the behaviour and conversation. The case is the same with many other qualities of the mind, body, or fortune; and this circumstance, as well as the double relations above mentioned, must be admitted to be of consequence in the production of these passions.

A second circumstance, which is of consequence in this affair, is the constancy and durableness of the object. What is very casual and inconstant, beyond the common course of human affairs, gives little joy, and less pride. We are not much satisfied with the thing itself; and are still less apt to feel any new degree of self-satisfaction upon its account. We foresee and anticipate its change; which makes us little satisfied with the thing itself: We compare it to ourselves, whose existence is more durable; by which means its inconstancy appears still greater. It seems ridiculous to make ourselves the object of a passion, on account of a quality or possession, which is of so much shorter duration, and attends us during so small a part of our existence.

A third circumstance, not to be neglected, is that the objects, in order to produce pride or self-value, must be peculiar to us, or at least common to us with a few others. The advantages of sun-shine, good weather, a happy climate, &c. distinguish us not from any of our companions, and give us no preference or superiority. The comparison, which we are every moment apt to make, presents no inference to our advantage; and we still remain, notwithstanding these enjoyments, on a level with all our friends and acquaintance.

As health and sickness vary incessantly to all men, and there is no one, who is solely or certainly fixed in either; these accidental blessings and calamities are in a manner separated from us, and are not considered as a foundation for vanity or humiliation. But wherever a malady of any kind is so rooted in our constitution, that we no longer entertain any hope of recovery, from that moment it damps our self-conceit, as is evident in old men, whom nothing mortifies more than the consideration of their age and infirmities. They endeavour, as long as possible, to conceal their blindness and deafness, their rheums and gouts: nor do they ever avow them without reluctance and uneasiness. And though young men are not ashamed of every head-ach or cold which they fall into; yet no topic is more proper to mortify human pride, and make us entertain a mean opinion of our nature, than this, that we are every moment of our lives subject to such infirmities. This proves, that bodily pain and sickness are in themselves proper causes of humility; though the custom of estimating every thing, by comparison, more than by its intrinsic worth and value, makes us overlook those calamities, which we find incident to every one, and causes us to form an idea of our merit and character, independent of them.

We are ashamed of such maladies as affect others, and are either dangerous or disagreeable to them. Of the epilepsy; because it gives horror to every one present: Of the itch; because it is infectious: Of the king's evil; because it often goes to posterity. Men always consider the sentiments of others in their judgment of themselves.

A fourth circumstance, which has an influence on these passions, is *general rules*; by which we form a notion of different ranks of men, suitably to the power or riches of which they are possessed; and this notion is not changed by any peculiarities of health or temper of the persons, which may deprive them of all enjoyment in their possessions. Custom readily carries us beyond the just bounds in our passions, as well as in our reasonings.

It may not be amiss to observe on this occasion, that the influence of general rules and maxims on the passions very much contributes to facilitate the effects of all the principles or internal mechanism, which we here explain. For it seems evident, that, if a person full grown, and of the same nature with ourselves, were on a sudden transported into our world, he would be much embarrassed with every object, and would not readily determine what degree of love or hatred, of pride or humility, or of any other passion should be excited by it. The passions are often varied by very inconsiderable principles; and these do not always play with perfect regularity, especially on the first trial. But as custom or practice has brought to light all these principles, and has settled the just value of every thing: this must certainly contribute to the easy production of the passions, and guide us, by means of general established rules, in the proportions, which we ought to observe in preferring one object to another. This remark may, perhaps, serve to obviate difficulties, that arise concerning some causes, which we here ascribe to particular passions, and which may be esteemed too refined to operate so universally and certainly, as they are found to do.

Sect. III.

1. In running over all the causes, which produce the passion of pride or that of humility; it would readily occur, that the same circumstance, if transferred from ourselves to another person, would render him the object of love or hatred, esteem or contempt. The virtue, genius, beauty, family, riches, and authority of others beget favourable sentiments in their behalf: and their vice, folly, deformity, poverty, and meanness excite the contrary sentiments. The

double relation of impressions and ideas still operates on these passions of love and hatred; as on the former of pride and humility. Whatever gives a separate pleasure or pain, and is related to another person or connected with him, makes him the object of our affection or disgust.

Hence too injury or contempt towards us is one of the greatest sources of our hatred; services or esteem, of our friendship.

2. Sometimes a relation to ourselves excites affection towards any person. But there is always here implied a relation of sentiments, without which the other relation would have no influence.[1]

A person, who is related to us, or connected with us, by blood, by similitude of fortune, of adventures, profession, or country, soon becomes an agreeable companion to us: because we enter easily and familiarly into his sentiments and conceptions: Nothing is strange or new to us: Our imagination, passing from self, which is ever intimately present to us, runs smoothly along the relation or connexion, and conceives with a full sympathy the person, who is nearly related to self. He renders himself immediately acceptable, and is at once on an easy footing with us: No distance, no reserve has place, where the person introduced is supposed so closely connected with us.

Relation has here the same influence as custom or acquaintance, in exciting affection; and from like causes. The ease and satisfaction, which, in both cases, attend our intercourse or commerce, is the source of the friendship.

3. The passions of love and hatred are always followed by, or rather conjoined with, benevolence and anger. It is this conjunction, which chiefly distinguishes these affections from pride and humility. For pride and humility are pure emotions in the soul, unattended with any desire, and not immediately exciting us to action. But love and hatred are not compleat within themselves, nor rest in that emotion, which they produce: but carry the mind to something farther. Love is always followed by a desire of happiness to the person beloved, and an aversion to his misery: As hatred produces a desire of the misery, and

---

[1] The affection of parents to children seems founded on an original instinct. The affection towards other relations depends on the principles here explained.

an aversion to the happiness of the person hated. These opposite desires seem to be originally and primarily conjoined with the passions of love and hatred. It is a constitution of nature, of which we can give no farther explication.

4. Compassion frequently arises, where there is no preceding esteem or friendship; and compassion is an uneasiness in the sufferings of another. It seems to spring from the intimate and strong conception of his sufferings; and our imagination proceeds by degrees, from the lively idea to the real feeling of another's misery.

Malice and envy also arise in the mind without any preceding hatred or injury; though their tendency is exactly the same with that of anger and ill-will. The comparison of ourselves with others seems to be the source of envy and malice. The more unhappy another is, the more happy do we ourselves appear in our own conception.

5. The similar tendency of compassion to that of benevolence, and of envy to anger, forms a very close relation between these two sets of passions: though of a different kind from that which was insisted on above. It is not a resemblance of feeling or sentiment, but a resemblance of tendency or direction. Its effect, however, is the same, in producing an association of passions. Compassion is seldom or never felt without some mixture of tenderness or friendship: and envy is naturally accompanied with anger or ill-will. To desire the happiness of another, from whatever motive, is a good preparative to affection: and to delight in another's misery almost unavoidably begets aversion towards him.

Even where interest is the source of our concern, it is commonly attended with the same consequences. A partner is a natural object of friendship; a rival of enmity.

6. Poverty, meanness, disappointment, produce contempt and dislike: But when these misfortunes are very great, or are represented to us in very strong colours, they excite compassion, and tenderness, and friendship. How is this contradiction to be accounted for? The poverty and meanness of another, in their common appearance, gives us uneasiness, by a species of imperfect sympathy; and this uneasiness produces aversion or dislike, from the resemblance of sentiment. But when we enter more intimately into another's concerns, and wish for his happiness, as well as feel

his misery, friendship or goodwill arises, from the similar tendency of the inclinations.

[1] A bankrupt, at first, while the idea of his misfortunes is fresh and recent, and while the comparison of his present unhappy situation with his former prosperity operates strongly upon us, meets with compassion and friendship. After these ideas are weakened or obliterated by time, he is in danger of compassion and contempt.

7. In respect, there is a mixture of humility, with the esteem or affection : In contempt, a mixture of pride.

The amorous passion is usually compounded of complacency in beauty, a bodily appetite, and friendship or affection. The close relation of these sentiments is very obvious, as well as their origin from each other, by means of that relation. Were there no other phaenomenon to reconcile us to the present theory, this alone, methinks, were sufficient.

SECT. IV

1. The present theory of the passions depends entirely on the double relations of sentiments and ideas, and the mutual assistance, which these relations lend to each other. It may not, therefore, be improper to illustrate these principles by some farther instances.

2. The virtues, talents, accomplishments, and possessions of others, make us love and esteem them : Because these objects excite a pleasing sensation, which is related to love ; and as they have also a relation or connexion with the person, this union of ideas forwards the union of sentiments, according to the foregoing reasoning.

But suppose, that the person, whom we love, is also related to us, by blood, country, or friendship ; it is evident, that a species of pride must also be excited by his accomplishments and possessions ; there being the same double relation, which we have all along insisted on. The person is related to us, or there is an easy transition of thought from him to us ; and sentiments, excited by his advantages and virtues, are agreeable, and consequently related to pride. Accordingly we find, that people are naturally vain of the good qualities or high fortune of their friends and countrymen.

[1] [This paragraph was added in Edition R.]

3. But it is observable, that, if we reverse the order of the passions, the same effect does not follow. We pass easily from love and affection to pride and vanity; but not from the latter passions to the former, though all the relations be the same. We love not those who are related to us, on account of our own merit; though they are naturally vain on account of our merit. What is the reason of this difference? The transition of the imagination to ourselves, from objects related to us, is always easy; both on account of the relation, which facilitates the transition, and because we there pass from remoter objects, to those which are contiguous. But in passing from ourselves to objects, related to us; though the former principle forwards the transition of thought, yet the latter opposes it; and consequently there is not the same easy transfusion of passions from pride to love as from love to pride.

4. The virtues, services, and fortune of one man inspire us readily with esteem and affection for another related to him. The son of our friend is naturally entitled to our friendship: The kindred of a very great man value themselves, and are valued by others, on account of that relation. The force of the double relation is here fully displayed.

5. The following are instances of another kind, where the operation of these principles may still be discovered. Envy arises from a superiority in others; but it is observable, that it is not the great disproportion between us, which exites that passion, but on the contrary, our proximity. A great disproportion cuts off the relation of the ideas, and either keeps us from comparing ourselves with what is remote from us, or diminishes the effects of the comparison.

A poet is not apt to envy a philosopher, or a poet of a different kind, of a different nation, or of a different age. All these differences, if they do not prevent, at least weaken the comparison, and consequently the passion.

This too is the reason, why all objects appear great or little, merely by a comparison with those of the same species. A mountain neither magnifies nor diminishes a horse in our eyes: But when a FLEMISH and a WELSH horse are seen together, the one appears greater and the other less, than when viewed apart.

From the same principle we may account for that remark of historians, that any party, in a civil war, or even factious division, always choose to call in a foreign enemy at any hazard, rather than submit to their fellow-citizens. GUICCI-ARDIN applies this remark to the wars in ITALY; where the relations between the different states are, properly speaking, nothing but of name, language, and contiguity. Yet even these relations, when joined with superiority, by making the comparison more natural, make it likewise more grievous, and cause men to search for some other superiority, which may be attended with no relation, and by that means, may have a less sensible influence on the imagination. When we cannot break the association, we feel a stronger desire to remove the superiority. This seems to be the reason, why travellers, though commonly lavish of their praise to the CHINESE and PERSIANS, take care to depreciate those neighbouring nations, which may stand upon a footing of rivalship with their native country.

6. The fine arts afford us parallel instances. Should an author compose a treatise, of which one part was serious and profound, another light and humorous; every one would condemn so strange a mixture, and would blame him for the neglect of all rules of art and criticism. Yet we accuse not PRIOR for joining his *Alma* and *Solomon* in the same volume; though that amiable poet has perfectly succeeded in the gaiety of the one, as well as in the melancholy of the other. Even suppose the reader should peruse these two compositions without any interval, he would feel little or no difficulty in the change of the passions. Why? but because he considers these performances as entirely different; and by that break in the ideas, breaks the progress of the affections, and hinders the one from influencing or contradicting the other.

An heroic and burlesque design, united in one picture, would be monstrous; though we place two pictures of so opposite a character in the same chamber, and even close together, without any scruple.

7. It needs be no matter of wonder, that the easy transition of the imagination should have such an influence on all the passions. It is this very circumstance, which forms all the relations and connexions amongst objects. We know no real connexion between one thing and another. We only know, that the idea of one thing is associated with that of another, and that the imagination makes an easy transition

between them. And as the easy transition of ideas, and that of sentiments mutually assist each other ; we might beforehand expect, that this principle must have a mighty influence on all our internal movements and affections. And experience sufficiently confirms the theory.

For, not to repeat all the foregoing instances : Suppose, that I were travelling with a companion through a country, to which we are both utter strangers ; it is evident, that, if the prospects be beautiful, the roads agreeable, and the fields finely cultivated ; this may serve to put me in good-humour, both with myself and fellow-traveller. But as the country has no connexion with myself or friend, it can never be the immediate cause either of self-value or of regard to him : And therefore, if I found not the passion on some other object, which bears to one of us a closer relation, my emotions are rather to be considered as the overflowings of an elevated or humane disposition, than as an established passion. But supposing the agreeable prospect before us to be surveyed either from his country-seat or from mine ; this new connexion of ideas gives a new direction to the sentiment of pleasure, derived from the prospect, and raises the emotion of regard or vanity, according to the nature of the connexion. There is not here, methinks, much room for doubt or difficulty.

Sect. V.

1. It seems evident, that reason, in a strict sense, as meaning the judgment of truth and falsehood, can never, of itself, be any motive to the will, and can have no influence but so far as it touches some passion or affection. *Abstract relations* of ideas are the object of curiosity, not of volition. And *matters of fact*, where they are neither good nor evil, where they neither excite desire nor aversion, are totally indifferent, and whether known or unknown, whether mistaken or rightly apprehended, cannot be regarded as any motive to action.

2. What is commonly, in a popular sense, called reason, and is so much recommended in moral discourses, is nothing but a general and a calm passion, which takes a comprehensive and a distant view of its object, and actuates the will, without exciting any sensible emotion. A man, we say, is diligent in his profession from reason ; that is, from a calm

desire of riches and a fortune. A man adheres to justice from reason; that is, from a calm regard to public good, or to a character with himself and others.

3. The same objects, which recommend themselves to reason in this sense of the word, are also the objects of what we call passion, when they are brought near to us, and acquire some other advantages, either of external situation, or congruity to our internal temper; and by that means excite a turbulent and sensible emotion. Evil, at a great distance, is avoided, we say, from reason: Evil, near at hand, produces aversion, horror, fear, and is the object of passion.

4. The common error of metaphysicians has lain in ascribing the direction of the will entirely to one of these principles, and supposing the other to have no influence. Men often act knowingly against their interest: It is not therefore the view of the greatest possible good which always influences them. Men often counteract a violent passion, in prosecution of their distant interests and designs: It is not therefore the present uneasiness alone, which determines them. In general, we may observe, that both these principles operate on the will; and where they are contrary, that either of them prevails, according to the general character or present disposition of the person. What we call *strength of mind* implies the prevalence of the calm passions above the violent; though we may easily observe, that there is no person so constantly possessed of this virtue, as never, on any occasion, to yield to the solicitation of violent affection and desire. From these variations of temper proceeds the great difficulty of deciding with regard to the future actions and resolutions of men, where there is any contrariety of motives and passions.

Sect. VI.

1. We shall here enumerate some of those circumstances, which render a passion calm or violent, which heighten or diminish any emotion.

It is a property in human nature, that any emotion, which attends a passion, is easily converted into it; though in their natures they be originally different from, and even contrary to each other. It is true, in order to cause a perfect union amongst passions, and make one produce the other, there is always required a double relation, according to the theory above delivered. But when two passions are already produced by their separate causes, and are both present in the mind, they readily mingle and unite; though they have but one relation, and sometimes without any. The predominant passion swallows up the inferior, and converts it into itself. The spirits, when once excited, easily receive a change in their direction; and it is natural to imagine, that this change will come from the prevailing affection. The connexion is in many cases closer between any two passions than between any passion and indifference.

When a person is once heartily in love, the little faults and caprices of his mistress, the jealousies and quarrels, to which that commerce is so subject: however unpleasant they be, and rather connected with anger and hatred; are yet found, in many instances, to give additional force to the prevailing passion. It is a common artifice of politicians, when they would affect any person very much by a matter of fact, of which they intend to inform him, first to excite his curiosity; delay as long as possible the satisfying of it; and by that means raise his anxiety and patience to the utmost, before they give him a full insight into the business. They know, that this curiosity will precipitate him into the passion, which they purpose to raise, and will assist the object in its influence on the mind. A soldier advancing to battle, is naturally inspired with courage and confidence, when he thinks on his friends and fellow-soldiers; and is struck with fear and terror, when he reflects on the enemy. Whatever new emotion therefore proceeds from the former, naturally encreases the courage; as the same emotion proceeding from the latter, augments the fear. Hence in martial discipline, the uniformity and lustre of habit, the regularity of figures and motions, with all the pomp and majesty of war, encourage ourselves and our allies; while the same objects in the enemy strike terror into us, though agreeable and beautiful in themselves.

Hope is, in itself, an agreeable passion, and allied to friendship and benevolence; yet is it able sometimes to blow up anger, when that is the predominant passion. *Spes addita suscitat iras.* VIRG.

2. Since passions, however independent, are naturally transfused into each other, if they be both present at the

same time; it follows, that when good or evil is placed in such a situation as to cause any particular emotion, besides its direct passion of desire or aversion, this latter passion must acquire new force and violence.

3. This often happens, when any object excites contrary passions. For it is observable, that an opposition of passions commonly causes a new emotion in the spirits, and produces more disorder than the concurrence of any two affections of equal force. This new emotion is easily converted into the predominant passion, and in many instances, is observed to encrease its violence, beyond the pitch, at which it would have arrived, had it met with no opposition. Hence we naturally desire what is forbid, and often take a pleasure in performing actions, merely because they are unlawful. The notion of duty, when opposite to the passions, is not always able to overcome them; and when it fails of that effect, is apt rather to encrease and irritate them, by producing an opposition in our motives and principles.

4. The same effect follows, whether the opposition arise from internal motives or external obstacles. The passion commonly acquires new force in both cases. The efforts, which the mind makes to surmount the obstacle, excite the spirits, and enliven the passion.

5. Uncertainty has the same effect as opposition. The agitation of the thought, the quick turns which it makes from one view to another, the variety of passions which succeed each other, according to the different views: All these produce an emotion in the mind; and this emotion transfuses itself into the predominant passion.

Security, on the contrary, diminishes the passions. The mind, when left to itself, immediately languishes; and in order to preserve its ardour, must be every moment supported by a new flow of passion. For the same reason, despair, though contrary to security, has a like influence.

6. Nothing more powerfully excites any affection than to conceal some part of its object, by throwing it into a kind of shade, which at the same time that it shows enough to prepossess us in favour of the object, leaves still some work for the imagination. Besides that obscurity is always attended with a kind of uncertainty; the effort, which the fancy makes to compleat the idea, rouzes the spirits, and gives an additional force to the passion.

7. As despair and security, though contrary, produce the same effects; so absence is observed to have contrary effects, and in different circumstances, either encreases or diminishes our affection. ROCHEFOUCAULT has very well remarked, that absence destroys weak passions, but encreases strong; as the wind extinguishes a candle, but blows up a fire. Long absence naturally weakens our idea, and diminishes the passion: But where the affection is so strong and lively as to support itself, the uneasiness, arising from absence, encreases the passion, and gives it new force and influence.

8. When the soul applies itself to the performance of any action, or the conception of any object, to which it is not accustomed, there is a certain unpliableness in the faculties, and a difficulty of the spirits moving in their new direction. As this difficulty excites the spirits, it is the source of wonder, surprize, and of all the emotions, which arise from novelty; and is, in itself, agreeable, like every thing which enlivens the mind to a moderate degree. But though surprize be agreeable in itself, yet, as it puts the spirits in agitation, it not only augments our agreeable affections, but also our painful, according to the foregoing principle. Hence every thing that is new, is most affecting, and gives us either more pleasure or pain, than what, strictly speaking, should naturally follow from it. When it often returns upon us, the novelty wears off; the passions subside; the hurry of the spirits is over; and we survey the object with greater tranquillity.

9. The imagination and affections have a close union together. The vivacity of the former gives force to the latter. Hence the prospect of any pleasure, with which we are acquainted, affects us more than any other pleasure, which we may own superior, but of whose nature we are *wholly* ignorant. Of the one we can form a particular and determinate idea. The other we conceive under the general notion of pleasure.

Any satisfaction, which we lately enjoyed, and of which the memory is fresh and recent, operates on the will with more violence, than another of which the traces are decayed and almost obliterated.

A pleasure, which is suitable to the way of life, in which we are engaged, excites more our desire and appetite than another, which is foreign to it.

Nothing is more capable of infusing any passion into the

mind, than eloquence, by which objects are represented in the strongest and most lively colours. The bare opinion of another, especially when enforced with passion, will cause an idea to have an influence upon us, though that idea might otherwise have been entirely neglected.

It is remarkable, that lively passions commonly attend a lively imagination. In this respect, as well as in others, the force of the passion depends as much on the temper of the person, as on the nature and situation of the object.

What is distant, either in place or time, has not equal influence with what is near and contiguous.

*_**   *_**   *_**

I pretend not to have here exhausted this subject. It is sufficient for my purpose, if I have made it appear, that, in the production and conduct of the passions, there is a certain regular mechanism, which is susceptible of as accurate a disquisition, as the laws of motion, optics, hydrostatics, or any part of natural philosophy.

AN

ENQUIRY

CONCERNING THE

PRINCIPLES

OF

MORALS.

AN ENQUIRY CONCERNING

THE

PRINCIPLES OF MORALS.

SECTION I.- *Of the General Principles of Morals.*

DISPUTES with men, pertinaciously obstinate in their principles, are, of all others, the most irksome ; except, perhaps,
those with persons, [1]entirely disingenuous, who really do not
believe the opinions they defend, but engage in the controversy, from affectation, from a spirit of opposition, or
from a desire of showing wit and ingenuity, superior to the
rest of mankind. The same blind adherence to their own
arguments is to be expected in both ; the same contempt of
their antagonists ; and the same passionate vehemence, in
inforcing sophistry and falsehood. And as reasoning is not
the source, whence either disputant derives his tenets ; it is
in vain to expect, that any logic, which speaks not to the
affections, will ever engage him to embrace sounder principles.

Those who have denied the reality of moral distinctions,
may be ranked among the disingenuous disputants ; nor is
it conceivable, that any human creature could ever seriously
believe, that all characters and actions were alike entitled to
the affection and regard of every one. The difference, which
nature has placed between one man and another, is so wide,
and this difference is still so much farther widened, by
education, example, and habit, that, where the opposite
extremes come at once under our apprehension, there is no
scepticism so scrupulous, and scarce any assurance so determined, as absolutely to deny all distinction between them.

[1] [Entirely disingenuous : added in Edition M.]

Let a man's insensibility be ever so great, he must often be touched with the images of RIGHT and WRONG; and let his prejudices be ever so obstinate, he must observe, that others are susceptible of like impressions. The only way, therefore, of converting an antagonist of this kind, is to leave him to himself. For, finding that no body keeps up the controversy with him, it is probable he will, at last, of himself, from mere weariness, come over to the side of common sense and reason.

There has been a controversy started of late, much better worth examination, concerning the general foundation of MORALS; whether they be derived from REASON, or from SENTIMENT; whether we attain the knowledge of them by a chain of argument and induction, or by an immediate feeling and finer internal sense; whether, like all sound judgment of truth and falsehood, they should be the same to every rational intelligent being; or whether, like the perception of beauty and deformity, they be founded entirely on the particular fabric and constitution of the human species.

The ancient philosophers, though they often affirm, that virtue is nothing but conformity to reason, yet, in general, seem to consider morals as deriving their existence from taste and sentiment. On the other hand, our modern enquirers, though they also talk much of the beauty of virtue, and deformity of vice, yet have commonly endeavoured to account for these distinctions by metaphysical reasonings, and by deductions from the most abstract principles of the understanding. Such confusion reigned in these subjects, that an opposition of the greatest consequence could prevail between one system and another, and even in the parts of almost each individual system; and yet no body, till very lately, was ever sensible of it. The elegant [1] Lord SHAFTESBURY, who first gave occasion to remark this distinction, and who, in general, adhered to the principles of the ancients, is not, himself, entirely free from the same confusion.

It must be acknowledged, that both sides of the question are susceptible of specious arguments. Moral distinctions, it may be said, are discernible by pure *reason*: Else, whence the many disputes that reign in common life, as well as in philosophy, with regard to this subject: The long chain of

[1] [Elegant and sublime: Editions G and K.]

proofs often produced on both sides ; the examples cited, the authorities appealed to, the analogies employed, the fallacies detected, the inferences drawn, and the several conclusions adjusted to their proper principles. Truth is disputable ; not taste : What exists in the nature of things is the standard of our judgment ; what each man feels within himself is the standard of sentiment. Propositions in geometry may be proved, systems in physics may be controverted ; but the harmony of verse, the tenderness of passion, the brilliancy of wit, must give immediate pleasure. No man reasons concerning another's beauty ; but frequently concerning the justice or injustice of his actions. In every criminal trial the first object of the prisoner is to disprove the facts alleged, and deny the actions imputed to him : The second to prove, that, even if these actions were real, they might be justified, as innocent and lawful. It is confessedly by deductions of the understanding, that the first point is ascertained : How can we suppose that a different faculty of the mind is employed in fixing the other ?

On the other hand, those who would resolve all moral determinations into *sentiment*, may endeavour to show, that it is impossible for reason ever to draw conclusions of this nature. To virtue, say they, it belongs to be *amiable*, and vice *odious*. This forms their very nature or essence. But can reason or argumentation distribute these different epithets to any subjects, and pronounce before-hand, that this must produce love, and that hatred ? Or what other reason can we ever assign for these affections, but the original fabric and formation of the human mind, which is naturally adapted to receive them ?

The end of all moral speculations is to teach us our duty ; and, by proper representations of the deformity of vice and beauty of virtue, beget correspondent habits, and engage us to avoid the one, and embrace the other. But is this ever to be expected from inferences and conclusions of the understanding, which of themselves have no hold of the affections, or set in motion the active powers of men ? They discover truths : But where the truths which they discover are indifferent, and beget no desire or aversion, they can have no influence on conduct and behaviour. What is honourable, what is fair, what is becoming, what is noble, what is generous, takes possession of the heart, and animates us to embrace and maintain it. What is intelligible, what is evident, what is probable, what is true, procures only the cool assent of the understanding; and gratifying a speculative curiosity, puts an end to our researches.

Extinguish all the warm feelings and prepossessions in favour of virtue, and all disgust or aversion to vice: Render men totally indifferent towards these distinctions; and morality is no longer a practical study, nor has any tendency to regulate our lives and actions.

These arguments on each side (and many more might be produced) are so plausible, that I am apt to suspect, they may, the one as well as the other, be solid and satisfactory, and that *reason* and *sentiment* concur in almost all moral determinations and conclusions. The final sentence, it is probable, which pronounces characters and actions amiable or odious, praise-worthy or blameable; that which stamps on them the mark of honour or infamy, approbation or censure; that which renders morality an active principle, and constitutes virtue our happiness, and vice our misery: It is probable, I say, that this final sentence depends on some internal sense or feeling, which nature has made universal in the whole species. For what else can have an influence of this nature? But in order to pave the way for such a sentiment, and give a proper discernment of its object, it is often necessary, we find, that much reasoning should precede, that nice distinctions be made, just conclusions drawn, distant comparisons formed, complicated relations examined, and general facts fixed and ascertained. Some species of beauty, especially the natural kinds, on their first appearance, command our affection and approbation; and where they fail of this effect, it is impossible for any reasoning to redress their influence, or adapt them better to our taste and sentiment. But in many orders of beauty, particularly those of the finer arts, it is requisite to employ much reasoning, in order to feel the proper sentiment; and a false relish may frequently be corrected by argument and reflection. There are just grounds to conclude, that moral beauty partakes much of this latter species, and demands the assistance of our intellectual faculties, in order to give it a suitable influence on the human mind.

But though this question, concerning the general principles of morals, be curious and important, it is needless for us, at

present, to employ farther care in our researches concerning
it. For if we can be so happy, in the course of this enquiry,
as to discover the true origin of morals, it will then easily
appear how far either sentiment or reason enters into all
determinations of this nature.[1] [2] In order to attain this
purpose, we shall endeavour to follow a very simple method :
We shall analyse that complication of mental qualities,
which form what, in common life, we call PERSONAL MERIT :
We shall consider every attribute of the mind, which renders
a man an object either of esteem and affection, or of hatred
and contempt ; every habit or sentiment or faculty, which, if
ascribed to any person, implies either praise or blame, and
may enter into any panegyric or satire of his character and
manners. The quick sensibility, which, on this head, is so
universal among mankind, gives a philosopher sufficient
assurance, that he can never be considerably mistaken in
framing the catalogue, or incur any danger of misplacing
the objects of his contemplation : He needs only enter into
his own breast for a moment, and consider whether or not he
should desire to have this or that quality ascribed to him,
and whether such or such an imputation would proceed from
a friend or an enemy. The very nature of language guides
us almost infallibly in forming a judgment of this nature ;
and as every tongue possesses one set of words which are
taken in a good sense, and another in the opposite, the least
acquaintance with the idiom suffices, without any reasoning,
to direct us in collecting and arranging the estimable or
blameable qualities of men. The only object of reasoning is
to discover the circumstances on both sides, which are common to these qualities : to observe that particular in which
the estimable qualities agree on the one hand, and the
blameable on the other ; and thence to reach the foundation
of ethics, and find those universal principles, from which all

---

[1] See Appendix I. Concerning Moral
Sentiment.
[2] [Editions G to N omit as far as
'ultimately derived,' and substitute the
following : Mean while, it will scarce
be possible for us, ere this contro versy is
fully decided, to proceed in that accurate manner, required in the sciences ;
by beginning with exact definitions of
virtue and vice, which are the objects
of our present enquiry. But we shall
do what may justly be esteemed as satisfactory. We shall consider the matter
as an object of experience. We shall
call *every quality or action of the mind,*
virtuous *which is attended with the general approbation of mankind ; and we
shall denominate vicious, every quality
which is the object of general hatred or
censure.* These qualities we shall endeavour to collect ; and after examining,
on both sides, the several circumstances,
in which they agree, 'tis hoped we may,
at last, reach the foundation of ethics,
and find those universal principles, *from
which all moral blame or approbation
is ultimately derived.*]

censure or approbation is ultimately derived. As this is a question of fact, not of abstract science, we can only expect success, by following the experimental method, and deducing general maxims from a comparison of particular instances. The other scientifical method, where a general abstract principle is first established, and is afterwards branched out into a variety of inferences and conclusions, may be more perfect in itself, but suits less the imperfection of human nature, and is a common source of illusion and mistake in this as well as in other subjects. Men are now cured of their passion for hypotheses and systems in natural philosophy, and will hearken to no arguments but those which are derived from experience. It is full time they should attempt a like reformation in all moral disquisitions ; and reject every system of ethics, however subtile or ingenious, which is not founded on fact and observation.

[1] We shall begin our enquiry on this head by the consideration of social virtues, benevolence and justice. The explication of them will probably give us an opening by which others may be accounted for.

SECTION II.[2] *Of Benevolence.*

PART I.

It may be esteemed, perhaps, a superfluous task to prove, that the benevolent or softer affections[3] are ESTIMABLE ; and wherever they appear, engage the approbation, and good-will of mankind. The epithets *sociable, good-natured, humane, merciful, grateful, friendly, generous, beneficent*, or their equivalents, are known in all languages, and universally express the highest merit, which *human nature* is capable of attaining. Where these amiable qualities are attended with birth and power and eminent abilities, and display themselves in the good government or useful instruction of mankind, they seem even to raise the possessors of them above the rank of *human nature*, and make them approach in some measure to the divine. Exalted capacity, undaunted courage, prosperous success ; these may only expose a hero or politician to the envy or ill-will of the public:

---

[1] [This paragraph was added in Edition O.]

[2] [In Editions G to Q this Section was introduced by paragraphs, forming Part

I. which subsequently appeared as Appendix II., Of Self-Love.]

[3] [Are VIRTUOUS engage the esteem, approbation, and &c: Editions G to N.]

But as soon as the praises are added of humane and benefi-cent; when instances are displayed of lenity, tenderness, or friendship: envy itself is silent, or joins the general voice of approbation and applause.

When PERICLES, the great ATHENIAN statesman and general, was on his death-bed, his surrounding friends, deeming him now insensible, began to indulge their sorrow for their expiring patron, by enumerating his great qualities and successes, his conquests and victories, the unusual length of his administration, and his nine trophies erected over the enemies of the republic. *You forget*, cries the dying hero, who had heard all, *you forget the most eminent of my praises, while you dwell so much on those vulgar advantages, in which fortune had a principal share. You have not observed, that no citizen has ever yet worne mourning on my account.*[1]

In men of more ordinary talents and capacity, the social virtues become, if possible, still more essentially requisite; there being nothing eminent, in that case, to compensate for the want of them, or preserve the person from our severest hatred, as well as contempt. A high ambition, an elevated courage, is apt, says CICERO, in less perfect cha-racters, to degenerate into a turbulent ferocity. The more social and softer virtues are there chiefly to be regarded. These are always good and amiable.[2]

The principal advantage, which JUVENAL discovers in the extensive capacity of the human species is, that it renders our benevolence also more extensive, and gives us larger opportunities of spreading our kindly influence than what are indulged to the inferior creation.[3] It must, indeed, be confessed, that by doing good only, can a man truly enjoy the advantages of being eminent. His exalted station, of itself, but the more exposes him to danger and tempest. His sole prerogative is to afford shelter to inferiors, who repose themselves under his cover and protection.

But I forget, that it is not my present business to recom-mend generosity and benevolence, or to paint, in their true colours, all the genuine charms of the social virtues. These, indeed, sufficiently engage every heart, on the first appre-hension of them; and it is difficult to abstain from some sally of panegyric, as often as they occur in discourse or reasoning. But our object here being more the speculative,

[1] PLUT. in PERICLE. 38.   [2] Cic. de Officiis, lib. i.   [3] Sat. XV. 159. & seq.

than the practical part of morals, it will suffice to remark, (what will readily, I believe, be allowed) that no qualities are more intitled to the general good-will and approbation of mankind than benevolence and humanity, friendship and gratitude, natural affection and public spirit, or whatever proceeds from a tender sympathy with others, and a generous concern for our kind and species. These, wherever they appear, seem to transfuse themselves, in a manner, into each beholder, and to call forth, in their own behalf, the same favourable and affectionate sentiments, which they exert on all around.

PART II.[1]

We may observe, that, in displaying the praises of any humane, beneficent man, there is one circumstance which never fails to be amply insisted on, namely, the happiness and satisfaction, derived to society from his intercourse and good offices. To his parents, we are apt to say, he endears himself by his pious attachment and duteous care, still more than by the connexions of nature. His children never feel his authority, but when employed for their advantage. With him, the ties of love are consolidated by beneficence and friendship. The ties of friendship approach, in a fond observance of each obliging office, to those of love and inclination. His domestics and dependants have in him a sure resource; and no longer dread the power of fortune, but so far as she exercises it over him. From him the hungry receive food, the naked cloathing, the ignorant and slothful skill and industry. Like the sun, an inferior minister of providence, he cheers, invigorates, and sustains the surrounding world.

If confined to private life, the sphere of his activity is narrower; but his influence is all benign and gentle. If exalted into a higher station, mankind and posterity reap the fruit of his labours.

As these topics of praise never fail to be employed, and with success, where we would inspire esteem for any one; may it not thence be concluded, that the UTILITY, resulting from the social virtues, forms, at least, a *part* of their merit, and is one source of that approbation and regard so universally paid to them?

[1] [Part III. in Editions G to Q.]

When we recommend even an animal or a plant as *useful* and *beneficial*, we give it an applause and recommendation suited to its nature. As, on the other hand, reflection on the baneful influence of any of these inferior beings always inspires us with the sentiment of aversion. The eye is pleased with the prospect of corn-fields and loaded vine-yards; horses grazing, and flocks pasturing: But flies the view of briars and brambles, affording shelter to wolves and serpents.

A machine, a piece of furniture, a vestment, a house well contrived for use and conveniency, is so far beautiful, and is contemplated with pleasure and approbation. An experienced eye is here sensible to many excellencies, which escape persons ignorant and uninstructed.

Can anything stronger be said in praise of a profession, such as merchandize or manufacture, than to observe the advantages which it procures to society? And is not a monk and inquisitor enraged when we treat his order as useless or pernicious to mankind?

The historian exults in displaying the benefit arising from his labours. The writer of romance alleviates or denies the bad consequences ascribed to his manner of composition.

In general, what praise is implied in the simple epithet *useful!* What reproach in the contrary!

Your Gods, says CICERO,[1] in opposition to the EPICUREANS, cannot justly claim any worship or adoration, with whatever imaginary perfections you may suppose them endowed. They are totally useless and unactive. Even the EGYPTIANS, whom you so much ridicule, never consecrated any animal but on account of its utility.

The sceptics assert,[2] though absurdly, that the origin of all religious worship was derived from the utility of inanimate objects, as the sun and moon, to the support and well-being of mankind. This is also the common reason assigned by historians, for the deification of eminent heroes and legis-lators.[3]

To plant a tree, to cultivate a field, to beget children; meritorious acts, according to the religion of ZOROASTER.

In all determinations of morality, this circumstance of public utility is ever principally in view; and wherever dis-

[1] De Nat. Deor. lib. i. 36.   [2] Sext. Emp. adversus Math. lib. ix.
[3] Diod. Sic. passim.   291. 18.

putes arise, either in philosophy or common life, concerning the bounds of duty, the question cannot, by any means, be decided with greater certainty, than by ascertaining, on any side, the true interests of mankind. If any false opinion, embraced from appearances, has been found to prevail; as soon as farther experience and sounder reasoning have given us juster notions of human affairs; we retract our first sentiment, and adjust anew the boundaries of moral good and evil.

Giving alms to common beggars is naturally praised; because it seems to carry relief to the distressed and indigent: But when we observe the encouragement thence arising to idleness and debauchery, we regard that species of charity rather as a weakness than a virtue.

Tyrannicide, or the assassination of usurpers and oppressive princes, was highly extolled in ancient times; because it both freed mankind from many of these monsters, and seemed to keep the others in awe, whom the sword or poinard could not reach. But history and experience having since convinced us, that this practice encreases the jealousy and cruelty of princes, a TIMOLEON and a BRUTUS, though treated with indulgence on account of the prejudices of their times, are now considered as very improper models for imitation.

Liberality in princes is regarded as a mark of beneficence: But when it occurs, that the homely bread of the honest and industrious is often thereby converted into delicious cates for the idle and the prodigal, we soon retract our heedless praises. The regrets of a prince, for having lost a day, were noble and generous: But had he intended to have spent it in acts of generosity to his greedy courtiers, it was better lost than misemployed after that manner.

Luxury, or a refinement on the pleasures and conveniencies of life, had long been supposed the source of every corruption in government, and the immediate cause of faction, sedition, civil wars, and the total loss of liberty. It was, therefore, universally regarded as a vice, and was an object of declamation to all satyrists, and severe moralists. Those, who prove, or attempt to prove, that such refinements rather tend to the encrease of industry, civility, and arts, regulate anew our *moral* as well as *political* sentiments, and represent, as laudable or innocent, what had formerly been regarded as pernicious and blameable.

Upon the whole, then, it seems undeniable, *that* nothing can bestow more merit on any human creature than the sentiment of benevolence in an eminent degree; and *that* a *part*, at least, of its merit arises from its tendency to promote the interests of our species, and bestow happiness on human society. We carry our view into the salutary consequences of such a character and disposition; and whatever has so benign an influence, and forwards so desirable an end, is beheld with complacency and pleasure. The social virtues are never regarded without their beneficial tendencies, nor viewed as barren and unfruitful. The happiness of mankind, the order of society, the harmony of families, the mutual support of friends, are always considered as the result of their gentle dominion over the breasts of men.

How considerable a *part* of their merit we ought to ascribe to their utility, will better appear from future disquisitions;[1] as well as the reason, why this circumstance has such a command over our esteem and approbation.[2]

SECTION III.—*Of Justice.*

PART I.

THAT Justice is useful to society, and consequently that *part* of its merit, at least, must arise from that consideration, it would be a superfluous undertaking to prove. That public utility is the *sole* origin of justice, and that reflections on the beneficial consequences of this virtue are the *sole* foundation of its merit; this proposition, being more curious and important, will better deserve our examination and enquiry.

Let us suppose, that nature has bestowed on the human race such profuse *abundance* of all *external* conveniencies, that, without any uncertainty in the event, without any care or industry on our part, every individual finds himself fully provided with whatever his most voracious appetites can want, or luxurious imagination wish or desire. His natural beauty, we shall suppose, surpasses all acquired ornaments: The perpetual clemency of the seasons renders useless all cloaths or covering: The raw herbage affords him the most delicious fare; the clear fountain, the richest beverage. No laborious occupation required: No tillage: No navigation.

[1] Sect. 3d and 4th. Of Justice: and Of Political Society. [2] Sect. 5th. Why Utility Pleases.

N 2

Music, poetry, and contemplation form his sole business :
Conversation, mirth, and friendship his sole amusement.

It seems evident, that, in such a happy state, every other
social virtue would flourish, and receive tenfold encrease ;
but the cautious, jealous virtue of justice would never once
have been dreamed of. For what purpose make a partition
of goods, where every one has already more than enough ?
Why give rise to property, where there cannot possibly be any
injury ? Why call this object *mine*, when, upon the seizing of
it by another, I need but stretch out my hand to possess
myself of what is equally valuable ? Justice, in that case,
being totally USELESS, would be an idle ceremonial, and
could never possibly have place in the catalogue of virtues.

We see, even in the present necessitous condition of mankind, that, wherever any benefit is bestowed by nature in an
unlimited abundance, we leave it always in common among
the whole human race, and make no subdivisions of right
and property. Water and air, though the most necessary of
all objects, are not challenged as the property of individuals ;
nor can any man commit injustice by the most lavish use and
enjoyment of these blessings. In fertile extensive countries,
with few inhabitants, land is regarded on the same footing.
And no topic is so much insisted on by those, who defend
the liberty of the seas, as the unexhausted use of them in
navigation. Were the advantages, procured by navigation,
as inexhaustible, these reasoners had never had any adversaries to refute ; nor had any claims ever been advanced of
a separate, exclusive dominion over the ocean.

It may happen, in some countries, at some periods, that
there be established a property in water, none in land ;[1] if
the latter be in greater abundance than can be used by the
inhabitants, and the former be found, with difficulty, and in
very small quantities.

Again ; suppose, that, though the necessities of human
race continue the same as at present, yet the mind is so enlarged, and so replete with friendship and generosity, that
every man has the utmost tenderness for every man, and feels
no more concern for his own interest than for that of his
fellows : It seems evident, that the USE of justice would, in
this case, be suspended by such an extensive benevolence,

[1] GENESIS, chap. xiii. and xxi.

nor would the divisions and barriers of property and obligation have ever been thought of. Why should I bind another, by a deed or promise, to do me any good office, when I know that he is already prompted, by the strongest inclination, to seek my happiness, and would, of himself, perform the desired service; except the hurt, he thereby receives, be greater than the benefit accruing to me? in which case, he knows, that, from my innate humanity and friendship, I should be the first to oppose myself to his imprudent generosity. Why raise land-marks between my neighbour's field and mine, when my heart has made no division between our interests; but shares all his joys and sorrows with the same force and vivacity as if originally my own? Every man, upon this supposition, being a second self to another, would trust all his interests to the discretion of every man; without jealousy, without partition, without distinction. And the whole human race would form only one family; where all would lie in common, and be used freely, without regard to property: but cautiously too, with as entire regard to the necessities of each individual, as if our own interests were most intimately concerned.

In the present disposition of the human heart, it would, perhaps, be difficult to find compleat instances of such enlarged affections; but still we may observe, that the case of families approaches towards it: and the stronger the mutual benevolence is among the individuals, the nearer it approaches: till all distinction of property be, in a great measure, lost and confounded among them. Between married persons, the cement of friendship is by the laws supposed so strong as to abolish all division of possessions: and has often, in reality, the force ascribed to it. And it is observable, that, during the ardour of new enthusiasms, when every principle is inflamed into extravagance, the community of goods has frequently been attempted: and nothing but experience of its inconveniencies, from the returning or disguised selfishness of men, could make the imprudent fanatics adopt anew the ideas of justice and of separate property. So true is it, that this virtue derives its existence entirely from its necessary *use* to the intercourse and social state of mankind.

To make this truth more evident, let us reverse the foregoing suppositions: and carrying every thing to the opposite extreme, consider what would be the effect of these new situations.   Suppose a society to fall into such want of all common necessaries, that the utmost frugality and industry cannot preserve the greater number from perishing, and the whole from extreme misery : It will readily, I believe, be admitted, that the strict laws of justice are suspended, in such a pressing emergence, and give place to the stronger motives of necessity and self-preservation.   Is it any crime, after a shipwreck, to seize whatever means or instrument of safety one can lay hold of, without regard to former limitations of property ?   Or if a city besieged were perishing with hunger ; can we imagine, that men will see any means of preservation before them, and lose their lives, from a scrupulous regard to what, in other situations, would be the rules of equity and justice ?   The USE and TENDENCY of that virtue is to procure happiness and security, by preserving order in society : But where the society is ready to perish from extreme necessity, no greater evil can be dreaded from violence and injustice ; and every man may now provide for himself by all the means, which prudence can dictate, or humanity permit.   The public, even in less urgent necessities, opens granaries, without the consent of proprietors ; as justly supposing, that the authority of magistracy may, consistent with equity, extend so far : But were any number of men to assemble, without the tye of laws or civil jurisdiction ; would an equal partition of bread in a famine, though effected by power and even violence, be regarded as criminal or injurious ?

Suppose likewise, that it should be a virtuous man's fate to fall into the society of ruffians, remote from the protection of laws and government ; what conduct must he embrace in that melancholy situation ?   He sees such a desperate rapaciousness prevail ; such a disregard to equity, such contempt of order, such stupid blindness to future consequences, as must immediately have the most tragical conclusion, and must terminate in destruction to the greater number, and in a total dissolution of society to the rest.   He, mean while, can have no other expedient than to arm himself, to whomever the sword he seizes, or the buckler, may belong : To make provision of all means of defence and security : And his particular regard to justice being no longer of USE to his own safety or that of others, he must consult the dictates of self-preservation alone, without concern for those who no longer merit his care and attention.

When any man, even in political society, renders himself, by his crimes, obnoxious to the public, he is punished by the laws in his goods and person ; that is, the ordinary rules of justice are, with regard to him, suspended for a moment, and it becomes equitable to inflict on him, for the *benefit* of society, what, otherwise, he could not suffer without wrong or injury.

The rage and violence of public war ; what is it but a suspension of justice among the warring parties, who perceive, that this virtue is now no longer of any *use* or advantage to them? The laws of war, which then succeed to those of equity and justice, are rules calculated for the *advantage* and *utility* of that particular state, in which men are now placed. And were a civilized nation engaged with barbarians, who observed no rules even of war ; the former must also suspend their observance of them, where they no longer serve to any purpose ; and must render every action or rencounter as bloody and pernicious as possible to the first aggressors.

Thus, the rules of equity or justice depend entirely on the particular state and condition, in which men are placed, and owe their origin and existence to that UTILITY, which results to the public from their strict and regular observance. Reverse, in any considerable circumstance, the condition of men : Produce extreme abundance or extreme necessity : Implant in the human breast perfect moderation and humanity, or perfect rapaciousness and malice : By rendering justice totally *useless*, you thereby totally destroy its essence, and suspend its obligation upon mankind.

The common situation of society is a medium amidst all these extremes. We are naturally partial to ourselves, and to our friends ; but are capable of learning the advantage resulting from a more equitable conduct. Few enjoyments are given us from the open and liberal hand of nature ; but by art, labour, and industry, we can extract them in great abundance. Hence the ideas of property become necessary in all civil society : Hence justice derives its usefulness to the public : And hence alone arises its merit and moral obligation.

These conclusions are so natural and obvious, that they

have not escaped even the poets, in their descriptions of the felicity, attending the golden age or the reign of SATURN. The seasons, in that first period of nature, were so temperate, if we credit these agreeable fictions, that there was no necessity for men to provide themselves with cloaths and houses, as a security against the violence of heat and cold: The rivers flowed with wine and milk: The oaks yielded honey; and nature spontaneously produced her greatest delicacies. Nor were these the chief advantages of that happy age. Tempests were not alone removed from nature; but those more furious tempests were unknown to human breasts, which now cause such uproar, and engender such confusion. Avarice, ambition, cruelty, selfishness, were never heard of: Cordial affection, compassion, sympathy, were the only movements with which the mind was yet acquainted. Even the punctilious distinction of *mine* and *thine* was banished from among that happy race of mortals, and carried with it the very notion of property and obligation, justice and injustice.

This *poetical* fiction of the *golden age* is, in some respects, of a piece with the *philosophical* fiction of the *state of nature*; only that the former is represented as the most charming and most peaceable condition, which can possibly be imagined; whereas the latter is painted out as a state of mutual war and violence, attended with the most extreme necessity. On the first origin of mankind, we are told, their ignorance and savage nature were so prevalent, that they could give no mutual trust, but must each depend upon himself, and his own force or cunning for protection and security. No law was heard of: No rule of justice known: No distinction of property regarded: Power was the only measure of right; and a perpetual war of all against all was the result of men's untamed selfishness and barbarity.[1]

---

[1] This fiction of a state of nature, as a state of war, was not first started by Mr. HOBBES, as is commonly imagined. PLATO endeavours to refute an hypothesis very like it in the 2nd, 3rd, and 4th books de republica. CICERO, on the contrary, supposes it certain and universally acknowledged in the following passage.[1] 'Quis enim vestrûm, judices, ignorat, ita naturam rerum tulisse, ut quodam tempore homines, nondum neque naturali, neque civili

---

[1] [Editions G to N add: Which is the only authority I shall cite for these reasonings; not imitating in this the example of PUFFENDORF, nor even that of GROTIUS, who think a verse from OVID or PLAUTUS or PETRONIUS a necessary warrant for every moral truth; or the example of Mr. WOOLASTON, who has constant recourse to HEBREW and ARABIC authors for the same purpose.]

Whether such a condition of human nature could ever exist, or if it did, could continue so long as to merit the appellation of a *state*, may justly be doubted. Men are necessarily born in a family-society, at least ; and are trained up by their parents to some rule of conduct and behaviour. But this must be admitted, that, if such a state of mutual war and violence was ever real, the suspension of all laws of justice, from their absolute inutility, is a necessary and infallible consequence.

The more we vary our views of human life, and the newer and more unusual the lights are, in which we survey it, the more shall we be convinced, that the origin here assigned for the virtue of justice is real and satisfactory.

Were there a species of creatures, intermingled with men, which, though rational, were possessed of such inferior strength, both of body and mind, that they were incapable of all resistance, and could never, upon the highest provocation, make us feel the effects of their resentment ; the necessary consequence, I think, is, that we should be bound, by the laws of humanity, to give gentle usage to these creatures, but should not, properly speaking, lie under any restraint of justice with regard to them, nor could they possess any right or property, exclusive of such arbitrary lords. Our intercourse with them could not be called society, which supposes a degree of equality ; but absolute command on the one side, and servile obedience on the other. Whatever we covet, they must instantly resign : Our permission is the only tenure, by which they hold their possessions : Our compassion and kindness the only check, by which they curb our lawless will : And as no inconvenience ever results from the exercise of a power, so firmly established in nature, the restraints of justice and property, being totally *useless*, would never have place in so unequal a confederacy.

jure descripto, fusi per agros, ac dispersi vagarentur tantumque haberent quantum manu ac viribus, per caedem ac vulnera, aut eripere, aut retinere potuissent ? Qui igitur primi virtute et consilio praestanti exstiterunt, ii perspecto genere humanae docilitatis atque ingenii, dissipatos, unum in locum congregarunt, eosque ex feritate illa ad justitiam ac mansuetudinem transduxerunt. Tum res ad communem utilitatem, quas publicas appellamus, tum conventicula hominum, quae postea civitates nominatae sunt, tum domicilia conjuncta, quas urbes dicamus, invento et divino et humano jure, moenibus saepserunt. Atque inter hanc vitam, perpolitam humanitate, et illam immanem, nihil tam interest quam JUS atque VIS. Horum utro uti nolimus, altero est utendum. Vim volumus extingui ? Jus valeat necesse est, id est, judicia, quibus omne jus continetur. Judicia displicent, aut nulla sunt ? Vis dominetur necesse est. Haec vident omnes.' *Pro* *S.tt.* l. 42.

This is plainly the situation of men, with regard to animals; and how far these may be said to possess reason, I leave it to others to determine. The great superiority of civilized Europeans above barbarous Indians, tempted us to imagine ourselves on the same footing with regard to them, and made us throw off all restraints of justice, and even of humanity, in our treatment of them. In many nations, the female sex are reduced to like slavery, and are rendered incapable of all property, in opposition to their lordly masters. But though the males, when united, have, in all countries, bodily force sufficient to maintain this severe tyranny; yet such are the insinuation, address, and charms of their fair companions, that women are commonly able to break the confederacy, and share with the other sex in all the rights and privileges of society.

Were the human species so framed by nature as that each individual possessed within himself every faculty, requisite both for his own preservation and for the propagation of his kind: Were all society and intercourse cut off between man and man, by the primary intention of the supreme Creator: It seems evident, that so solitary a being would be as much incapable of justice, as of social discourse and conversation. Where mutual regards and forbearance serve to no manner of purpose, they would never direct the conduct of any reasonable man. The headlong course of the passions would be checked by no reflection on future consequences. And as each man is here supposed to love himself alone, and to depend only on himself and his own activity for safety and happiness, he would, on every occasion, to the utmost of his power, challenge the preference above every other being, to none of which he is bound by any ties, either of nature or of interest.

But suppose the conjunction of the sexes to be established in nature, a family immediately arises; and particular rules being found requisite for its subsistence, these are immediately embraced; though without comprehending the rest of mankind within their prescriptions. Suppose, that several families unite together into one society, which is totally disjoined from all others, the rules, which preserve peace and order, enlarge themselves to the utmost extent of that society; but becoming then entirely useless, lose their force when carried one step farther. But again suppose, that several distinct societies maintain a kind of intercourse for mutual convenience and advantage, the boundaries of justice still grow larger, in proportion to the largeness of men's views, and the force of their mutual connexions. History, experience, reason sufficiently instruct us in this natural progress of human sentiments, and in the gradual enlargement of our regards to justice, in proportion as we become acquainted with the extensive utility of that virtue.

PART II.

If we examine the *particular* laws, by which justice is directed, and property determined; we shall still be presented with the same conclusion. The good of mankind is the only object of all these laws and regulations. Not only it is requisite, for the peace and interest of society, that men's possessions should be separated: but the rules, which we follow, in making the separation, are such as can best be contrived to serve farther the interests of society.

We shall suppose, that a creature, possessed of reason, but unacquainted with human nature, deliberates with himself what RULES of justice or property would best promote public interest, and establish peace and security among mankind: His most obvious thought would be, to assign the largest possessions to the most extensive virtue, and give every one the power of doing good, proportioned to his inclination. In a perfect theocracy, where a being, infinitely intelligent, governs by particular volitions, this rule would certainly have place, and might serve to the wisest purposes: But were mankind to execute such a law; so great is the uncertainty of merit, both from its natural obscurity, and from the self-conceit of each individual, that no determinate rule of conduct would ever result from it: and the total dissolution of society must be the immediate consequence. Fanatics may suppose, *that dominion is founded on grace*, and *that saints alone inherit the earth*: but the civil magistrate very justly puts these sublime theorists on the same footing with common robbers, and teaches them by the severest discipline, that a rule, which, in speculation, may seem the most advantageous to society, may yet be found, in practice, totally pernicious and destructive.

That there were *religious* fanatics of this kind in ENGLAND, during the civil wars, we learn from history; though it is probable, that the obvious *tendency* of these principles excited such horror in mankind, as soon obliged the dangerous enthusiasts to renounce, or at least conceal their tenets. Perhaps, the *levellers*, who claimed an equal distribution of property, were a kind of *political* fanatics, which arose from the religious species, and more openly avowed their pretensions; as carrying a more plausible appearance, of being practicable in themselves, as well as useful to human society.

It must, indeed, be confessed, that nature is so liberal to mankind, that, were all her presents equally divided among the species, and improved by art and industry, every individual would enjoy all the necessaries, and even most of the comforts of life; nor would ever be liable to any ills, but such as might accidentally arise from the sickly frame and constitution of his body. It must also be confessed, that, wherever we depart from this equality, we rob the poor of more satisfaction than we add to the rich, and that the slight gratification of a frivolous vanity, in one individual, frequently costs more than bread to many families, and even provinces. It may appear withal, that the rule of equality, as it would be highly *useful*, is not altogether *impracticable*; but has taken place, at least in an imperfect degree, in some republics; particularly that of SPARTA; where it was attended, it is said, with the most beneficial consequences. Not to mention, that the AGRARIAN laws, so frequently claimed in ROME, and carried into execution in many GREEK cities, proceeded, all of them, from a general idea of the utility of this principle.

But historians, and even common sense, may inform us, that, however specious these ideas of *perfect* equality may seem, they are really, at bottom, *impracticable*; and were they not so, would be extremely *pernicious* to human society. Render possessions ever so equal, men's different degrees of art, care, and industry will immediately break that equality. Or if you check these virtues, you reduce society to the most extreme indigence; and instead of preventing want and beggary in a few, render it unavoidable to the whole community. The most rigorous inquisition too is requisite to watch every inequality on its first appearance; and the most severe jurisdiction, to punish and redress it. But besides, that so much authority must soon degenerate into tyranny, and be exerted with great partialities; who can possibly be possessed of it, in such a situation as is here supposed? Perfect equality of possessions, destroying all subordination, weakens extremely the authority of magistracy, and must reduce all power nearly to a level, as well as property.

We may conclude, therefore, that, in order to establish laws for the regulation of property, we must be acquainted with the nature and situation of man; must reject appearances, which may be false, though specious; and must search for those rules, which are, on the whole, most *useful* and *beneficial.* Vulgar sense and slight experience are sufficient for this purpose; where men give not way to too selfish avidity, or too extensive enthusiasm.

Who sees not, for instance, that whatever is produced or improved by a man's art or industry ought, for ever, to be secured to him, in order to give encouragement to such *useful* habits and accomplishments? That the property ought also to descend to children and relations, for the same *useful* purpose? That it may be alienated by consent, in order to beget that commerce and intercourse, which is so *beneficial* to human society? And that all contracts and promises ought carefully to be fulfilled, in order to secure mutual trust and confidence, by which the general *interest* of mankind is so much promoted?

Examine the writers on the laws of nature; and you will always find, that, whatever principles they set out with, they are sure to terminate here at last, and to assign, as the ultimate reason for every rule which they establish, the convenience and necessities of mankind. A concession thus extorted, in opposition to systems, has more authority, than if it had been made in prosecution of them.

What other reason, indeed, could writers ever give, why this must be *mine* and that *yours*; since uninstructed nature, surely, never made any such distinction? The objects, which receive those appellations, are, of themselves, foreign to us: they are totally disjoined and separated from us; and nothing but the general interests of society can form the connexion.

Sometimes, the interests of society may require a rule of justice in a particular case; but may not determine any particular rule, among several, which are all equally beneficial. In that case, the slightest *analogies* are laid hold of, in order to prevent that indifference and ambiguity, which would be the source of perpetual dissention. Thus possession alone, and first possession, is supposed to convey property, where no body else has any preceding claim and pretension. Many of the reasonings of lawyers are of this analogical nature, and depend on very slight connexions of the imagination.

Does any one scruple, in extraordinary cases, to violate all regard to the private property of individuals, and sacrifice to public interest a distinction, which had been established for the sake of that interest? The safety of the people is the supreme law: All other particular laws are subordinate to it, and dependant on it: And if, in the *common* course of things, they be followed and regarded; it is only because the public safety and interest *commonly* demand so equal and impartial an administration.

Sometimes both *utility* and *analogy* fail, and leave the laws of justice in total uncertainty. Thus, it is highly requisite, that prescription or long possession should convey property; but what number of days or months or years should be sufficient for that purpose, it is impossible for reason alone to determine. *Civil laws* here supply the place of the natural *code*, and assign different terms for prescription, according to the different *utilities*, proposed by the legislator. Bills of exchange and promissory notes, by the laws of most countries, prescribe sooner than bonds, and mortgages, and contracts of a more formal nature.

In general, we may observe, that all questions of property are subordinate to authority of civil laws, which extend, restrain, modify, and alter the rules of natural justice, according to the particular *convenience* of each community. The laws have, or ought to have, a constant reference to the constitution of government, the manners, the climate, the religion, the commerce, the situation of each society. A late author [1] of genius, as well as learning, has prosecuted this subject at large, and has established, from these principles, a system of political knowledge, which abounds in ingenious and brilliant thoughts, and is not wanting in solidity.[2]

---

[1] [Editions G and K read: Of great genius as well as extensive learning, the best system of political knowledge that, perhaps, has ever yet been communicated to the world.]

[2] The author of *L'Esprit des Loix.*

This illustrious writer, however, sets out with a different theory, and supposes all right to be founded on certain *rapports* or relations; which is a system, that, in my opinion, never will be reconciled with true philosophy. Father

What is a man's property? Any thing, which it is lawful for him, and for him alone, to use. *But what rule have we, by which we can distinguish these objects?* Here we must have recourse to statutes, customs, precedents, analogies, and a hundred other circumstances; some of which are constant and inflexible, some variable and arbitrary. But the ultimate point, in which they all professedly terminate, is, the interest and happiness of human society. Where this enters not into consideration, nothing can appear more whimsical, unnatural, and even superstitious, than all or most of the laws of justice and of property.

Those, who ridicule vulgar superstitions, and expose the folly of particular regards to meats, days, places, postures, apparel, have an easy task; while they consider all the qualities and relations of the objects, and discover no adequate cause for that affection or antipathy, veneration or horror, which have so mighty an influence over a considerable part of mankind. A SYRIAN would have starved rather than taste pigeon; an EGYPTIAN would not have approached bacon: But if these species of food be examined by the senses of sight, smell, or taste, or scrutinized by the sciences

---

MALEBRANCHE, as far as I can learn, was the first that started this abstract theory of morals, which was afterwards adopted by CUDWORTH, CLARKE, and others; and as it excludes all sentiment, and pretends to found every thing on reason, it has not wanted followers in this philosophic age. See Section 1. and Appendix I. With regard to justice, the virtue here treated of, the inference against this theory seems short and conclusive. Property is allowed to be dependent on civil laws; civil laws are allowed to have no other object, but the interest of society: This therefore must be allowed to be the sole foundation of property and justice. Not to mention, that our obligation itself to obey the magistrate and his laws is founded on nothing but the interests of society.

If the ideas of justice, sometimes, do not follow the dispositions of civil law; we shall find, that these cases, instead of objections, are confirmations of the theory delivered above. Where a civil law is so perverse as to cross all the interests of society, it loses all its authority, and men judge by the ideas of natural justice, which are conformable to those interests. Sometimes also civil laws, for useful purposes, require a ceremony or form to any deed; and where that is wanting, their decrees run contrary to the usual tenor of justice; but one who takes advantage of such chicanes, is not commonly regarded as an honest man. Thus, the interests of society require, that contracts be fulfilled; and there is not a more material article either of natural or civil justice: But the omission of a trifling circumstance will often, by law, invalidate a contract, *in foro humano*, but not *in foro conscientiæ*, as divines express themselves. In these cases, the magistrate is supposed only to withdraw his power of enforcing the right, not to have altered the right. Where his intention extends to the right, and is conformable to the interests of society; it never fails to alter the right; a clear proof of the origin of justice and of property, as assigned above.

[The reference to CUDWORTH was added in Edition O.]

of chymistry, medicine, or physics ; no difference is ever found between them and any other species, nor can that precise circumstance be pitched on, which may afford a just foundation for the religious passion. A fowl on Thursday is lawful food ; on Friday abominable : Eggs, in this house, and in this diocese, are permitted during Lent ; a hundred paces farther, to eat them is a damnable sin. This earth or building, yesterday was profane ; to-day, by the muttering of certain words, it has become holy and sacred. Such reflections as these, in the mouth of a philosopher, one may safely say, are too obvious to have any influence ; because they must always, to every man, occur at first sight : and where they prevail not, of themselves, they are surely obstructed by education, prejudice, and passion, not by ignorance or mistake.

It may appear to a careless view, or rather a too abstracted reflection, that there enters a like superstition into all the sentiments of justice : and that, if a man expose its object, or what we call property, to the same scrutiny of sense and science, he will not, by the most accurate enquiry, find any foundation for the difference made by moral sentiment. I may lawfully nourish myself from this tree ; but the fruit of another of the same species, ten paces off, it is criminal for me to touch. Had I worne this apparel an hour ago, I had merited the severest punishment ; but a man, by pronouncing a few magical syllables, has now rendered it fit for my use and service. Were this house placed in the neighbouring territory, it had been immoral for me to dwell in it ; but being built on this side of the river, it is subject to a different municipal law, and, [1] by its becoming mine, I incur no blame or censure. The same species of reasoning, it may be thought, which so successfully exposes superstition, is also applicable to justice ; nor is it possible, in the one case more than in the other, to point out, in the object, that precise quality or circumstance, which is the foundation of the sentiment.

But there is this material difference between *superstition* and *justice*, that the former is frivolous, useless, and burdensome ; the latter is absolutely requisite to the well-being of mankind and existence of society. When we abstract from this circum-

---

[1] [By its becoming mine : added in Edition Q.]

stance (for it is too apparent ever to be overlooked) it must be confessed, that all regards to right and property, seem entirely without foundation, as much as the grossest and most vulgar superstition. Were the interests of society nowise concerned, it is as unintelligible, why another's articulating certain sounds implying consent, should change the nature of my actions with regard to a particular object, as why the reciting of a liturgy by a priest, in a certain habit and posture, should dedicate a heap of brick and timber, and render it, thenceforth and for ever, sacred.[1]

[1] It is evident, that the will or consent alone never transfers property, nor causes the obligation of a promise (for the same reasoning extends to both) but the will must be expressed by words or signs, in order to impose a tye upon any man. The expression being once brought in as subservient to the will, soon becomes the principal part of the promise; nor will a man be less bound by his word, though he secretly give a different direction to his intention, and with-hold the assent of his mind. But though the expression makes, on most occasions, the whole of the promise, yet it does not always so; and one who should make use of any expression, of which he knows not the meaning, and which he uses without any sense of the consequences, would not certainly be bound by it. Nay, though he know its meaning, yet if he use it in jest only, and with such signs as evidently show, that he has no serious intention of binding himself, he would not lie under any obligation of performance; but it is necessary, that the words be a perfect expression of the will, without any contrary signs. Nay, even this we must not carry so far as to imagine, that one, whom, by our quickness of understanding, we conjecture, from certain signs, to have an intention of deceiving us, is not bound by his expression or verbal promise, if we accept of it; but must limit this conclusion to those cases where the signs are of a different nature from those of deceit. All these contradictions are easily accounted for, if justice arise entirely from its usefulness to society; but will never be explained on any other hypothesis.

It is remarkable, that the moral decisions of the *Jesuits* and other relaxed casuists, were commonly formed in prosecution of some such subtilties of reasoning as are here pointed out, and proceed as much from the habit of scholastic refinement as from any corruption of the heart, if we may follow the authority of Mons. Bayle. See his Dictionary, article Loyola. And why has the indignation of mankind risen so high against these casuists; but because every one perceived, that human society could not subsist were such practices authorized, and that morals must always be handled with a view to public interest, more than philosophical regularity? If the secret direction of the intention, said every man of sense, could invalidate a contract; where is our security? And yet a metaphysical schoolman might think, that where an intention was supposed to be requisite, if that intention really had not place, no consequence ought to follow, and no obligation be imposed. The casuistical subtilties may not be greater than the subtilties of lawyers, hinted at above; but as the former are *pernicious*, and the latter *innocent* and even *necessary*, this is the reason of the very different reception they meet with from the world.

[2] It is a doctrine of the church of Rome, that the priest, by a secret direction of his intention, can invalidate any sacrament. This position is derived from a strict and regular prosecution of the obvious truth, that empty words alone, without any meaning or intention in the speaker, can never be attended with any effect. If the same conclusion be not admitted in reasonings concerning civil contracts, where

[2] [This paragraph was added in Edition O.]

These reflections are far from weakening the obligations of justice, or diminishing any thing from the most sacred attention to property. On the contrary, such sentiments must acquire new force from the present reasoning. For what stronger foundation can be desired or conceived for any duty, than to observe, that human society, or even human nature could not subsist, without the establishment of it; and will still arrive at greater degrees of happiness and perfection, the more inviolable the regard is, which is paid to that duty? [1]

The dilemma seems obvious: As justice evidently tends to promote public utility and to support civil society, the sentiment of justice is either derived from our reflecting on that tendency, or like hunger, thirst, and other appetites, resentment, love of life, attachment to offspring, and other passions, arises from a simple original instinct in the human breast, which nature has implanted for like salutary purposes. [2] If the latter be the case, it follows, that property, which is the object of justice, is also distinguished by a simple, original instinct, and is not ascertained by any argument or reflection. But who is there that ever heard of such an instinct? Or is this a subject, in which new discoveries can be made? We may as well attempt to discover, in the body, new senses, which had before escaped the observation of all mankind.

But farther, though it seems a very simple proposition to say, that nature, by an instinctive sentiment, distinguishes property, yet in reality we shall find, that there are required for that purpose ten thousand different instincts, and these employed about objects of the greatest intricacy and nicest discernment. For when a definition of *property* is required, that relation is found to resolve itself into any possession acquired by occupation, by industry, by prescription, by in-

the affair is allowed to be of so much less consequence than the eternal salvation of thousands, it proceeds entirely from men's sense of the danger and inconvenience of the doctrine in the former case: And we may thence observe, that however positive, arrogant, and dogmatical any superstition may appear, it never can convey any thorough persuasion of the reality of its objects, or put them, in any degree, on a balance with the common incidents of life, which we learn from daily observation and experimental reasoning.

[1] [Edition G omits all between this point and the concluding paragraph of the section.]

[2] [Edition N omits the preceding sentence, and reads: If justice arose from a simple, original instinct in the human breast, without any reflection, even on those obvious interests of society, which absolutely require that virtue, it follows, &c.]

heritance, by contract, &c. Can we think, that nature, by an original instinct, instructs us in all these methods of acquisition?

These words too, inheritance and contract, stand for ideas infinitely complicated; and to define them exactly, a hundred volumes of laws, and a thousand volumes of commentators, have not been found sufficient. Does nature, whose instincts in men are all simple, embrace such complicated and artificial objects, and create a rational creature, without trusting any thing to the operation of his reason?

But even though all this were admitted, it would not be satisfactory. Positive laws can certainly transfer property. Is it by another original instinct, that we recognize the authority of kings and senates, and mark all the boundaries of their jurisdiction? Judges too, even though their sentence be erroneous and illegal, must be allowed, for the sake of peace and order, to have decisive authority, and ultimately to determine property. Have we original, innate ideas of prætors and chancellors and juries? Who sees not, that all these institutions arise merely from the necessities of human society?

All birds of the same species, in every age and country, build their nests alike: In this we see the force of instinct. Men, in different times and places, frame their houses differently: Here we perceive the influence of reason and custom. A like inference may be drawn from comparing the instinct of generation and the institution of property.

How great soever the variety of municipal laws, it must be confessed, that their chief out-lines pretty regularly concur; because the purposes, to which they tend, are every where exactly similar. In like manner, all houses have a roof and walls, windows and chimneys; though diversified in their shape, figure, and materials. The purposes of the latter, directed to the conveniencies of human life, discover not more plainly their origin from reason and reflection, than do those of the former, which point all to a like end.

I need not mention the variations, which all the rules of property receive from the finer turns and connexions of the imagination, and from the subtilties and abstractions of law-topics and reasonings. There is no possibility of reconciling this observation to the notion of original instincts.

What alone will beget a doubt concerning the theory, on

which I insist, is the influence of education and acquired habits, by which we are so accustomed to blame injustice, that we are not, in every instance, conscious of any immediate reflection on the pernicious consequences of it. The views the most familiar to us are apt, for that very reason, to escape us; and what we have very frequently performed from certain motives, we are apt likewise to continue mechanically, without recalling, on every occasion, the reflections, which first determined us. The convenience, or rather necessity, which leads to justice, is so universal, and every where points so much to the same rules, that the habit takes place in all societies; and it is not without some scrutiny, that we are able to ascertain its true origin. The matter, however, is not so obscure, but that, even in common life, we have, every moment, recourse to the principle of public utility, and ask, *What must become of the world, if such practices prevail? How could society subsist under such disorders?* Were the distinction or separation of possessions entirely useless, can any one conceive, that it ever should have obtained in society?

Thus we seem, upon the whole, to have attained a knowledge of the force of that principle here insisted on, and can determine what degree of esteem or moral approbation may result from reflections on public interest and utility. The necessity of justice to the support of society is the SOLE foundation of that virtue; and since no moral excellence is more highly esteemed, we may conclude, that this circumstance of usefulness has, in general, the strongest energy, and most entire command over our sentiments. It must, therefore, be the source of a considerable part of the merit ascribed to humanity, benevolence, friendship, public spirit, and other social virtues of that stamp; as it is the SOLE source of the moral approbation paid to fidelity, justice, veracity, integrity, and those other estimable and useful qualities and principles. It is entirely agreeable to the rules of philosophy, and even of common reason; where any principle has been found to have a great force and energy in one instance, to ascribe to it a like energy in all similar instances. [1]This indeed is NEWTON's chief rule of philosophizing.[2]

---

[1] [This sentence is printed as a note in Editions G to P; and they also call it the *second* rule.]

[2] Principia, lib. iii.

Section IV.—*Of Political Society.*

HAD every man sufficient *sagacity* to perceive, at all times, the strong interest, which binds him to the observance of justice and equity, and *strength of mind* sufficient to persevere in a steady adherence to a general and a distant interest, in opposition to the allurements of present pleasure and advantage; there had never, in that case, been any such thing as government or political society, but each man, following his natural liberty, had lived in entire peace and harmony with all others. What need of positive law where natural justice is, of itself, a sufficient restraint? Why create magistrates, where there never arises any disorder or iniquity? Why abridge our native freedom, when, in every instance, the utmost exertion of it is found innocent and beneficial? It is evident, that, if government were totally useless, it never could have place, and that the SOLE foundation of the duty of ALLEGIANCE is the *advantage*, which it procures to society, by preserving peace and order among mankind.

When a number of political societies are erected, and maintain a great intercourse together, a new set of rules are immediately discovered to be *useful* in that particular situation; and accordingly take place under the title of LAWS of NATIONS. Of this kind are, the sacredness of the person of ambassadors, abstaining from poisoned arms, quarter in war, with others of that kind, which are plainly calculated for the *advantage* of states and kingdoms, in their intercourse with each other.

The rules of justice, such as prevail among individuals, are not entirely suspended among political societies. All princes pretend a regard to the rights of other princes; and some, no doubt, without hypocrisy. Alliances and treaties are every day made between independent states, which would only be so much waste of parchment, if they were not found, by experience, to have *some* influence and authority. But here is the difference between kingdoms and individuals. Human nature cannot, by any means, subsist, without the association of individuals; and that association never could have place, were no regard paid to the laws of equity and justice. Disorder, confusion, the war of all against all, are the necessary consequences of such a licentious conduct.

But nations can subsist without intercourse. They may even subsist, in some degree, under a general war. The observance of justice, though useful among them, is not guarded by so strong a necessity as among individuals; and the *moral obligation* holds proportion with the *usefulness*. All politicians will allow, and most philosophers, that REASONS of STATE may, in particular emergencies, dispense with the rules of justice, and invalidate any treaty or alliance, where the strict observance of it would be prejudicial, in a considerable degree, to either of the contracting parties. But nothing less than the most extreme necessity, it is confessed, can justify individuals in a breach of promise, or an invasion of the properties of others.

In a confederated commonwealth, such as the ACHÆAN republic of old, or the SWISS Cantons and United Provinces in modern times; as the league has here a peculiar *utility*, the conditions of union have a peculiar sacredness and authority, and a violation of them would be regarded as no less, or even as more criminal, than any private injury or injustice.

The long and helpless infancy of man requires the combination of parents for the subsistence of their young; and that combination requires the virtue of CHASTITY or fidelity to the marriage bed. Without such a *utility*, it will readily be owned, that such a virtue would never have been thought of.[1]

An infidelity of this nature is much more *pernicious* in *women* than in *men*. Hence the laws of chastity are much stricter over the one sex than over the other.

These rules have all a reference to generation; and yet women past child-bearing are no more supposed to be exempted from them than those in the flower of their youth

---

[1] The only solution, which PLATO gives to all the objections, that might be raised against the community of women, established in his imaginary commonwealth, is Κάλλιστα γὰρ δὴ τοῦτο καὶ λέγεται καὶ λελέξεται, ὅτι τὸ μὲν ὠφέλιμον καλόν, Τὸ δὲ βλαβερὸν αἰσχρόν. Svite enim istud & dicitur & dicitur, Id. quod utile sit honestum esse, quod autem inutile sit turpe esse. De Rep. lib. 5. p. 457. ex edit. Ser. And this maxim will admit of no doubt, where public utility is concerned; which is PLATO's meaning. And indeed to what other purpose do all the ideas of chastity and modesty serve? *Nisi utile est quod facimus, frustra est gloria*, says PHÆDRUS, 3. 17. 12. Καλὸν τῶν βλαβερῶν οὐδέν, says PLUTARCH *de vitiosa pudore*, 529. F. Nihil eorum quæ damnosa sunt, pulchrum est. The same was the opinion of the Stoics. Φασιν οὖν οἱ Στωικοὶ ἀγαθὸν εἶναι ὠφέλειαν ἢ οὐχ ἕτεραν ὠφελείας, ὠφέλειαν μὲν λέγοντες τὴν ἀρετὴν καὶ τὴν σπουδαίαν πρᾶξιν. SEXT. EMP. lib. 3. cap. 20.

and beauty. *General rules* are often extended beyond the principle, whence they first arise; and this in all matters of taste and sentiment. It is a vulgar story at PARIS, that, during the rage of the MISSISSIPPI, a hump-backed fellow went every day into the RUE DE QUINCEMPOIX, where the stock-jobbers met in great crowds, and was well paid for allowing them to make use of his hump as a desk, in order to sign their contracts upon it. Would the fortune, which he raised by this expedient, make him a handsome fellow; though it be confessed, that personal beauty arises very much from ideas of utility? The imagination is influenced by associations of ideas; which, though they arise at first from the judgment, are not easily altered by every particular exception that occurs to us. To which we may add, in the present case of chastity, that the example of the old would be pernicious to the young; and that women, continually foreseeing that a certain time would bring them the liberty of indulgence, would naturally advance that period, and think more lightly of this whole duty, so requisite to society.

SECT. IV.

Those who live in the same family have such frequent opportunities of licence of this kind, that nothing could preserve purity of manners, were marriage allowed, among the nearest relations, or any intercourse of love between them ratified by law and custom. INCEST, therefore, being *pernicious* in a superior degree, has also a superior turpitude and moral deformity annexed to it.

What is the reason, why, by the ATHENIAN laws, one might marry a half-sister by the father, but not by the mother? Plainly this: The manners of the ATHENIANS were so reserved, that a man was never permitted to approach the women's apartment, even in the same family, unless where he visited his own mother. His step-mother and her children were as much shut up from him as the women of any other family, and there was as little danger of any criminal correspondence between them. Uncles and nieces, for a like reason, might marry at ATHENS; but neither these, nor half-brothers and sisters, could contract that alliance at ROME, where the intercourse was more open between the sexes. Public utility is the cause of all these variations.

To repeat, to a man's prejudice, any thing that escaped him in private conversation, or to make any such use of his private letters, is highly blamed. The free and social inter-course of minds must be extremely checked, where no such rules of fidelity are established.

Even in repeating stories, whence we can foresee no ill consequences to result, the giving of one's author is regarded as a piece of indiscretion, if not of immorality. These stories, in passing from hand to hand, and receiving all the usual variations, frequently come about to the persons con-cerned, and produce animosities and quarrels among people, whose intentions are the most innocent and inoffensive.

To pry into secrets, to open or even read the letters of others, to play the spy upon their words and looks and actions; what habits more inconvenient in society? What habits, of consequence, more blameable?

This principle is also the foundation of most of the laws of good manners; a kind of lesser morality, calculated for the ease of company and conversation. Too much or too little ceremony are both blamed, and every thing, which pro-motes ease, without an indecent familiarity, is useful and laudable.

Constancy in friendships, attachments, and familiarities, is commendable, and is requisite to support trust and good correspondence in society. But in places of general, though casual concourse, where the pursuit of health and pleasure brings people promiscuously together, public conveniency has dispensed with this maxim; and custom there promotes an unreserved conversation for the time, by indulging the privilege of dropping afterwards every indifferent acquaint-ance, without breach of civility or good manners.

Even in societies, which are established on principles the most immoral, and the most destructive to the interests of the general society, there are required certain rules, which a species of false honour, as well as private interest, engages the members to observe. Robbers and pirates, it has often been remarked, could not maintain their pernicious con-federacy, did they not establish a new distributive justice among themselves, and recal those laws of equity, which they have violated with the rest of mankind.

I hate a drinking companion, says the GREEK proverb, who never forgets. The follies of the last debauch should be buried in eternal oblivion, in order to give full scope to the follies of the next.

Among nations, where an immoral gallantry, if covered with a thin veil of mystery, is, in some degree, authorised by custom, there immediately arise a set of rules, calculated for the conveniency of that attachment. The famous court or parliament of love in PROVENCE formerly decided all difficult cases of this nature.

In societies for play, there are laws required for the conduct of the game; and these laws are different in each game. The foundation, I own, of such societies is frivolous; and the laws are, in a great measure, though not altogether, capricious and arbitrary. So far is there a material difference between them and the rules of justice, fidelity, and loyalty. The general societies of men are absolutely requisite for the subsistence of the species; and the public conveniency, which regulates morals, is inviolably established in the nature of man, and of the world, in which he lives. The comparison, therefore, in these respects, is very imperfect. We may only learn from it the necessity of rules, wherever men have any intercourse with each other.

They cannot even pass each other on the road without rules. Waggoners, coachmen, and postilions have principles, by which they give the way; and these are chiefly founded on mutual ease and convenience. Sometimes also they are arbitrary, at least dependent on a kind of capricious analogy, like many of the reasonings of lawyers.[1]

To carry the matter farther, we may observe, that it is impossible for men so much as to murder each other without statutes, and maxims, and an idea of justice and honour. War has its laws as well as peace; and even that sportive kind of war, carried on among wrestlers, boxers, cudgel-players, gladiators, is regulated by fixed principles. Common interest and utility beget infallibly a standard of right and wrong among the parties concerned.

[1] That the lighter machine yield to the heavier, and, in machines of the same kind, that the empty yield to the loaded: this rule is founded on convenience. That those who are going to the capital take place of those who are coming from it: this seems to be founded on some idea of the dignity of the great city, and of the preference of the future to the past. From like reasons, among foot-walkers, the right-hand intitles a man to the wall, and prevents jostling, which peaceable people find very disagreeable and inconvenient.

Sect. V.—*Why Utility pleases.*

PART I.

It seems so natural a thought to ascribe to their utility the praise, which we bestow on the social virtues, that one would expect to meet with this principle every where in moral writers, as the chief foundation of their reasoning and enquiry. In common life, we may observe, that the circumstance of utility is always appealed to; nor is it supposed, that a greater eulogy can be given to any man, than to display his usefulness to the public, and enumerate the services, which he has performed to mankind and society. What praise, even of an inanimate form, if the regularity and elegance of its parts destroy not its fitness for any useful purpose! And how satisfactory an apology for any disproportion or seeming deformity, if we can show the necessity of that particular construction for the use intended! A ship appears more beautiful to an artist, or one moderately skilled in navigation, where its prow is wide and swelling beyond its poop, than if it were framed with a precise geometrical regularity, in contradiction to all the laws of mechanics. A building, whose doors and windows were exact squares, would hurt the eye by that very proportion; as ill adapted to the figure of a human creature, for whose service the fabric was intended. What wonder then, that a man, whose habits and conduct are hurtful to society, and dangerous or pernicious to every one who has an intercourse with him, should, on that account, be an object of disapprobation, and communicate to every spectator the strongest sentiment of disgust and hatred.[1]

[1] We ought not to imagine, because an inanimate object may be useful as well as a man, that therefore it ought also, according to this system, to merit the appellation of *virtuous*. The sentiments, excited by utility, are, in the two cases, very different; and the one is mixed with affection, esteem, approbation, &c. and not the other. In like manner, an inanimate object may have good colour and proportions as well as a human figure. But can we ever be in love with the former? There are a numerous set of passions and sentiments, of which thinking rational beings are, by the original constitution of nature, the only proper objects: And though the very same qualities be transferred to an insensible, inanimate being, they will not excite the same sentiments. The beneficial qualities of herbs and minerals are, indeed, sometimes called their *virtues*; but this is an effect of the caprice of language, which ought not to be regarded in reasoning. For though there be a species of approbation attending even inanimate objects when beneficial, yet this sentiment is so weak, and so different from that which is directed to beneficent magistrates or statesmen, that they ought not to be ranked under the same class or appellation.

A very small variation of the object, even where the same qualities are pre-

But perhaps the difficulty of accounting for these effects of usefulness, or its contrary, has kept philosophers from admitting them into their systems of ethics, and has induced them rather to employ any other principle, in explaining the origin of moral good and evil. But it is no just reason for rejecting any principle, confirmed by experience, that we cannot give a satisfactory account of its origin, nor are able to resolve it into other more general principles. And if we would employ a little thought on the present subject, we need be at no loss to account for the influence of utility, and to deduce it from principles, the most known and avowed in human nature.

From the apparent usefulness of the social virtues, it has readily been inferred by sceptics, both ancient and modern, that all moral distinctions arise from education, and were, at first, invented, and afterwards encouraged, by the art of politicians, in order to render men tractable, and subdue their natural ferocity and selfishness, which incapacitated them for society. This principle, indeed, of precept and education, must so far be owned to have a powerful influence, that it may frequently encrease or diminish, beyond their natural standard, the sentiments of approbation or dislike; and may even, in particular instances, create, without any natural principle, a new sentiment of this kind; as is evident in all superstitious practices and observances: But that *all* moral affection or dislike arises from this origin, will never surely be allowed by any judicious enquirer. Had nature made no such distinction, founded on the original constitution of the mind, the words, *honourable* and *shameful*, *lovely* and *odious*, *noble* and *despicable*, had never had place in any language: nor could politicians, had they invented these terms, ever have been able to render them intelligible, or make them convey any idea to the audience. So that nothing can be more superficial than this paradox of the sceptics; and it were well, if, in the abstruser studies of logic and metaphysics, we could as easily obviate the cavils of that sect. as in the practical and more intelligible sciences of politics and morals.

The social virtues must, therefore, be allowed to have a

served, will destroy a sentiment. Thus, the same beauty, transferred to a different sex, excites no amorous passion, where nature is not extremely perverted.

natural beauty and amiableness, which, at first, antecedent
to all precept or education, recommends them to the esteem
of uninstructed mankind, and engages their affections. And
as the public utility of these virtues is the chief circumstance, whence they derive their merit, it follows, that the
end, which they have a tendency to promote, must be some
way agreeable to us, and take hold of some natural affection.
It must please, either from considerations of self-interest, or
from more generous motives and regards.

It has often been asserted, that, as every man has a strong
connexion with society, and perceives the impossibility of his
solitary subsistence, he becomes, on that account, favourable
to all those habits or principles, which promote order in society, and insure to him the quiet possession of so inestimable
a blessing. As much as we value our own happiness and
welfare, as much must we applaud the practice of justice and
humanity, by which alone the social confederacy can be maintained, and every man reap the fruits of mutual protection
and assistance.

This deduction of morals from self-love, or a regard to
private interest, is an obvious thought, and has not arisen
wholly from the wanton sallies and sportive assaults of the
sceptics. To mention no others, POLYBIUS, one of the gravest
and most judicious, as well as most moral writers of antiquity,
has assigned this selfish origin to all our sentiments of virtue.[1]
But though the solid, practical sense of that author, and his
aversion to all vain subtilties, render his authority on the
present subject very considerable; yet is not this an affair to
be decided by authority, and the voice of nature and experience seems plainly to oppose the selfish theory.

We frequently bestow praise on virtuous actions, performed
in very distant ages and remote countries; where the utmost
subtilty of imagination would not discover any appearance of
self-interest, or find any connexion of our present happiness
and security with events so widely separated from us.

A generous, a brave, a noble deed, performed by an adver-

---

[1] Undutifulness to parents is disap-
proved of by mankind, προορωμένους τὸ
μέλλον, καὶ συλλογιζομένους, ὅτι τὸ
παραπλήσιον ἑκάστοις αὐτῶν συγκυρήσει.
Ingratitude for a like reason (though
he seems there to mix a more generous
regard) σιναγανακτοῦντας μὲν τῷ πέλας,
ἀναφέροντες δ᾽ ἐπ᾽ αὐτοὺς τὸ παραπλήσιον.

ἐξ ὧν ὑπογίγνεταί τις ἔννοια παρ᾽ ἑκάστῳ
τοῦ καθήκοντος δυνάμεως καὶ θεωρίας.
Lib. vi. cap. 6. Perhaps the historian
only meant, that our sympathy and humanity was more enlivened, by our considering the similarity of our case with
that of the person suffering; which is a
just sentiment.

sary, commands our approbation; while in its consequences it may be acknowledged prejudicial to our particular interest.

Where private advantage concurs with general affection for virtue, we readily perceive and avow the mixture of these distinct sentiments, which have a very different feeling and influence on the mind. We praise, perhaps, with more alacrity, where the generous, humane action contributes to our particular interest: But the topics of praise, which we insist on, are very wide of this circumstance. And we may attempt to bring over others to our sentiments, without endeavouring to convince them, that they reap any advantage from the actions which we recommend to their approbation and applause.

Frame the model of a praise-worthy character, consisting of all the most amiable moral virtues: Give instances, in which these display themselves after an eminent and extraordinary manner: You readily engage the esteem and approbation of all your audience, who never so much as enquire in what age and country the person lived, who possessed these noble qualities: A circumstance, however, of all others, the most material to self-love, or a concern for our own individual happiness.

Once on a time, a statesman, in the shock and contest of parties, prevailed so far as to procure, by his eloquence, the banishment of an able adversary; whom he secretly followed, offering him money for his support during his exile, and soothing him with topics of consolation in his misfortunes. *Alas!* cries the banished statesman, *with what regret must I leave my friends in this city, where even enemies are so generous!* Virtue, though in an enemy, here pleased him: And we also give it the just tribute of praise and approbation; nor do we retract these sentiments, when we hear, that the action passed at ATHENS, about two thousand years ago, and that the persons' names were ESCHINES and DEMOSTHENES.

What is that to me? There are few occasions, when this question is not pertinent: And had it that universal, infallible influence supposed, it would turn into ridicule every composition, and almost every conversation, which contain any praise or censure of men and manners.

It is but a weak subterfuge, when pressed by these facts and arguments, to say, that we transport ourselves, by the force of imagination, into distant ages and countries, and consider the advantage, which we should have reaped from these characters, had we been contemporaries, and had any commerce with the persons. It is not conceivable, how a *real* sentiment or passion can ever arise from a known *imaginary* interest; especially when our *real* interest is still kept in view, and is often acknowledged to be entirely distinct from the imaginary, and even sometimes opposite to it.

A man, brought to the brink of a precipice, cannot look down without trembling; and the sentiment of *imaginary* danger actuates him, in opposition to the opinion and belief of *real* safety. But the imagination is here assisted by the presence of a striking object; and yet prevails not, except it be also aided by novelty, and the unusual appearance of the object. Custom soon reconciles us to heights and precipices, and wears off these false and delusive terrors. The reverse is observable in the estimates, which we form of characters and manners; and the more we habituate ourselves to an accurate scrutiny of morals, the more delicate feeling do we acquire of the most minute distinctions between vice and virtue. Such frequent occasion, indeed, have we, in common life, to pronounce all kinds of moral determinations, that no object of this kind can be new or unusual to us; nor could any *false* views or prepossessions maintain their ground against an experience, so common and familiar. Experience being chiefly what forms the association of ideas, it is impossible, that any association could establish and support itself, in direct opposition to that principle.

Usefulness is agreeable, and engages our approbation. This is a matter of fact, confirmed by daily observation. But, *useful?* For what? For some body's interest, surely. Whose interest then? Not our own only: For our approbation frequently extends farther. It must, therefore, be the interest of those, who are served by the character or action approved of; and these we may conclude, however remote, are not totally indifferent to us. By opening up this principle, we shall discover one great source of moral distinctions.

PART II.

Self-love is a principle in human nature of such extensive energy, and the interest of each individual is, in general, so closely connected with that of the community, that those philosophers were excusable, who fancied, that all our concern for the public might be resolved into a concern for our own happiness and preservation. They saw every moment, instances of approbation or blame, satisfaction or displeasure towards characters and actions; they denominated the objects of these sentiments, *virtues*, or *vices*; they observed, that the former had a tendency to encrease the happiness, and the latter the misery of mankind; they asked, whether it were possible that we could have any general concern for society, or any disinterested resentment of the welfare or injury of others; they found it simpler to consider all these sentiments as modifications of self-love; and they discovered a pretence, at least, for this unity of principle, in that close union of interest, which is so observable between the public and each individual.

But notwithstanding this frequent confusion of interests, it is easy to attain what natural philosophers, after lord BACON, have affected to call the *experimentum crucis*, or that experiment, which points out the right way in any doubt or ambiguity. We have found instances, in which private interest was separate from public; in which it was even contrary: And yet we observed the moral sentiment to continue, notwithstanding this disjunction of interests. And wherever these distinct interests sensibly concurred, we always found a sensible encrease of the sentiment, and a more warm affection to virtue, and detestation of vice, or what we properly call, *gratitude* and *revenge*. Compelled by these instances, we must renounce the theory, which accounts for every moral sentiment by the principle of self-love. We must adopt a more public affection, and allow, that the interests of society are not, even on their own account, entirely indifferent to us. Usefulness is only a tendency to a certain end; and it is a contradiction in terms, that any thing pleases as means to an end, where the end itself no wise affects us. If usefulness, therefore, be a source of moral sentiment, and if this usefulness be not always considered with a reference to self; it follows, that every thing, which contributes to the happiness of society, recommends itself directly to our approbation and good-will. Here is a principle, which accounts, in great part, for the origin of morality: And what need we seek for abstruse and remote systems, when there occurs one so obvious and natural?[1]

---

[1] It is needless to push our researches so far as to ask, why we have humanity or a fellow-feeling with others. It s sufficient, that this is experienced to be

Have we any difficulty to comprehend the force of humanity and benevolence? Or to conceive, that the very aspect of happiness, joy, prosperity, gives pleasure; that of pain, suffering, sorrow, communicates uneasiness? The human countenance, says HORACE,[1] borrows smiles or tears from the human countenance. Reduce a person to solitude, and he loses all enjoyment, except either of the sensual or speculative kind; and that because the movements of his heart are not forwarded by correspondent movements in his fellow-creatures. The signs of sorrow and mourning, though arbitrary, affect us with melancholy; but the natural symptoms, tears and cries and groans, never fail to infuse compassion and uneasiness. And if the effects of misery touch us in so lively a manner; can we be supposed altogether insensible or indifferent towards its causes; when a malicious or treacherous character and behaviour are presented to us?

We enter, I shall suppose, into a convenient, warm, well-contrived apartment: We necessarily receive a pleasure from its very survey; because it presents us with the pleasing ideas of ease, satisfaction, and enjoyment. The hospitable, good-humoured, humane landlord appears. This circumstance surely must embellish the whole: nor can we easily forbear reflecting, with pleasure, on the satisfaction which results to every one from his intercourse and good-offices.

His whole family, by the freedom, ease, confidence, and calm enjoyment, diffused over their countenances, sufficiently express their happiness. I have a pleasing sympathy in the prospect of so much joy, and can never consider the source of it, without the most agreeable emotions

He tells me, that an oppressive and powerful neighbour had attempted to dispossess him of his inheritance, and had long disturbed all his innocent and social pleasures. I feel

---

a principle in human nature. We must stop somewhere in our examination of causes; and there are, in every science, some general principles, beyond which we cannot hope to find any principle more general. No man is absolutely indifferent to the happiness and misery of others. The first has a natural tendency to give pleasure; the second, pain. This every one may find in himself. It is not probable, that these principles can be resolved into principles more simple and universal, whatever attempts may have been made to that purpose. But if it were possible, it belongs not to the present subject; and we may here safely consider these principles as original: Happy, if we can render all the consequences sufficiently plain and perspicuous!

[1] Uti ridentibus arrident, ita flentibus adflent
Humani vultus. HOR. A. P. 101.

an immediate indignation arise in me against such violence and injury.

But it is no wonder, he adds, that a private wrong should proceed from a man, who had enslaved provinces, depopulated cities, and made the field and scaffold stream with human blood. I am struck with horror at the prospect of so much misery, and am actuated by the strongest antipathy against its author.

In general, it is certain, that, wherever we go, whatever we reflect on or converse about, every thing still presents us with the view of human happiness or misery, and excites in our breast a sympathetic movement of pleasure or uneasiness. In our serious occupations, in our careless amusements, this principle still exerts its active energy.

A man, who enters the theatre, is immediately struck with the view of so great a multitude, participating of one common amusement; and experiences, from their very aspect, a superior sensibility or disposition of being affected with every sentiment, which he shares with his fellow-creatures.

He observes the actors to be animated by the appearance of a full audience, and raised to a degree of enthusiasm, which they cannot command in any solitary or calm moment.

Every movement of the theatre, by a skilful poet, is communicated, as it were by magic, to the spectators; who weep, tremble, resent, rejoice, and are enflamed with all the variety of passions, which actuate the several personages of the drama.

Where any event crosses our wishes, and interrupts the happiness of the favourite characters, we feel a sensible anxiety and concern. But where their sufferings proceed from the treachery, cruelty, or tyranny of an enemy, our breasts are affected with the liveliest resentment against the author of these calamities.

It is here esteemed contrary to the rules of art to represent any thing cool and indifferent. A distant friend, or a confident, who has no immediate interest in the catastrophe, ought, if possible, to be avoided by the poet; as communicating a like indifference to the audience, and checking the progress of the passions.

Few species of poetry are more entertaining than *pastoral*; and every one is sensible, that the chief source of its pleasure arises from those images of a gentle and tender tranquillity.

which it represents in its personages, and of which it communicates a like sentiment to the reader. SANNAZARIUS, who transferred the scene to the sea-shore, though he presented the most magnificent object in nature, is confessed to have erred in his choice. The idea of toil, labour, and danger, suffered by the fishermen, is painful; by an unavoidable sympathy, which attends every conception of human happiness or misery.

When I was twenty, says a FRENCH poet, OVID was my favourite: Now I am forty, I declare for HORACE. We enter, to be sure, more readily into sentiments, which resemble those we feel every day: But no passion, when well represented, can be entirely indifferent to us; because there is none, of which every man has not, within him, at least the seeds and first principles. It is the business of poetry to bring every affection near to us by lively imagery and representation, and make it look like truth and reality: A certain proof, that, wherever that reality is found, our minds are disposed to be strongly affected by it.

Any recent event or piece of news, by which the fate of states, provinces, or many individuals is affected, is extremely interesting even to those whose welfare is not immediately engaged. Such intelligence is propagated with celerity, heard with avidity, and enquired into with attention and concern. The interest of society appears, on this occasion, to be, in some degree, the interest of each individual. The imagination is sure to be affected; though the passions excited may not always be so strong and steady as to have great influence on the conduct and behaviour.

The perusal of a history seems a calm entertainment; but would be no entertainment at all, did not our hearts beat with correspondent movements to those which are described by the historian.

THUCYDIDES and GUICCIARDIN support with difficulty our attention; while the former describes the trivial rencounters of the small cities of GREECE, and the latter the harmless wars of PISA. The few persons interested, and the small interest fill not the imagination, and engage not the affections. The deep distress of the numerous ATHENIAN army before SYRACUSE; the danger, which so nearly threatens VENICE; these excite compassion; these move terror and anxiety.

The indifferent, uninteresting stile of SUETONIUS, equally with the masterly pencil of TACITUS, may convince us of the cruel depravity of NERO or TIBERIUS: But what a difference of sentiment! While the former coldly relates the facts; and the latter sets before our eyes the venerable figures of a SORANUS and a THRASEA, intrepid in their fate, and only moved by the melting sorrows of their friends and kindred. What sympathy then touches every human heart! What indignation against the tyrant, whose causeless fear or unprovoked malice gave rise to such detestable barbarity!

If we bring these subjects nearer: If we remove all suspicion of fiction and deceit: What powerful concern is excited, and how much superior, in many instances, to the narrow attachments of self-love and private interest! Popular sedition, party zeal, a devoted obedience to factious leaders; these are some of the most visible, though less laudable effects of this social sympathy in human nature.

The frivolousness of the subject too, we may observe, is not able to detach us entirely from what carries an image of human sentiment and affection.

When a person stutters, and pronounces with difficulty, we even sympathize with this trivial uneasiness, and suffer for him. And it is a rule in criticism, that every combination of syllables or letters, which gives pain to the organs of speech in the recital, appears also, from a species of sympathy, harsh and disagreeable to the ear. Nay, when we run over a book with our eye, we are sensible of such unharmonious composition; because we still imagine, that a person recites it to us, and suffers from the pronunciation of these jarring sounds. So delicate is our sympathy!

Easy and unconstrained postures and motions are always beautiful: An air of health and vigour is agreeable: Cloaths which warm, without burdening the body; which cover, without imprisoning the limbs, are well-fashioned. In every judgment of beauty, the feelings of the person affected enter into consideration, and communicate to the spectator similar touches of pain or pleasure.[1] What wonder, then, if we can pronounce no judgment concerning the character and conduct

---

[1] 'Decentior equus cujus astricta sunt ilia; sed idem velocior. Pulcher aspectu sit athleta, cujus lacertos exercitatio expressit; idem certamini paratior. Nunquam enim species ab utilitate dividitur. Sed hoc quidem discernere modici judicii est.' QUINTILIAN Inst. lib. viii. cap. 3.

I 2

of men, without considering the tendencies of their actions, and the happiness or misery which thence arises to society? What association of ideas would ever operate, were that principle here totally unactive.[1]

If any man from a cold insensibility, or narrow selfishness of temper, is unaffected with the images of human happiness or misery, he must be equally indifferent to the images of vice and virtue: As, on the other hand, it is always found, that a warm concern for the interests of our species is attended with a delicate feeling of all moral distinctions; a strong resentment of injury done to men; a lively approbation of their welfare. In this particular, though great superiority is observable of one man above another; yet none are so entirely indifferent to the interest of their fellow-creatures, as to perceive no distinctions of moral good and evil, in consequence of the different tendencies of actions and principles. How, indeed, can we suppose it possible in any one, who wears a human heart, that if there be subjected to his censure, one character or system of conduct, which is beneficial, and another, which is pernicious, to his species or community, he will not so much as give a cool preference to the former. or ascribe to it the smallest merit or regard? Let us suppose such a person ever so selfish; let private interest have ingrossed ever so much his attention; yet in instances, where that is not concerned, he must unavoidably feel *some* propensity to the good of mankind, and make it an object of choice, if every thing else be equal. Would any man, who is walking along, tread as willingly on another's gouty toes, whom he has no quarrel with, as on the hard flint and pavement? There is here surely a difference in the case. We surely take

---

[1] In proportion to the station which a man possesses, according to the relations in which he is placed; we always expect from him a greater or less degree of good, and when disappointed, blame his inutility; and much more do we blame him, if any ill or prejudice arise from his conduct and behaviour. When the interests of one country interfere with those of another, we estimate the merits of a statesman by the good or ill, which results to his own country from his measures and councils, without regard to the prejudice which he brings on his enemies and rivals. His fellow-citizens are the objects, which lie nearest the eye, while we determine his character. And as nature has implanted in every one a superior affection to his own country, we never expect any regard to distant nations, where a competition arises. Not to mention, that while every man consults the good of his own community, we are sensible, that the general interest of mankind is better promoted, than by loose indeterminate views to the good of a species, whence no beneficial action could ever result, for want of a duly limited object, on which they could exert themselves.

into consideration the happiness and misery of others, in weighing the several motives of action, and incline to the former, where no private regards draw us to seek our own promotion or advantage by the injury of our fellow-creatures. And if the principles of humanity are capable, in many instances, of influencing our actions, they must, at all times, have *some* authority over our sentiments, and give us a general approbation of what is useful to society, and blame of what is dangerous or pernicious. The degrees of these sentiments may be the subject of controversy; but the reality of their existence, one should think, must be admitted, in every theory or system.

A creature, absolutely malicious and spiteful, were there any such in nature, must be worse than indifferent to the images of vice and virtue. All his sentiments must be inverted, and directly opposite to those, which prevail in the human species. Whatever contributes to the good of mankind, as it crosses the constant bent of his wishes and desires, must produce uneasiness and disapprobation; and on the contrary, whatever is the source of disorder and misery in society, must, for the same reason, be regarded with pleasure and complacency. TIMON, who, probably from his affected spleen, more than any inveterate malice, was denominated the man-hater, embraced ALCIBIADES, with great fondness. *Go on my boy! cried he, acquire the confidence of the people: You will one day, I foresee, be the cause of great calamities to them* [1]: Could we admit the two principles of the MANICHEANS, it is an infallible consequence, that their sentiments of human actions, as well as of every thing else, must be totally opposite, and that every instance of justice and humanity, from its necessary tendency, must please the one deity and displease the other. All mankind so far resemble the good principle, that, where interest or revenge or envy perverts not our disposition, we are always inclined, from our natural philanthropy, to give the preference to the happiness of society, and consequently to virtue, above its opposite. Absolute, unprovoked, disinterested malice has never, perhaps, place in any human breast; or if it had, must there pervert all the sentiments of morals, as well as the feelings of humanity. If the cruelty of NERO be allowed entirely voluntary, and not rather the

[1] Plutarch in vita Alc. c. 16.

effect of constant fear and resentment; it is evident, that TIGELLINUS, preferably to SENECA or BURRHUS, must have possessed his steady and uniform approbation.

A statesman or patriot, who serves our own country, in our own time, has always a more passionate regard paid to him, than one whose beneficial influence operated on distant ages or remote nations; where the good, resulting from his generous humanity, being less connected with us, seems more obscure, and affects us with a less lively sympathy. We may own the merit to be equally great, though our sentiments are not raised to an equal height, in both cases. The judgment here corrects the inequalities of our internal emotions and perceptions; in like manner, as it preserves us from error, in the several variations of images, presented to our external senses. The same object, at a double distance, really throws on the eye a picture of but half the bulk; yet we imagine that it appears of the same size in both situations; because we know, that, on our approach to it, its image would expand on the eye, and that the difference consists not in the object itself, but in our position with regard to it. And, indeed, without such a correction of appearances, both in internal and external sentiment, men could never think or talk steadily on any subject; while their fluctuating situations produce a continual variation on objects, and throw them into such different and contrary lights and positions.[1]

The more we converse with mankind, and the greater social intercourse we maintain, the more shall we be familiarized to these general preferences and distinctions, without which our conversation and discourse could scarcely be rendered intelligible to each other. Every man's interest is peculiar to himself, and the aversions and desires, which result from it,

---

[1] For a like reason, the tendencies of actions and characters, not their real accidental consequences, are alone regarded in our determinations or general judgments; though in our real feeling or sentiment, we cannot help paying greater regard to one whose station, joined to virtue, renders him really useful to society, than to one, who exerts the social virtues only in good intentions and benevolent affections. Separating the character from the fortune, by an easy and necessary effort of thought, we pronounce these persons alike, in our esteem, the real

praise. The judgment corrects or endeavours to correct the appearance: But is not able entirely to prevail over sentiment.

Why is this peach-tree said to be better than that other; but because it produces more or better fruit? And would not the same praise be given it, though snails or vermin had destroyed the peaches, before they came to full maturity? In morals too, is not *the tree known by the fruit?* And cannot we easily distinguish between nature and accident, in the one case as well as in the other?

cannot be supposed to affect others in a like degree. General language, therefore, being formed for general use, must be moulded on some more general views, and must affix the epithets of praise or blame, in conformity to sentiments, which arise from the general interests of the community. And if these sentiments, in most men, be not so strong as those, which have a reference to private good; yet still they must make some distinction, even in persons the most depraved and selfish; and must attach the notion of good to a beneficent conduct, and of evil to the contrary. Sympathy, we shall allow, is much fainter than our concern for ourselves, and sympathy with persons remote from us, much fainter than that with persons near and contiguous; but for this very reason, it is necessary for us, in our calm judgments and discourse concerning the characters of men, to neglect all these differences, and render our sentiments more public and social. Besides, that we ourselves often change our situation in this particular, we every day meet with persons, who are in a situation different from us, and who could never converse with us, were we to remain constantly in that position and point of view, which is peculiar to ourselves. The intercourse of sentiments, therefore, in society and conversation, makes us form some general unalterable standard, by which we may approve or disapprove of characters and manners. And though the heart takes not part with those general notions, nor regulates all its love and hatred, by the universal, abstract differences of vice and virtue, without regard to self, or the persons with whom we are more intimately connected; yet have these moral differences a considerable influence, and being sufficient, at least, for discourse, serve all our purposes in company, in the pulpit, on the theatre, and in the schools.[1]

Thus, in whatever light we take this subject, the merit, ascribed to the social virtues, appears still uniform, and arises chiefly from that regard, which the natural sentiment of benevolence engages us to pay to the interests of mankind and society. If we consider the principles of the human make,

---

[1] It is wisely ordained by nature, that private connexions should commonly prevail over universal views and considerations; otherwise our affections and actions would be dissipated and lost, for want of a proper limited object. Thus a small benefit done to ourselves, or our near friends, excites more lively sentiments of love and approbation than a great benefit done to a distant commonwealth: But still we know here, as in all the senses, to correct these inequalities by reflection, and retain a general standard of vice and virtue, founded chiefly on general usefulness.

such as they appear to daily experience and observation, we must, *à priori*, conclude it impossible for such a creature as man to be totally indifferent to the well or ill-being of his fellow-creatures, and not readily, of himself, to pronounce, where nothing gives him any particular byass, that what promotes their happiness is good, what tends to their misery is evil, without any farther regard or consideration. Here then are the faint rudiments, at least, or out-lines, of a *general* distinction between actions; and in proportion as the humanity of the person is supposed to encrease, his connexion with those who are injured or benefited, and his lively conception of their misery or happiness; his consequent censure or approbation acquires proportionable vigour. There is no necessity, that a generous action, barely mentioned in an old history or remote gazette, should communicate any strong feelings of applause and admiration. Virtue, placed at such a distance, is liked a fixed star, which, though to the eye of reason, it may appear as luminous as the sun in his meridian, is so infinitely removed, as to affect the senses, neither with light nor heat. Bring this virtue nearer, by our acquaintance or connexion with the persons, or even by an eloquent recital of the case: our hearts are immediately caught, our sympathy enlivened, and our cool approbation converted into the warmest sentiments of friendship and regard. These seem necessary and infallible consequences of the general principles of human nature, as discovered in common life and practice.

Again: reverse these views and reasonings: Consider the matter *à posteriori*; and weighing the consequences, enquire if the merit of social virtue be not, in a great measure, derived from the feelings of humanity, with which it affects the spectators. It appears to be matter of fact, that the circumstance of *utility*, in all subjects, is a source of praise and approbation: That it is constantly appealed to in all moral decisions concerning the merit and demerit of actions: That it is the *sole* source of that high regard paid to justice, fidelity, honour, allegiance, and chastity: That it is inseparable from all the other social virtues, humanity, generosity, charity, affability, lenity, mercy, and moderation: And, in a word, that it is a foundation of the chief part of morals, which has a reference to mankind and our fellow-creatures.

It appears also, that, in our general approbation of characters and manners, the useful tendency of the social virtues

moves us not by any regards to self-interest, but has an influence much more universal and extensive. It appears, that
a tendency to public good, and to the promoting of peace,
harmony, and order in society, does always, by affecting
the benevolent principles of our frame, engage us on the
side of the social virtues. And it appears, as an additional
confirmation, that these principles of humanity and sympathy
enter so deeply into all our sentiments, and have so powerful
an influence, as may enable them to excite the strongest
censure and applause. The present theory is the simple
result of all these inferences, each of which seems founded
on uniform experience and observation.

Were it doubtful, whether there were any such principle
in our nature as humanity or a concern for others, yet when
we see, in numberless instances, that whatever has a tendency to promote the interests of society, is so highly
approved of, we ought thence to learn the force of the benevolent principle : since it is impossible for any thing to please
as means to an end, where the end is totally indifferent. On
the other hand, were it doubtful, whether there were, implanted in our nature, any general principle of moral blame
and approbation, yet when we see, in numberless instances,
the influence of humanity, we ought thence to conclude, that
it is impossible, but that every thing, which promotes the
interest of society, must communicate pleasure, and what
is pernicious give uneasiness. But when these different
reflections and observations concur in establishing the same
conclusion, must they not bestow an undisputed evidence
upon it ?

It is however hoped, that the progress of this argument
will bring a farther confirmation of the present theory, by
showing the rise of other sentiments of esteem and regard
from the same or like principles.

SECTION VI.—*Of Qualities Useful to Ourselves.*

PART I.[1]

IT seems evident, that where a quality or habit is subjected
to our examination, if it appear, in any respect, prejudicial
to the person possessed of it, or such as incapacitates him

---

[1] [In Editions G to N this Section   Part I, which subsequently appeared as
was introduced by paragraphs, forming   Appendix IV, Of some Verbal Disputes.

for business and action, it is instantly blamed, and ranked among his faults and imperfections. Indolence, negligence, want of order and method, obstinacy, fickleness, rashness, credulity; these qualities were never esteemed by any one indifferent to a character; much less, extolled as accomplishments or virtues. The prejudice, resulting from them, immediately strikes our eye, and gives us the sentiment of pain and disapprobation.

No quality, it is allowed, is absolutely either blameable or praise-worthy. It is all according to its degree. A due medium, say the PERIPATETICS, is the characteristic of virtue. But this medium is chiefly determined by utility. A proper celerity, for instance, and dispatch in business, is commendable. When defective, no progress is ever made in the execution of any purpose: When excessive, it engages us in precipitate and ill-concerted measures and enterprises: By such reasonings, we fix the proper and commendable mediocrity in all moral and prudential disquisitions; and never lose view of the advantages, which result from any character or habit.

Now as these advantages are enjoyed by the person possessed of the character, it can never be *self-love* which renders the prospect of them agreeable to us, the spectators, and prompts our esteem and approbation. No force of imagination can convert us into another person, and make us fancy, that we, being that person, reap benefit from those valuable qualities, which belong to him. Or if it did, no celerity of imagination could immediately transport us back, into ourselves, and make us love and esteem the person, as different from us. Views and sentiments, so opposite to known truth, and to each other, could never have place, at the same time, in the same person. All suspicion, therefore, of selfish regards, is here totally excluded. It is a quite different principle, which actuates our bosom, and interests us in the felicity of the person whom we contemplate. Where his natural talents and acquired abilities give us the prospect of elevation, advancement, a figure in life, prosperous success, a steady command over fortune, and the execution of great or advantageous undertakings; we are struck with such agreeable images, and feel a complacency and regard immediately arise towards him. The ideas of happiness, joy, triumph, prosperity, are connected with every circumstance of his character, and diffuse over our minds a pleasing sentiment of sympathy and humanity.[1]

Let us suppose a person originally framed so as to have no manner of concern for his fellow-creatures, but to regard the happiness and misery of all sensible beings with greater indifference than even two contiguous shades of the same colour. Let us suppose, if the prosperity of nations were laid on the one hand, and their ruin on the other, and he were desired to choose; that he would stand, like the schoolman's ass, irresolute and undetermined, between equal motives; or rather, like the same ass between two pieces of wood or marble, without any inclination or propensity to either side. The consequence, I believe, must be allowed just, that such a person, being absolutely unconcerned, either for the public good of a community or the private utility of others, would look on every quality, however pernicious, or however beneficial, to society, or to its possessor, with the same indifference as on the most common and uninteresting object.

But if, instead of this fancied monster, we suppose a *man* to form a judgment or determination in the case, there is to him a plain foundation of preference, where every thing else is equal; and however cool his choice may be, if his heart be selfish, or if the persons interested be remote from him; there must still be a choice or distinction between what is useful, and what is pernicious. Now this distinction is the same in all its parts, with the *moral distinction*, whose foundation has been so often, and so much in vain, enquired after. The same endowments of the mind, in every circumstance, are agreeable to the sentiment of morals and to that of humanity; the same temper is susceptible of high degrees

[1] One may venture to affirm, that there is no human creature, to whom the appearance of happiness (where envy or revenge has no place) does not give pleasure, that of misery, uneasiness. This seems inseparable from our make and constitution. But they are only the more generous minds, that are thence prompted to seek zealously the good of others, and to have a real passion for their welfare. With men of narrow and ungenerous spirits, this sympathy goes not beyond a slight feeling of the imagination, which serves only to excite sentiments of complacency or censure, and makes them apply to the object either honourable or dishonourable appellations. A griping miser, for instance, praises extremely *industry* and *frugality* even in others, and sets them, in his estimation, above all the other virtues. He knows the good that results from them, and feels that species of happiness with a more lively sympathy, than any other you could represent to him; though perhaps he would not part with a shilling to make the fortune of the industrious man, whom he praises so highly.

of the one sentiment and of the other ; and the same alteration in the objects, by their nearer approach or by connexions,
enlivens the one and the other.   By all the rules of philosophy, therefore, we must conclude, that these sentiments
are originally the same ; since, in each particular, even the
most minute, they are governed by the same laws, and are
moved by the same objects.

Why do philosophers infer, with the greatest certainty,
that the moon is kept in its orbit by the same force of gravity,
that makes bodies fall near the surface of the earth, but
because these effects are, upon computation, found similar
and equal?   And must not this argument bring as strong
conviction, in moral as in natural disquisitions?

To prove, by any long detail, that all the qualities, useful
to the possessor, are approved of, and the contrary censured,
would be superfluous.   The least reflection on what is every
day experienced in life, will be sufficient.   We shall only
mention a few instances, in order to remove, if possible, all
doubt and hesitation.

The quality, the most necessary for the execution of any
useful enterprise, is DISCRETION; by which we carry on
a safe intercourse with others, give due attention to our own
and to their character, weigh each circumstance of the
business which we undertake, and employ the surest and
safest means for the attainment of any end or purpose.   To
a CROMWELL, perhaps or a DE RETZ, discretion may appear
an alderman-like virtue, as Dr. SWIFT calls it ; and being
incompatible with those vast designs, to which their courage
and ambition prompted them, it might really, in them, be a
fault or imperfection.   But in the conduct of ordinary life,
no virtue is more requisite, not only to obtain success, but to
avoid the most fatal miscarriages and disappointments.   The
greatest parts without it, as observed by an elegant writer,
may be fatal to their owner; as POLYPHEMUS, deprived of
his eye, was only the more exposed, on account of his enormous strength and stature.

The best character, indeed, were it not rather too perfect
for human nature, is that which is not swayed by temper of
any kind ; but alternately employs enterprise and caution,
as each is *useful* to the particular purpose intended.   Such
is the excellence which ST. EVREMOND ascribes to mareschal
TURENNE, who displayed every campaign, as he grew older,

more temerity in his military enterprises; and being now, from long experience, perfectly acquainted with every incident in war, he advanced with greater firmness and security, in a road so well known to him. Fabius, says MACHIAVEL, was cautious; Scipio enterprising: And both succeeded, because the situation of the ROMAN affairs, during the command of each, was peculiarly adapted to his genius; but both would have failed, had these situations been reversed. He is happy, whose circumstances suit his temper; but he is more excellent, who can suit his temper to any circumstances.

What need is there to display the praises of INDUSTRY, and to extol its advantages, in the acquisition of power and riches, or in raising what we call a *fortune* in the world? The tortoise, according to the fable, by his perseverance, gained the race of the hare, though possessed of much superior swiftness. A man's time, when well husbanded, is like a cultivated field, of which a few acres produce more of what is useful to life, than extensive provinces, even of the richest soil, when over-run with weeds and brambles.

But all prospect of success in life, or even of tolerable subsistence, must fail, where a reasonable FRUGALITY is wanting. The heap, instead of encreasing, diminishes daily, and leaves its possessor so much more unhappy, as, not having been able to confine his expences to a large revenue, he will still less be able to live contentedly on a small one. The souls of men, according to PLATO[1], inflamed with impure appetites, and losing the body, which alone afforded means of satisfaction, hover about the earth, and haunt the places where their bodies are deposited; possessed with a longing desire to recover the lost organs of sensation. So may we see worthless prodigals, having consumed their fortune in wild debauches, thrusting themselves into every plentiful table, and every party of pleasure, hated even by the vicious, and despised even by fools.

The one extreme of frugality is *avarice*, which, as it both deprives a man of all use of his riches, and checks hospitality and every social enjoyment, is justly censured on a double account. *Prodigality*, the other extreme, is commonly more hurtful to a man himself; and each of these extremes is blamed above the other, according to the temper of the person

[1] Phædo. 81.

who censures, and according to his greater or less sensibility to pleasure, either social or sensual.

¹QUALITIES often derive their merit from complicated sources. *Honesty, fidelity, truth,* are praised for their immediate tendency to promote the interests of society; but after those virtues are once established upon this foundation, they are also considered as advantageous to the person himself, and as the source of that trust and confidence, which can alone give a man any consideration in life. One becomes contemptible, no less than odious, when he forgets the duty, which, in this particular, he owes to himself as well as to society.

Perhaps, this consideration is one *chief* source of the high blame, which is thrown on any instance of failure among women in point of *chastity.* The greatest regard, which can be acquired by that sex, is derived from their fidelity; and a woman becomes cheap and vulgar, loses her rank, and is exposed to every insult, who is deficient in this particular. The smallest failure is here sufficient to blast her character. A female has so many opportunities of secretly indulging these appetites, that nothing can give us security but her absolute modesty and reserve; and where a breach is once made, it can scarcely ever be fully repaired. If a man behave with cowardice on one occasion, a contrary conduct reinstates him in his character. But by what action can a woman, whose behaviour has once been dissolute, be able to assure us, that she has formed better resolutions, and has self-command enough to carry them into execution?

All men, it is allowed, are equally desirous of happiness; but few are successful in the pursuit: One considerable cause is the want of STRENGTH of MIND, which might enable them to resist the temptation of present ease or pleasure, and carry them forward in the search of more distant profit and enjoyment. Our affections, on a general prospect of their objects, form certain rules of conduct, and certain measures of preference of one above another: And these decisions, though really the result of our calm passions and propensities, (for what else can pronounce any object eligible or the contrary?) are yet said, by a natural abuse of terms, to be the determinations of pure *reason* and reflection. But when some of these objects approach nearer to us, or acquire the advan-

¹ [This paragraph and the next were added in Edition N.]

tages of favourable lights and positions, which catch the heart or imagination: our general resolutions are frequently confounded, a small enjoyment preferred, and lasting shame and sorrow entailed upon us. And however poets may employ their wit and eloquence, in celebrating present pleasure, and rejecting all distant views to fame, health, or fortune; it is obvious, that this practice is the source of all dissoluteness and disorder, repentance and misery. A man of a strong and determined temper adheres tenaciously to his general resolutions, and is neither seduced by the allurements of pleasure, nor terrified by the menaces of pain; but keeps still in view those distant pursuits, by which he, at once, ensures his happiness and his honour.

Self-satisfaction, at least in some degree, is an advantage, which equally attends the FOOL and the WISE MAN: But it is the only one; nor is there any other circumstance in the conduct of life, where they are upon an equal footing. Business, books, conversation; for all of these, a fool is totally incapacitated, and except condemned by his station to the coarsest drudgery, remains a *useless* burthen upon the earth. Accordingly, it is found, that men are extremely jealous of their character in this particular; and many instances are seen of profligacy and treachery, the most avowed and unreserved; none of bearing patiently the imputation of ignorance and stupidity. DICAEARCHUS, the MACEDONIAN general, who, as POLYBIUS tells us [1], openly erected one altar to impiety, another to injustice, in order to bid defiance to mankind; even he, I am well assured, would have started at the epithet of *fool*, and have meditated revenge for so injurious an appellation. Except the affection of parents, the strongest and most indissoluble bond in nature, no connexion has strength sufficient to support the disgust arising from this character. Love itself, which can subsist under treachery, ingratitude, malice, and infidelity, is immediately extinguished by it, when perceived and acknowledged: nor are deformity and old age more fatal to the dominion of that passion. So dreadful are the ideas of an utter incapacity for any purpose or undertaking, and of continued error and misconduct in life!

When it is asked, whether a quick or a slow apprehension be most valuable? Whether one, that, at first view, penetrates

* Lib. xvii. cap. 35.

far into a subject, but can perform nothing upon study; or a contrary character, which must work out every thing by dint of application? Whether a clear head or a copious invention? Whether a profound genius or a sure judgment? In short, what character, or peculiar turn of understanding is more excellent than another? It is evident, that we can answer none of these questions. without considering which of those qualities capacitates a man best for the world, and carries him farthest in any undertaking.

If refined sense and exalted sense be not so *useful* as common sense, their rarity, their novelty, and the nobleness of their objects make some compensation, and render them the admiration of mankind : As gold, though less serviceable than iron, acquires, from its scarcity, a value, which is much superior.

The defects of judgment can be supplied by no art or invention; but those of MEMORY frequently may, both in business and in study, by method and industry, and by diligence in committing every thing to writing; and we scarcely ever hear a short memory given as a reason for a man's failure in any undertaking. But in ancient times, when no man could make a figure without the talent of speaking, and when the audience were too delicate to bear such crude, undigested harangues as our extemporary orators offer to public assemblies; the faculty of memory was then of the utmost consequence, and was accordingly much more valued than at present. Scarce any great genius is mentioned in antiquity, who is not celebrated for this talent; and CICERO enumerates it among the other sublime qualities of CÆSAR himself.[1]

Particular customs and manners alter the usefulness of qualities : They also alter their merit. Particular situations and accidents have, in some degree, the same influence. He will always be more esteemed, who possesses those talents and accomplishments, which suit his station and profession, than he whom fortune has misplaced in the part which she has assigned him. The private or selfish virtues are, in this respect, more arbitrary than the public and social. In other respects, they are, perhaps, less liable to doubt and controversy.

Fuit in illo ingenium, ratio, memoria, literæ, cura, cogitatio, diligentia, &c. PHILIP. 2. 45.

In this kingdom, such continued ostentation, of late years, has prevailed among men in *active* life with regard to *public spirit*, and among those in *speculative* with regard to *benevolence*; and so many false pretensions to each have been, no doubt, detected, that men of the world are apt, without any bad intention, to discover a sullen incredulity on the head of those moral endowments, and even sometimes absolutely to deny their existence and reality. In like manner, I find, that, of old, the perpetual cant of the *Stoics* and *Cynics* concerning *virtue*, their magnificent professions and slender performances, bred a disgust in mankind; and LUCIAN, who, though licentious with regard to pleasure, is yet, in other respects, a very moral writer, cannot, sometimes, talk of virtue, so much boasted, without betraying symptoms of spleen and irony.[1] But surely this peevish delicacy, whenceever it arises, can never be carried so far as to make us deny the existence of every species of merit, and all distinction of manners and behaviour. Besides *discretion, caution, enterprise, industry, assiduity, frugality, economy, good-sense, prudence, discernment*; besides these endowments, I say, whose very names force an avowal of their merit, there are many others, to which the most determined scepticism cannot, for a moment, refuse the tribute of praise and approbation. *Temperance, sobriety, patience, constancy, perseverance, forethought, considerateness, secrecy, order, insinuation, address, presence of mind, quickness of conception, facility of expression*; these, and a thousand more of the same kind, no man will ever deny to be excellencies and perfections. As their merit consists in their tendency to serve the person, possessed of them, without any magnificent claim to public and social desert, we are the less jealous of their pretensions, and readily admit them into the catalogue of laudable qualities. We are not sensible, that, by this concession, we have paved the way for all the other moral excellencies, and cannot confidently hesitate any longer, with regard to disinterested benevolence, patriotism, and humanity.

It seems, indeed, certain, that first appearances are here, as usual, extremely deceitful, and that it is more difficult, in a

[1] Ἀρετήν τινα καὶ ἀσώματα καὶ λήρους μεγάλῃ τῇ φωνῇ ξυνειρόντων. Luc. Timon. 9. Again. Καὶ συναγάγοντες (οἱ φιλόσοφοι) εὐεξαπάτητα μειράκια τήν τε πολυθρύλλητον ἀρετὴν τραγῳδοῦσι. Ica-

ΡΟ-ΜΕΝ. 30. In another place. Ἡ ποῦ γάρ ἐστιν ἡ πολυθρύλλητος ἀρετή, καὶ φύσις, καὶ εἱμαρμένη, καὶ τύχη, ἀνυπόστατα καὶ κενὰ πραγμάτων ὀνόματα. Deor. Concil. 13.

speculative way, to resolve into self-love the merit, which we ascribe to the selfish virtues above-mentioned, than that even of the social virtues, justice and beneficence. For this latter purpose, we need but say, that whatever conduct promotes the good of the community is loved, praised, and esteemed by the community, on account of that utility and interest, of which every one partakes: And though this affection and regard be, in reality, gratitude, not self-love, yet a distinction, even of this obvious nature, may not readily be made by superficial reasoners; and there is room, at least, to support the cavil and dispute for a moment. But as qualities, which tend only to the utility of their possessor without any reference to us, or to the community, are yet esteemed and valued; by what theory or system can we account for this sentiment from self-love, or deduce it from that favourite origin? There seems here a necessity for confessing that the happiness and misery of others are not spectacles entirely indifferent to us; but that the view of the former, whether in its causes or effects, like sun-shine or the prospect of well-cultivated plains, (to carry our pretensions no higher) communicates a secret joy and satisfaction; the appearance of the latter, like a lowering cloud or barren landskip, throws a melancholy damp over the imagination. And this concession being once made, the difficulty is over; and a natural unforced interpretation of the phænomena of human life will afterwards, we may hope, prevail among all speculative enquirers.

PART II.[1]

It may not be improper, in this place, to examine the influence of bodily endowments, and of the goods of fortune, over our sentiments of regard and esteem, and to consider whether these phænomena fortify or weaken the present theory. [2]It will naturally be expected, that the beauty of the body, as is supposed by all ancient moralists, will be similar, in some respects, to that of the mind; and that every kind of esteem, which is paid to a man, will have something similar in its origin, whether it arise from his mental endowments, or from the situation of his exterior circumstances.

It is evident, that one considerable source of *beauty* in all

---

[1] [Part 3 in Editions G to N.]   Edition N, which, however, stops at
[2] [This sentence was added in   'origin.']

animals is the advantage, which they reap from the particular structure of their limbs and members, suitably to the particular manner of life, to which they are by nature destined. The just proportions of a horse, described by XENOPHON and VIRGIL, are the same, that are received at this day by our modern jockeys; because the foundation of them is the same, namely, experience of what is detrimental or useful in the animal.

Broad shoulders, a lank belly, firm joints, taper legs; all these are beautiful in our species, because signs of force and vigour. Ideas of utility and its contrary, though they do not entirely determine what is handsome or deformed, are evidently the source of a considerable part of approbation or dislike.

In ancient times, bodily strength and dexterity, being of greater *use* and importance in war, was also much more esteemed and valued, than at present. Not to insist on HOMER and the poets, we may observe, that historians scruple not to mention *force of body* among the other accomplishments even of EPAMINONDAS, whom they acknowledge to be the greatest hero, statesman, and general of all the GREEKS.[1] A like praise is given to POMPEY, one of the greatest of the ROMANS.[2] This instance is similar to what we observed above, with regard to memory.

What derision and contempt, with both sexes, attend *impotence*; while the unhappy object is regarded as one deprived of so capital a pleasure in life, and at the same time, as disabled from communicating it to others. *Barrenness* in women, being also a species of *inutility*, is a reproach, but not in the same degree: Of which the reason is very obvious, according to the present theory.[3]

[1] DIODORUS SICULUS, lib. 15, 88. It may not be improper to give the character of EPAMINONDAS, as drawn by the historian, in order to show the ideas of perfect merit, which prevailed in those ages. In other illustrious men, says he, you will observe, that each possessed some one shining quality, which was the foundation of his fame. In EPAMINONDAS all the *virtues* are found united; force of body, eloquence of expression, vigour of mind, contempt of riches, gentleness of disposition, and *what is chiefly to be regarded*, courage and conduct in war.

[2] *Cum alacribus, saltu; cum velocibus,*

cursu; cum validis recte certabat. SALLUST apud VEGET.—De Re Mil. 19.

[3] [Edition G adds in a note: To the same Purpose, we may observe a Phænomenon, which might appear somewhat trivial and ludicrous; if any Thing could be trivial, which portray'd Conclusions of such Importance; or ludicrous, which was employ'd in a philosophical Reasoning. 'Tis a general Remark, that those we call good *Fellows* Men, who have either signaliz'd themselves by their amorous Exploits, or whose Make of Body or other symptoms promise any extraordinary Vigour of that kind, are well receiv'd by the fair sex, and

Q 2

There is no rule in painting or statuary more indispensible than that of balancing the figures, and placing them with the greatest exactness on their proper center of gravity. A figure, which is not justly balanced, is ugly; because it conveys the disagreeable ideas of fall, harm, and pain[1].

A disposition or turn of mind, which qualifies a man to rise in the world, and advance his fortune, is entitled to esteem and regard, as has already been explained. It may, therefore, naturally be supposed, that the actual possession of riches and authority will have a considerable influence over these sentiments.

Let us examine any hypothesis, by which we can account for the regard paid to the rich and powerful: We shall find none satisfactory, but that which derives it from the enjoyment communicated to the spectator by the images of prosperity, happiness, ease, plenty, authority, and the gratification of every appetite. Self-love, for instance, which some affect so much to consider as the source of every sentiment, is plainly insufficient for this purpose. Where no good-will or friendship appears, it is difficult to conceive on what we can found our hope of advantage from the riches of others; though we naturally respect the rich, even before they discover any such favourable disposition towards us.

We are affected with the same sentiments, when we lie so much out of the sphere of their activity, that they cannot even be supposed to possess the power of serving us. A prisoner of war, in all civilised nations, is treated with a regard suited to his condition; and riches, it is evident, go far towards fixing the condition of any person. If birth and

naturally engage the Affections even of those whose Virtue or Situation prevents any Design of ever giving Employment to those Talents. The Imagination is pleas'd with these Conceptions, and entering with Satisfaction into the Ideas of so favourite an Enjoyment, feels a Complacency and Good-will towards the Person. A like Principle operating more extensively, is the general Source of more Affection and Approbation.]

[1] All men are equally liable to pain and disease and sickness; and may again recover health and ease. These circumstances, as they make no distinction between one man and another, are no source of pride or humility, regard or contempt. But comparing our own species to superior ones, it is a very mortifying consideration, that we should all be so liable to diseases and infirmities; and divines accordingly employ this topic, in order to depress self-conceit and vanity. They would have more success, if the common bent of our thoughts were not perpetually turned to compare ourselves with others. The infirmities of old age are mortifying; because a comparison with the young may take place. The king's evil is industriously concealed, because it affects others, and is often transmitted to posterity. The case is nearly the same with such diseases as convey any nauseous or frightful images; the epilepsy, for instance, ulcers, sores, scabs, etc.

quality enter for a share, this still affords us an argument to our present purpose. For what is it we call a man of birth, but one who is descended from a long succession of rich and powerful ancestors, and who acquires our esteem by his connexion with persons whom we esteem? His ancestors, therefore, though dead, are respected, in some measure, on account of their riches; and consequently, without any kind of expectation.

But not to go so far as prisoners of war or the dead, to find instances of this disinterested regard of riches; we may only observe, with a little attention, those phænomena, which occur in common life and conversation. A man, who is himself, we shall suppose, of a competent fortune, and of no profession, being introduced to a company of strangers, naturally treats them with different degrees of respect, as he is informed of their different fortunes and conditions; though it is impossible that he can so suddenly propose, and perhaps he would not accept of, any pecuniary advantage from them. A traveller is always admitted into company, and meets with civility, in proportion as his train and equipage speak him a man of great or moderate fortune. In short, the different ranks of men are, in a great measure, regulated by riches; and that with regard to superiors as well as inferiors, strangers as well as acquaintance.

What remains, therefore, but to conclude, that, as riches are desired for ourselves only as the means of gratifying our appetites, either at present or in some imaginary future period; they beget esteem in others merely from their having that influence. This indeed is their very nature or essence: They have a direct reference to the commodities, conveniencies, and pleasures of life: The bill of a banker, who is broke, or gold in a desart island, would otherwise be full as valuable. When we approach a man, who is, as we say, at his ease, we are presented with the pleasing ideas of plenty, satisfaction, cleanliness, warmth; a chearful house, elegant furniture, ready service, and whatever is desirable in meat, drink, or apparel. On the contrary, when a poor man appears, the disagreeable images of want, penury, hard labour, dirty furniture, coarse or ragged cloaths, nauseous meat and distasteful liquor, immediately strike our fancy. What else do we mean by saying that one is rich, the other poor? And as regard or contempt is the natural consequence of those different situations in life; it is easily seen what additional light and evidence this throws on our preceding theory, with regard to all moral distinctions.[1]

A man, who has cured himself of all ridiculous prepossessions, and is fully, sincerely, and steadily convinced, from experience as well as philosophy, that the difference of fortune makes less difference in happiness than is vulgarly imagined; such a one does not measure out degrees of esteem according to the rent-rolls of his acquaintance. He may, indeed, externally pay a superior deference to the great lord above the vassal; because riches are the most convenient, being the most fixed and determinate, source of distinction: But his internal sentiments are more regulated by the personal characters of men, than by the accidental and capricious favours of fortune.

In most countries of EUROPE, family, that is, hereditary riches, marked with titles and symbols from the sovereign, is the chief source of distinction. In ENGLAND, more regard is paid to present opulence and plenty. Each practice has its advantages and disadvantages. Where birth is respected, unactive, spiritless minds remain in haughty indolence, and dream of nothing but pedigrees and genealogies: The generous and ambitious seek honour and authority and reputation and favour. Where riches are the chief idol, corruption, venality, rapine prevail: Arts, manufactures, commerce, agriculture flourish. The former prejudice, being favourable to military virtue, is more suited to monarchies. The latter, being the chief spur to industry, agrees better with a republican government. And we accordingly find, that each of these forms of government, by varying the *utility* of those customs, has commonly a proportionable effect on the sentiments of mankind.

---

[1] There is something extraordinary, and seemingly unaccountable in the operation of our passions, when we consider the fortune and situation of others. Very often another's advancement and prosperity produces envy, which has a strong mixture of hatred, and arises chiefly from the comparison of ourselves with the person. At the very same time, or at least in very short intervals, we may feel the passion of respect, which is a species of affection or good-will, with a mixture of humility. On the other hand, the misfortunes of our fellows often cause pity, which has in it a strong mixture of good-will. This sentiment of pity is nearly allied to contempt, which is a species of dislike, with a mixture of pride. I only point out these phenomena, as a subject of speculation to such as are curious with regard to moral enquiries. It is sufficient for the present purpose to observe in general, that power and riches commonly cause respect, poverty and meanness contempt, though particular views and incidents may sometimes raise the passions of envy and of pity.

SECT. VII. – *Of Qualities immediately agreeable to Ourselves.*

WHOEVER has passed an evening with serious melancholy people, and has observed how suddenly the conversation was animated, and what sprightliness diffused itself over the countenance, discourse, and behaviour of every one, on the accession of a good-humoured, lively companion; such a one will easily allow, that CHEARFULNESS carries great merit with it, and naturally conciliates the good-will of mankind. No quality, indeed, more readily communicates itself to all around; because no one has a greater propensity to display itself, in jovial talk and pleasant entertainment. The flame spreads through the whole circle; and the most sullen and morose are often caught by it. That the melancholy hate the merry, even though HORACE says it, I have some difficulty to allow: because I have always observed, that, where the jollity is moderate and decent, serious people are so much the more delighted, as it dissipates the gloom, with which they are commonly oppressed; and gives them an unusual enjoyment.

From this influence of chearfulness, both to communicate itself, and to engage approbation, we may perceive, that there is another set of mental qualities, which, without any utility or any tendency to farther good, either of the community or of the possessor, diffuse a satisfaction on the beholders, and procure friendship and regard. Their immediate sensation, to the person possessed of them, is agreeable: Others enter into the same humour, and catch the sentiment, by a contagion or natural sympathy: And as we cannot forbear loving whatever pleases, a kindly emotion arises towards the person, who communicates so much satisfaction. He is a more animating spectacle: His presence diffuses over us more serene complacency and enjoyment: Our imagination, entering into his feelings and disposition, is affected in a more agreeable manner, than if a melancholy, dejected, sullen, anxious temper were presented to us. Hence the affection and approbation, which attend the former: The aversion and disgust, with which we regard the latter.[1]

---

[1] There is no man, who, on particular occasions, is not affected with all the disagreeable passions, fear, anger, dejection, grief, melancholy, anxiety.

Few men would envy the character, which CÆSAR gives of
CASSIUS.

> He loves no play,
> As thou do'st, ANTHONY: He hears no music:
> Seldom he smiles; and smiles in such a sort,
> As if he mock'd himself, and scorn'd his spirit
> That could be mov'd to smile at any thing.

Not only such men, as CÆSAR adds, are commonly *dangerous*,
but also, having little enjoyment within themselves, they can
never become agreeable to others, or contribute to social
entertainment. In all polite nations and ages, a relish for
pleasure, if accompanied with temperance and decency, is
esteemed a considerable merit, even in the greatest men;
and becomes still more requisite in those of inferior rank
and character. It is an agreeable representation, which a
FRENCH writer gives of the situation of his own mind in this
particular, *Virtue I love*, says he, *without austerity: Pleasure,
without effeminacy: And life, without fearing its end.*[1]

Who is not struck with any signal instance of GREAT-
NESS of MIND or Dignity of Character; with elevation of
sentiment, disdain of slavery, and with that noble pride and
spirit, which arises from conscious virtue? The sublime,
says LONGINUS, is often nothing but the echo or image of
magnanimity; and where this quality appears in any one,
even though a syllable be not uttered, it excites our applause
and admiration; as may be observed of the famous silence
of AJAX in the ODYSSEY, which expresses more noble disdain
and resolute indignation, than any language can convey.[2]

Were I ALEXANDER, said PARMENIO, *I would accept of these
offers made by* DARIUS. *So would I too*, replied ALEXANDER,
were I PARMENIO. This saying is admirable, says LONGINUS,
from a like principle.[3]

Go! cries the same hero to his soldiers, when they refused
to follow him to the INDIES, *go tell your countrymen, that
you left* ALEXANDER *compleating the conquest of the world.*
'ALEXANDER,' said the Prince of CONDÉ, who always

&c. But these, so far as they are
natural, and universal, make no difference between one man and another, and
can never be the object of blame. It
is only when the disposition gives a
propensity to any of these disagreeable
passions, that they disfigure the character, and by giving uneasiness, con-

vey the sentiment of disapprobation to
the spectator.

[1] 'J'aime la vertu, sans rudesse;
    J'aime le plaisir, sans molesse;
    J'aime la vie, & n'en crains point
la fin.' ST. ÉVREMOND.
[2] Cap. 9.
[3] Idem.

admired this passage, 'abandoned by his soldiers, among
'Barbarians, not yet fully subdued, felt in himself such a
'dignity and right of empire, that he could not believe it
'possible, that any one would refuse to obey him. Whether
'in EUROPE or in ASIA, among GREEKS or PERSIANS, all was
'indifferent to him: Wherever he found men, he fancied he
'should find subjects.'

The 'confident of MEDEA in the tragedy recommends
caution and submission; and enumerating all the distresses
of that unfortunate heroine, asks her, what she has to support her against her numerous and implacable enemies.
Myself, replies she; *Myself, I say, and it is enough.* BOILEAU
justly recommends this passage as an instance of true
sublime.[2]

When PHOCION, the modest, the gentle PHOCION, was led
to execution, he turned to one of his fellow-sufferers, who
was lamenting his own hard fate. *Is it not glory enough for
you*, says he, *that you die with* PHOCION? [3]

Place in opposition the picture, which TACITUS draws of
VITELLIUS, fallen from empire, prolonging his ignominy
from a wretched love of life, delivered over to the merciless
rabble; tossed, buffeted, and kicked about; constrained, by
their holding a poinard under his chin, to raise his head,
and expose himself to every contumely. What abject infamy! What low humiliation! Yet even here, says the
historian, he discovered some symptoms of a mind not
wholly degenerate. To a tribune, who insulted him, he
replied, *I am still your emperor.*[4]

We never excuse the absolute want of spirit and dignity
of character, or a proper sense of what is due to one's self,
in society and the common intercourse of life. This vice
constitutes what we properly call *meanness*; when a man can
submit to the basest slavery, in order to gain his ends; fawn
upon those who abuse him; and degrade himself by intimacies and familiarities with undeserving inferiors. A certain
degree of generous pride or self-value is so requisite, that

---

[1] ['Confidant' in several Editions.]
[2] Reflexion 10 sur Longin.
[3] PLUTARCH in PHOC. 36.
[4] Tacit. hist. lib. iii. 84. The author
entering upon the narration, says,
*Laniata veste, foedum spectaculum duce-
batur, multis increpantibus, nullo inla-
crimante: deformitas exitus misericor-*
diam abstulerat. To enter thoroughly
into this method of thinking, we must
make allowance for the ancient maxims,
that no one ought to prolong his life
after it became dishonourable; but, as
he had always a right to dispose of it,
it then became a duty to part with it.

the absence of it in the mind displeases, after the same manner as the want of a nose, eye, or any of the most material features of the face or members of the body.[1]

The utility of COURAGE, both to the public and to the person possessed of it, is an obvious foundation of merit: But to any one who duly considers of the matter, it will appear, that this quality has a peculiar lustre, which it derives wholly from itself, and from that noble elevation inseparable from it. Its figure, drawn by painters and by poets, displays, in each feature, a sublimity and daring confidence: which catches the eye, engages the affections, and diffuses, by sympathy, a like sublimity of sentiment over every spectator.

Under what shining colours does DEMOSTHENES[2] represent PHILIP; where the orator apologizes for his own administration, and justifies that pertinacious love of liberty, with which he had inspired the ATHENIANS. 'I beheld PHILIP,' says he, 'he with whom was your contest, resolutely, while ' in pursuit of empire and dominion, exposing himself to ' every wound; his eye gored, his neck wrested, his arm, ' his thigh pierced, whatever part of his body fortune should ' seize on, that cheerfully relinquishing: provided that, with ' what remained, he might live in honour and renown. And ' shall it be said, that he, born in PELLA, a place heretofore ' mean and ignoble, should be inspired with so high an ' ambition and thirst of fame: While you, ATHENIANS, &c.' These praises excite the most lively admiration; but the views presented by the orator, carry us not, we see, beyond the hero himself, nor ever regard the future advantageous consequences of his valour.

The martial temper of the ROMANS, inflamed by continual wars, had raised their esteem of courage so high, that, in their language, it was called *virtue*, by way of excellence and of distinction from all other moral qualities. *The* SUEVI,

[1] The absence of a virtue may often be a vice; and that of the highest kind; as in the instance of ingratitude, as well as meanness. Where we expect a beauty, the disappointment gives an uneasy sensation, and produces a real deformity. An abjectness of character, likewise, is disgustful and contemptible in another view. Where a man has no sense of value in himself, we are not likely to have any higher esteem of him. And if the same person, who crouches to his superiors, is insolent to his inferiors (as often happens), this contrariety of behaviour, instead of correcting the former vice, aggravates it extremely by the addition of a vice still more odious. See sect. 8. Of Qualities immediately agreeable to Others.

[2] Pro corona, 217.

in the opinion of TACITUS,[1] *dressed their hair with a laudable intent: Not for the purpose of loving or being loved: They adorned themselves only for their enemies, and in order to appear more terrible.* A sentiment of the historian, which would sound a little oddly in other nations and other ages.

The SCYTHIANS, according to HERODOTUS,[2] after scalping their enemies, dressed the skin like leather, and used it as a towel; and whoever had the most of those towels was most esteemed among them. So much had martial bravery, in that nation, as well as in many others, destroyed the sentiments of humanity: a virtue surely much more useful and engaging.

It is indeed observable, that, among all uncultivated nations, who have not, as yet, had full experience of the advantages attending beneficence, justice, and the social virtues, courage is the predominant excellence; what is most celebrated by poets, recommended by parents and instructors, and admired by the public in general. The ethics of HOMER are, in this particular, very different from those of FENELON, his elegant imitator; and such as were well suited to an age, when one hero, as remarked by THUCYDIDES,[3] could ask another, without offence, whether he were a robber or not. Such also, very lately, was the system of ethics, which prevailed in many barbarous parts of IRELAND; if we may credit SPENCER, in his judicious account of the state of that kingdom.[4]

Of the same class of virtues with courage is that undisturbed philosophical TRANQUILLITY, superior to pain, sorrow, anxiety, and each assault of adverse fortune. Conscious of his own virtue, say the philosophers, the sage elevates himself above every accident of life: and securely placed in the temple of wisdom, looks down on inferior mortals, engaged in pursuit of honours, riches, reputation, and every frivolous enjoyment. These pretensions, no doubt, when stretched to the utmost, are, by far, too magnificent for human nature. They carry, however, a

---

[1] De moribus Germ. 38.
[2] Lib. iv. 64.   [3] Lib. i. 5.
[4] It is a common use, says he, amongst their gentlemen's sons, that, as soon as they are able to use their weapons, they strait gather to themselves three or four stragglers or kern, with whom wandering a while up and down idly the country, taking only meat, he at last falleth into some bad occasion, that shall be offered; which being once made known, he is thenceforth counted a man of worth, in whom there is courage.

grandeur with them, which seizes the spectator, and strikes
him with admiration.   And the nearer we can approach in
practice, to this sublime tranquillity and indifference (for we
must distinguish it from a stupid insensibility) the more
secure enjoyment shall we attain within ourselves, and the
more greatness of mind shall we discover to the world.   The
philosophical tranquillity may, indeed, be considered only as
a branch of magnanimity.

Who admires not SOCRATES; his perpetual serenity and
contentment, amidst the greatest poverty and domestic
vexations; his resolute contempt of riches, and his magnanimous care of preserving liberty, while he refused all
assistance from his friends and disciples, and avoided even
the dependence of an obligation? EPICTETUS had not so
much as a door to his little house or hovel; and therefore,
soon lost his iron lamp, the only furniture which he had
worth taking.   But resolving to disappoint all robbers for
the future, he supplied its place with an earthen lamp, of
which he very peaceably kept possession ever after.

Among the ancients, the heroes in philosophy, as well as
those in war and patriotism, have a grandeur and force of
sentiment, which astonishes our narrow souls, and is rashly
rejected as extravagant and supernatural.   They, in their
turn, I allow, would have had equal reason to consider as
romantic and incredible, the degree of humanity, clemency,
order, tranquillity, and other social virtues, to which, in the
administration of government, we have attained in modern
times, had any one been then able to have made a fair
representation of them.   Such is the compensation, which
nature, or rather education, has made in the distribution of
excellencies and virtues, in those different ages.

The merit of BENEVOLENCE, arising from its utility,
and its tendency to promote the good of mankind, has been
already explained, and is, no doubt, the source of a _con-
siderable_ part of that esteem, which is so universally paid to
it.   But it will also be allowed, that the very softness and
tenderness of the sentiment, its engaging endearments, its
fond expressions, its delicate attentions, and all that flow of
mutual confidence and regard, which enters into a warm
attachment of love and friendship: It will be allowed, I say,
that these feelings, being delightful in themselves, are
necessarily communicated to the spectators, and melt them

into the same fondness and delicacy. The tear naturally starts in our eye on the apprehension of a warm sentiment of this nature: Our breast heaves, our heart is agitated, and every humane tender principle of our frame is set in motion, and gives us the purest and most satisfactory enjoyment.

When poets form descriptions of ELYSIAN fields, where the blessed inhabitants stand in no need of each other's assistance, they yet represent them as maintaining a constant intercourse of love and friendship, and sooth our fancy with the pleasing image of these soft and gentle passions. The idea of tender tranquillity in a pastoral ARCADIA is agreeable from a like principle, as has been observed above.[1]

Who would live amidst perpetual wrangling, and scolding, and mutual reproaches? The roughness and harshness of these emotions disturb and displease us: We suffer by contagion and sympathy; nor can we remain indifferent spectators, even though certain, that no pernicious consequences would ever follow from such angry passions.

As a certain proof, that the whole merit of benevolence is not derived from its usefulness, we may observe, that, in a kind way of blame, we say, a person is *too good*; when he exceeds his part in society, and carries his attention for others beyond the proper bounds. In like manner, we say a man is *too high-spirited, too intrepid, too indifferent about fortune*: Reproaches, which really, at bottom, imply more esteem than many panegyrics. Being accustomed to rate the merit and demerit of characters chiefly by their useful or pernicious tendencies, we cannot forbear applying the epithet of blame, when we discover a sentiment, which rises to a degree, that is hurtful: But it may happen, at the same time, that its noble elevation, or its engaging tenderness so seizes the heart, as rather to encrease our friendship and concern for the person.[2]

The amours and attachments of HARRY the IVth of FRANCE, during the civil wars of the league, frequently hurt his interest and his cause; but all the young, at least, and amorous, who can sympathize with the tender passions, will allow, that this very weakness (for they will readily call it

---

[1] Sect. v. Part 2. Why Utility pleases.

[2] Cheerfulness could scarce admit of blame from its excess, were it not that dissolute mirth, without a proper cause or subject, is a sure symptom and characteristic of folly, and on that account disgustful.

such) chiefly endears that hero, and interests them in his fortunes.

The excessive bravery and resolute inflexibility of CHARLES the XIIth ruined his own country, and infested all his neighbours ; but have such splendour and greatness in their appearance, as strikes us with admiration ; and they might, in some degree, be even approved of, if they betray not sometimes too evident symptoms of madness and disorder.

The ATHENIANS pretended to the first invention of agriculture and of laws ; and always valued themselves extremely on the benefit thereby procured to the whole race of mankind.   They also boasted, and with reason, of their warlike enterprizes ; particularly against those innumerable fleets and armies of PERSIANS, which invaded GREECE during the reigns of DARIUS and XERXES.   But though there be no comparison, in point of utility, between these peaceful and military honours ; yet we find, that the orators, who have writ such elaborate panegyrics on that famous city, have chiefly triumphed in displaying the warlike atchievements. LYSIAS, THUCYDIDES, PLATO, and ISOCRATES discover, all of them, the same partiality ; which, though condemned by calm reason and reflection, appears so natural in the mind of man.

It is observable, that the great charm of poetry consists in lively pictures of the sublime passions, magnanimity, courage, disdain of fortune ; or those of the tender affections, love and friendship ; which warm the heart, and diffuse over it similar sentiments and emotions.   And though all kinds of passion, even the most disagreeable, such as grief and anger, are observed, when excited by poetry, to convey a satisfaction, from a mechanism of nature, not easy to be explained : Yet those more elevated or softer affections have a peculiar influence, and please from more than one cause or principle. Not to mention, that they alone interest us in the fortune of the persons represented, or communicate any esteem and affection for their character.

And can it possibly be doubted, that this talent itself of poets, to move the passions, this PATHETIC and SUBLIME of sentiment, is a very considerable merit ; and being enhanced by its extreme rarity, may exalt the person possessed of it, above every character of the age in which he lives ? The prudence, address, steadiness, and benign government of Augustus, adorned with all the splendour of his noble birth and imperial crown, render him but an unequal competitor for fame with Virgil, who lays nothing into the opposite scale but the divine beauties of his poetical genius.

The very sensibility to these beauties, or a DELICACY of taste, is itself a beauty in any character; as conveying the purest, the most durable, and most innocent of all enjoyments.

These are some instances of the several species of merit, that are valued for the immediate pleasure, which they communicate to the person possessed of them. No views of utility or of future beneficial consequences enter into this sentiment of approbation; yet is it of a kind similar to that other sentiment, which arises from views of a public or private utility. The same social sympathy, we may observe, or fellow-feeling with human happiness or misery, gives rise to both; and this analogy, in all the parts of the present theory, may justly be regarded as a confirmation of it.

SECT. VIII.—*Of Qualities immediately agreeable to Others.*[1]

As the mutual shocks, in *society*, and the oppositions of interest and self-love have constrained mankind to establish the laws of *justice*; in order to preserve the advantages of mutual assistance and protection: In like manner, the eternal contrarieties, in *company*, of men's pride and self-conceit, have introduced the rules of GOOD-MANNERS or POLITENESS; in order to facilitate the intercourse of minds, and an undisturbed commerce and conversation. Among well-bred people, a mutual deference is affected: Contempt of others disguised: Authority concealed: Attention given to each in his turn: And an easy stream of conversation maintained, without vehemence, without interruption, without eagerness for victory, and without any airs of superiority. These attentions and regards are immediately *agreeable* to others, abstracted from any consideration of utility or beneficial tendencies: They conciliate affection, promote esteem,

[1] It is the nature, and, indeed, the definition of virtue, that it is *a quality of the mind agreeable to or approved of by every one, who considers or contemplates it.* But some qualities produce pleasure, because they are useful to society, or useful or agreeable to the person himself; others produce it more immediately: Which is the case with the class of virtues here considered.

and extremely enhance the merit of the person, who regulates his behaviour by them.

Many of the forms of breeding are arbitrary and casual: But the thing expressed by them is still the same. A SPANIARD goes out of his own house before his guest, to signify that he leaves him master of all. In other countries, the landlord walks out last, as a common mark of deference and regard.

But, in order to render a man perfect *good company*, he must have WIT and INGENUITY as well as good-manners. What wit is, it may not be easy to define; but it is easy surely to determine, that it is a quality immediately *agreeable* to others, and communicating, on its first appearance, a lively joy and satisfaction to every one who has any comprehension of it. The most profound metaphysics, indeed, might be employed, in explaining the various kinds and species of wit; and many classes of it, which are now received on the sole testimony of taste and sentiment, might, perhaps, be resolved into more general principles. But this is sufficient for our present purpose, that it does affect taste and sentiment, and bestowing an immediate enjoyment, is a sure source of approbation and affection.

In countries, where men pass most of their time in conversation, and visits, and assemblies, these *companionable* qualities, so to speak, are of high estimation, and form a chief part of personal merit. In countries, where men live a more domestic life, and either are employed in business, or amuse themselves in a narrower circle of acquaintance, the more solid qualities are chiefly regarded. Thus, I have often observed, that, among the FRENCH, the first questions, with regard to a stranger, are, *Is he polite? Has he wit?* In our own country, the chief praise bestowed, is always that of a *good-natured, sensible fellow.*

In conversation, the lively spirit of dialogue is *agreeable*, even to those who desire not to have any share in the discourse: Hence the teller of long stories, or the pompous declaimer, is very little approved of. But most men desire likewise their turn in the conversation, and regard, with a very evil eye, that *loquacity*, which deprives them of a right they are naturally so jealous of.

There is a sort of harmless *liars*, frequently to be met with in company, who deal much in the marvellous. Their usual intention is to please and entertain; but as men are most delighted with what they conceive to be truth, these people mistake extremely the means of pleasing, and incur universal blame. Some indulgence, however, to lying or fiction is given in *humorous* stories; because it is there really agreeable and entertaining; and truth is not of any importance.

Eloquence, genius of all kinds, even good sense, and sound reasoning, when it rises to an eminent degree, and is employed upon subjects of any considerable dignity and nice discernment; all these endowments seem immediately agreeable, and have a merit distinct from their usefulness. Rarity, likewise, which so much enhances the price of every thing, must set an additional value on these noble talents of the human mind.

Modesty may be understood in different senses, even abstracted from chastity, which has been already treated of. It sometimes means that tenderness and nicety of honour, that apprehension of blame, that dread of intrusion or injury towards others, that PUDOR, which is the proper guardian of every kind of virtue, and a sure preservative against vice and corruption. But its most usual meaning is when it is opposed to *impudence* and *arrogance*, and expresses a diffidence of our own judgment, and a due attention and regard for others. In young men chiefly, this quality is a sure sign of good sense; and is also the certain means of augmenting that endowment, by preserving their ears open to instruction, and making them still grasp after new attainments. But it has a farther charm to every spectator; by flattering every man's vanity, and presenting the appearance of a docile pupil, who receives, with proper attention and respect, every word they utter.

Men have, in general, a much greater propensity to over-value than under-value themselves; notwithstanding the opinion of ARISTOTLE.[1] This makes us more jealous of the excess on the former side, and causes us to regard, with a peculiar indulgence, all tendency to modesty and self-diffidence; as esteeming the danger less of falling into any vicious extreme of that nature. It is thus, in countries, where men's bodies are apt to exceed in corpulency, personal

---

[1] Ethic. ad Nicomachum. iv. 3, 37.

beauty is placed in a much greater degree of slenderness, than in countries, where that is the most usual defect. Being so often struck with instances of one species of deformity, men think they can never keep at too great a distance from it, and wish always to have a leaning to the opposite side. In like manner, were the door opened to self-praise, and were MONTAIGNE'S maxim observed, that one should say as frankly, *I have sense, I have learning, I have courage, beauty, or wit* ; as it is sure we often think so ; were this the case, I say, every one is sensible, that such a flood of impertinence would break in upon us, as would render society wholly intolerable. For this reason custom has established it as a rule, in common societies, that men should not indulge themselves in self-praise, or even speak much of themselves ; and it is only among intimate friends or people of very manly behaviour, that one is allowed to do himself justice. No body finds fault with MAURICE, Prince of ORANGE, for his reply to one, who asked him, whom he esteemed the first general of the age, *The marquis of* SPINOLA, said he, *is the second.* Though it is observable, that the self-praise implied is here better implied, than if it had been directly expressed, without any cover or disguise.

He must be a very superficial thinker, who imagines, that all instances of mutual deference are to be understood in earnest, and that a man would be more esteemable for being ignorant of his own merits and accomplishments. A small bias towards modesty, even in the internal sentiment, is favourably regarded, especially in young people ; and a strong bias is required, in the outward behaviour : But this excludes not a noble pride and spirit, which may openly display itself in its full extent, when one lies under calumny or oppression of any kind. The generous contumacy of SOCRATES, as CICERO calls it, has been highly celebrated in all ages ; and when joined to the usual modesty of his behaviour, forms a shining character. IPHICRATES, the ATHENIAN, being accused of betraying the interests of his country, asked his accuser, *Would you*, says he, *have, on a like occasion, been guilty of that crime ? By no means*, replied the other. *And can you then imagine*, cried the hero, *that* IPHICRATES *would be guilty ?*[1] In short, a generous spirit and self-value, well founded, decently disguised, and courageously supported under dis-

[1] QUINCTIL. lib. v. cap. 12.

tress and calumny, is a great excellency, and seems to derive its merit from the noble elevation of its sentiment, or its immediate agreeableness to its possessor. In ordinary characters, we approve of a bias towards modesty, which is a quality immediately agreeable to others: The vicious excess of the former virtue, namely, insolence or haughtiness, is immediately disagreeable to others: The excess of the latter is so to the possessor. Thus are the boundaries of these duties adjusted.

A desire of fame, reputation, or a character with others, is so far from being blameable, that it seems inseparable from virtue, genius, capacity, and a generous or noble disposition. An attention even to trivial matters, in order to please, is also expected and demanded by society; and no one is surprised, if he find a man in company, to observe a greater elegance of dress and more pleasant flow of conversation, than when he passes his time at home, and with his own family. Wherein, then, consists VANITY, which is so justly regarded as a fault or imperfection. It seems to consist chiefly in such an intemperate display of our advantages, honours, and accomplishments; in such an importunate and open demand of praise and admiration, as is offensive to others, and encroaches too far on *their* secret vanity and ambition. It is besides a sure symptom of the want of true dignity and elevation of mind, which is so great an ornament in any character. For why that impatient desire of applause; as if you were not justly entitled to it, and might not reasonably expect, that it would for ever attend you? Why so anxious to inform us of the great company which you have kept; the obliging things which were said to you; the honours, the distinctions which you met with; as if these were not things of course, and what we could readily, of ourselves, have imagined, without being told of them?

DECENCY, or a proper regard to age, sex, character, and station in the world, may be ranked among the qualities, which are immediately agreeable to others, and which, by that means, acquire praise and approbation. An effeminate behaviour in a man, a rough manner in a woman: these are ugly because unsuitable to each character, and different from the qualities which we expect in the sexes. It is as if a tragedy abounded in comic beauties, or a comedy in tragic. The disproportions hurt the eye, and convey a disagreeable sentiment to the spectators, the source of blame and disapprobation. This is that *indecorum*, which is explained so much at large by CICERO in his Offices.

Among the other virtues, we may also give CLEANLINESS a place; since it naturally renders us agreeable to others, and is no inconsiderable source of love and affection. No one will deny, that a negligence in this particular is a fault; and as faults are nothing but smaller vices, and this fault can have no other origin than the uneasy sensation, which it excites in others; we may, in this instance, seemingly so trivial, clearly discover the origin of moral distinctions, about which the learned have involved themselves in such mazes of perplexity and error.

But besides all the *agreeable* qualities, the origin of whose beauty, we can, in some degree explain and account for, there still remains something mysterious and inexplicable, which conveys an immediate satisfaction to the spectator, but how, or why, or for what reason, he cannot pretend to determine. There is a MANNER, a grace, an ease, a genteelness, an I-know-not-what, which some men possess above others, which is very different from external beauty and comeliness, and which, however, catches our affection almost as suddenly and powerfully. And though this *manner* be chiefly talked of in the passion between the sexes, where the concealed magic is easily explained, yet surely much of it prevails in all our estimation of characters, and forms no inconsiderable part of personal merit. This class of accomplishments, therefore, must be trusted entirely to the blind, but sure testimony of taste and sentiment; and must be considered as a part of ethics, left by nature to baffle all the pride of philosophy, and make her sensible of her narrow boundaries and slender acquisitions.

We approve of another, because of his wit, politeness, modesty, decency, or any agreeable quality which he possesses; although he be not of our acquaintance, nor has ever given us any entertainment, by means of these accomplishments. The idea, which we form of their effect on his acquaintance, has an agreeable influence on our imagination, and gives us the sentiment of approbation. This principle enters into all the judgments, which we form concerning manners and characters.

Sect. IX.—*Conclusion.*

PART I.

It may justly appear surprising, that any man, in so late an age, should find it requisite to prove, by elaborate reasoning, ¹that PERSONAL MERIT consists altogether in the possession of mental qualities, *useful* or *agreeable* to the *person himself* or to *others*. It might be expected, that this principle would have occurred even to the first rude, unpractised enquirers concerning morals, and been received from its own evidence, without any argument or disputation. Whatever is valuable in any kind, so naturally classes itself under the division of *useful* or *agreeable*, the *utile* or the *dulce*, that it is not easy to imagine, why we should ever seek farther, or consider the question as a matter of nice research or enquiry. And as every thing useful or agreeable must possess these qualities with regard either to the *person himself* or to *others*, the compleat delineation or description of merit seems to be performed as naturally as a shadow is cast by the sun, or an image is reflected upon water. If the ground, on which the shadow is cast, be not broken and uneven; nor the surface, from which the image is reflected, disturbed and confused; a just figure is immediately presented, without any art or attention. And it seems a reasonable presumption, that systems and hypotheses have perverted our natural understanding; when a theory, so simple and obvious, could so long have escaped the most elaborate examination.

But however the case may have fared with philosophy; in common life, these principles are still implicitly maintained, nor is any other topic of praise or blame ever recurred to, when we employ any panegyric or satire, any applause or censure of human action and behaviour. If we observe men, in every intercourse of business or pleasure, in every discourse and conversation; we shall find them no where, except in the schools, at any loss upon this subject. What so natural, for instance, as the following dialogue? You are very happy, we shall suppose one to say, addressing himself to another, that you have given your daughter to Cleanthes.

¹ [That Virtue or Personal Merit: Editions G to N.]

He is a man of honour and humanity. Every one, who has any intercourse with him, is sure of *fair* and *kind* treatment.[1] I congratulate you too, says another on the promising expectations of this son-in-law; whose assiduous application to the study of the laws, whose quick penetration and early knowledge both of men and business, prognosticate the greatest honours and advancement.[2] You surprise me, replies a third, when you talk of CLEANTHES as a man of business and application. I met him lately in a circle of the gayest company, and he was the very life and soul of our conversation: So much wit with good manners; so much gallantry without affectation; so much ingenious knowledge so genteelly delivered, I have never before observed in any one.[3] You would admire him still more, says a fourth, if you knew him more familiarly. That chearfulness, which you might remark in him, is not a sudden flash struck out by company: It runs through the whole tenor of his life, and preserves a perpetual serenity on his countenance, and tranquillity in his soul. He has met with severe trials, misfortunes as well as dangers; and by his greatness of mind, was still superior to all of them.[4] The image, gentlemen, which you have here delineated of CLEANTHES, cry'd I, is that of accomplished merit. Each of you has given a stroke of the pencil to his figure; and you have unawares exceeded all the pictures drawn by GRATIAN or CASTIGLIONE. A philosopher might select this character as a model of perfect virtue.

And as every quality, which is useful or agreeable to ourselves or others, is, in common life, allowed to be a part of personal merit; so no other will ever be received, where men judge of things by their natural, unprejudiced reason, without the delusive glosses of superstition and false religion. Celibacy, fasting, penance, mortification, self-denial, humility, silence, solitude, and the whole train of monkish virtues; for what reason are they every where rejected by men of sense, but because they serve to no manner of purpose; neither advance a man's fortune in the world, nor render him a more valuable member of society: neither qualify him for the entertainment of company, nor increase his power of self-enjoyment? We observe, on the contrary, that they

[1] Qualities useful to others.
[2] Qualities useful to the person himself. Section VI.
[3] Qualities immediately agreeable to others. Section VIII.
[4] Qualities immediately agreeable to the person himself. Section VII.

cross all these desirable ends; stupify the understanding and harden the heart, obscure the fancy and sour the temper. We justly, therefore, transfer them to the opposite column, and place them in the catalogue of vices; nor has any superstition force sufficient among men of the world, to pervert entirely these natural sentiments. A gloomy, hair-brained enthusiast, after his death, may have a place in the calendar; but will scarcely ever be admitted, when alive, into intimacy and society, except by those who are as delirious and dismal as himself.

It seems a happiness in the present theory, that it enters not into that vulgar dispute concerning the *degrees* of benevolence or self-love, which prevail in human nature; a dispute which is never likely to have any issue, both because men, who have taken part, are not easily convinced, and because the phænomena, which can be produced on either side, are so dispersed, so uncertain, and subject to so many interpretations, that it is scarcely possible accurately to compare them, or draw from them any determinate inference or conclusion. It is sufficient for our present purpose, if it be allowed, what surely, without the greatest absurdity, cannot be disputed, that there is some benevolence, however small, infused into our bosom; some spark of friendship for human kind; some particle of the dove, kneaded into our frame, along with the elements of the wolf and serpent. Let these generous sentiments be supposed ever so weak; let them be insufficient to move even a hand or finger of our body; they must still direct the determinations of our mind, and where every thing else is equal, produce a cool preference of what is useful and serviceable to mankind, above what is pernicious and dangerous. A *moral distinction*, therefore, immediately arises; a general sentiment of blame and approbation; a tendency, however faint, to the objects of the one, and a proportionable aversion to those of the other. Nor will those reasoners, who so earnestly maintain the predominant selfishness of human kind, be any wise scandalized at hearing of the weak sentiments of virtue, implanted in our nature. On the contrary, they are found as ready to maintain the one tenet as the other; and their spirit of satire (for such it appears, rather than of corruption) naturally gives rise to both opinions; which have, indeed, a great and almost an indissoluble connexion together.

Avarice, ambition, vanity, and all passions vulgarly, though improperly, comprized under the denomination of *self-love*, are here excluded from our theory concerning the origin of morals, not because they are too weak, but because they have not a proper direction, for that purpose. The notion of morals, implies some sentiment common to all mankind, which recommends the same object to general approbation, and makes every man, or most men, agree in the same opinion or decision concerning it. It also implies some sentiment, so universal and comprehensive as to extend to all mankind, and render the actions and conduct, even of the persons the most remote, an object of applause or censure, according as they agree or disagree with that rule of right which is established. These two requisite circumstances belong alone to the sentiment of humanity here insisted on. The other passions produce, in every breast, many strong sentiments of desire and aversion, affection and hatred; but these neither are felt so much in common, nor are so comprehensive, as to be the foundation of any general system and established theory of blame or approbation.

When a man denominates another his *enemy*, his *rival*, his *antagonist*, his *adversary*, he is understood to speak the language of self-love, and to express sentiments, peculiar to himself, and arising from his particular circumstances and situation. But when he bestows on any man the epithets of *vicious* or *odious* or *depraved*, he then speaks another language, and expresses sentiments, in which, he expects, all his audience are to concur with him. He must here, therefore, depart from his private and particular situation, and must chuse a point of view, common to him with others: He must move some universal principle of the human frame, and touch a string, to which all mankind have an accord and symphony. If he mean, therefore, to express, that this man possesses qualities, whose tendency is pernicious to society, he has chosen this common point of view, and has touched the principle of humanity, in which every man, in some degree, concurs. While the human heart is compounded of the same elements as at present, it will never be wholly indifferent to public good, nor entirely unaffected with the tendency of characters and manners. And though this affection of humanity may not generally be esteemed so strong as vanity or ambition, yet, being common to all men, it can alone be the foundation of morals, or of any general system of blame or praise. One man's ambition is not another's ambition; nor will the same event or object satisfy both: But the humanity of one man is the humanity of every one; and the same object touches this passion in all human creatures.

But the sentiments, which arise from humanity, are not only the same in all human creatures, and produce the same approbation or censure; but they also comprehend all human creatures; nor is there any one whose conduct or character is not, by their means, an object, to every one, of censure or approbation. On the contrary, those other passions, commonly denominated selfish, both produce different sentiments in each individual, according to his particular situation; and also contemplate the greater part of mankind with the utmost indifference and unconcern. Whoever has a high regard and esteem for me flatters my vanity; whoever expresses contempt mortifies and displeases me: But as my name is known but to a small part of mankind, there are few, who come within the sphere of this passion, or excite, on its account, either my affection or disgust. But if you represent a tyrannical, insolent, or barbarous behaviour, in any country or in any age of the world: I soon carry my eye to the pernicious tendency of such a conduct, and feel the sentiment of repugnance and displeasure towards it. No character can be so remote as to be, in this light, wholly indifferent to me. What is beneficial to society or to the person himself must still be preferred. And every quality or action, of every human being, must, by this means, be ranked under some class or denomination, expressive of general censure or applause.

What more, therefore, can we ask to distinguish the sentiments, dependant on humanity, from those connected with any other passion, or to satisfy us, why the former are the origin of morals, not the latter? Whatever conduct gains my approbation, by touching my humanity, procures also the applause of all mankind, by affecting the same principle in them: But what serves my avarice or ambition pleases these passions in me alone, and affects not the avarice and ambition of the rest of mankind. There is no circumstance of conduct in any man, provided it have a beneficial tendency, that is not agreeable to my humanity, however remote the person : But every man, so far removed as neither to cross nor serve my avarice and ambition, is regarded as wholly indifferent by those passions. The distinction, therefore, between these species of sentiment being so great and evident, language must soon be moulded upon it, and must invent a peculiar set of terms, in order to express those universal sentiments of censure or approbation, which arise from humanity, or from views of general usefulness and its contrary. VIRTUE and VICE become then known : Morals are recognized : Certain general ideas are framed of human conduct and behaviour : Such measures are expected from men, in such situations : This action is determined to be conformable to our abstract rule ; that other, contrary. And by such universal principles are the particular sentiments of self-love frequently controuled and limited.[1]

From instances of popular tumults, seditions, factions, panics, and of all passions, which are shared with a multitude ; we may learn the influence of society, in exciting and supporting any emotion ; while the most ungovernable disorders are raised, we find, by that means, from the slightest and most frivolous occasions. SOLON was no very cruel, though perhaps, an unjust legislator, who punished neuters in civil wars ; and few, I believe, would, in such cases, incur the penalty, were their affection and discourse allowed sufficient to absolve them. No selfishness, and scarce any philosophy, have their force sufficient to support a total coolness and indifference ; and he must be more or less than man, who kindles not in the common blaze. What

[1] It seems certain, both from reason and experience, that a rude, untaught savage regulates chiefly his love and hatred by the ideas of private utility and injury, and has but faint conceptions of a general rule or system of behaviour. The man who stands opposite to him in battle, he hates heartily, not only for the present moment, which is almost unavoidable, but for ever after ; nor is he satisfied without the most extreme punishment and vengeance. But we, accustomed to society, and to more enlarged reflections, consider, that this man is serving his own country and community ; that any man, in the same situation, would do the same ; that we ourselves, in like circumstances, observe a like conduct ; that, in general human society is best supported on such maxims : And by these suppositions and views, we correct, in some measure, our ruder and narrower passions. And though much of our friendship and enmity be still regulated by private considerations of benefit and harm, we pay, at least, this homage to general rules, which we are accustomed to respect, that we commonly pervert our adversary's conduct, by imputing malice or injustice to him, in order to give vent to those passions, which arise from self-love and private interest. When the heart is full of rage, it never wants pretences of this nature ; though sometimes as frivolous, as those from which HORACE, being almost crushed by the fall of a tree, affects to accuse of parricide the first planter of it.

wonder, then, that moral sentiments are found of such influence in life; though springing from principles, which may appear, at first sight, somewhat small and delicate? But these principles, we must remark, are social and universal: They form, in a manner, the *party* of human-kind against vice or disorder, its common enemy : And as the benevolent concern for others is diffused, in a greater or less degree, over all men, and is the same in all, it occurs more frequently in discourse, is cherished by society and conversation, and the blame and approbation, consequent on it, are thereby rouzed from that lethargy, into which they are probably lulled, in solitary and uncultivated nature. Other passions, though perhaps originally stronger, yet being selfish and private, are often overpowered by its force, and yield the dominion of our breast to those social and public principles.

Another spring of our constitution, that brings a great addition of force to moral sentiment, is, the love of fame ; which rules, with such uncontrolled authority, in all generous minds, and is often the grand object of all their designs and undertakings. By our continual and earnest pursuit of a character, a name, a reputation in the world, we bring our own deportment and conduct frequently in review, and consider how they appear in the eyes of those who approach and regard us. This constant habit of surveying ourselves, as it were, in reflection, keeps alive all the sentiments of right and wrong, and begets, in noble natures, a certain reverence for themselves as well as others ; which is the surest guardian of every virtue. The animal conveniencies and pleasures sink gradually in their value ; while every inward beauty and moral grace is studiously acquired, and the mind is accomplished in every perfection, which can adorn or embellish a rational creature.

Here is the most perfect morality with which we are acquainted : Here is displayed the force of many sympathies. Our moral sentiment is itself a feeling chiefly of that nature: And our regard to a character with others seems to arise only from a care of preserving a character with ourselves ; and in order to attain this end, we find it necessary to prop our tottering judgment on the correspondent approbation of mankind.

But, that we may accommodate matters, and remove, if possible, every difficulty, let us allow all these reasonings to be false. Let us allow, that, when we resolve the pleasure, which arises from views of utility, into the sentiments of humanity and sympathy, we have embraced a wrong hypothesis. Let us confess it necessary to find some other explication of that applause, which is paid to objects, whether inanimate, animate, or rational, if they have a tendency to promote the welfare and advantage of mankind. However difficult it be to conceive, that an object is approved of on account of its tendency to a certain end, while the end itself is totally indifferent; let us swallow this absurdity, and consider what are the consequences. The preceding delineation or definition [1] of PERSONAL MERIT must still retain its evidence and authority : It must still be allowed, that every quality of the mind, which is *useful* or *agreeable* to the *person himself* or to *others*, communicates a pleasure to the spectator, engages his esteem, and is admitted under the honourable denomination of virtue or merit. Are not justice, fidelity, honour, veracity, allegiance, chastity, esteemed solely on account of their tendency to promote the good of society? Is not that tendency inseparable from humanity, benevolence, lenity, generosity, gratitude, moderation, tenderness, friendship, and all the other social virtues? Can it possibly be doubted, that industry, discretion, frugality, secrecy, order, perseverance, forethought, judgment, and this whole class of virtues and accomplishments, of which many pages would not contain the catalogue: can it be doubted, I say, that the tendency of these qualities to promote the interest and happiness of their possessor, is the sole foundation of their merit? Who can dispute that a mind, which supports a perpetual serenity and chearfulness, a noble dignity and undaunted spirit, a tender affection and goodwill to all around ; as it has more enjoyment within itself, is also a more animating and rejoicing spectacle, than if dejected with melancholy, tormented with anxiety, irritated with rage, or sunk into the most abject baseness and degeneracy? And as to the qualities, immediately *agreeable to others*, they speak sufficiently for themselves ; and he must be unhappy, indeed, either in his own temper, or in his situation and company, who has never perceived the charms of a facetious wit or flowing affability, of a delicate modesty or decent genteelness of address and manner.

[1] [of Virtue: Editions G to N.]

I am sensible, that nothing can be more unphilosophical than to be positive or dogmatical on any subject; and that, even if *excessive* scepticism could be maintained, it would not be more destructive to all just reasoning and enquiry. I am convinced, that, where men are the most sure and arrogant, they are commonly the most mistaken, and have there given reins to passion, without that proper deliberation and suspence, which can alone secure them from the grossest absurdities. Yet, I must confess, that this enumeration puts the matter in so strong a light, that I cannot, *at present*, be more assured of any truth, which I learn from reasoning and argument, than that personal merit consists entirely in the usefulness or agreeableness of qualities to the person himself possessed of them, or to others, who have any intercourse with him. But when I reflect, that, though the bulk and figure of the earth have been measured and delineated, though the motions of the tides have been accounted for, the order and œconomy of the heavenly bodies subjected to their proper laws, and INFINITE itself reduced to calculation: yet men still dispute concerning the foundation of their moral duties: When I reflect on this, I say, I fall back into diffidence and scepticism, and suspect, that an hypothesis, so obvious, had it been a true one, would, long ere now, have been received by the unanimous suffrage and consent of mankind.

PART II.

Having expressed the moral *approbation* attending merit or virtue,[1] there remains nothing, but briefly to consider our interested *obligation* to it, and to enquire, whether every man, who has any regard to his own happiness and welfare, will not best find his account in the practice of every moral duty. If this can be clearly ascertained from the foregoing theory, we shall have the satisfaction to reflect, that we have advanced principles, which not only, it is hoped, will stand the test of reasoning and enquiry, but may contribute to the amendment of men's lives, and their improvement in morality and social virtue. And though the philosophical truth of any proposition by no means depends on its tendency to promote the interests of society; yet a man has but a bad grace, who delivers a theory, however true, which, he must

---

[1] [Edition G omits the preceding clause.]

confess, leads to a practice dangerous and pernicious. Why rake into those corners of nature, which spread a nuisance all around? Why dig up the pestilence from the pit, in which it is buried? The ingenuity of your researches may be admired; but your systems will be detested : And mankind will agree, if they cannot refute them, to sink them, at least, in eternal silence and oblivion. Truths, which are *pernicious* to society, if any such there be, will yield to errors, which are salutary and *advantageous.*

But what philosophical truths can be more advantageous to society, than those here delivered, which represent virtue in all her genuine and most engaging charms, and make us approach her with ease, familiarity, and affection? The dismal dress falls off, with which many divines, and some philosophers have covered her; and nothing appears but gentleness, humanity, beneficence, affability; nay even, at proper intervals, play, frolic, and gaiety. She talks not of useless austerities and rigours, suffering and self-denial. She declares, that her sole purpose is, to make her votaries and all mankind, during every instant of their existence, if possible, cheerful and happy; nor does she ever willingly part with any pleasure but in hopes of ample compensation in some other period of their lives. The sole trouble, which she demands, is that of just calculation, and a steady preference of the greater happiness. And if any austere pretenders approach her, enemies to joy and pleasure, she either rejects them as hypocrites and deceivers; or if she admit them in her train, they are ranked however, among the least favoured of her votaries.

And, indeed, to drop all figurative expression, what hopes can we ever have of engaging mankind to a practice, which we confess full of austerity and rigour? Or what theory of morals can ever serve any useful purpose, unless it can show, by a particular detail, that all the duties, which it recommends, are also the true interest of each individual? The peculiar advantage of the foregoing system seems to be, that it furnishes proper mediums for that purpose.

That the virtues which are immediately *useful* or *agreeable* to the person possessed of them, are desirable in a view to self-interest, it would surely be superfluous to prove. Moralists, indeed, may spare themselves all the pains, which they often take in recommending these duties. To what purpose collect arguments to evince, that temperance is advantageous, and the excesses of pleasure hurtful? When it appears, that these excesses are only denominated such, because they are hurtful; and that, if unlimited use of strong liquors, for instance, no more impaired health or the faculties of mind and body than the use of air or water, it would not be a whit more vicious or blameable.

It seems equally superfluous to prove, that the *companionable* virtues of good manners and wit, decency and genteelness, are more desirable than the contrary qualities. Vanity alone, without any other consideration, is a sufficient motive to make us wish for the possession of these accomplishments. No man was ever willingly deficient in this particular. All our failures here proceed from bad education, want of capacity, or a perverse and unpliable disposition. Would you have your company coveted, admired, followed; rather than hated, despised, avoided? Can any one seriously deliberate in the case? As no enjoyment is sincere, without some reference to company and society; so no society can be agreeable, or even tolerable, where a man feels his presence unwelcome, and discovers all around him symptoms of disgust and aversion.

But why, in the greater society or confederacy of mankind, should not the case be the same as in particular clubs and companies? Why is it more doubtful, that the enlarged virtues of humanity, generosity, beneficence, are desirable with a view to happiness and self-interest, than the limited endowments of ingenuity and politeness? Are we apprehensive, lest those social affections interfere, in a greater and more immediate degree than any other pursuits, with private utility, and cannot be gratified, without some important sacrifice of honour and advantage? If so, we are but ill instructed in the nature of the human passions, and are more influenced by verbal distinctions than by real differences.

Whatever contradiction may vulgarly be supposed between the *selfish* and *social* sentiments or dispositions, they are really no more opposite than selfish and ambitious, selfish and revengeful, selfish and vain. It is requisite, that there be an original propensity of some kind, in order to be a basis to self-love, by giving a relish to the objects of its pursuit; and none more fit for this purpose than benevolence or humanity. The goods of fortune are spent in one gratification or another: The miser, who accumulates his annual income, and lends it out at interest, has really spent it in the gratification of his avarice. And it would be difficult to show, why a man is more a loser by a generous action, than by any other method of expence; since the utmost which he can attain, by the most elaborate selfishness, is the indulgence of some affection.

Now if life, without passion, must be altogether insipid and tiresome; let a man suppose that he has full power of modelling his own disposition, and let him deliberate what appetite or desire he would choose for the foundation of his happiness and enjoyment. Every affection, he would observe, when gratified by success, gives a satisfaction proportioned to its force and violence : but besides this advantage, common to all, the immediate feeling of benevolence and friendship, humanity and kindness, is sweet, smooth, tender, and agreeable, independent of all fortune and accidents. These virtues are besides attended with a pleasing consciousness or remembrance, and keep us in humour with ourselves as well as others; while we retain the agreeable reflection of having done our part towards mankind and society. And though all men show a jealousy of our success in the pursuits of avarice and ambition; yet are we almost sure of their good-will and good-wishes, so long as we persevere in the paths of virtue, and employ ourselves in the execution of generous plans and purposes. What other passion is there where we shall find so many advantages united; an agreeable sentiment, a pleasing consciousness, a good reputation? But of these truths, we may observe, men are, of themselves, pretty much convinced; nor are they deficient in their duty to society, because they would not wish to be generous, friendly, and humane; but because they do not feel themselves such.

Treating vice with the greatest candour, and making it all possible concessions, we must acknowledge, that there is not, in any instance, the smallest pretext for giving it the preference above virtue, with a view to self-interest; except, perhaps, in the case of justice, where a man, taking things in a certain light, may often seem to be a loser by his integrity. And though it is allowed, that, without a regard to property, no society could subsist; yet, according to the imperfect way in which human affairs are conducted, a sensible knave, in particular incidents, may think, that an act of iniquity or infidelity will make a considerable addition to his fortune, without causing any considerable breach in the social union and confederacy. That *honesty is the best policy*, may be a good general rule; but is liable to many exceptions: And he, it may, perhaps, be thought, conducts himself with most wisdom, who observes the general rule, and takes advantage of all the exceptions.

I must confess, that, if a man think, that this reasoning much requires an answer, it will be a little difficult to find any, which will to him appear satisfactory and convincing. If his heart rebel not against such pernicious maxims, if he feel no reluctance to the thoughts of villany or baseness, he has indeed lost a considerable motive to virtue; and we may expect, that his practice will be answerable to his speculation. But in all ingenuous natures, the antipathy to treachery and roguery is too strong to be counterbalanced by any views of profit or pecuniary advantage. Inward peace of mind, consciousness of integrity, a satisfactory review of our own conduct; these are circumstances very requisite to happiness, and will be cherished and cultivated by every honest man, who feels the importance of them.

Such a one has, besides, the frequent satisfaction of seeing knaves, with all their pretended cunning and abilities, betrayed by their own maxims; and while they purpose to cheat with moderation and secrecy, a tempting incident occurs, nature is frail, and they give into the snare; whence they can never extricate themselves, without a total loss of reputation, and the forfeiture of all future trust and confidence with mankind.

But were they ever so secret and successful, the honest man, if he has any tincture of philosophy, or even common observation and reflection, will discover that they themselves are, in the end, the greatest dupes, and have sacrificed the invaluable enjoyment of a character, with themselves at least, for the acquisition of worthless toys and gewgaws. How little is requisite to supply the *necessities* of nature? And in a view to *pleasure*, what comparison between the unbought satisfaction of conversation, society, study, even health and the common beauties of nature, but above all the peaceful reflection on one's own conduct: What comparison, I say, between these, and the feverish, empty amusements of luxury and expence? These natural pleasures, indeed, are really without price; both because they are below all price in their attainment, and above it in their enjoyment.

Appendix I.—*Concerning Moral Sentiment.*

If the foregoing hypothesis be received, it will now be easy for us to determine the question first started,[1] concerning the general principles of morals; and though we postponed the decision of that question, lest it should then involve us in intricate speculations, which are unfit for moral discourses, we may resume it at present, and examine how far either *reason* or *sentiment* enters into all decisions of praise or censure.

One principal foundation of moral praise being supposed to lie in the usefulness of any quality or action; it is evident, that *reason* must enter for a considerable share in all decisions of this kind; since nothing but that faculty can instruct us in the tendency of qualities and actions, and point out their beneficial consequences to society and to their possessor. In many cases, this is an affair liable to great controversy: Doubts may arise; opposite interests may occur; and a preference must be given to one side, from very nice views, and a small overbalance of utility. This is particularly remarkable in questions with regard to justice: as is, indeed, natural to suppose, from that species of utility, which attends this virtue.[2] Were every single instance of justice, like that of benevolence, useful to society; this would be a more simple state of the case, and seldom liable to great controversy. But as single instances of justice are often pernicious in their first and immediate tendency, and as the advantage to society results only from the observance of the general rule, and from the concurrence and combination of several persons in the same equitable conduct; the case here becomes more intricate and involved. The various circumstances of society; the various consequences of any practice; the various interests, which may be proposed: These, on

---

[1] Sect. I. Of the General Principles of Morals.

[2] See Appendix III. Some farther Considerations with regard to Justice.

many occasions, are doubtful, and subject to great discussion and enquiry. The object of municipal laws is to fix all the questions with regard to justice: The debates of civilians; the reflections of politicians; the precedents of history and public records, are all directed to the same purpose. And a very accurate *reason* or *judgment* is often requisite, to give the true determination, amidst such intricate doubts arising from obscure or opposite utilities.

But though reason, when fully assisted and improved, be sufficient to instruct us in the pernicious or useful tendency of qualities and actions; it is not alone sufficient to produce any moral blame or approbation. Utility is only a tendency to a certain end; and were the end totally indifferent to us, we should feel the same indifference towards the means. It is requisite a *sentiment* should here display itself, in order to give a preference to the useful above the pernicious tendencies. This sentiment can be no other than a feeling for the happiness of mankind, and a resentment of their misery; since these are the different ends which virtue and vice have a tendency to promote. Here, therefore, *reason* instructs us in the several tendencies of actions, and *humanity* makes a distinction in favour of those which are useful and beneficial.

This partition between the faculties of understanding and sentiment, in all moral decisions, seems clear from the preceding hypothesis. But I shall suppose that hypothesis false: It will then be requisite to look out for some other theory, that may be satisfactory; and I dare venture to affirm, that none such will ever be found, so long as we suppose reason to be the sole source of morals. To prove this, it will be proper to weigh the five following considerations.

I. It is easy for a false hypothesis to maintain some appearance of truth, while it keeps wholly in generals, makes use of undefined terms, and employs comparisons, instead of instances. This is particularly remarkable in that philosophy, which ascribes the discernment of all moral distinctions to reason alone, without the concurrence of sentiment. It is impossible that, in any particular instance, this hypothesis can so much as be rendered intelligible; whatever specious figure it may make in general declamations and discourses. Examine the crime of *ingratitude*, for instance: which has place, wherever we observe good-will, expressed and known, together with good-offices performed, on the one side, and a

APP. I.

return of ill-will or indifference, with ill-offices or neglect or. the other: Anatomize all these circumstances, and examine, by your reason alone, in what consists the demerit or blame: You never will come to any issue or conclusion.

Reason judges either of *matter of fact* or of *relations*. Enquire then, *first*, where is that matter of fact, which we here call *crime*; point it out; determine the time of its existence; describe its essence or nature; explain the sense or faculty, to which it discovers itself. It resides in the mind of the person, who is ungrateful. He must, therefore, feel it, and be conscious of it. But nothing is there, except the passion of ill-will or absolute indifference. You cannot say, that these, of themselves, always, and in all circumstances, are crimes. No: They are only crimes, when directed towards persons, who have before expressed and displayed good-will towards us. Consequently, we may infer, that the crime of ingratitude is not any particular individual *fact*; but arises from a complication of circumstances, which, being presented to the spectator, excites the *sentiment* of blame, by the particular structure and fabric of his mind.

This representation, you say, is false. Crime, indeed, consists not in a particular *fact*, of whose reality we are assured by *reason*: But it consists in certain *moral relations*, discovered by reason, in the same manner as we discover, by reason, the truths of geometry or algebra. But what are the relations, I ask, of which you here talk? In the case stated above, I see first good-will and good-offices in one person; then ill-will and ill-offices in the other. Between these, there is the relation of *contrariety*. Does the crime consist in that relation? But suppose a person bore me ill-will or did me ill-offices; and I, in return, were indifferent towards him, or did him good-offices: Here is the same relation of *contrariety*; and yet my conduct is often highly laudable. Twist and turn this matter as much as you will, you can never rest the morality on relation; but must have recourse to the decisions of sentiment.

When it is affirmed, that two and three are equal to the half of ten; this relation of equality, I understand perfectly. I conceive, that if ten be divided into two parts, of which one has as many units as the other; and if any of these parts be compared to two added to three, it will contain as many units as that compound number. But when you draw thence a comparison to moral relations, I own that I am altogether at a loss to understand you. A moral action, a crime, such as ingratitude, is a complicated object. Does morality consist in the relation of its parts to each other. How? After what manner? Specify the relation: Be more particular and explicit in your propositions; and you will easily see their falsehood.

No, say you, the morality consists in the relation of actions to the rule of right; and they are denominated good or ill, according as they agree or disagree with it. What then is this rule of right? In what does it consist? How is it determined? By reason, you say, which examines the moral relations of actions. So that moral relations are determined by the comparison of actions to a rule. And that rule is determined by considering the moral relations of objects. Is not this fine reasoning?

All this is metaphysics, you cry: That is enough: There needs nothing more to give a strong presumption of falsehood. Yes, reply I: Here are metaphysics surely: But they are all on your side, who advance an abstruse hypothesis, which can never be made intelligible, nor quadrate with any particular instance or illustration. The hypothesis which we embrace is plain. It maintains, that morality is determined by sentiment. It defines virtue to be *whatever mental action or quality gives to a spectator the pleasing sentiment of approbation*; and vice the contrary. We then proceed to examine a plain matter of fact, to wit, what actions have this influence: We consider all the circumstances, in which these actions agree: And thence endeavour to extract some general observations with regard to these sentiments. If you call this metaphysics, and find any thing abstruse here, you need only conclude, that your turn of mind is not suited to the moral sciences.

II. When a man, at any time, deliberates concerning his own conduct (as, whether he had better, in a particular emergence, assist a brother or a benefactor), he must consider these separate relations, with all the circumstances and situations of the persons, in order to determine the superior duty and obligation: And in order to determine the proportion of lines in any triangle, it is necessary to examine the nature of that figure, and the relations which its several parts bear to each other. But notwithstanding this appearing similarity in the two cases, there is, at bottom, an extreme difference between them. A speculative reasoner concerning triangles or circles considers the several known and given relations of the parts of these figures; and thence infers some unknown relation, which is dependent on the former. But in moral deliberations, we must be acquainted, before-hand, with all the objects, and all their relations to each other; and from a comparison of the whole, fix our choice or approbation. No new fact to be ascertained : No new relation to be discovered. All the circumstances of the case are supposed to be laid before us, ere we can fix any sentence of blame or approbation. If any material circumstance be yet unknown or doubtful, we must first employ our enquiry or intellectual faculties to assure us of it; and must suspend for a time all moral decision or sentiment. While we are ignorant, whether a man were aggressor or not, how can we determine whether the person who killed him, be criminal or innocent? But after every circumstance, every relation is known, the understanding has no farther room to operate, nor any object on which it could employ itself. The approbation or blame, which then ensues, cannot be the work of the judgment, but of the heart; and is not a speculative proposition or affirmation, but an active feeling or sentiment. In the disquisitions of the understanding, from known circumstances and relations, we infer some new and unknown. In moral decisions, all the circumstances and relations must be previously known; and the mind, from the contemplation of the whole, feels some new impression of affection or disgust, esteem or contempt, approbation or blame.

Hence the great difference between a mistake of *fact* and one of *right*; and hence the reason why the one is commonly criminal and not the other. When Œdipus killed Laius, he was ignorant of the relation, and from circumstances, innocent and involuntary, formed erroneous opinions concerning the action which he committed. But when Nero killed Agrippina, all the relations between himself and the person, and all the circumstances of the fact, were previously known to him: But the motive of revenge, or fear, or interest, prevailed in his savage heart over the sentiments of duty and humanity. And when we express that detestation against him, to which he, himself, in a little time,

became insensible; it is not, that we see any relations, of
which he was ignorant; but that, from the rectitude of our
disposition, we feel sentiments, against which he was
hardened, from flattery and a long perseverance in the most
enormous crimes. In these sentiments, then, not in a
discovery of relations of any kind, do all moral determinations consist. Before we can pretend to form any decision
of this kind, every thing must be known and ascertained on
the side of the object or action. Nothing remains but to
feel, on our part, some sentiment of blame or approbation;
whence we pronounce the action criminal or virtuous.

III. This doctrine will become still more evident, if we
compare moral beauty with natural, to which, in many
particulars, it bears so near a resemblance. It is on the
proportion, relation, and position of parts, that all natural
beauty depends; but it would be absurd thence to infer,
that the perception of beauty, like that of truth in geometrical problems, consists wholly in the perception of
relations, and was performed entirely by the understanding
or intellectual faculties. In all the sciences, our mind, from
the known relations, investigates the unknown: But in all
decisions of taste or external beauty, all the relations are
before-hand obvious to the eye; and we thence proceed to
feel a sentiment of complacency or disgust, according to the
nature of the object, and disposition of our organs.

EUCLID has fully explained all the qualities of the circle;
but has not, in any proposition, said a word of its beauty.
The reason is evident. The beauty is not a quality of the
circle. It lies not in any part of the line, whose parts are
equally distant from a common center. It is only the effect,
which that figure produces upon the mind, whose peculiar
fabric or structure renders it susceptible of such sentiments.
In vain would you look for it in the circle, or seek it, either
by your senses or by mathematical reasonings, in all the
properties of that figure.

Attend to PALLADIO and PERRAULT, while they explain all
the parts and proportions of a pillar: They talk of the
cornice and frieze and base and entablature and shaft and
architrave; and give the description and position of each of
these members. But should you ask the description and
position of its beauty, they would readily reply, that the
beauty is not in any of the parts or members of a pillar, but

results from the whole, when that complicated figure is presented to an intelligent mind, susceptible to those finer sensations. 'Till such a spectator appear, there is nothing but a figure of such particular dimensions and proportions: From his sentiments alone arise its elegance and beauty.

Again; attend to CICERO, while he paints the crimes of a VERRES or a CATILINE; you must acknowledge that the moral turpitude results, in the same manner, from the contemplation of the whole, when presented to a being, whose organs have such a particular structure and formation. The orator may paint rage, insolence, barbarity on the one side: Meekness, suffering, sorrow, innocence on the other: But if you feel no indignation or compassion arise in you from this complication of circumstances, you would in vain ask him, in what consists the crime or villany, which he so vehemently exclaims against: At what time, or on what subject it first began to exist: And what has a few months afterwards become of it, when every disposition and thought of all the actors is totally altered, or annihilated. No satisfactory answer can be given to any of these questions, upon the abstract hypothesis of morals; and we must at last acknowledge, that the crime or immorality is no particular fact or relation, which can be the object of the understanding: But arises entirely from the sentiment of disapprobation, which, by the structure of human nature, we unavoidably feel on the apprehension of barbarity or treachery.

IV. Inanimate objects may bear to each other all the same relations, which we observe in moral agents; though the former can never be the object of love or hatred, nor are consequently susceptible of merit or iniquity. A young tree, which over-tops and destroys its parent,[1] stands in all the same relations with NERO, when he murdered AGRIPPINA; and if morality consisted merely in relations, would, no doubt, be equally criminal.

V. It appears evident, that the ultimate ends of human actions can never, in any case, be accounted for by *reason*, but recommend themselves entirely to the sentiments and affections of mankind, without any dependance on the intellectual faculties. Ask a man, *why he uses exercise*; he will answer, *because he desires to keep his health*. If you then enquire, *why he desires health*, he will readily reply, *because*

---

[1] [From whose seed it sprung: Editions G & K.]

sickness is painful. If you push your enquiries farther, and desire a reason, *why he hates pain*, it is impossible he can ever give any. This is an ultimate end, and is never referred to any other object.

Perhaps, to your second question, *why he desires health*, he may also reply, that *it is necessary for the exercise of his calling.* If you ask, *why he is anxious on that head*, he will answer, *because he desires to get money.* If you demand *Why? It is the instrument of pleasure*, says he. And beyond this it is an absurdity to ask for a reason. It is impossible there can be a progress *in infinitum*; and that one thing can always be a reason, why another is desired. Something must be desirable on its own account, and because of its immediate accord or agreement with human sentiment and affection.

Now as virtue is an end, and is desirable on its own account, without fee or reward, merely, for the immediate satisfaction which it conveys; it is requisite that there should be some sentiment, which it touches; some internal taste or feeling, or whatever you please to call it, which distinguishes moral good and evil, and which embraces the one and rejects the other.

Thus the distinct boundaries and offices of *reason* and of *taste* are easily ascertained. The former conveys the knowledge of truth and falsehood: The latter gives the sentiment of beauty and deformity, vice and virtue. The one discovers objects, as they really stand in nature, without addition or diminution: The other has a productive faculty, and gilding or staining all natural objects with the colours, borrowed from internal sentiment, raises, in a manner, a new creation. Reason, being cool and disengaged, is no motive to action, and directs only the impulse received from appetite or inclination, by showing us the means of attaining happiness or avoiding misery: Taste, as it gives pleasure or pain, and thereby constitutes happiness or misery, becomes a motive to action, and is the first spring or impulse to desire and volition. From circumstances and relations, known or supposed, the former leads us to the discovery of the concealed and unknown: After all circumstances and relations are laid before us, the latter makes us feel from the whole a new sentiment of blame or approbation. The standard of the one, being founded on the nature of things, is eternal and inflexible, even by the will of the Supreme Being: The standard of the other, arising from the internal frame and constitution of animals, is ultimately derived from that Supreme Will, which bestowed on each being its peculiar nature, and arranged the several classes and orders of existence.

APPENDIX II.[1]—*Of Self-love.*

THERE is a principle, supposed to prevail among many, which is utterly incompatible with all virtue or moral sentiment; and as it can proceed from nothing but the most depraved disposition, so in its turn it tends still further to encourage that depravity. This principle is, that all *benevolence* is mere hypocrisy, friendship a cheat, public spirit a farce, fidelity a snare to procure trust and confidence; and that, while all of us, at bottom, pursue only our private interest, we wear these fair disguises, in order to put others off their guard, and expose them the more to our wiles and machinations. What heart one must be possessed of who professes such principles, and who feels no internal sentiment that belies so pernicious a theory, it is easy to imagine: And also, what degree of affection and benevolence he can bear to a species, whom he represents under such odious colours, and supposes so little susceptible of gratitude or any return of affection. Or if we should not ascribe these principles wholly to a corrupted heart, we must, at least, account for them from the most careless and precipitate examination. Superficial reasoners, indeed, observing many false pretences among mankind, and feeling, perhaps, no very strong restraint in their own disposition, might draw a general and a hasty conclusion, that all is equally corrupted, and that men, different from all other animals, and indeed from all other species of existences, admit of no degrees of good or bad but are, in every instance, the same creatures under different disguises and appearances.

There is another principle, somewhat resembling the former; which has been much insisted on by philosophers, and has been the foundation of many a system; that, whatever affection one may feel, or imagine he feels for others, no passion is, or can be disinterested; that the most generous friendship, however sincere, is a modification of self-love; and that, even unknown to ourselves, we seek only our own gratification, while we appear the most deeply engaged in schemes for the liberty and happiness of mankind. By a turn of imagination, by a refinement of reflection, by an enthusiasm of passion, we seem to take part in the interests of others, and imagine ourselves divested of all selfish considerations: But, at bottom, the most generous patriot and most niggardly miser, the bravest hero and most abject coward, have, in every action, an equal regard to their own happiness and welfare.

Whoever concludes from the seeming tendency of this opinion, that those, who make profession of it, cannot possibly feel the true sentiments of benevolence, or have any regard for genuine virtue, will often find himself, in practice, very much mistaken. Probity and honour were no strangers to EPICURUS and his sect. ATTICUS and HORACE seem to have enjoyed from nature, and cultivated by reflection, as generous and friendly dispositions as any disciple of the austerer schools. And among the modern, HOBBES and LOCKE, who maintained the selfish system of morals, lived irreproachable lives; though the former lay not under any restraint of religion, which might supply the defects of his philosophy.

An EPICUREAN or a HOBBIST readily allows, that there is such a thing as friendship in the world, without hypocrisy or disguise; though he may attempt, by a philosophical chymistry, to resolve the elements of this passion, if I may so speak, into those of another, and explain every affection to be self-love, twisted and moulded, by a particular turn of imagination, into a variety of appearances. But as the same turn of imagination prevails not in every man, nor gives the same direction to the original passion; this is sufficient, even according to the selfish system, to make the widest difference in human characters, and denominate one man virtuous and humane, another vicious and meanly interested. I esteem the man, whose self-love, by whatever means, is so directed as to give him a concern for others, and render him serviceable to society: As I hate or despise him, who has no regard to any thing beyond his own gratifications and enjoyments. In vain would you suggest, that these characters, though seemingly opposite, are, at bottom, the same, and that a very inconsiderable turn of thought forms the whole difference between them. Each character, notwithstanding these inconsiderable differences, appears to me, in practice, pretty durable and untransmutable. And I find not in this more than in other subjects, that the natural sentiments, arising from the general appearances of things, are easily destroyed by subtile reflections concerning the minute origin of these appearances. Does not the lively, chearful colour of a countenance inspire me with complacency and pleasure; even though I learn from philosophy, that all difference of complexion arises from the most minute differences of thickness, in the most minute parts of the skin; by means of which a superficies is qualified to reflect one of the original colours of light, and absorb the others?

But though the question, concerning the universal or partial selfishness of man be not so material, as is usually imagined, to morality and practice, it is certainly of consequence in the speculative science of human nature, and is a proper object of curiosity and enquiry. It may not, therefore, be unsuitable, in this place, to bestow a few reflections upon it.[1]

The most obvious objection to the selfish hypothesis, is, that, as it is contrary to common feeling and our most unprejudiced notions, there is required the highest stretch of philosophy to establish so extraordinary a paradox. To the most careless observer, there appear to be such dispositions as benevolence and generosity; such affections as love, friendship, compassion, gratitude. These sentiments have their causes, effects, objects, and operations, marked by common language and observation, and plainly distinguished from those of the selfish passions. And as this is the obvious appearance of things, it must be admitted; till some hypothesis be discovered, which, by penetrating deeper into human nature, may prove the former affections to be

[1] Benevolence naturally divides into two kinds, the *general* and the *particular*. The first is, where we have no friendship or connexion or esteem for the person, but feel only a general sympathy with him or a compassion for his pains, and a congratulation with his pleasures. The other species of benevolence is founded on an opinion of virtue, on services done us, or on some particular connexions. Both these sentiments must be allowed real in human nature; but whether they will resolve into some nice considerations of self-love, is a question more curious than important. The former sentiment, to wit, that of general benevolence, or humanity, or sympathy, we shall have occasion frequently to treat of in the course of this enquiry; and I assume it as real, from general experience, without any other proof.

nothing but modifications of the latter. All attempts of this kind have hitherto proved fruitless, and seem to have proceeded entirely, from that love of *simplicity*, which has been the source of much false reasoning in philosophy. I shall not here enter into any detail on the present subject. Many able philosophers have shown the insufficiency of these systems. And I shall take for granted what, I believe, the smallest reflection will make evident to every impartial enquirer.

But the nature of the subject furnishes the strongest presumption, that no better system will ever, for the future, be invented, in order to account for the origin of the benevolent from the selfish affections, and reduce all the various emotions of the human mind to a perfect simplicity. The case is not the same in this species of philosophy as in physics. Many an hypothesis in nature, contrary to first appearances, has been found, on more accurate scrutiny, solid and satisfactory. Instances of this kind are so frequent, that a judicious, as well as witty philosopher,[1] has ventured to affirm, if there be more than one way, in which any phaenomenon may be produced, that there is a general presumption for its arising from the causes, which are the least obvious and familiar. But the presumption always lies on the other side, in all enquiries concerning the origin of our passions, and of the internal operations of the human mind. The simplest and most obvious cause, which can there be assigned for any phaenomenon, is probably the true one. When a philosopher, in the explication of his system, is obliged to have recourse to some very intricate and refined reflections, and to suppose them essential to the production of any passion or emotion, we have reason to be extremely on our guard against so fallacious an hypothesis. The affections are not susceptible of any impression from the refinements of reason or imagination; and it is always found, that a vigorous exertion of the latter faculties, necessarily, from the narrow capacity of the human mind, destroys all activity in the former. Our predominant motive or intention is, indeed, frequently concealed from ourselves, when it is mingled and confounded with other motives, which the mind, from vanity or self-conceit, is desirous of supposing more prevalent: But there is no instance, that a conceal-

[1] Mons. Fontenelle.

ment of this nature has ever arisen from the abstruseness and intricacy of the motive. A man, that has lost a friend and patron, may flatter himself, that all his grief arises from generous sentiments, without any mixture of narrow or interested considerations : But a man, that grieves for a valuable friend, who needed his patronage and protection ; how can we suppose, that his passionate tenderness arises from some metaphysical regards to a self-interest, which has no foundation or reality ? We may as well imagine, that minute wheels and springs, like those of a watch, give motion to a loaded waggon, as account for the origin of passion from such abstruse reflections.

Animals are found susceptible of kindness, both to their own species and to ours ; nor is there, in this case, the least suspicion of disguise or artifice. Shall we account for all *their* sentiments too, from refined deductions of self-interest ? Or if we admit a disinterested benevolence in the inferior species, by what rule of analogy can we refuse it in the superior ?

Love between the sexes begets a complacency and good-will, very distinct from the gratification of an appetite. Tenderness to their offspring, in all sensible beings, is commonly able alone to counter-balance the strongest motives of self-love, and has no manner of dependance on that affection. What interest can a fond mother have in view, who loses her health by assiduous attendance on her sick child, and afterwards languishes and dies of grief, when freed, by its death, from the slavery of that attendance ?

Is gratitude no affection of the human breast, or is that a word merely, without any meaning or reality ? Have we no satisfaction in one man's company above another's, and no desire of the welfare of our friend, even though absence or death should prevent us from all participation in it ? Or what is it commonly, that gives us any participation in it, even while alive and present, but our affection and regard to him ?

These and a thousand other instances are marks of a general benevolence in human nature, where no *real* interest binds us to the object. And how an *imaginary* interest, known and avowed for such, can be the origin of any passion or emotion, seems difficult to explain. No satisfactory hypothesis of this kind has yet been discovered ; nor is there the smallest probability, that the future industry of men will ever be attended with more favourable success.

But farther, if we consider rightly of the matter, we shall find, that the hypothesis, which allows of a disinterested benevolence, distinct from self-love, has really more *simplicity* in it, and is more conformable to the analogy of nature, than that which pretends to resolve all friendship and humanity into this latter principle. There are bodily wants or appetites, acknowledged by every one, which necessarily precede all sensual enjoyment, and carry us directly to seek possession of the object. Thus, hunger and thirst have eating and drinking for their end; and from the gratification of these primary appetites arises a pleasure, which may become the object of another species of desire or inclination, that is secondary and interested. In the same manner, there are mental passions, by which we are impelled immediately to seek particular objects, such as fame, or power, or vengeance, without any regard to interest; and when these objects are attained, a pleasing enjoyment ensues, as the consequence of our indulged affections. Nature must, by the internal frame and constitution of the mind, give an original propensity to fame, ere we can reap any pleasure from that acquisition, or pursue it from motives of self-love, and a desire of happiness. If I have no vanity, I take no delight in praise: If I be void of ambition, power gives me no enjoyment: If I be not angry, the punishment of an adversary is totally indifferent to me. In all these cases, there is a passion, which points immediately to the object, and constitutes it our good or happiness; as there are other secondary passions, which afterwards arise, and pursue it as a part of our happiness, when once it is constituted such by our original affections. Were there no appetite of any kind antecedent to self-love, that propensity could scarcely ever exert itself; because we should, in that case, have felt few and slender pains or pleasures, and have little misery or happiness to avoid or to pursue.

Now where is the difficulty in conceiving, that this may likewise be the case with benevolence and friendship, and that, from the original frame of our temper, we may feel a desire of another's happiness or good, which, by means of that affection, becomes our own good, and is afterwards pursued, from the combined motives of benevolence and self-enjoyment? Who sees not that vengeance, from the force alone of passion, may be so eagerly pursued, as to make us knowingly neglect every consideration of ease, interest, or safety; and, like some vindictive animals, infuse our very souls into the wounds we give an enemy[1]? And what a malignant philosophy must it be, that will not allow, to humanity and friendship, the same privileges, which are undisputably granted to the darker passions of enmity and resentment? Such a philosophy is more like a satyr than a true delineation or description of human nature; and may be a good foundation for paradoxical wit and raillery, but is a very bad one for any serious argument or reasoning.

APPENDIX III.[2]—*Some farther Considerations with regard to Justice.*

THE intention of this Appendix is to give some more particular explication of the origin and nature of Justice, and to mark some differences between it and the other virtues.

The social virtues of humanity and benevolence exert their influence immediately, by a direct tendency or instinct, which chiefly keeps in view the simple object, moving the affections, and comprehends not any scheme or system, nor the consequences resulting from the concurrence, imitation, or example of others. A parent flies to the relief of his child; transported by that natural sympathy, which actuates him, and which affords no leisure to reflect on the sentiments or conduct of the rest of mankind in like circumstances. A generous man chearfully embraces an opportunity of serving his friend; because he then feels himself under the dominion of the beneficent affections, nor is he concerned whether any other person in the universe were ever before actuated by such noble motives, or will ever afterwards prove their influence. In all these cases, the social passions have in view a single individual object, and pursue the safety or happiness alone of the person loved and esteemed. With this they are satisfied: In this, they acquiesce. And as the good, resulting from their benign influence, is in itself compleat and entire, it also excites the moral sentiment of approbation, without any reflection on

---

[1] Animasque in vulnere ponunt. VIRG. Geor. 4, 238. Dum alteri noceat, sui negligens, says SENECA of Anger. De   Ira. l. i. 1.

[2] [Appendix ii. in Editions G to Q.]

farther consequences, and without any more enlarged views AP. III
of the concurrence or imitation of the other members of
society. On the contrary, were the generous friend or disinterested patriot to stand alone in the practice of beneficence; this would rather enhance his value in our eyes, and
join the praise of rarity and novelty to his other more exalted
merits.

The case is not the same with the social virtues of justice
and fidelity. They are highly useful, or indeed absolutely
necessary to the well-being of mankind: But the benefit,
resulting from them, is not the consequence of every individual single act; but arises from the whole scheme or
system, concurred in by the whole, or the greater part of
the society. General peace and order are the attendants of
justice or a general abstinence from the possessions of others:
But a particular regard to the particular right of one individual citizen may frequently, considered in itself, be productive of pernicious consequences. The result of the
individual acts is here, in many instances, directly opposite
to that of the whole system of actions; and the former may
be extremely hurtful, while the latter is, to the highest
degree, advantageous. Riches, inherited from a parent, are,
in a bad man's hand, the instrument of mischief. The right
of succession may, in one instance, be hurtful. Its benefit
arises only from the observance of the general rule; and it
is sufficient, if compensation be thereby made for all the ills
and inconveniencies, which flow from particular characters
and situations.

Cyrus, young and unexperienced, considered only the individual case before him, and reflected on a limited fitness
and convenience, when he assigned the long coat to the tall
boy, and the short coat to the other of smaller size. His
governor instructed him better; while he pointed out more
enlarged views and consequences, and informed his pupil of
the general, inflexible rules, necessary to support general
peace and order in society.

The happiness and prosperity of mankind, arising from
the social virtue of benevolence and its subdivisions, may be
compared to a wall, built by many hands; which still rises
by each stone, that is heaped upon it, and receives increase
proportional to the diligence and care of each workman.
The same happiness, raised by the social virtue of justice and

APP. III. its subdivisions, may be compared to the building of a vault, where each individual stone would, of itself, fall to the ground ; nor is the whole fabric supported but by the mutual assistance and combination of its corresponding parts.

All the laws of nature, which regulate property, as well as all civil laws, are general, and regard alone some essential circumstances of the case, without taking into consideration the characters, situations, and connexions of the person concerned, or any particular consequences which may result from the determination of these laws, in any particular case which offers. They deprive, without scruple, a beneficent man of all his possessions, if acquired by mistake, without a good title ; in order to bestow them on a selfish miser, who has already heaped up immense stores of superfluous riches. Public utility requires, that property should be regulated by general inflexible rules ; and though such rules are adopted as best serve the same end of public utility, it is impossible for them to prevent all particular hardships, or make beneficial consequences result from every individual case. It is sufficient, if the whole plan or scheme be necessary to the support of civil society, and if the balance of good, in the main, do thereby preponderate much above that of evil. Even the general laws of the universe, though planned by infinite wisdom, cannot exclude all evil or inconvenience, in every particular operation.

It has been asserted by some, that justice arises from HUMAN CONVENTIONS, and proceeds from the voluntary choice, consent, or combination of mankind. If by *convention* be here meant a *promise* (which is the most usual sense of the word) nothing can be more absurd than this position. The observance of promises is itself one of the most considerable parts of justice ; and we are not surely bound to keep our word, because we have given our word to keep it. But if by convention be meant a sense of common interest ; which sense each man feels in his own breast, which he remarks in his fellows, and which carries him, in concurrence with others, into a general plan or system of actions, which tends to public utility ; it must be owned, that, in this sense, justice arises from human conventions. For if it be allowed (what is, indeed, evident) that the particular consequences of a particular act of justice may be hurtful to the public as well as to individuals ; it follows, that every man, in embracing that virtue, must have an eye to the whole plan or system, and must expect the concurrence of his fellows in the same conduct and behaviour. Did all his views terminate in the consequences of each act of his own, his benevolence and humanity, as well as his self-love, might often prescribe to him measures of conduct very different from those, which are agreeable to the strict rules of right and justice.

Thus two men pull the oars of a boat by common convention, for common interest, without any promise or contract: Thus gold and silver are made the measures of exchange; thus speech and words and language are fixed by human convention and agreement. Whatever is advantageous to two or more persons, if all perform their part; but what loses all advantage, if only one perform, can arise from no other principle. There would otherwise be no motive for any one of them to enter into that scheme of conduct.[1]

The word, *natural*, is commonly taken in so many senses, and is of so loose a signification, that it seems vain to dispute, whether justice be natural or not. If self-love, if benevolence be natural to man; if reason and forethought be also natural; then may the same epithet be applied to justice, order, fidelity, property, society. Men's inclination, their necessities lead them to combine; their understanding and experience tell them, that this combination is impossible, where each governs himself by no rule, and pays no regard to the possessions of others: And from these passions and reflections conjoined, as soon as we observe like passions and reflections in others, the sentiment of justice, throughout all ages, has infallibly and certainly had place, to some degree or other, in every individual of the human species. In so sagacious an animal, what necessarily arises from the exer-

---

[1] This theory concerning the origin of property, and consequently of justice, is, in the main, the same with that hinted at and adopted by GROTIUS. 'Hinc discimus, quæ fuerit causa, ob quam a primæva communione rerum primo mobilium, deinde & immobilium discessum est: nimirum quod cum non contenti homines vesci sponte natis, antra habitare, corpore aut nudo agere, aut corticibus arborum ferarumve pellibus vestito, vitæ genus exquisitus delegissent, industria opus fuit, quam singuli rebus singulis adhiberent: Quo minus autem fructus in commune conferrentur, primum obstitit locorum, in quæ homines discesserunt, distantia, deinde justitiæ & amoris defectus, per quem fiebat, ut nec in labore, nec in consumtione fructuum, quæ debebat, æqualitas servaretur. Simul discimus, quomodo res in proprietatem iverint; non animi actu solo, neque enim scire alii poterant, quid alii suum esse vellent, ut eo abstinerent, & idem velle plures poterant: sed pacto quodam aut expresso, ut per divisionem, aut tacito, ut per occupationem.' De Jure Belli & Pacis. Lib. ii. cap. 2. § 2, art. 4 & 5.

APP. III. tion of his intellectual faculties, may justly be esteemed natural.[1]

Among all civilized nations, it has been the constant endeavour to remove every thing arbitrary and partial from the decision of property, and to fix the sentence of judges by such general views and considerations, as may be equal to every member of the society. For besides, that nothing could be more dangerous than to accustom the bench, even in the smallest instance, to regard private friendship or enmity; it is certain, that men, where they imagine, that there was no other reason for the preference of their adversary but personal favour, are apt to entertain the strongest ill-will against the magistrates and judges. When natural reason, therefore, points out no fixed view of public utility, by which a controversy of property can be decided, positive laws are often framed to supply its place, and direct the procedure of all courts of judicature. Where these too fail, as often happens, precedents are called for; and a former decision, though given itself without any sufficient reason, justly becomes a sufficient reason for a new decision. If direct laws and precedents be wanting, imperfect and indirect ones are brought in aid; and the controverted case is ranged under them, by analogical reasonings and comparisons, and similitudes, and correspondencies, which are often more fanciful than real. In general, it may safely be affirmed, that jurisprudence is, in this respect, different from all the sciences; and that in many of its nicer questions, there cannot properly be said to be truth or falsehood on either side. If one pleader bring the case under any former law or precedent, by a refined analogy or comparison; the opposite pleader is not at a loss to find an opposite analogy or comparison: And the preference given by the judge is often founded more on taste and imagination than on any solid argument. Public utility is the general object of all courts of judicature; and this utility too requires a stable rule in all controversies. But where

---

[1] Natural may be opposed, either to what is *unusual, miraculous,* or *artificial*. In the two former senses, justice and property are undoubtedly natural. But as they suppose reason, forethought, design, and a social union and confederacy among men, perhaps, that epithet cannot strictly, in the last sense, be applied to them. Had men lived without society, property had never been known, and neither justice nor injustice had ever existed. But society among human creatures, had been impossible, without reason, and forethought. Inferior animals, that unite, are guided by instinct, which supplies the place of reason. But all these disputes are merely verbal.

several rules, nearly equal and indifferent, present themselves,
it is a very slight turn of thought, which fixes the decision
in favour of either party.[1]

[1] That there be a separation or distinction of possessions, and that this separation be steady and constant; this is absolutely required by the interests of society, and hence the origin of justice and property. What possessions are assigned to particular persons; this is, generally speaking, pretty indifferent; and is often determined by very frivolous views and considerations. We shall mention a few particulars.

Were a society formed among several independent members, the most obvious rule, which could be agreed on, would be to annex property to *present* possession, and leave every one a right to what he at present enjoys. The relation of possession, which takes place between the person and the object, naturally draws on the relation of property.

For a like reason, occupation or first possession becomes the foundation of property.

Where a man bestows labour and industry upon any object, which before belonged to no body; as in cutting down and shaping a tree, in cultivating a field, &c., the alteration which he produces, causes a relation between him and the object, and naturally engages us to annex it to him by the new relation of property. This cause here concurs with the public utility, which consists in the encouragement given to industry and labour.

Perhaps too, private humanity towards the possessor, concurs in this instance, with the other motives, and engages us to leave with him what he has acquired by his sweat and labour; and what he has flattered himself in the constant enjoyment of. For though private humanity can, by no means, be the origin of justice; since the latter virtue so often contradicts the former; yet when the rule of separate and constant possession is once formed by the indispensible necessities of society, private humanity, and an aversion to the doing a hardship to another may, in a particular instance, give rise to a particular rule of property.

I am much inclined to think, that the right of succession or inheritance much depends on those connexions of the imagination, and that the relation to a former proprietor begetting a relation to the object, is the cause why the property is transferred to a man after the death of his kinsman. It is true; industry is more encouraged by the transference of possession to children or near relations: But this consideration will only have place in a cultivated society; whereas the right of succession is regarded even among the greatest Barbarians.

Acquisition of property by *accession* can be explained no way but by having recourse to the relations and connexions of the imagination.

The property of rivers, by the laws of most nations, and by the natural turn of our thought, is attributed to the proprietors of their banks, excepting such vast rivers as the RHINE or the DANUBE, which seem too large to follow as an accession to the property of the neighbouring fields. Yet even these rivers are considered as the property of that nation, through whose dominions they run; the idea of a nation being of a suitable bulk to correspond with them, and bear them such a relation in the fancy.

The accessions, which are made to land, bordering upon rivers, follow the land, say the civilians, provided it be made by what they call *alluvion*, that is, insensibly and imperceptibly; which are circumstances, that assist the imagination in the conjunction.

Where there is any considerable portion torn at once from one bank and added to another, it becomes not *his* property, whose land it falls on, till it unite with the land, and till the trees and plants have spread their roots into both. Before that, the thought does not sufficiently join them.

In short, we must ever distinguish between the necessity of a separation and constancy in men's possession, and the rules, which assign particular objects to particular persons. The first necessity is obvious, strong, and invincible: The latter may depend on a public utility more light and frivolous, on the sentiment of private humanity and aversion to private hardship, on positive laws, on precedents, analogies, and very fine connexions and turns of the imagination. [This note was added in Edition K.]

APP. III.
'We may just observe, before we conclude this subject, that, after the laws of justice are fixed by views of general utility, the injury, the hardship, the harm, which result to any individual from a violation of them, enter very much into consideration, and are a great source of that universal blame, which attends every wrong or iniquity. By the laws of society this coat, this horse, is mine, and *ought* to remain perpetually in my possession : I reckon on the secure enjoyment of it : By depriving me of it, you disappoint my expectations, and doubly displease me, and offend every bystander. It is a public wrong, so far as the rules of equity are violated : It is a private harm, so far as an individual is injured. And though the second consideration could have no place, were not the former previously established : For otherwise the distinction of *mine* and *thine* would be unknown in society : Yet there is no question, but the regard to general good is much enforced by the respect to particular. What injures the community, without hurting any individual, is often more lightly thought of. But where the greatest public wrong is also conjoined with a considerable private one, no wonder the highest disapprobation attends so iniquitous a behaviour.

APPENDIX IV.[2]—*Of some Verbal Disputes.*

NOTHING is more usual than for philosophers to encroach upon the province of grammarians ; and to engage in disputes of words, while they imagine, that they are handling controversies of the deepest importance and concern.[3] It was in order to avoid altercations so frivolous and endless, that I endeavoured to state with the utmost caution the object of

[1] [Some copies of Edition G do not contain this paragraph. In others, the page having been torn out, a new page was inserted, containing the paragraph.]

[2] [This appears as Part i. of Section vi., Of Qualities useful to Ourselves, in Editions G to N.]

[3] [Editions G to M omit from this point to 'It seems indeed certain, &c.' p. 281, and substitute as follows :—

Thus, were we here to assert or to deny, *that all laudable qualities of the mind were to be consider'd as virtues or moral attributes*, many would imagine that we had enter'd upon one of the profoundest speculations of Ethics ; tho' 'tis probable, all the while, that the greatest part of the dispute would be found entirely verbal. To avoid, therefore, all frivolous subtilties and altercations, as much as possible, we shall content ourselves with observing, *first*, that, in common life, the sentiments of censure or approbation, produced by mental qualities of every kind, are very similar ; and *secondly*, that all antient Moralists (the best models), in treating of them, make little or no difference amongst them.

Edition N omits as far as 'Were we to say, &c.' p. 280, and substitutes as follows : Thus were we to seek an exact definition or description of those mental qualities,which are denominated *virtues* : we might be somewhat at a loss, and might find ourselves at first involved in inextricable difficulties.]

our present enquiry; and proposed simply to collect on the one hand, a list of those mental qualities which are the object of love or esteem, and form a part of personal merit, and on the other hand, a catalogue of those qualities, which are the object of censure or reproach, and which detract from the character of the person, possessed of them; subjoining some reflections concerning the origin of these sentiments of praise or blame. On all occasions, where there might arise the least hesitation, I avoided the terms *virtue* and *vice*; because some of those qualities, which I classed among the objects of praise, receive, in the ENGLISH language, the appellation of *talents*, rather than of virtues; as some of the blameable or censurable qualities are often called *defects*, rather than vices. It may now, perhaps, be expected, that, before we conclude this moral enquiry, we should exactly separate the one from the other; should mark the precise boundaries of virtues and talents, vices and defects; and should explain the reason and origin of that distinction. But in order to excuse myself from this undertaking, which would, at last, prove only a grammatical enquiry, I shall subjoin the four following reflections, which shall contain all that I intend to say on the present subject.

First, I do not find, that in the ENGLISH, or any other modern tongue, the boundaries are exactly fixed between virtues and talents, vices and defects, or that a precise definition can be given of the one as contradistinguished from the other. Were we to say, for instance, that the esteemable qualities alone, which are voluntary, are entitled to the appellation of virtues; we should soon recollect the qualities of courage, equanimity, patience, self-command; with many others, which almost every language classes under this appellation, though they depend little or not at all on our choice. Should we affirm, that the qualities alone, which prompt us to act our part in society, are entitled to that honourable distinction; it must immediately occur, that these are indeed the most valuable qualities, and are commonly denominated the *social* virtues; but that this very epithet supposes, that there are also virtues of another species.[1] Should we lay hold of the distinction between *intellectual* and *moral* endow-

[1] [Edition N appends the following note.

It seems to me, that in our language there are always said to be virtues of many different kinds; but when a man is said to be *virtuous* or is denominated a man of virtue, we chiefly regard his social qualities, which are indeed the most valuable. They are called the *virtues* by way of excellence.]

APP. IV. ments, and affirm the last alone to be the real and genuine virtues, because they alone lead to action; we should find, that many of those qualities, usually called intellectual virtues, such as prudence, penetration, discernment, discretion, had also a considerable influence on conduct. The distinction between the *heart* and the *head* may also be adopted: The qualities of the first may be defined such as in their immediate exertion are accompanied with a feeling or sentiment; and these alone may be called the genuine virtues. But industry, frugality, temperance, secrecy, perseverance, and many other laudable powers or habits, generally stiled virtues, are exerted without any immediate sentiment in the person possessed of them; and are only known to him by their effects. It is fortunate, amidst all this seeming perplexity, that the question, being merely verbal, cannot possibly be of any importance. A moral, philosophical discourse needs not enter into all these caprices of language, which are so variable in different dialects, and in different ages of the same dialect.[1] But on the whole, it seems to me, that, though it is always allowed, that there are virtues of many different kinds, yet, when a man is called *virtuous*, or is denominated a man of virtue, we chiefly regard his social qualities, which are, indeed, the most valuable. It is, at the same time, certain, that any remarkable defect in courage, temperance, œconomy, industry, understanding, dignity of mind, would bereave even a very good-natured, honest man of this honourable appellation. Who did ever say, except by way of irony, that such a one was a man of great virtue, but an egregious blockhead?

But, *secondly*, it is no wonder, that languages should not be very precise in marking the boundaries between virtues and talents, vices and defects; since there is so little distinction made in our internal estimation of them. It seems indeed certain, that the *sentiment* of conscious worth, the self-satisfaction proceeding from a review of a man's own

---

[1] [For the next four sentences Edition N substitutes as follows:—
It may happen, that, in treating of ethics, we may sometimes mention laudable qualities, which the English tongue does not always rank under the appellation of virtue; but we do it only because we are at a loss how to draw the exact line between the one and the other; or at least because we consider the question as merely grammatical. And the more fully to justify our practice in this particular, we shall endeavour to make it appear, *first*, that in common life, the sentiments of censure or approbation, produced by mental qualities of every kind, are nearly similar; and *secondly*, that all antient moralists, (the best models) in treating of them, make little or no difference among them.]

conduct and character; it seems certain, I say, that this sentiment, which, though the most common of all others, has no proper name in our language,[1] arises from the endowments of courage and capacity, industry and ingenuity, as well as from any other mental excellencies. Who, on the other hand, is not deeply mortified with reflecting on his own folly and dissoluteness, and feels not a secret sting or compunction, whenever his memory presents any past occurrence, where he behaved with stupidity or ill-manners? No time can efface the cruel ideas of a man's own foolish conduct, or of affronts, which cowardice or imprudence has brought upon him. They still haunt his solitary hours, damp his most aspiring thoughts, and show him, even to himself, in the most contemptible and most odious colours imaginable.

What is there too we are more anxious to conceal from others than such blunders, infirmities, and meannesses, or more dread to have exposed by raillery and satire? And is not the chief object of vanity, our bravery or learning, our wit or breeding, our eloquence or address, our taste or abilities? These we display with care, if not with ostentation; and we commonly show more ambition of excelling in them, than even in the social virtues themselves, which are, in reality, of such superior excellence. Good-nature and honesty, especially the latter, are so indispensably required, that, though the greatest censure attends any violation of these duties, no eminent praise follows such common instances of them, as seem essential to the support of human society. And hence the reason, in my opinion, why, though men often extol so liberally the qualities of their heart, they are shy in commending the endowments of their head: Because the latter virtues, being supposed more rare and extraordinary, are observed to be the more usual objects of pride and self-conceit; and when boasted of, beget a strong suspicion of these sentiments.

It is hard to tell, whether you hurt a man's character most by calling him a knave or a coward, and whether a beastly

---

[1] The term, pride, is commonly taken in a bad sense; but this sentiment seems indifferent, and may be either good or bad, according as it is well or ill founded, and according to the other circumstances which accompany it. The FRENCH express this sentiment by the term, *amour propre*, but as they also express self-love as well as vanity, by the same term, there arises thence a great confusion in ROCHEFOUCAULT, and many of their moral writers.

APP. IV.

glutton or drunkard be not as odious and contemptible, as a selfish, ungenerous miser. Give me my choice, and I would rather, for my own happiness and self-enjoyment, have a friendly, humane heart, than possess all the other virtues of DEMOSTHENES and PHILIP united: But I would rather pass with the world for one endowed with extensive genius and intrepid courage, and should thence expect stronger instances of general applause and admiration. The figure which a man makes in life, the reception which he meets with in company, the esteem paid him by his acquaintance; all these advantages depend as much upon his good sense and judgment, as upon any other part of his character. Had a man the best intentions in the world, and were the farthest removed from all injustice and violence, he would never be able to make himself be much regarded, without a moderate share, at least, of parts and understanding.

What is it then we can here dispute about? If sense and courage, temperance and industry, wisdom and knowledge confessedly form a considerable part of *personal merit*: if a man, possessed of these qualities, is both better satisfied with himself, and better entitled to the goodwill, esteem, and services of others, than one entirely destitute of them; if, in short, the *sentiments* are similar, which arise from these endowments and from the social virtues; is there any reason for being so extremely scrupulous about a *word*, or disputing whether they be entitled to the denomination of virtues?[1] It may, indeed, be pretended, that the sentiment of approbation, which those accomplishments produce, besides its being *inferior*, is also somewhat *different* from that, which attends the virtues of justice and humanity. But this seems not a sufficient reason for ranking them entirely under different classes and appellations. The character of CÆSAR and that of CATO, as drawn by SALLUST, are both of them virtuous, in the strictest and most limited sense of the word; but in a

---

[1] [Editions G to M add in a note: It seems to me, that in our language, courage, temperance, industry, frugality, &c., according to popular stile, are called *virtues*; but when a man is said to be *virtuous*, or is denominated a man of virtue, we chiefly regard his social qualities. 'Tis needless for a moral, philosophical discourse to enter into all these caprices of language, which are so variable in different dialects, and in different ages of the same dialect. The *sentiments* of men, being more uniform, as well as more important, are a fitter subject of speculation: Tho' at the same time, we may just observe, that wherever the social virtues are talked of, 'tis plainly imply'd, by this distinction, that there are also other virtues of a different nature.]

different way: Nor are the sentiments entirely the same, which arise from them. The one produces love: the other, esteem: The one is amiable; the other awful: We should wish to meet the one character in a friend; the other we should be ambitious of in ourselves. In like manner the approbation, which attends temperance or industry or frugality, may be somewhat different from that which is paid to the social virtues, without making them entirely of a different species. And, indeed, we may observe, that these endowments, more than the other virtues, produce not, all of them, the same kind of approbation. Good sense and genius beget esteem and regard: Wit and humour excite love and affection.[1]

Most people, I believe, will naturally, without premeditation, assent to the definition of the elegant and judicious poet.

> Virtue (for mere good-nature is a fool)
> Is sense and spirit with humanity.[2]

What pretensions has a man to our generous assistance or good offices, who has dissipated his wealth in profuse expences, idle vanities, chimerical projects, dissolute pleasures, or extravagant gaming? These vices (for we scruple not to call them such) bring misery unpitied, and contempt on every one addicted to them.

ACHÆUS, a wise and prudent prince, fell into a fatal snare, which cost him his crown and life, after having used every reasonable precaution to guard himself against it. On that

---

[1] Love and esteem are nearly the same passion, and arise from similar causes. The qualities, which produce both, are such as communicate pleasure. But where this pleasure is severe and serious; or where its object is great and makes a strong impression, or where it produces any degree of humility and awe: In all these cases, the passion, which arises from the pleasure, is more properly denominated esteem than love. Benevolence attends both: But is connected with love in a more eminent degree. There seems to be still a stronger mixture of pride in contempt than of humility in esteem; and the reason would not be difficult to one, who studied accurately the passions. All these various mixtures and compositions and appearances of sentiment form a very curious subject of speculation, but are wide of our present purpose. Throughout this enquiry, we always consider in general, what qualities are a subject of praise or of censure, without entering into all the minute differences of sentiment, which they excite. It is evident, that whatever is contemned, is also disliked, as well as what is hated; and here we endeavour to take objects, according to their most simple views and appearances. These sciences are but too apt to appear abstract to common readers, even with all the precautions which we can take to clear them from superfluous speculations, and bring them down to every capacity.

[2] Armstrong: The Art of preserving Health. Book I.

APP. IV.account, says the historian, he is a just object of regard and compassion: His betrayers alone of hatred and contempt.[1]

The precipitate flight and improvident negligence of POMPEY, at the beginning of the civil wars, appeared such notorious blunders to CICERO, as quite palled his friendship towards that great man. *In the same manner, says he, as want of cleanliness, decency, or discretion in a mistress are found to alienate our affections.* For so he expresses himself, where he talks, not in the character of a philosopher, but in that of a statesman and man of the world, to his friend ATTICUS.[2]

But the same CICERO, in imitation of all the ancient moralists, when he reasons as a philosopher, enlarges very much his ideas of virtue, and comprehends every laudable quality or endowment of the mind, under that honourable appellation. [3] This leads to the *third* reflection, which we proposed to make, to wit, that the ancient moralists, the best models, made no material distinction among the different species of mental endowments and defects, but treated all alike under the appellation of virtues and vices, and made them indiscriminately the object of their moral reasonings. The *prudence* explained in CICERO's *Offices*,[4] is that sagacity, which leads to the discovery of truth, and preserves us from error and mistake. *Magnanimity, temperance, decency,* are there also at large discoursed of. And as that eloquent moralist followed the common received division of the four cardinal virtues, our social duties form but one head, in the general distribution of his subject.[5]

[1] POLYBIUS, lib. viii. cap. 2, 8 & 9.
[2] Lib. ix. epist. 10, 2.
[3] [This sentence was added in Edition O.]
[4] Lib. i. cap. 6.
[5] The following passage of CICERO is worth quoting, as being the most clear and express to our purpose, that anything can be imagined, and, in a dispute, which is chiefly verbal, must, on account of the author, carry an authority, from which there can be no appeal.

'Virtus autem, quæ est per se ipsa laudabilis, et sine qua nihil laudari potest, tamen habet plures partes, quarum alia est alia ad laudationem aptior. Sunt enim aliæ virtutes, quæ videntur in moribus hominum et quadam comitate ac beneficentia positæ: aliæ, quæ in ingenii aliqua facultate, aut animi magnitudine ac robore. Nam clementia, justitia, benignitas, fides, fortitudo in periculis communibus, jucunda est auditu in laudationibus. Omnes enim hæ virtutes non tam ipsis, qui eas in se habent, quam generi hominum fructuosæ putantur. Sapientia et magnitudo animi, qua omnes res humanæ tenues et pro nihilo putantur; et in cogitando vis quædam ingenii et ipsa eloquentia admirationis habet non minus, jucunditatis minus. Ipsos enim magis videtur, quos laudamus, quam illos, apud quos laudamus, ornare ac tueri; sed tamen in laudando jungenda sunt etiam hæc genera virtutum. Ferunt enim aures hominum, cum illa quæ jucunda et grata, tum etiam illa, quæ mirabilia sunt in virtute, laudari.' *De Orat. lib. 2. cap.* 84

We need only peruse the titles of chapters in ARISTOTLE'S Ethics to be convinced, that he ranks courage, temperance, magnificence, magnanimity, modesty, prudence, and a manly openness, among the virtues, as well as justice and friendship.

To *sustain* and to *abstain*, that is, to be patient and continent, appeared to some of the ancients a summary comprehension of all morals.

EPICTETUS has scarcely ever mentioned the sentiment of humanity and compassion, but in order to put his disciples on their guard against it. The virtue of the *Stoics* seems to consist chiefly in a firm temper, and a sound understanding. With them, as with SOLOMON and the eastern moralists, folly and wisdom are equivalent to vice and virtue.

Men will praise thee, says DAVID,[1] when thou dost well unto thyself. I hate a wise man, says the GREEK poet, who is not wise to himself.[2]

PLUTARCH is no more cramped by systems in his philosophy than in his history. Where he compares the great men of GREECE and ROME, he fairly sets in opposition all their blemishes and accomplishments of whatever kind, and omits nothing considerable, which can either depress or exalt their characters. His moral discourses contain the same free and natural censure of men and manners.

The character of HANNIBAL, as drawn by LIVY,[3] is esteemed partial, but allows him many eminent virtues. Never was there a genius, says the historian, more equally fitted for those opposite offices of commanding and obeying; and it were, therefore, difficult to determine whether he rendered himself *dearer* to the general or to the army. To none would HASDRUBAL entrust more willingly the conduct of any dangerous enterprize; under none, did the soldiers discover more courage and confidence. Great boldness in facing danger; great prudence in the midst of it. No labour could fatigue his body or subdue his mind. Cold and heat were indifferent to him: Meat and drink he sought as supplies to

---

I suppose, if CICERO were now alive, it would be found difficult to fetter his moral sentiments by narrow systems; or persuade him, that no qualities were to be admitted as *virtues*, or acknowledged to be a part of *personal merit*, but what were recommended by *The Whole Duty of Man*. [This note was added in Edition Q.]

[1] Psalm 49th.
[2] Μισῶ σοφιστὴν ὅστις οὐδ' αὑτῷ σοφός. EURIPIDES. Fr. 111. [Edition G gives as the reference: Incert. apud Lucianum, apologia pro mercede conductis. Edition K does the same in the Text, but makes the correction in the Errata.]
[3] Lib. xxi. cap. 4.

the necessities of nature, not as gratifications of his voluptuous appetites: Waking or rest he used indiscriminately, by night or by day.——These great VIRTUES were balanced by great VICES: Inhuman cruelty; perfidy more than *punic*; no truth, no faith, no regard to oaths, promises, or religion.

The character of ALEXANDER the Sixth, to be found in GUICCIARDIN,[1] is pretty similar, but juster; and is a proof, that even the moderns, where they speak naturally, hold the same language with the ancients. In this pope, says he, there was a singular capacity and judgment: Admirable prudence; a wonderful talent of persuasion; and in all momentous enterprizes, a diligence and dexterity incredible. But these *virtues* were infinitely overbalanced by his *vices*; no faith, no religion, insatiable avarice, exorbitant ambition, and a more than barbarous cruelty.

POLYBIUS,[2] reprehending TIMÆUS for his partiality against AGATHOCLES, whom he himself allows to be the most cruel and impious of all tyrants, says: If he took refuge in SYRACUSE, as asserted by that historian, flying the dirt and smoke and toil of his former profession of a potter; and if proceeding from such slender beginnings, he became master, in a little time, of all SICILY; brought the CARTHAGINIAN state into the utmost danger; and at last died in old age, and in possession of sovereign dignity: Must he not be allowed something prodigious and extraordinary, and to have possessed great talents and capacity for business and action? His historian, therefore, ought not to have alone related what tended to his reproach and infamy; but also what might redound to his PRAISE and HONOUR.

In general, we may observe, that the distinction of voluntary or involuntary was little regarded by the ancients in their moral reasonings; where they frequently treated the question as very doubtful, *whether virtue could be taught or not?*[3] They justly considered, that cowardice, meanness, levity, anxiety, impatience, folly, and many other qualities of the mind, might appear ridiculous and deformed, contemptible and odious, though independent of the will. Nor could it

---

[1] Lib. i.
[2] Lib. xii. 15.
[3] Vid. PLATO in MENONE, SENECA *de Otio sap. cap.* 31. So also HORACE,

Virtutem doctrina paret, naturane donet.
Epist. lib. i. ep. 18, 100. ÆSCHINIS SOCRATICUS. Dial. i. [The reference to Æs. Soc. was added in Edition O.]

be supposed, at all times, in every man's power to attain every kind of mental, more than of exterior beauty.

[1] And here there occurs the *fourth* reflection which I purposed to make, in suggesting the reason, why modern philosophers have often followed a course, in their moral enquiries, so different from that of the ancients. In later times, philosophy of all kinds, especially ethics, have been more closely united with theology than ever they were observed to be among the Heathens; and as this latter science admits of no terms of composition, but bends every branch of knowledge to its own purpose, without much regard to the phaenomena of nature, or to the unbiassed sentiments of the mind, hence reasoning, and even language, have been warped from their natural course, and distinctions have been endeavoured to be established, where the difference of the objects was, in a manner, imperceptible. Philosophers, or rather divines under that disguise, treating all morals, as on a like footing with civil laws, guarded by the sanctions of reward and punishment, were necessarily led to render this circumstance, of *voluntary* or *involuntary*, the foundation of their whole theory. Every one may employ *terms* in what sense he pleases: But this, in the mean time, must be allowed, that *sentiments* are every day experienced of blame and praise, which have objects beyond the dominion of the will or choice, and of which it behoves us, if not as moralists, as speculative philosophers at least, to give some satisfactory theory and explication.

A blemish, a fault, a vice, a crime; these expressions seem to denote different degrees of censure and disapprobation; which are, however, all of them, at the bottom, pretty nearly of the same kind or species. The explication of one will easily lead us into a just conception of the others;[2] and it is of greater consequence to attend to things than to verbal appellations. That we owe a duty to ourselves is confessed even in the most vulgar system of morals; and it must be of consequence to examine that duty, in order to see, whether it bears any affinity to that which we owe to society. It is probable, that the approbation, attending the observance of both, is of a similar nature, and arises from similar principles; whatever appellation we may give to either of these excellencies.

[1] [This sentence and the next do not occur in Editions G to N, which resume: But modern philosophers, treating, &c.]

[2] [The remainder of the paragraph was added in Edition N.]

A DIALOGUE.[1]

My friend, PALAMEDES, who is as great a rambler in his principles as in his person, and who has run over, by study and travel, almost every region of the intellectual and material world, surprized me lately with an account of a nation, with whom, he told me, he had passed a considerable part of his life, and whom, he found, in the main, a people extremely civilized and intelligent.

There is a country, said he, in the world, called FOURLI, no matter for its longitude or latitude, whose inhabitants have ways of thinking, in many things, particularly in morals, diametrically opposite to ours. When I came among them, I found that I must submit to double pains; first to learn the meaning of the terms in their language, and then to know the import of those terms, and the praise or blame attached to them. After a word had been explained to me, and the character, which it expressed, had been described, I concluded, that such an epithet must necessarily be the greatest reproach in the world; and was extremely surprized to find one in a public company, apply it to a person, with whom he lived in the strictest intimacy and friendship. *You fancy*, said I, one day, to an acquaintance, *that* CHANGUIS *is your mortal enemy: I love to extinguish quarrels; and I must, therefore, tell you, that I heard him talk of you in the most obliging manner.* But to my great astonishment, when I repeated CHANGUIS's words, though I had both remembered and understood them perfectly, I found, that they were taken for the most mortal affront, and that I had very innocently rendered the breach between these persons altogether irreparable.

As it was my fortune to come among this people on a very advantageous footing, I was immediately introduced to the best company; and being desired by ALCHEIC to live with him, I readily accepted of his invitation; as I found him universally

[1] [For the Author's opinion of this Dialogue, see 'History of the Editions,' Vol. III. p. 52.—ED.]

esteemed for his personal merit, and indeed regarded by every one in FOURLI, as a perfect character.

One evening he invited me, as an amusement, to bear him company in a serenade, which he intended to give to GULKI, with whom, he told me, he was extremely enamoured; and I soon found that his taste was not singular : For we met many of his rivals, who had come on the same errand. I very naturally concluded, that this [1] mistress of his must be one of the finest women in town; and I already felt a secret inclination to see her, and be acquainted with her. But as the moon began to rise, I was much surprized to find, that we were in the midst of the university, where GULKI studied : And I was somewhat ashamed for having attended my friend, on such an errand.

I was afterwards told, that ALCHEIC's choice of GULKI was very much approved of by all the good company in town; and that it was expected, while he gratified his own passion, he would perform to that young man the same good office, which he had himself owed to ELCOUF. It seems ALCHEIC had been very handsome in his youth, had been courted by many lovers; but had bestowed his favours chiefly on the sage ELCOUF; to whom he was supposed to owe, in a great measure, the astonishing progress which he had made in philosophy and virtue.

It gave me some surprize, that ALCHEIC's wife (who by-the-by happened also to be his sister) was no wise scandalized at this species of infidelity.

Much about the same time I discovered (for it was not attempted to be kept a secret from me or any body) that ALCHEIC was a murderer and a parricide, and had put to death an innocent person, the most nearly connected with him, and whom he was bound to protect and defend by all the ties of nature and humanity. When I asked, with all the caution and deference imaginable, what was his motive for this action; he replied coolly, that he was not then so much at ease in his circumstances as he is at present, and that he had acted, in that particular, by the advice of all his friends.

Having heard ALCHEIC's virtue so extremely celebrated, I pretended to join him in the general voice of acclamation, and only asked, by way of curiosity, as a stranger, which of all his noble actions was most highly applauded; and I soon found, that all sentiments were united in giving the preference to the

[1] [This flame of his: Editions G and K.]

assassination of USBEK. This USBEK had been to the last moment ALCHEIC'S intimate friend, had laid many high obligations upon him, had even saved his life on a certain occasion, and had, by his will, which was found after the murder, made him heir to a considerable part of his fortune. ALCHEIC, it seems, conspired with about twenty or thirty more, most of them also USBEK's friends; and falling all together on that unhappy man, when he was not aware, they had torne him with a hundred wounds; and given him that reward for all his past favours and obligations. USBEK, said the general voice of the people, had many great and good qualities: His very vices were shining, magnificent, and generous: But this action of ALCHEIC's sets him far above USBEK in the eyes of all judges of merit; and is one of the noblest that ever perhaps the sun shone upon.

Another part of ALCHEIC's conduct, which I also found highly applauded, was his behaviour towards CALISH, with whom he was joined in a project or undertaking of some importance. CALISH, being a passionate man, gave ALCHEIC, one day, a sound drubbing; which he took very patiently, waited the return of CALISH's good-humour, kept still a fair correspondence with him; and by that means brought the affair, in which they were joined, to a happy issue, and gained to himself immortal honour by his remarkable temper and moderation.

I have lately received a letter from a correspondent in FOURLI, by which I learn, that, since my departure, ALCHEIC, falling into a bad state of health, has fairly hanged himself; and has died universally regretted and applauded in that country. So virtuous and noble a life, says each FOURLIAN, could not be better crowned than by so noble an end; and ALCHEIC has proved by this, as well as by all his other actions, what was his constant principle during his life, and what he boasted of near his last moments, that a wise man is scarcely inferior to the great god, VITZLI. This is the name of the supreme deity among the FOURLIANS.

The notions of this people, continued PALAMEDES, are as extraordinary with regard to good-manners and sociableness, as with regard to morals. My friend ALCHEIC formed once a party for my entertainment, composed of all the prime wits and philosophers of FOURLI; and each of us brought his mess along with him to the place where we assembled. I observed one of them to be worse provided than the rest, and offered him a share of my mess, which happened to be a roasted pullet : And I could not but remark, that he and all the rest of the company smiled at my simplicity. I was told, that ALCHEIC had once so much interest with his club as to prevail with them to eat in common, and that he had made use of an artifice for that purpose. He persuaded those, whom he observed to be *worst* provided, to offer their mess to the company ; after which, the others, who had brought more delicate fare, were ashamed not to make the same offer. This is regarded as so extraordinary an event, that it has since, as I learn, been recorded in the history of ALCHEIC's life, composed by one of the greatest geniuses of FOURLI.

Pray, said I, PALAMEDES, when you were at FOURLI, did you also learn the art of turning your friends into ridicule, by telling them strange stories, and then laughing at them, if they believed you. I assure you, replied he, had I been disposed to learn such a lesson, there was no place in the world more proper. My friend, so often mentioned, did nothing, from morning to night, but sneer, and banter, and rally ; and you could scarcely ever distinguish, whether he were in jest or earnest. But you think then, that my story is improbable ; and that I have used, or rather abused the privilege of a traveller. To be sure, said I, you were but in jest. Such barbarous and savage manners are not only incompatible with a civilized, intelligent people, such as you said these were ; but are scarcely compatible with human nature. They exceed all we ever read of, among the MINGRELIANS, and TOPINAMBOUES.

Have a care, cried he, have a care ! You are not aware that you are speaking blasphemy, and are abusing your favourites, the GREEKS, especially the ATHENIANS, whom I have couched, all along, under these bizarre names I employed. If you consider aright, there is not one stroke of the foregoing character, which might not be found in the man of highest merit at ATHENS, without diminishing in the least from the brightness of his character. The amours of the GREEKS, their marriages[1], and the exposing of their children cannot but strike you immediately. The death of USBEK is an exact counter-part to that of CÆSAR.

---

[1] The laws of ATHENS allowed a man to marry his sister by the father. SOLON's law forbid pæderasty to slaves, as being an act of too great dignity for such mean persons.

All to a trifle, said I, interrupting him: You did not mention that USBEK was an usurper.

I did not, replied he; lest you should discover the parallel I aimed at. But even adding this circumstance, we should make no scruple, according to our sentiments of morals, to denominate BRUTUS, and CASSIUS, ungrateful traitors and assassins: Though you know, that they are, perhaps, the highest characters of all antiquity; and the ATHENIANS erected statues to them; which they placed near those of HARMODIUS and ARISTOGITON, their own deliverers. And if you think this circumstance, which you mention, so material to absolve these patriots, I shall compensate it by another, not mentioned, which will equally aggravate their crime. A few days before the execution of their fatal purpose, they all swore fealty to CÆSAR; and protesting to hold his person ever sacred, they touched the altar with those hands, which they had already armed for his destruction.[1]

I need not remind you of the famous and applauded story of THEMISTOCLES, and of his patience towards EURYBIADES, the SPARTAN, his commanding officer, who, heated by debate, lifted his cane to him in a council of war (the same thing as if he had cudgelled him), *Strike!* cries the ATHENIAN, *strike! but hear me.*

You are too good a scholar not to discover the ironical SOCRATES and his ATHENIAN club in my last story; and you will certainly observe, that it is exactly copied from XENOPHON, with a variation only of the names.[2] And I think I have fairly made it appear, that an ATHENIAN man of merit might be such a one as with us would pass for incestuous, a parricide, an assassin, an ungrateful, perjured traitor, and something else too abominable to be named; not to mention his rusticity and ill-manners. And having lived in this manner, his death might be entirely suitable: He might conclude the scene by a desperate act of self-murder, and die with the most absurd blasphemies in his mouth. And notwithstanding all this, he shall have statues, if not altars, erected to his memory; poems and orations shall be composed in his praise; great sects shall be proud of calling themselves by his name; and the most distant posterity shall blindly continue their admiration: Though

[1] APPIAN. Bell. Civ. lib. ii. 106. SUETONIUS in vit. CÆSARIS. 84.
[2] Mem. Soc. lib. iii. 11. 1.

were such a one to arise among themselves, they would justly
regard him with horror and execration.

I might have been aware, replied I, of your artifice.
You seem to take pleasure in this topic : and are indeed the
only man I ever knew, who was well acquainted with the
ancients, and did not extremely admire them. But instead
of attacking their philosophy, their eloquence, or poetry, the
usual subjects of controversy between us, you now seem to
impeach their morals, and accuse them of ignorance in a
science, which is the only one, in my opinion, in which they
are not surpassed by the moderns. Geometry, physics,
astronomy, anatomy, botany, geography, navigation ; in these
we justly claim the superiority : But what have we to oppose
to their moralists ? Your representation of things is fallacious. You have no indulgence for the manners and customs of different ages. Would you try a GREEK or ROMAN
by the common law of ENGLAND ? Hear him defend himself
by his own maxims ; and then pronounce.

There are no manners so innocent or reasonable, but may
be rendered odious or ridiculous, if measured by a standard,
unknown to the persons; especially, if you employ a little
art or eloquence, in aggravating some circumstances, and
extenuating others, as best suits the purpose of your discourse. All these artifices may easily be retorted on you.
Could I inform the ATHENIANS, for instance, that there was
a nation, in which adultery, both active and passive, so to
speak, was in the highest vogue and esteem : In which every
man of education chose for his mistress a married woman,
the wife, perhaps, of his friend and companion ; and valued
himself upon these infamous conquests, as much as if he
had been several times a conqueror in boxing or wrestling
at the *Olympic* games : In which every man also took a
pride in his tameness and facility with regard to his own
wife, and was glad to make friends or gain interest by
allowing her to prostitute her charms ; and even, without
any such motive, gave her full liberty and indulgence : I
ask, what sentiments the ATHENIANS would entertain of such
a people ; they who never mentioned the crime of adultery
but in conjunction with robbery and poisoning ? Which
would they admire most, the villany or the meanness of such
a conduct ?

Should I add, that the same people were as proud of their

slavery and dependance as the ATHENIANS of their liberty; and though a man among them were oppressed, disgraced, impoverished, insulted, or imprisoned by the tyrant, he would still regard it as the highest merit to love, serve, and obey him; and even to die for his smallest glory or satisfaction: These noble GREEKS would probably ask me, whether I spoke of a human society, or of some inferior, servile species.

It was then I might inform my ATHENIAN audience, that these people, however, wanted not spirit and bravery. If a man, say I, though their intimate friend, should throw out, in a private company, a raillery against them, nearly approaching any of those, with which your generals and demagogues every day regale each other, in the face of the whole city, they never can forgive him; but in order to revenge themselves, they oblige him immediately to run them through the body, or be himself murdered. And if a man, who is an absolute stranger to them, should desire them, at the peril of their own life, to cut the throat of their bosom-companion, they immediately obey, and think themselves highly obliged and honoured by the commission. These are their maxims of honour: This is their favourite morality.

But though so ready to draw their sword against their friends and countrymen; no disgrace, no infamy, no pain, no poverty will ever engage these people to turn the point of it against their own breast. A man of rank would row in the gallies, would beg his bread, would languish in prison, would suffer any tortures; and still preserve his wretched life. Rather than escape his enemies by a generous contempt of death, he would infamously receive the same death from his enemies, aggravated by their triumphant insults, and by the most exquisite sufferings.

It is very usual too, continued I, among this people to erect jails, where every art of plaguing and tormenting the unhappy prisoners is carefully studied and practised: And in these jails it is usual for a parent voluntarily to shut up several of his children; in order, that another child, whom he owns to have no greater or rather less merit than the rest, may enjoy his whole fortune, and wallow in every kind of voluptuousness and pleasure. Nothing so virtuous in their opinion as this barbarous partiality.

But what is more singular in this whimsical nation, say I

to the ATHENIANS, is, that a frolic of yours during the SATURNALIA[1], when the slaves are served by their masters, is seriously continued by them throughout the whole year, and throughout the whole course of their lives ; accompanied too with some circumstances, which still farther augment the absurdity and ridicule. Your sport only elevates for a few days those whom fortune has thrown down, and whom she too, in sport, may really elevate for ever above you : But this nation gravely exalts those, whom nature has subjected to them, and whose inferiority and infirmities are absolutely incurable. The women, though without virtue, are their masters and sovereigns : These they reverence, praise, and magnify : To these, they pay the highest deference and respect : And in all places and all times, the superiority of the females is readily acknowledged and submitted to by every one, who has the least pretensions to education and politeness. Scarce any crime would be so universally detested as an infraction of this rule.

You need go no further, replied PALAMEDES ; I can easily conjecture the people whom you aim at. The strokes, with which you have painted them, are pretty just; and yet you must acknowledge, that scarce any people are to be found, either in ancient or modern times, whose national character is, upon the whole, less liable to exception. But I give you thanks for helping me out with my argument. I had no intention of exalting the moderns at the expence of the ancients. I only meant to represent the uncertainty of all these judgments concerning characters; and to convince you, that fashion, vogue, custom, and law, were the chief foundation of all moral determinations. The ATHENIANS surely, were a civilized, intelligent people, if ever there were one ; and yet their man of merit might, in this age, be held in horror and execration. The FRENCH are also, without doubt, a very civilized, intelligent people; and yet their man of merit might, with the ATHENIANS, be an object of the highest contempt and ridicule, and even hatred. And what renders the matter more extraordinary : These two people are supposed to be the most similar in their national character of any in ancient and modern times ; and while the

<hr>

[1] The GREEKS kept the feast of SATURN or CHRONUS, as well as the ROMANS. See LUCIAN. Epist. SATURN.

ENGLISH flatter themselves that they resemble the ROMANS, their neighbours on the continent draw the parallel between themselves and those polite GREEKS. What wide difference, therefore, in the sentiments of morals, must be found between civilized nations and Barbarians, or between nations whose characters have little in common? How shall we pretend to fix a standard for judgments of this nature?

By tracing matters, replied I, a little higher, and examining the first principles, which each nation establishes, of blame or censure. The RHINE flows north, the RHONE south; yet both spring from the *same* mountain, and are also actuated, in their opposite directions, by the *same* principle of gravity. The different inclinations of the ground, on which they run, cause all the difference of their courses.

In how many circumstances would an ATHENIAN and a FRENCH man of merit certainly resemble each other? Good sense, knowledge, wit, eloquence, humanity, fidelity, truth, justice, courage, temperance, constancy, dignity of mind: These you have all omitted; in order to insist only on the points, in which they may, by accident, differ. Very well: I am willing to comply with you; and shall endeavour to account for these differences from the most universal, established principles of morals.

The GREEK loves, I care not to examine more particularly. I shall only observe, that, however blameable, they arose from a very innocent cause, the frequency of the gymnastic exercises among that people; and were recommended, though absurdly, as the source of friendship, sympathy, mutual attachment, and fidelity ;[1] qualities esteemed in all nations and all ages.

The marriage of half-brothers and sisters seems no great difficulty. Love between the nearer relations is contrary to reason and public utility; but the precise point, where we are to stop, can scarcely be determined by natural reason: and is therefore a very proper subject for municipal law or custom. If the ATHENIANS went a little too far on the one side, the canon law has surely pushed matters a great way into the other extreme.[2]

Had you asked a parent at ATHENS, why he bereaved

[1] PLAT. symp. p. 182. Ex edit. SER.   See Enquiry Sec. IV. Of Political Society.

his child of that life, which he had so lately given it. It is because I love it, he would reply ; and regard the poverty which it must inherit from me, as a greater evil than death, which it is not capable of dreading, feeling, or resenting.[1]

How is public liberty, the most valuable of all blessings, to be recovered from the hands of an usurper or tyrant, if his power shields him from public rebellion, and our scruples from private vengeance ? That his crime is capital by law, you acknowledge : And must the highest aggravation of his crime, the putting of himself above law, form his full se-curity ? You can reply nothing, but by showing the great inconveniencies of assassination ; which could any one have proved clearly to the ancients, he had reformed their senti-ments in this particular.

Again, to cast your eye on the picture which I have drawn of modern manners; there is almost as great difficulty, I acknowledge, to justify FRENCH as GREEK gallantry; except only, that the former is much more natural and agreeable than the latter. But our neighbours, it seems, have resolved to sacrifice some of the domestic to the sociable pleasures: and to prefer ease, freedom, and an open commerce, to a strict fidelity and constancy. These ends are both good, and are somewhat difficult to reconcile ; nor need we be surprised, if the customs of nations incline too much, sometimes to the one side, sometimes to the other.

The most inviolable attachment to the laws of our country is every where acknowledged a capital virtue; and where the people are not so happy, as to have any legislature but a single person, the strictest loyalty is, in that case, the truest patriotism.

Nothing surely can be more absurd and barbarous than the practice of duelling ; but those, who justify it, say, that it begets civility and good-manners. And a duellist, you may observe, always values himself upon his courage, his sense of honour, his fidelity and friendship ; qualities, which are here indeed very oddly directed, but which have been esteemed universally, since the foundation of the world.

Have the gods forbid self-murder ? An ATHENIAN allows, that it ought to be forborn. Has the Deity permitted it ?

---

[1] PLUT. de amore prolis, sub fine.

A FRENCHMAN allows, that death is preferable to pain and infamy.

You see then, continued I, that the principles upon which men reason in morals are always the same; though the conclusions which they draw are often very different. That they all reason aright with regard to this subject, more than with regard to any other, it is not incumbent on any moralist to show. It is sufficient, that the original principles of censure or blame are uniform, and that erroneous conclusions can be corrected by sounder reasoning and larger experience. Though many ages have elapsed since the fall of GREECE and ROME; though many changes have arrived in religion, language, laws, and customs; none of these revolutions has ever produced any considerable innovation in the primary sentiments of morals, more than in those of external beauty. Some minute differences, perhaps, may be observed in both. HORACE[1] celebrates a low forehead, and ANACREON joined eye-brows:[2] but the APOLLO and the VENUS of antiquity are still our models for male and female beauty: in like manner as the character of SCIPIO continues our standard for the glory of heroes, and that of CORNELIA for the honour of matrons.

It appears, that there never was any quality recommended by any one, as a virtue or moral excellence, but on account of its being *useful*, or *agreeable* to a man *himself*, or to *others*. For what other reason can ever be assigned for praise or approbation? Or where would be the sense of extolling a *good* character or action, which, at the same time, is allowed to be *good for nothing?* All the differences, therefore, in morals, may be reduced to this one general foundation, and may be accounted for by the different views, which people take of these circumstances.

Sometimes men differ in their judgment about the usefulness of any habit or action: Sometimes also the peculiar circumstances of things render one moral quality more useful than others, and give it a peculiar preference.

It is not surprising, that, during a period of war and disorder, the military virtues should be more celebrated than the pacific, and attract more the admiration and attention

---

[1] Epist. lib. i. epist. 7, 26. Also lib. i. ode 33, 5.

[2] Ode 28. PETRONIUS (cap. 126) joins both these circumstances as beauties.

of mankind. 'How usual is it,' says TULLY,[1] 'to find CIM-
BRIANS, CELTIBERIANS, and other Barbarians, who bear, with
inflexible constancy, all the fatigues and dangers of the field;
but are immediately dispirited under the pain and hazard of
a languishing distemper: While, on the other hand, the
GREEKS patiently endure the slow approaches of death, when
armed with sickness and disease; but timorously fly his
presence, when he attacks them violently with swords and
falchions!' So different is even the same virtue of courage
among warlike or peaceful nations! And indeed, we may
observe, that, as the difference between war and peace is the
greatest that arises among nations and public societies, it
produces also the greatest variations in moral sentiment, and
diversifies the most our ideas of virtue and personal merit.

Sometimes too, magnanimity, greatness of mind, disdain
of slavery, inflexible rigour and integrity, may better suit
the circumstances of one age than those of another, and
have a more kindly influence, both on public affairs, and on a
man's own safety and advancement. Our idea of merit,
therefore, will also vary a little with these variations; and
LABEO, perhaps, be censured for the same qualities, which
procured CATO the highest approbation.

A degree of luxury may be ruinous and pernicious in a
native of SWITZERLAND, which only fosters the arts, and
encourages industry in a FRENCHMAN or ENGLISHMAN. We
are not, therefore, to expect, either the same sentiments,
or the same laws in BERNE, which prevail in LONDON or
PARIS.

Different customs have also some influence as well as
different utilities; and by giving an early biass to the mind,
may produce a superior propensity, either to the useful or
the agreeable qualities; to those which regard self, or those
which extend to society. These four sources of moral sentiment
still subsist; but particular accidents may, at one time,
make any one of them flow with greater abundance than at
another.

The customs of some nations shut up the women from
all social commerce: Those of others make them so essential
a part of society and conversation, that, except where business
is transacted, the male-sex alone are supposed almost wholly

[1] Tusc. Quaest. lib. ii. 27.

incapable of mutual discourse and entertainment. As this difference is the most material that can happen in private life, it must also produce the greatest variation in our moral sentiments.

Of all nations in the world, where polygamy was not allowed, the GREEKS seem to have been the most reserved in their commerce with the fair sex, and to have imposed on them the strictest laws of modesty and decency. We have a strong instance of this in an oration of LYSIAS.[1] A widow injured, ruined, undone, calls a meeting of a few of her nearest friends and relations; and though never before accustomed, says the orator, to speak in the presence of men, the distress of her circumstances constrained her to lay the case before them. The very opening of her mouth in such company required, it seems, an apology.

When DEMOSTHENES prosecuted his tutors, to make them refund his patrimony, it became necessary for him, in the course of the law-suit, to prove that the marriage of APHOBUS's sister with ONETER was entirely fraudulent, and that, notwithstanding her sham marriage, she had lived with her brother at ATHENS for two years past, ever since her divorce from her former husband. And it is remarkable, that though these were people of the first fortune and distinction in the city, the orator could prove this fact no way, but by calling for her female slaves to be put to the question, and by the evidence of one physician, who had seen her in her brother's house during her illness.[2] So reserved were GREEK manners.

We may be assured, that an extreme purity of manners was the consequence of this reserve. Accordingly we find, that, except the fabulous stories of an HELEN and a CLYTEMNESTRA, there scarcely is an instance of any event in the GREEK history, which proceeded from the intrigues of women. On the other hand, in modern times, particularly in a neighbouring nation, the females enter into all transactions and all management of church and state: And no man can expect success, who takes not care to obtain their good graces. HARRY the third, by incurring the displeasure of the fair, endangered his crown, and lost his life, as much as by his indulgence to heresy.

It is needless to dissemble: The consequence of a very free commerce between the sexes, and of their living much

---

[1] Orat. 32, 898.   [2] In Oneter. p. 873-4.

together, will often terminate in intrigues and gallantry. We must sacrifice somewhat of the *useful*, if we be very anxious to obtain all the *agreeable* qualities; and cannot pretend to reach alike every kind of advantage. Instances of licence, daily multiplying, will weaken the scandal with the one sex, and teach the other, by degrees, to adopt the famous maxim of LA FONTAINE, with regard to female infidelity, *that if one knows it, it is but a small matter; if one knows it not, it is nothing.*[1]

Some people are inclined to think, that the best way of adjusting all differences, and of keeping the proper medium between the *agreeable* and the *useful* qualities of the sex, is to live with them after the manner of the ROMANS and the ENGLISH (for the customs of these two nations seem similar in this respect[2]); that is, without gallantry,[3] and without jealousy. By a parity of reason, the customs of the SPANIARDS and of the ITALIANS of an age ago (for the present are very different) must be the worst of any; because they favour both gallantry and jealousy.

Nor will these different customs of nations affect the one sex only: Their idea of personal merit in the males must also be somewhat different with regard, at least, to conversation, address, and humour. The one nation, where the men live much apart, will naturally more approve of prudence; the other of gaiety. With the one simplicity of manners will be in the highest esteem; with the other, politeness. The one will distinguish themselves by good-sense and judgment; the other, by taste and delicacy. The eloquence of the former will shine most in the senate; that of the other, on the theatre.

These, I say, are the *natural* effects of such customs. For it must be confessed, that chance has a great influence on national manners; and many events happen in society, which are not to be accounted for by general rules. Who could imagine, for instance, that the ROMANS, who lived freely

---

[1] Quand on le sçait, c'est peu de chose; Quand on l'ignore, ce n'est rien.

[2] During the time of the emperors, the ROMANS seem to have been more given to intrigues and gallantry than the ENGLISH are at present: And the women of condition, in order to retain their lovers, endeavoured to fix a name of reproach on those who were addicted to wenching and low amours. They were called ANCILLARIOLI. See SENECA de beneficiis. Lib. 1. cap. 9. See also MARTIAL. lib. 12. epig. 58.

[3] The gallantry here meant is that of amours and attachments, not that of complaisance, which is as much paid to the fair-sex in ENGLAND as in any other country.

with their women, should be very indifferent about music, and esteem dancing infamous: While the GREEKS, who never almost saw a woman but in their own houses, were continually piping, singing, and dancing?

The differences of moral sentiment, which naturally arise from a republican or monarchical government, are also very obvious; as well as those which proceed from general riches or poverty, union or faction, ignorance or learning. I shall conclude this long discourse with observing, that different customs and situations vary not the original ideas of merit (however they may, some consequences) in any very essential point, and prevail chiefly with regard to young men, who can aspire to the agreeable qualities, and may attempt to please. The MANNER, the ORNAMENTS, the GRACES, which succeed in this shape, are more arbitrary and casual: But the merit of riper years is almost every where the same; and consists chiefly in integrity, humanity, ability, knowledge, and the other more solid and useful qualities of the human mind.

What you insist on, replied PALAMEDES, may have some foundation, when you adhere to the maxims of common life and ordinary conduct. Experience and the practice of the world readily correct any great extravagance on either side. But what say you to *artificial* lives and manners? How do you reconcile the maxims, on which, in different ages and nations, these are founded?

What do you understand by *artificial* lives and manners? said I. I explain myself, replied he. You know, that religion had, in ancient times, very little influence on common life, and that, after men had performed their duty in sacrifices and prayers at the temple, they thought, that the gods left the rest of their conduct to themselves, and were little pleased or offended with those virtues or vices, which only affected the peace and happiness of human society. In those ages, it was the business of philosophy alone to regulate men's ordinary behaviour and deportment; and accordingly, we may observe, that this being the sole principle, by which a man could elevate himself above his fellows, it acquired a mighty ascendant over many, and produced great singularities of maxims and of conduct. At present, when philosophy has lost the allurement of novelty, it has no such extensive influence; but seems to confine itself mostly to speculations in the closet; in the same manner, as the ancient religion was limited to sacrifices in the temple. Its place is now supplied by the modern religion, which inspects our whole conduct, and prescribes an universal rule to our actions, to our words, to our very thoughts and inclinations; a rule so much the more austere, as it is guarded by infinite, though distant, rewards and punishments; and no infraction of it can ever be concealed or disguised.

DIOGENES is the most celebrated model of extravagant philosophy. Let us seek a parallel to him in modern times. We shall not disgrace any philosophic name by a comparison with the DOMINICS or LOYOLAS, or any canonized monk or friar. Let us compare him to PASCAL, a man of parts and genius as well as DIOGENES himself; and perhaps too, a man of virtue, had he allowed his virtuous inclinations to have exerted and displayed themselves.

The foundation of DIOGENES's conduct was an endeavour to render himself an independent being as much as possible, and to confine all his wants and desires and pleasures within himself and his own mind: The aim of PASCAL was to keep a perpetual sense of his dependence before his eyes, and never to forget his numberless wants and infirmities. The ancient supported himself by magnanimity, ostentation, pride, and the idea of his own superiority above his fellow-creatures. The modern made constant profession of humility and abasement, of the contempt and hatred of himself; and endeavoured to attain these supposed virtues, as far as they are attainable. The austerities of the GREEK were in order to inure himself to hardships, and prevent his ever suffering: Those of the FRENCHMAN were embraced merely for their own sake, and in order to suffer as much as possible. The philosopher indulged himself in the most beastly pleasures, even in public: The saint refused himself the most innocent, even in private. The former thought it his duty to love his friends, and to rail at them, and reprove them, and scold them: The latter endeavoured to be absolutely indifferent towards his nearest relations, and to love and speak well of his enemies. The great object of DIOGENES's wit was every kind of superstition, that is every kind of religion known in his time. The mortality of the soul was his standard principle; and even his sentiments of a divine providence seem to have been licentious. The most ridiculous superstitions directed PASCAL's faith and practice; and an extreme contempt of this life, in comparison of the future, was the chief foundation of his conduct.

In such a remarkable contrast do these two men stand: Yet both of them have met with general admiration in their different ages, and have been proposed as models of imitation. Where then is the universal standard of morals, which you talk of? And what rule shall we establish for the many different, nay contrary sentiments of mankind?

An experiment, said I, which succeeds in the air, will not always succeed in a vacuum. When men depart from the maxims of common reason, and affect these *artificial* lives, as you call them, no one can answer for what will please or displease them. They are in a different element from the rest of mankind; and the natural principles of their mind play not with the same regularity, as if left to themselves, free from the illusions of religious superstition or philosophical enthusiasm.

THE

NATURAL HISTORY

OF

RELIGION.

THE

NATURAL HISTORY OF RELIGION.[1]

———◦◦◦———

INTRODUCTION.

As every enquiry, which regards religion, is of the utmost importance, there are two questions in particular, which challenge our attention, to wit, that concerning its foundation in reason, and that concerning its origin in human nature. Happily, the first question, which is the most important, admits of the most obvious, at least, the clearest solution. The whole frame of nature bespeaks an intelligent author; and no rational enquirer can, after serious reflection, suspend his belief a moment with regard to the primary principles of genuine Theism and Religion. But the other question, concerning the origin of religion in human nature, is exposed to some more difficulty. The belief of invisible, intelligent power has been very generally diffused over the human race, in all places and in all ages; but it has neither perhaps been so universal as to admit of no exception, nor has it been, in any degree, uniform in the ideas, which it has suggested. Some nations have been discovered, who entertained no sentiments of Religion, if travellers and historians may be credited; and no two nations, and scarce any two men, have ever agreed precisely in the same sentiments. It would appear, therefore, that this preconception springs not from an original instinct or primary impression of nature, such as gives rise to self-love, affection between the sexes, love of progeny, gratitude, resentment; since every instinct of this kind has been found absolutely universal in all nations and ages, and has always a precise determinate object, which it inflexibly pursues. The first religious principles must be

---

[1] [For the circumstances attending the publication of this Treatise, see 'History of the Editions,' Vol. III. p. 60 *et seq.*—ED.]

secondary; such as may easily be perverted by various accidents and causes, and whose operation too, in some cases,
may, by an extraordinary concurrence of circumstances, be
altogether prevented. What those principles are, which
give rise to the original belief, and what those accidents and
causes are, which direct its operation, is the subject of our
present enquiry.

SECT. I.—*That Polytheism was the primary Religion of Men.*

It appears to me, that, if we consider the improvement of
human society, from rude beginnings to a state of greater
perfection, polytheism or idolatry was, and necessarily must
have been, the first and most ancient religion of mankind.
This opinion I shall endeavour to confirm by the following
arguments.

It is a matter of fact incontestable, that about 1,700 years
ago all mankind were [1] polytheists. The doubtful and
sceptical principles of a few philosophers, or the theism, and
that too not entirely pure, of one or two nations, form no
objection worth regarding. Behold then the clear testimony
of history. The farther we mount up into antiquity, the
more do we find mankind plunged into [2] polytheism. No
marks, no symptoms of any more perfect religion. The
most ancient records of human race still present us with
that system as the popular and established creed. The
north, the south, the east, the west, give their unanimous
testimony to the same fact. What can be opposed to so full
an evidence?

As far as writing or history reaches, mankind, in ancient
times, appear universally to have been polytheists. Shall we
assert, that, in more ancient times, before the knowledge of
letters, or the discovery of any art or science, men entertained the principles of pure theism? That is, while they
were ignorant and barbarous, they discovered truth: But fell
into error, as soon as they acquired learning and politeness.

But in this assertion you not only contradict all appearance
of probability, but also our present experience concerning
the principles and opinions of barbarous nations. The
savage tribes of AMERICA, AFRICA, and ASIA are all idolaters.

---

[1] [Idolaters: Editions L to Q.]   [2] [Idolatry: Editions L to Q.]

Not a single exception to this rule. Insomuch, that, were a traveller to transport himself into any unknown region; if he found inhabitants cultivated with arts and science, though even upon that supposition there are odds against their being theists, yet could he not safely, till farther inquiry, pronounce any thing on that head: But if he found them ignorant and barbarous, he might beforehand declare them idolaters; and there scarcely is a possibility of his being mistaken.

It seems certain, that, according to the natural progress of human thought, the ignorant multitude must first entertain some groveling and familiar notion of superior powers, before they stretch their conception to that perfect Being, who bestowed order on the whole frame of nature. We may as reasonably imagine, that men inhabited palaces before huts and cottages, or studied geometry before agriculture: as assert that the Deity appeared to them a pure spirit, omniscient, omnipotent, and omnipresent, before he was apprehended to be a powerful, though limited being, with human passions and appetites, limbs and organs. The mind rises gradually, from inferior to superior: By abstracting from what is imperfect, it forms an idea of perfection: And slowly distinguishing the nobler parts of its own frame from the grosser, it learns to transfer only the former, much elevated and refined, to its divinity. Nothing could disturb this natural progress of thought, but some obvious and invincible argument, which might immediately lead the mind into the pure principles of theism, and make it overleap, at one bound, the vast interval which is interposed between the human and the divine nature. But though I allow, that the order and frame of the universe, when accurately examined, affords such an argument; yet I can never think, that this consideration could have an influence on mankind, when they formed their first rude notions of religion.

The causes of such objects, as are quite familiar to us, never strike our attention or curiosity; and however extraordinary or surprising these objects in themselves, they are passed over, by the raw and ignorant multitude, without much examination or enquiry. ADAM, rising at once, in paradise, and in the full perfection of his faculties, would naturally, as represented by MILTON, be astonished at the glorious appearances of nature, the heavens, the air, the earth, his own organs and members; and would be led to ask, whence this wonderful scene arose. But a barbarous, necessitous animal (such as a man is on the first origin of society), pressed by such numerous wants and passions, has no leisure to admire the regular face of nature, or make enquiries concerning the cause of those objects, to which from his infancy he has been gradually accustomed. On the contrary, the more regular and uniform, that is, the more perfect nature appears, the more is he familiarized to it, and the less inclined to scrutinize and examine it. A monstrous birth excites his curiosity, and is deemed a prodigy. It alarms him from its novelty; and immediately sets him a trembling, and sacrificing, and praying. But an animal, compleat in all its limbs and organs, is to him an ordinary spectacle, and produces no religious opinion or affection. Ask him, whence that animal arose; he will tell you, from the copulation of its parents. And these, whence? From the copulation of theirs. A few removes satisfy his curiosity, and set the objects at such a distance, that he entirely loses sight of them. Imagine not, that he will so much as start the question, whence the first animal; much less, whence the whole system or united fabric of the universe arose. Or, if you start such a question to him, expect not, that he will employ his mind with any anxiety about a subject, so remote, so uninteresting, and which so much exceeds the bounds of his capacity.

But farther, if men were at first led into the belief of one Supreme Being, by reasoning from the frame of nature, they could never possibly leave that belief, in order to embrace [1] polytheism; but the same principles of reason, which at first produced and diffused over mankind, so magnificent an opinion, must be able, with greater facility, to preserve it. The first invention and proof of any doctrine is much more difficult than the supporting and retaining of it.

There is a great difference between historical facts and speculative opinions; nor is the knowledge of the one propagated in the same manner with that of the other. An historical fact, while it passes by oral tradition from eye-witnesses and contemporaries, is disguised in every successive narration, and may at last retain but very small, if any, re-

[1] [Idolatry: Editions L to Q.]

semblance of the original truth, on which it was founded. The frail memories of men, their love of exaggeration, their supine carelessness; these principles, if not corrected by books and writing, soon pervert the account of historical events; where argument or reasoning has little or no place, nor can ever recal the truth, which has once escaped those narrations. It is thus the fables of HERCULES, THESEUS, BACCHUS are supposed to have been originally founded in true history, corrupted by tradition. But with regard to speculative opinions, the case is far otherwise. If these opinions be founded on arguments so clear and obvious as to carry conviction with the generality of mankind, the same arguments, which at first diffused the opinions, will still preserve them in their original purity. If the arguments be more abstruse, and more remote from vulgar apprehension, the opinions will always be confined to a few persons; and as soon as men leave the contemplation of the arguments, the opinions will immediately be lost and be buried in oblivion. Whichever side of this dilemma we take, it must appear impossible, that theism could, from reasoning, have been the primary religion of human race, and have afterwards, by its corruption, given birth to polytheism and to all the various superstitions of the heathen world. Reason, when obvious, prevents these corruptions: When abstruse, it keeps the principles entirely from the knowledge of the vulgar, who are alone liable to corrupt any principle or opinion.

SECT. II.—*Origin of Polytheism.*

If we would, therefore, indulge our curiosity, in enquiring concerning the origin of religion, we must turn our thoughts towards ¹ polytheism, the primitive religion of uninstructed mankind.

Were men led into the apprehension of invisible, intelligent power by a contemplation of the works of nature, they could never possibly entertain any conception but of one single being, who bestowed existence and order on this vast machine, and adjusted all its parts, according to one regular plan or connected system. For though, to persons of a certain turn of mind, it may not appear altogether absurd, that several independent beings, endowed with superior wis-

¹ [Idolatry or polytheism: Essay . . . I. . . ?]

dom, might conspire in the contrivance and execution of one regular plan; yet is this a merely arbitrary supposition, which, even if allowed possible, must be confessed neither to be supported by probability nor necessity. All things in the universe are evidently of a piece. Every thing is adjusted to every thing. One design prevails throughout the whole. And this uniformity leads the mind to acknowledge one author; because the conception of different authors, without any distinction of attributes or operations, serves only to give perplexity to the imagination, without bestowing any satisfaction on the understanding. [1] The statue of LAOCOON, as we learn from PLINY, was the work of three artists : But it is certain, that, were we not told so, we should never have imagined, that a groupe of figures, cut from one stone, and united in one plan, was not the work and contrivance of one statuary. To ascribe any single effect to the combination of several causes, is not surely a natural and obvious supposition.

On the other hand, if, leaving the works of nature, we trace the footsteps of invisible power in the various and contrary events of human life, we are necessarily led into polytheism and to the acknowledgment of several limited and imperfect deities. Storms and tempests ruin what is nourished by the sun. The sun destroys what is fostered by the moisture of dews and rains. War may be favourable to a nation, whom the inclemency of the seasons afflicts with famine. Sickness and pestilence may depopulate a kingdom, amidst the most profuse plenty. The same nation is not, at the same time, equally successful by sea and by land. And a nation, which now triumphs over its enemies, may anon submit to their more prosperous arms. In short, the conduct of events, or what we call the plan of a particular providence, is so full of variety and uncertainty, that, if we suppose it immediately ordered by any intelligent beings, we must acknowledge a contrariety in their designs and intentions, a constant combat of opposite powers, and a repentance or change of intention in the same power, from impotence or levity. Each nation has its tutelar deity. Each element is subjected to its invisible power or agent. The province of each god is separate from that of another. Nor are the

[1] [The remainder of the paragraph was given as a note in Editions I. to P.]

operations of the same god always certain and invariable. To-day he protects: To-morrow he abandons us. Prayers and sacrifices, rites and ceremonies, well or ill performed, are the sources of his favour or enmity, and produce all the good or ill fortune, which are to be found amongst mankind.

We may conclude, therefore, that, in all nations, which have embraced polytheism,[1] the first ideas of religion arose not from a contemplation of the works of nature, but from a concern with regard to the events of life, and from the incessant hopes and fears, which actuate the human mind. Accordingly, we find, that all idolaters, having separated the provinces of their deities, have recourse to that invisible agent, to whose authority they are immediately subjected, and whose province it is to superintend that course of actions, in which they are, at any time, engaged. JUNO is invoked at marriages; LUCINA at births. NEPTUNE receives the prayers of seamen; and MARS of warriors. The husbandman cultivates his field under the protection of CERES; and the merchant acknowledges the authority of MERCURY. Each natural event is supposed to be governed by some intelligent agent; and nothing prosperous or adverse can happen in life, which may not be the subject of peculiar prayers or thanksgivings.[2]

It must necessarily, indeed, be allowed, that, in order to carry men's intention beyond the present course of things, or lead them into any inference concerning invisible intelligent power, they must be actuated by some passion, which prompts their thought and reflection; some motive, which urges their first enquiry. But what passion shall we here have recourse to, for explaining an effect of such mighty consequence? Not speculative curiosity surely, or the pure love of truth. That motive is too refined for such gross apprehensions; and would lead men into enquiries concerning the frame of nature, a subject too large and comprehensive for their narrow capacities. No passions, therefore, can be

[1] [Polytheism or idolatry: Editions L to Q.]

[2] 'Fragilis & laboriosa mortalitas in partes ista digessit, infirmitatis suæ memor, ut portionibus coleret quisque, quo maxime indigeret.' PLIN. lib. ii. cap. 5. So early as HESIOD's time there were 30,000 deities. Oper. & Dier. lib.i. ver. 250. But the task to be performed by these seems still too great for that number. The provinces of the deities were so subdivided, that there was even a god of Sneezing. See ARIST. Probl. sect. 33. cap. 7. The province too and dignity of each was augmenting several deities.

supposed to work upon such barbarians, but the ordinary affections of human life ; the anxious concern for happiness, the dread of future misery, the terror of death, the thirst of revenge, the appetite for food and other necessaries. Agitated by hopes and fears of this nature, especially the latter, men scrutinize, with a trembling curiosity, the course of future causes, and examine the various and contrary events of human life. And in this disordered scene, with eyes still more disordered and astonished, they see the first obscure traces of divinity.

SECT. III.—*The same subject continued.*

We are placed in this world, as in a great theatre, where the true springs and causes of every event are entirely concealed from us ; nor have we either sufficient wisdom to foresee, or power to prevent those ills, with which we are continually threatened. We hang in perpetual suspence between life and death, health and sickness, plenty and want ; which are distributed amongst the human species by secret and unknown causes, whose operation is oft unexpected, and always unaccountable. These *unknown causes*, then, become the constant object of our hope and fear ; and while the passions are kept in perpetual alarm by an anxious expectation of the events, the imagination is equally employed in forming ideas of those powers, on which we have so entire a dependance. Could men anatomize nature, according to the most probable, at least the most intelligible philosophy, they would find, that these causes are nothing but the particular fabric and structure of the minute parts of their own bodies and of external objects ; and that, by a regular and constant machinery, all the events are produced, about which they are so much concerned. But this philosophy exceeds the comprehension of the ignorant multitude, who can only conceive the *unknown causes* in a general and confused manner ; though their imagination, perpetually employed on the same subject, must labour to form some particular and distinct idea of them. The more they consider these causes themselves, and the uncertainty of their operation, the less satisfaction do they meet with in their researches ; and, however unwilling, they must at last have abandoned so arduous an attempt, were it not for a propen-

sity in human nature, which leads into a system, that gives
them some satisfaction.

There is an universal tendency among mankind to conceive all beings like themselves, and to transfer to every
object, those qualities, with which they are familiarly acquainted, and of which they are intimately conscious. We
find human faces in the moon, armies in the clouds; and by
a natural propensity, if not corrected by experience and
reflection, ascribe malice or good-will to every thing, that
hurts or pleases us. Hence the frequency and beauty of the
prosopopœia in poetry; where trees, mountains and streams
are personified, and the inanimate parts of nature acquire
sentiment and passion. And though these poetical figures
and expressions gain not on the belief, they may serve, at
least, to prove a certain tendency in the imagination, without which they could neither be beautiful nor natural. Nor
is a river-god or hamadryad always taken for a mere poetical
or imaginary personage; but may sometimes enter into the
real creed of the ignorant vulgar; while each grove or field
is represented as possessed of a particular *genius* or invisible
power, which inhabits and protects it. Nay, philosophers
cannot entirely exempt themselves from this natural frailty;
but have oft ascribed to inanimate matter the horror of a
vacuum, sympathies, antipathies, and other affections of
human nature. The absurdity is not less, while we cast our
eyes upwards; and transferring, as is too usual, human
passions and infirmities to the deity, represent him as jealous
and revengeful, capricious and partial, and, in short, a wicked
and foolish man, in every respect but his superior power and
authority. No wonder, then, that mankind, being placed in
such an absolute ignorance of causes, and being at the same
time so anxious concerning their future fortune, should
immediately acknowledge a dependence on invisible powers,
possessed of sentiment and intelligence. The *unknown causes*,
which continually employ their thought, appearing always
in the same aspect, are all apprehended to be of the same
kind or species. Nor is it long before we ascribe to them
thought and reason and passion, and sometimes even the
limbs and figures of men, in order to bring them nearer to a
resemblance with ourselves.

In proportion as any man's course of life is governed by
accident, we always find, that he encreases in superstition;

as may particularly be observed of gamesters and sailors,
who, though, of all mankind, the least capable of serious
reflection, abound most in frivolous and superstitious apprehensions. The gods, says CORIOLANUS in DIONYSIUS,[1] have
an influence in every affair; but above all, in war; where
the event is so uncertain. All human life, especially before
the institution of order and good government, being subject
to fortuitous accidents; it is natural, that superstition should
prevail every where in barbarous ages, and put men on the
most earnest enquiry concerning those invisible powers, who
dispose of their happiness or misery. Ignorant of astronomy
and the anatomy of plants and animals, and too little curious
to observe the admirable adjustment of final causes; they
remain still unacquainted with a first and supreme creator,
and with that infinitely perfect spirit, who alone, by his
almighty will, bestowed order on the whole frame of nature.
Such a magnificent idea is too big for their narrow conceptions, which can neither observe the beauty of the work,
nor comprehend the grandeur of its author. They suppose
their deities, however potent and invisible, to be nothing but
a species of human creatures, perhaps raised from among
mankind, and retaining all human passions and appetites,
together with corporeal limbs and organs. Such limited
beings, though masters of human fate, being, each of them,
incapable of extending his influence every where, must be
vastly multiplied, in order to answer that variety of events,
which happen over the whole face of nature. Thus every
place is stored with a crowd of local deities; and thus
polytheism has prevailed, and still prevails, among the
greatest part of uninstructed mankind.[2]

Any of the human affections may lead us into the notion
of invisible, intelligent power; hope as well as fear, gratitude
as well as affliction: But if we examine our own hearts, or
observe what passes around us, we shall find, that men are

[1] Lib. viii. 33.
The following lines of EURIPIDES
are so much to the present purpose,
that I cannot forbear quoting them:

Οὐκ ἔστιν οὐδὲν πιστὸν, οὔτ' εὐδοξία.
Οὔτ' αὖ καλῶς πράσσοντα μὴ πράξειν
κακῶς.
Φύρουσι δ' αὐθ' οἱ θεοὶ πάλιν τε καὶ
πρόσω,

Ταραγμὸν ἐντιθέντες, ὡς ἀγνωσίᾳ
Σέβωμεν αὐτούς.   HECUBA. 956.

'There is nothing secure in the world;
no glory, no prosperity. The gods toss
all life into confusion; mix every thing
with its reverse; that all of us, from
our ignorance and uncertainty, may pay
them the more worship and reverence.'

much oftener thrown on their knees by the melancholy than by the agreeable passions. Prosperity is easily received as our due, and few questions are asked concerning its cause or author. It begets cheerfulness and activity and alacrity and a lively enjoyment of every social and sensual pleasure: And during this state of mind, men have little leisure or inclination to think of the unknown invisible regions. On the other hand, every disastrous accident alarms us, and sets us on enquiries concerning the principles whence it arose: Apprehensions spring up with regard to futurity: And the mind, sunk into diffidence, terror, and melancholy, has recourse to every method of appeasing those secret intelligent powers, on whom our fortune is supposed entirely to depend.

No topic is more usual with all popular divines than to display the advantages of affliction, in bringing men to a due sense of religion; by subduing their confidence and sensuality, which, in times of prosperity, make them forgetful of a divine providence. Nor is this topic confined merely to modern religions. The ancients have also employed it. *Fortune has never liberally, without envy*, says a GREEK historian,[1] *bestowed an unmixed happiness on mankind; but with all her gifts has ever conjoined some disastrous circumstance, in order to chastize men into a reverence for the gods, whom, in a continued course of prosperity, they are apt to neglect and forget.*

What age or period of life is the most addicted to superstition? The weakest and most timid. What sex? The same answer must be given. *The leaders and examples of every kind of superstition*, says STRABO,[2] *are the women. These excite the men to devotion and supplications, and the observance of religious days. It is rare to meet with one that lives apart from the females, and yet is addicted to such practices. And nothing can, for this reason, be more improbable, than the account given of an order of men among the* GETES, *who practised celibacy, and were notwithstanding the most religious fanatics.* A method of reasoning, which would lead us to entertain a bad idea of the devotion of monks: did we not know by an experience, not so common, perhaps, in STRABO's days, that one may practise celibacy, and profess chastity; and yet maintain the closest connexions and most entire sympathy with that timorous and pious sex.

[1] Diod. Sic. lib. iii. 47.   [2] Lib. vi. 297.

SECT. IV.—*Deities not considered as creators or formers of the world.*

The only point of theology, in which we shall find a consent of mankind almost universal, is, that there is invisible, intelligent power in the world: But whether this power be supreme or subordinate, whether confined to one being, or distributed among several, what attributes, qualities, connexions, or principles of action ought to be ascribed to those beings; concerning all these points, there is the widest difference in the popular systems of theology. Our ancestors in EUROPE, before the revival of letters, believed, as we do at present, that there was one supreme God, the author of nature, whose power, though in itself uncontroulable, was yet often exerted by the interposition of his angels and subordinate ministers, who executed his sacred purposes. But they also believed, that all nature was full of other invisible powers; fairies, goblins, elves, sprights; beings, stronger and mightier than men, but much inferior to the celestial natures, who surround the throne of God. Now, suppose, that any one, in those ages, had denied the existence of God and of his angels; would not his impiety justly have deserved the appellation of atheism, even though he had still allowed, by some odd capricious reasoning, that the popular stories of elves and fairies were just and well-grounded? The difference, on the one hand, between such a person and a genuine theist is infinitely greater than that, on the other, between him and one that absolutely excludes all invisible intelligent power. And it is a fallacy, merely from the casual resemblance of names, without any conformity of meaning, to rank such opposite opinions under the same denomination.

To any one, who considers justly of the matter, it will appear, that the gods of all polytheists are no better than the elves or fairies of our ancestors, and merit as little any pious worship or veneration. These pretended religionists are really a kind of superstitious atheists, and acknowledge no being, that corresponds to our idea of a deity. No first principle of mind or thought: No supreme government and administration: No divine contrivance or intention in the fabric of the world.

The CHINESE, when [1] their prayers are not answered, beat their idols. The deities of the LAPLANDERS are any large stone which they meet with of an extraordinary shape.[2] The EGYPTIAN mythologists, in order to account for animal worship, said, that the gods, pursued by the violence of earthborn men, who were their enemies, had formerly been obliged to disguise themselves under the semblance of beasts.[3] The CAUNII, a nation in the Lesser ASIA, resolving to admit no strange gods among them, regularly, at certain seasons, assembled themselves compleatly armed, beat the air with their lances, and proceeded in that manner to their frontiers; in order, as they said, to expel the foreign deities.[4] *Not even the immortal gods*, said some GERMAN nations to CÆSAR, *are a match for the* SUEVI.[5]

Many ills, says DIONE in HOMER to VENUS wounded by DIOMEDE, many ills, my daughter, have the gods inflicted on men: And many ills, in return, have men inflicted on the gods.[6] We need but open any classic author to meet with these gross representations of the deities; and LONGINUS[7] with reason observes, that such ideas of the divine nature, if literally taken, contain a true atheism.

Some writers[8] have been surprized, that the impieties of ARISTOPHANES should have been tolerated, nay publicly acted and applauded by the ATHENIANS; a people so superstitious and so jealous of the public religion, that, at that very time, they put SOCRATES to death for his imagined incredulity. But these writers do not consider, that the ludicrous, familiar images, under which the gods are represented by that comic poet, instead of appearing impious, were the genuine lights in which the ancients conceived their divinities. What conduct can be more criminal or mean, than that of JUPITER in the AMPHITRION? Yet that play, which represented his gallante exploits, was supposed so agreeable to him, that it was always acted in ROME by public authority, when the state was threatened with pestilence, famine, or any general calamity.[9] The ROMANS supposed, that, like all old letchers,

---

[1] Pere le Compte.
[2] Regnard, Voiage de Laponie.
[3] Diod. Sic. lib. i. 86. Lucian. de Sacrificiis. 14. Ovid alludes to the same tradition. Metam. lib. v. l. 321. So also MANILIUS, lib. iv. 800.
[4] Herodot. lib i. 172.
[5] Cæs. Comment. de bello Gallico, lib. iv. 7.
[6] Lib. v. 382.
[7] Cap. ix.
[8] Pere Brumoy, Theatre des Grecs & Fontenelle, Histoire des Oracles.
[9] Arnob. lib. vii. 597 ll.

he would be highly pleased with the recital of his former feats of prowess and vigour, and that no topic was so proper, upon which to flatter his vanity.

The LACEDEMONIANS, says XENOPHON,[1] always, during war, put up their petitions very early in the morning, in order to be beforehand with their enemies, and, by being the first solicitors, pre-engage the gods in their favour. We may gather from SENECA,[2] that it was usual, for the votaries in the temples, to make interest with the beadle or sexton, that they might have a seat near the image of the deity, in order to be the best heard in their prayers and applications to him. The TYRIANS, when besieged by ALEXANDER, threw chains on the statue of HERCULES, to prevent that deity from deserting to the enemy.[3] AUGUSTUS, having twice lost his fleet by storms, forbad NEPTUNE to be carried in procession along with the other gods; and fancied, that he had sufficiently revenged himself by that expedient.[4] After GERMANICUS's death, the people were so enraged at their gods, that they stoned them in their temples; and openly renounced all allegiance to them.[5]

To ascribe the origin and fabric of the universe to these imperfect beings never enters into the imagination of any polytheist or idolater. HESIOD, whose writings, with those of HOMER, contained the canonical system of the heavens;[6] HESIOD, I say, supposes gods and men to have sprung equally from the unknown powers of nature.[7] And throughout the whole theogony of that author, PANDORA is the only instance of creation or a voluntary production; and she too was formed by the gods merely from despight to PROMETHEUS, who had furnished men with stolen fire from the celestial regions.[8] The ancient mythologists, indeed, seem throughout to have rather embraced the idea of generation than that of creation or formation; and to have thence accounted for the origin of this universe.

OVID, who lived in a learned age, and had been instructed by philosophers in the principles of a divine creation or formation of the world; finding, that such an idea would not

[1] De Laced. Rep. 13.
[2] Epist. xli.
[3] Quint. Curtius, lib. iv. cap. 3. Diod. Sic. lib. xvii. 11.
[4] Suet. in vita Aug. cap. 16.
[5] Id. in vita Cal. cap. 5.
[6] Herodot. lib. ii. 53. Lucian, Jupiter confutatus, de luctu, Saturn, &c.
[7] Ὡς ὁμόθεν γεγάασι θεοὶ θνητοί τ᾽ ἄνθρωποι. Hes. Opera & Dies. l. 108.
[8] Theog. l. 570.

agree with the popular mythology, which he delivers, leaves it, in a manner, loose and detached from his system. *Quisquis fuit ille Deorum?*[1] Whichever of the gods it was, says he, that dissipated the chaos, and introduced order into the universe. It could neither be SATURN, he knew, nor JUPITER, nor NEPTUNE, nor any of the received deities of paganism. His theological system had taught him nothing upon that head; and he leaves the matter equally undetermined.

DIODORUS SICULUS,[2] beginning his work with an enumeration of the most reasonable opinions concerning the origin of the world, makes no mention of a deity or intelligent mind; though it is evident from his history, that he was much more prone to superstition than to irreligion. And in another passage,[3] talking of the ICHTHYOPHAGI, a nation in INDIA, he says, that, there being so great difficulty in accounting for their descent, we must conclude them to be *aborigines*, without any beginning of their generation, propagating their race from all eternity; as some of the physiologers, in treating of the origin of nature, have justly observed. ' But in such subjects as these,' adds the historian, ' which exceed all human capacity, it may well happen, that those, who discourse the most, know the least; reaching a specious appearance of truth in their reasonings, while extremely wide of the real truth and matter of fact.'

A strange sentiment in our eyes, to be embraced by a professed and zealous religionist![4] But it was merely by accident, that the question concerning the origin of the world did ever in ancient times enter into religious systems, or was treated of by theologers. The philosophers alone made profession of delivering systems of this kind; and it was pretty late too before these bethought themselves of having recourse to a mind or supreme intelligence, as the first cause of all. So far was it from being esteemed profane in those days to account for the origin of things without a deity, that THALES, ANAXIMENES, HERACLITUS, and others, who embraced that system of cosmogony, past unquestioned;

[1] Metamorph. lib. i. l. 32.
[2] Lib. i. 6 *et seq.*
[3] Lib. iii. 20.
[4] The same author, who can thus account for the origin of the world without a Deity, esteems it impious to explain from physical causes, the common accidents of life, earthquakes, inundations, and tempests: and devoutly ascribes these to the anger of JUPITER or NEPTUNE. A plain proof whence he derived his ideas of religion. See Lib. xv. c. 48. p. 364. Ex cap. RHODOMANNI.

Y 2

while ANAXAGORAS, the first undoubted theist among the philosophers, was perhaps the first that ever was accused of atheism.[1]

We are told by SEXTUS EMPIRICUS,[2] that EPICURUS, when a boy, reading with his preceptor these verses of HESIOD,

> Eldest of beings, *chaos* first arose ;
> Next *earth*, wide-stretch'd, the *seat* of all :

the young scholar first betrayed his inquisitive genius, by asking, *And chaos whence?* But was told by his preceptor, that he must have recourse to the philosophers for a solution of such questions. And from this hint EPICURUS left philology and all other studies, in order to betake himself to that science, whence alone he expected satisfaction with regard to these sublime subjects.

The common people were never likely to push their researches so far, or derive from reasoning their systems of religion; when philologers and mythologists, we see, scarcely ever discovered so much penetration. And even the philosophers, who discoursed of such topics, readily assented to the grossest theory, and admitted the joint origin of gods and men from night and chaos ; from fire, water, air, or whatever they established to be the ruling element.

Nor was it only on their first origin, that the gods were supposed dependent on the powers of nature. Throughout the whole period of their existence they were subjected to the dominion of fate or destiny. *Think of the force of necessity,* says AGRIPPA to the ROMAN people, *that force, to which even the gods must submit.*[3] And the Younger PLINY[4], agreeably to this way of thinking, tells us, that amidst the darkness, horror, and confusion, which ensued upon the first eruption of VESUVIUS, several concluded, that all nature was going to

---

[1] It will be easy to give a reason, why THALES, ANAXIMANDER, and those early philosophers, who really were atheists, might be very orthodox in the pagan creed; and why ANAXAGORAS and SOCRATES, though real theists, must naturally, in ancient times, be esteemed impious. The blind, unguided powers of nature, if they could produce men, might also produce such beings as JUPITER and NEPTUNE, who being the most powerful, intelligent existences in the world, would be proper objects of worship. But where a supreme intelligence, the first cause of all, is admitted, these capricious beings, if they exist at all, must appear very subordinate and dependent, and consequently be excluded from the rank of deities. PLATO (de leg. lib. x. 886 D.) assigns this reason for the imputation thrown on ANAXAGORAS, namely, his denying the divinity of the stars, planets, and other created objects.

[2] Adversus MATHEM. lib. 480.

[3] DIONYS. HALIC. lib. vi. 54.

[4] Epist. lib. vi.

wrack, and that gods and men were perishing in one common ruin.

It is great complaisance, indeed, if we dignify with the name of religion such an imperfect system of theology, and put it on a level with later systems, which are founded on principles more just and more sublime. For my part, I can scarcely allow the principles even of MARCUS AURELIUS, PLUTARCH, and some other *Stoics* and *Academics*, though much more refined than the pagan superstition, to be worthy of the honourable appellation of theism. For if the mythology of the heathens resemble the ancient EUROPEAN system of spiritual beings, excluding God and angels, and leaving only fairies and sprights; the creed of these philosophers may justly be said to exclude a deity, and to leave only angels and fairies.

SECT. V.—*Various Forms of Polytheism: Allegory, Hero-Worship.*

But it is chiefly our present business to consider the gross polytheism[1] of the vulgar, and to trace all its various appearances, in the principles of human nature, whence they are derived.

Whoever learns by argument, the existence of invisible intelligent power, must reason from the admirable contrivance of natural objects, and must suppose the world to be the workmanship of that divine being, the original cause of all things. But the vulgar polytheist, so far from admitting that idea, deifies every part of the universe, and conceives all the conspicuous productions of nature, to be themselves so many real divinities. The sun, moon, and stars, are all gods according to his system: Fountains are inhabited by nymphs, and trees by hamadryads: Even monkies, dogs, cats, and other animals often become sacred in his eyes, and strike him with a religious veneration. And thus, however strong men's propensity to believe invisible, intelligent power in nature, their propensity is equally strong to rest their attention on sensible, visible objects; and in order to reconcile these opposite inclinations, they are led to unite the invisible power with some visible object.

The distribution also of distinct provinces to the several deities is apt to cause some allegory, both physical and moral,

[1] [Polytheism and idolatry: Editions L to Q.]

to enter into the vulgar systems of polytheism. The god of war will naturally be represented as furious, cruel, and impetuous: The god of poetry as elegant, polite, and amiable: The god of merchandise, especially in early times, as thievish and deceitful. The allegories, supposed in HOMER and other mythologists, I allow, have often been so strained, that men of sense are apt entirely to reject them, and to consider them as the production merely of the fancy and conceit of critics and commentators. But that allegory really has place in the heathen mythology is undeniable even on the least reflection. CUPID the son of VENUS; the Muses the daughters of Memory; PROMETHEUS, the wise brother, and EPIMETHEUS the foolish; HYGIEIA or the goddess of health descended from ÆSCULAPIUS or the god of Physic: Who sees not, in these, and in many other instances, the plain traces of allegory? When a god is supposed to preside over any passion, event, or system of actions, it is almost unavoidable to give him a genealogy, attributes, and adventures, suitable to his supposed powers and influence; and to carry on that similitude and comparison, which is naturally so agreeable to the mind of man.

Allegories, indeed, entirely perfect, we ought not to expect as the productions of ignorance and superstition; there being no work of genius that requires a nicer hand, or has been more rarely executed with success. That *Fear* and *Terror* are the sons of MARS is just; but why by VENUS?[1] That *Harmony* is the daughter of VENUS is regular; but why by MARS?[2] That *Sleep* is the brother of *Death* is suitable; but why describe him as enamoured of one of the Graces?[3] And since the ancient mythologists fall into mistakes so gross and palpable, we have no reason surely to expect such refined and long-spun allegories, as some have endeavoured to deduce from their fictions.

[4]LUCRETIUS was plainly seduced by the strong appearance of allegory, which is observable in the pagan fictions. He first addresses himself to VENUS as to that generating power, which animates, renews, and beautifies the universe: But is soon betrayed by the mythology into incoherencies, while he prays to that allegorical personage to appease the furies of her lover MARS: An idea not drawn from allegory, but from

[1] HESIOD. Theog l. 935.
[2] Id. ibid. & PLUT. in vita PELOP. 19.
[3] ILIAD. xiv. 267.
[4] [This paragraph is given as a note in Editions L t P

the popular religion, and which LUCRETIUS, as an EPICUREAN, could not consistently admit of.

The deities of the vulgar are so little superior to human creatures, that, where men are affected with strong sentiments of veneration or gratitude for any hero or public benefactor, nothing can be more natural than to convert him into a god, and fill the heavens, after this manner, with continual recruits from among mankind. Most of the divinities of the ancient world are supposed to have once been men, and to have been beholden for their *apotheosis* to the admiration and affection of the people. The real history of their adventures, corrupted by tradition, and elevated by the marvellous, became a plentiful source of fable; especially in passing through the hands of poets, allegorists, and priests, who successively improved upon the wonder and astonishment of the ignorant multitude.

Painters too and sculptors came in for their share of profit in the sacred mysteries; and furnishing men with sensible representations of their divinities, whom they cloathed in human figures, gave great encrease to the public devotion, and determined its object. It was probably for want of these arts in rude and barbarous ages, that men deified plants, animals, and even brute, unorganized matter; and rather than be without a sensible object of worship, affixed divinity to such ungainly forms. Could any statuary of SYRIA, in early times, have formed a just figure of APOLLO, the conic stone, HELIOGABALUS, had never become the object of such profound adoration, and been received as a representation of the solar deity.[1]

STILPO was banished by the council of AREOPAGUS, for affirming that the MINERVA in the citadel was no divinity; but the workmanship of PHIDIAS, the sculptor.[2] What degree of reason must we expect in the religious belief of the vulgar in other nations; when ATHENIANS and AREOPAGITES could entertain such gross conceptions?

These then are the general principles of polytheism, founded in human nature, and little or nothing dependent on caprice and accident. As the *causes*, which bestow happiness or misery, are, in general, very little known and very uncertain, our anxious concern endeavours to attain a determinate idea

---

[1] HERODIAN. lib. v. 3. 10. JUPITER AMMON is represented by CURTIUS as a deity of the same kind. lib. iv. cap. 7. The ARABIANS and PESSINUNTIANS adored also shapeless unformed stones as their deity. ARNOB. lib. vi. 196 A. So much did their folly exceed that of the EGYPTIANS.

[2] DIOD. LAERT. lib. ii. 116.

of them ; and finds no better expedient than to represent them
as intelligent voluntary agents, like ourselves ; only somewhat
superior in power and wisdom.   The limited influence of these
agents, and their great proximity to human weakness, introduce the various distribution and division of their authority ;
and thereby give rise to allegory. The same principles naturally
deify mortals, superior in power, courage, or understanding,
and produce hero-worship ; together with fabulous history and
mythological tradition, in all its wild and unaccountable forms.
And as an invisible spiritual intelligence is an object too
refined for vulgar apprehension, men naturally affix it to some
sensible representation ; such as either the more conspicuous
parts of nature, or the statues, images, and pictures, which a
more refined age forms of its divinities.

Almost all idolaters, of whatever age or country, concur in
these general principles and conceptions ; and even the particular characters and provinces, which they assign to their
deities, are not extremely different.[1]   The GREEK and ROMAN
travellers and conquerors, without much difficulty, found their
own deities every where ; and said, This is MERCURY, that
VENUS ; this MARS, that NEPTUNE ; by whatever title the
strange gods might be denominated. The goddess HERTHA
of our SAXON ancestors seems to be no other, according to
TACITUS,[2] than the *Mater Tellus* of the ROMANS ; and his conjecture was evidently just.

SECT. VI.—*Origin of Theism from Polytheism.*

The doctrine of one supreme deity, the author of nature, is
very ancient, has spread itself over great and populous nations,
and among them has been embraced by all ranks and conditions of men : But whoever thinks that it has owed its success
to the prevalent force of those invincible reasons, on which it
is undoubtedly founded, would show himself little acquainted
with the ignorance and stupidity of the people, and their
incurable prejudices in favour of their particular superstitions.
Even at this day, and in EUROPE, ask any of the vulgar, why
he believes in an omnipotent creator of the world ; he will
never mention the beauty of final causes, of which he is wholly
ignorant : He will not hold out his hand, and bid you contem-

[1] See CÆSAR of the religion of the GAULS, De bello Gallico, lib. vi. 17.
[2] De moribus GERM. 40.

plate the suppleness and variety of joints in his fingers, their bending all one way, the counterpoise which they receive from the thumb, the softness and fleshy parts of the inside of his hand, with all the other circumstances, which render that member fit for the use, to which it was destined. To these he has been long accustomed; and he beholds them with listlessness and unconcern. He will tell you of the sudden and unexpected death of such a one: The fall and bruise of such another: The excessive drought of this season: The cold and rains of another. These he ascribes to the immediate operation of providence: And such events, as, with good reasoners, are the chief difficulties in admitting a supreme intelligence, are with him the sole arguments for it.

Many theists, even the most zealous and refined, have denied a *particular* providence, and have asserted, that the Sovereign mind or first principle of all things, having fixed general laws, by which nature is governed, gives free and uninterrupted course to these laws, and disturbs not, at every turn, the settled order of events by particular volitions. From the beautiful connexion, say they, and rigid observance of established rules, we draw the chief argument for theism; and from the same principles are enabled to answer the principal objections against it. But so little is this understood by the generality of mankind, that, wherever they observe any one to ascribe all events to natural causes, and to remove the particular interposition of a deity, they are apt to suspect him of the grossest infidelity. *A little philosophy*, says lord BACON, *makes men atheists: A great deal reconciles them to religion.* For men, being taught, by superstitious prejudices, to lay the stress on a wrong place; when that fails them, and they discover, by a little reflection, that the course of nature is regular and uniform, their whole faith totters, and falls to ruin. But being taught, by more reflection, that this very regularity and uniformity is the strongest proof of design and of a supreme intelligence, they return to that belief, which they had deserted; and they are now able to establish it on a firmer and more durable foundation.

Convulsions in nature, disorders, prodigies, miracles, though the most opposite to the plan of a wise superintendent, impress mankind with the strongest sentiments of religion; the causes of events seeming then the most unknown and unaccountable. Madness, fury, rage, and an inflamed imagination, though they sink men nearest to the level of beasts, are, for a like reason, often supposed to be the only dispositions, in which we can have any immediate communication with the Deity.

We may conclude, therefore, upon the whole, that, since the vulgar, in nations, which have embraced the doctrine of theism, still build it upon irrational and superstitious principles, they are never led into that opinion by any process of argument, but by a certain train of thinking, more suitable to their genius and capacity.

It may readily happen, in an idolatrous nation, that though men admit the existence of several limited deities, yet is there some one God, whom, in a particular manner, they make the object of their worship and adoration. They may either suppose, that, in the distribution of power and territory among the gods, their nation was subjected to the jurisdiction of that particular deity; or reducing heavenly objects to the model of things below, they may represent one god as the prince or supreme magistrate of the rest, who, though of the same nature, rules them with an authority, like that which an earthly sovereign exercises over his subjects and vassals. Whether this god, therefore, be considered as their peculiar patron, or as the general sovereign of heaven, his votaries will endeavour, by every art, to insinuate themselves into his favour; and supposing him to be pleased, like themselves, with praise and flattery, there is no eulogy or exaggeration, which will be spared in their addresses to him. In proportion as men's fears or distresses become more urgent, they still invent new strains of adulation; and even he who outdoes his predecessor in swelling up the titles of his divinity, is sure to be outdone by his successor in newer and more pompous epithets of praise. Thus they proceed; till at last they arrive at infinity itself, beyond which there is no farther progress: And it is well, if, in striving to get farther, and to represent a magnificent simplicity, they run not into inexplicable mystery, and destroy the intelligent nature of their deity, on which alone any rational worship or adoration can be founded. While they confine themselves to the notion of a perfect being, the creator of the world, they coincide, by chance, with the principles of reason and true philosophy; though they are guided to that notion, not by reason, of which they are in a

great measure incapable, but by the adulation and fears of
the most vulgar superstition.

We often find, amongst barbarous nations, and even sometimes amongst civilized, that, when every strain of flattery
has been exhausted towards arbitrary princes, when every
human quality has been applauded to the utmost; their
servile courtiers represent them, at last, as real divinities,
and point them out to the people as objects of adoration.
How much more natural, therefore, is it, that a limited deity,
who at first is supposed only the immediate author of the
particular goods and ills in life, should in the end be represented as sovereign maker and modifier of the universe?

Even where this notion of a supreme deity is already
established; though it ought naturally to lessen every other
worship, and abase every object of reverence, yet if a nation
has entertained the opinion of a subordinate tutelar divinity,
saint, or angel; their addresses to that being gradually rise
upon them, and encroach on the adoration due to their
supreme deity. The Virgin Mary, ere checked by the
reformation, had proceeded, from being merely a good
woman, to usurp many attributes of the Almighty: God
and St. NICHOLAS go hand in hand, in all the prayers and
petitions of the MUSCOVITES.

Thus the deity, who, from love, converted himself into a
bull, in order to carry off EUROPA; and who, from ambition,
dethroned his father, SATURN, became the OPTIMUS MAXIMUS
of the heathens. [1]Thus, the God of ABRAHAM, ISAAC, and
JACOB, became the supreme deity or JEHOVAH of the JEWS.

[2]The JACOBINS, who denied the immaculate conception,
have ever been very unhappy in their doctrine, even though
political reasons have kept the ROMISH church from con-
demning it. The CORDELIERS have run away with all the
popularity. But in the fifteenth century, as we learn from
BOULAINVILLIERS,[3] an ITALIAN *Cordelier* maintained, that,
during the three days, when CHRIST was interred, the hypo-
static union was dissolved, and that his human nature was

---

[1] [For this sentence the Proof reads:
Thus the deity, whom the vulgar Jews
conceived only as the God of *Abraham,
Isaac,* and *Jacob,* became their *Jehovah*
and Creator of the world.

Editions I. to N read: Thus, notwithstanding the sublime idea suggested
by *Moses* and the inspired writers,

many vulgar *Jews* seem still to have
conceived the supreme Being as a more
topical deity or national protector.]

[2] [This paragraph is given as a note
to the word "Almighty" in the last paragraph but one, in Editions I. to P.]

[3] *Histoire abregée,* p. 199.

not a proper object of adoration, during that period. Without the art of divination, one might foretel, that so gross and impious a blasphemy would not fail to be anathematized by the people. It was the occasion of great insults on the part of the JACOBINS; who now got some recompense for their misfortunes in the war about the immaculate conception.

Rather than relinquish this propensity to adulation, religionists, in all ages, have involved themselves in the greatest absurdities and contradictions.

HOMER, in one passage, calls OCEANUS and TETHYS the original parents of all things, conformably to the established mythology and tradition of the GREEKS: Yet, in other passages, he could not forbear complimenting JUPITER, the reigning deity, with that magnificent appellation; and accordingly denominates him the father of gods and men. He forgets, that every temple, every street was full of the ancestors, uncles, brothers, and sisters of this JUPITER; who was in reality nothing but an upstart parricide and usurper. A like contradiction is observable in HESIOD; and is so much the less excusable, as his professed intention was to deliver a true genealogy of the gods.

Were there a religion (and we may suspect Mahometanism of this inconsistence) which sometimes painted the Deity in the most sublime colours, as the creator of heaven and earth; sometimes [1] degraded him nearly to a level with human creatures in his powers and faculties; while at the same time it ascribed to him suitable infirmities, passions, and partialities, of the moral kind: That religion, after it was extinct, would also be cited as an instance of those contradictions, which arise from the gross, vulgar, natural conceptions of mankind, opposed to their continual propensity towards flattery and exaggeration. Nothing indeed would prove more strongly the divine origin of any religion, than to find (and happily this is the case with Christianity) that it is free from a contradiction, so incident to human nature.

---

[1] [The Proof reads: 'Sometimes degraded him so far to a level with human creatures as to represent him wrestling with a man, walking in the cool of the evening, showing his back parts, and descending from heaven to inform himself of what passes on earth: while, &c.' The pen is drawn through all from 'as' to 'earth:' and for 'so far' the margin gives 'nearly.']

SECT. VII.—*Confirmation of this Doctrine.*

It appears certain, that, though the original notions of the vulgar represent the Divinity as a limited being, and consider him only as the particular cause of health or sickness; plenty or want; prosperity or adversity; yet when more magnificent ideas are urged upon them, they esteem it dangerous to refuse their assent. Will you say, that your deity is finite and bounded in his perfections; may be overcome by a greater force; is subject to human passions, pains, and infirmities; has a beginning, and may have an end? This they dare not affirm; but thinking it safest to comply with the higher encomiums, they endeavour, by an affected ravishment and devotion, to ingratiate themselves with him. As a confirmation of this, we may observe, that the assent of the vulgar is, in this case, merely verbal, and that they are incapable of conceiving those sublime qualities, which they seemingly attribute to the Deity. Their real idea of him, notwithstanding their pompous language, is still as poor and frivolous as ever.

That original intelligence, say the MAGIANS, who is the first principle of all things, discovers himself *immediately* to the mind and understanding alone; but has placed the sun as his image in the visible universe; and when that bright luminary diffuses its beams over the earth and the firmament, it is a faint copy of the glory, which resides in the higher heavens. If you would escape the displeasure of this divine being, you must be careful never to set your bare foot upon the ground, nor spit into a fire, nor throw any water upon it, even though it were consuming a whole city.[1] Who can express the perfections of the Almighty? say the Mahometans. Even the noblest of his works, if compared to him, are but dust and rubbish. How much more must human conception fall short of his infinite perfections? His smile and favour renders men for ever happy: and to obtain it for your children, the best method is to cut off from them, while infants, a little bit of skin, about half the breadth of a farthing. Take two bits of cloth,[2] say the *Roman catholics*, about an inch or

---

[1] Hyde de Relig. veterum PERSARUM.   [2] Called the Scapulaire.

an inch and a half square, join them by the corners with two strings or pieces of tape about sixteen inches long, throw this over your head, and make one of the bits of cloth lie upon your breast, and the other upon your back, keeping them next your skin : There is not a better secret for recommending yourself to that infinite Being, who exists from eternity to eternity.

The GETES, commonly called immortal, from their steady belief of the soul's immortality, were genuine theists and unitarians. They affirmed ZAMOLXIS, their deity, to be the only true god; and asserted the worship of all other nations to be addressed to mere fictions and chimeras. But were their religious principles any more refined, on account of these magnificent pretensions? Every fifth year they sacrificed a human victim, whom they sent as a messenger to their deity, in order to inform him of their wants and necessities. And when it thundered, they were so provoked, that, in order to return the defiance, they let fly arrows at him, and declined not the combat as unequal. Such at least is the account, which HERODOTUS gives of the theism of the immortal GETES.[1]

SECT. VIII.—*Flux and reflux of Polytheism and Theism.*

It is remarkable, that the principles of religion have a kind of flux and reflux in the human mind, and that men have a natural tendency to rise from idolatry to theism, and to sink again from theism into idolatry. The vulgar, that is, indeed, all mankind, a few excepted, being ignorant and uninstructed, never elevate their contemplation to the heavens, or penetrate by their disquisitions into the secret structure of vegetable or animal bodies; so far as to discover a supreme mind or original providence, which bestowed order on every part of nature. They consider these admirable works in a more confined and selfish view; and finding their own happiness and misery to depend on the secret influence and unforeseen concurrence of external objects, they regard, with perpetual attention, the *unknown causes*, which govern all these natural events, and distribute pleasure and pain, good and ill, by their powerful, but silent, operation. The

[1] Lib. iv. 94.

unknown causes are still appealed to on every emergence; and in this general appearance or confused image, are the perpetual objects of human hopes and fears, wishes and apprehensions. By degrees, the active imagination of men, uneasy in this abstract conception of objects, about which it is incessantly employed, begins to render them more particular, and to clothe them in shapes more suitable to its natural comprehension. It represents them to be sensible, intelligent beings, like mankind; actuated by love and hatred, and flexible by gifts and entreaties, by prayers and sacrifices. Hence the origin of religion: And hence the origin of idolatry or polytheism.

But the same anxious concern for happiness, which begets the idea of these invisible, intelligent powers, allows not mankind to remain long in the first simple conception of them; as powerful, but limited beings; masters of human fate, but slaves to destiny and the course of nature. Men's exaggerated praises and compliments still swell their idea upon them; and elevating their deities to the utmost bounds of perfection, at last beget the attributes of unity and infinity, simplicity and spirituality. Such refined ideas, being somewhat disproportioned to vulgar comprehension, remain not long in their original purity; but require to be supported by the notion of inferior mediators or subordinate agents, which interpose between mankind and their supreme deity. These demi-gods or middle beings, partaking more of human nature, and being more familiar to us, become the chief objects of devotion, and gradually recal that idolatry, which had been formerly banished by the ardent prayers and panegyrics of timorous and indigent mortals. But as these idolatrous religions fall every day into grosser and more vulgar conceptions, they at last destroy themselves, and by the vile representations, which they form of their deities, make the tide turn again towards theism. But so great is the propensity, in this alternate revolution of human sentiments, to return back to idolatry, that the utmost precaution is not able effectually to prevent it. And of this, some theists, particularly the JEWS and MAHOMETANS, have been sensible; as appears by their banishing all the arts of statuary and painting, and not allowing the representations, even of human figures, to be taken by marble or colours: lest the common infirmity of mankind should thence produce idolatry. The feeble apprehensions of men cannot be satisfied with conceiving their deity as a pure spirit and perfect intelligence; and yet their natural terrors keep them from imputing to him the least shadow of limitation and imperfection. They fluctuate between these opposite sentiments. The same infirmity still drags them downwards, from an omnipotent and spiritual deity, to a limited and corporeal one, and from a corporeal and limited deity to a statue or visible representation. The same endeavour at elevation still pushes them upwards, from the statue or material image to the invisible power; and from the invisible power to an infinitely perfect deity, the creator and sovereign of the universe.

SECT. IX.—*Comparison of these Religions, with regard to Persecution and Toleration.*

Polytheism or idolatrous worship, being founded entirely in vulgar traditions, is liable to this great inconvenience, that any practice or opinion, however barbarous or corrupted, may be authorized by it; and full scope is given, for knavery to impose on credulity, till morals and humanity be expelled the religious systems of mankind. At the same time, idolatry is attended with this evident advantage, that, by limiting the powers and functions of its deities, it naturally admits the gods of other sects and nations to a share of divinity, and renders all the various deities, as well as rites, ceremonies, or traditions, compatible with each other.[1] Theism is opposite both in its advantages and disadvantages. As that system supposes one sole deity, the perfection of reason and goodness, it should, if justly prosecuted, banish every thing frivolous, unreasonable, or inhuman from religious worship, and set before men the most illustrious example, as well as the most commanding motives, of justice and benevolence. These mighty advantages are not indeed over-balanced (for that is not

---

[1] VERRIUS FLACCUS, cited by PLINY, lib. xxviii. cap. 2. affirmed, that it was usual for the ROMANS before they laid siege to any town, to invocate the tutelar deity of the place, and by promising him greater honours than those he at present enjoyed, bribe him to betray his old friends and votaries. The name of the tutelar deity of ROME was for this reason kept a most religious mystery; lest the enemies of the republic should be able, in the same manner, to draw him over to their service. For without the name, they thought, nothing of that kind could be practised. PLINY says, that the common form of invocation was preserved to his time in the ritual of the pontiffs. And MACROBIUS has transmitted a copy of it from the secret things of SAMMONICUS SERENUS.

possible), but somewhat diminished, by inconveniencies, which arise from the vices and prejudices of mankind. While one sole object of devotion is acknowledged, the worship of other deities is regarded as absurd and impious. Nay, this unity of object seems naturally to require the unity of faith and ceremonies, and furnishes designing men with a pretence for representing their adversaries as profane, and the objects of divine as well as human vengeance. For as each sect is positive that its own faith and worship are entirely acceptable to the deity, and as no one can conceive, that the same being should be pleased with different and opposite rites and principles; the several sects fall naturally into animosity, and mutually discharge on each other that sacred zeal and rancour, the most furious and implacable of all human passions.

The tolerating spirit of idolaters, both in ancient and modern times, is very obvious to any one, who is the least conversant in the writings of historians or travellers. When the oracle of DELPHI was asked, what rites or worship was most acceptable to the gods? Those which are legally established in each city, replied the oracle.[1] Even priests, in those ages, could, it seems, allow salvation to those of a different communion. The ROMANS commonly adopted the gods of the conquered people; and never disputed the attributes of those local and national deities, in whose territories they resided. The religious wars and persecutions of the EGYPTIAN idolaters are indeed an exception to this rule; but are accounted for by ancient authors from reasons singular and remarkable. Different species of animals were the deities of the different sects among the EGYPTIANS; and the deities being in continual war, engaged their votaries in the same contention. The worshippers of dogs could not long remain in peace with the adorers of cats or wolves.[2] But where that reason took not place, the EGYPTIAN superstition was not so incompatible as is commonly imagined: since we learn from HERODOTUS,[3] that very large contributions were given by AMASIS towards rebuilding the temple of DELPHI.

The intolerance of almost all religions, which have maintained the unity of God, is as remarkable as the contrary principle of polytheists. The implacable narrow spirit of the JEWS is well known. MAHOMETANISM set out with still

[1] Xenoph. Memor. lib. i. 3. 1   [2] Plutarch. de Isid. & Osir. p. 72.   [3] 180.

more bloody principles ; and even to this day, deals out damnation, though not fire and faggot, to all other sects.   And if, among CHRISTIANS, the ENGLISH and DUTCH have embraced the principles of toleration, this singularity has proceeded from the steady resolution of the civil magistrate, in opposition to the continued efforts of priests and bigots.

The disciples of ZOROASTER shut the doors of heaven against all but the MAGIANS.[1] Nothing could more obstruct the progress of the PERSIAN conquests, than the furious zeal of that nation against the temples and images of the GREEKS. And after the overthrow of that empire we find ALEXANDER, as a polytheist, immediately re-establishing the worship of the BABYLONIANS, which their former princes, as monotheists, had carefully abolished.[2]   Even the blind and devoted attachment of that conqueror to the GREEK superstition hindered not but he himself sacrificed according to the BABYLONISH rites and ceremonies.[3]

So sociable is polytheism, that the utmost fierceness and antipathy, which it meets with in an opposite religion, is scarcely able to disgust it, and keep it at a distance.   AUGUSTUS praised extremely the reserve of his grandson, CAIUS CÆSAR, when this latter prince, passing by JERUSALEM, deigned not to sacrifice according to the JEWISH law.   But for what reason did AUGUSTUS so much approve of this conduct ?   Only, because that religion was by the PAGANS esteemed ignoble and barbarous.[1]

I may venture to affirm, that few corruptions of idolatry and polytheism are more pernicious to society than this corruption of theism,[5] when carried to the utmost height. The human sacrifices of the CARTHAGINIANS, MEXICANS, and many barbarous nations,[6] scarcely exceed the inquisition and persecutions of ROME and MADRID.   For be-

---

[1] Hyde de Relig. vet Persarum.
[2] Arrian. de Exped, lib. iii. 16.   Id. lib. vii. 17.
[3] Id. ibid.
[4] Sueton. in vita Aug. c. 93.
[5] *Corruptio optimi pessima.*
[6] Most nations have fallen into this guilt of human sacrifices; though, perhaps, this impious superstition has never prevailed very much in any civilized nation, unless we except the CARTHAGINIANS.   For the TYRIANS soon abolished it.   A sacrifice is conceived as a present ; and any present is delivered to their deity by destroying it and rendering it useless to men ; by burning what is solid, pouring out the liquid, and killing the animate.   For want of a better way of doing him service, we do ourselves an injury ; and fancy that we thereby express, at least, the heartiness of our good-will and adoration.   Thus our mercenary devotion deceives ourselves, and imagines it deceives the deity.

sides, that the effusion of blood may not be so great in the former case as in the latter; besides this, I say, the human victims, being chosen by lot, or by some exterior signs, affect not, in so considerable a degree, the rest of the society. Whereas virtue, knowledge, love of liberty, are the qualities, which call down the fatal vengeance of inquisitors; and when expelled, leave the society in the most shameful ignorance, corruption, and bondage. The illegal murder of one man by a tyrant is more pernicious than the death of a thousand by pestilence, famine, or any undistinguishing calamity.

In the temple of DIANA at ARICIA near ROME, whoever murdered the present priest, was legally entitled to be installed his successor.[1] A very singular institution! For, however barbarous and bloody the common superstitions often are to the laity, they usually turn to the advantage of the holy order.

SECT. X.—*With regard to courage or abasement.*

From the comparison of theism and idolatry, we may form some other observations, which will also confirm the vulgar observation, that the corruption of the best things gives rise to the worst.

Where the deity is represented as infinitely superior to mankind, this belief, though altogether just, is apt, when joined with superstitious terrors, to sink the human mind into the lowest submission and abasement, and to represent the monkish virtues of mortification, penance, humility, and passive suffering, as the only qualities which are acceptable to him. But where the gods are conceived to be only a little superior to mankind, and to have been, many of them, advanced from that inferior rank, we are more at our ease in our addresses to them, and may even, without profaneness, aspire sometimes to a rivalship and emulation of them. Hence activity, spirit, courage, magnanimity, love of liberty, and all the virtues which aggrandize a people.

The heroes in paganism correspond exactly to the saints in popery and holy dervises in MAHOMETANISM. The place of HERCULES, THESEUS, HECTOR, ROMULUS, is now supplied by DOMINIC, FRANCIS, ANTHONY, and BENEDICT. Instead of the destruction of monsters, the subduing of tyrants, the defence of our native country; whippings and fastings,

cowardice and humility, abject submission and slavish obedience, are become the means of obtaining celestial honours
among mankind.

One great incitement to the pious ALEXANDER in his warlike expeditions was his rivalship of HERCULES and BACCHUS,
whom he justly pretended to have excelled.[1]   BRASIDAS, that
generous and noble SPARTAN, after falling in battle, had heroic
honours paid him by the inhabitants of AMPHIPOLIS, whose
defence he had embraced.[2]   And in general, all founders of
states and colonies among the GREEKS were raised to this
inferior rank of divinity, by those who reaped the benefit of
their labours.

This gave rise to the observation of MACHIAVEL[3], that the
doctrines of the CHRISTIAN religion (meaning the catholic ;
for he knew no other) which recommend only passive courage
and suffering, had subdued the spirit of mankind, and had
fitted them for slavery and subjection.   An observation, which
would certainly be just, were there not many other circumstances in human society which controul the genius and
character of a religion.

BRASIDAS seized a mouse, and being bit by it, let it go.
There is nothing so contemptible, said he, *but what may be safe,
if it has but courage to defend itself.*[4]   BELLARMINE patiently
and humbly allowed the fleas and other odious vermin to prey
upon him.   *We shall have heaven*, said he, *to reward us for our
sufferings : But these poor creatures have nothing but the enjoyment of the present life.*[5]   Such difference is there between the
maxims of a GREEK hero and a CATHOLIC saint.

SECT. XI.—*With regard to reason or absurdity.*

Here is another observation to the same purpose, and a new
proof that the corruption of the best things begets the worst.
If we examine, without prejudice, the ancient heathen mythology, as contained in the poets, we shall not discover in it
any such monstrous absurdity, as we may at first be apt to
apprehend.   Where is the difficulty in conceiving, that the
same powers or principles, whatever they were, which formed
this visible world, men and animals, produced also a species

[1] Arrian passim.
[2] Thucyd. lib. v. 11.
[3] Discorsi, lib. vi.
[4] Plut. Apopth.
[5] Bayle, Article BELLARMINE.

of intelligent creatures, of more refined substance and greater authority than the rest? That these creatures may be capricious, revengeful, passionate, voluptuous, is easily conceived; nor is any circumstance more apt, among ourselves, to engender such vices, than the licence of absolute authority. And in short, the whole mythological system is so natural, that, in the vast variety of planets and worlds, contained in this universe, it seems more than probable, that, somewhere or other, it is really carried into execution.

The chief objection to it with regard to this planet, is, that it is not ascertained by any just reason or authority. The ancient tradition, insisted on by heathen priests and theologers, is but a weak foundation; and transmitted also such a number of contradictory reports, supported, all of them, by equal authority, that it became absolutely impossible to fix a preference amongst them. A few volumes, therefore, must contain all the polemical writings of pagan priests: And their whole theology must consist more of traditional stories and superstitious practices than of philosophical argument and controversy.

But where theism forms the fundamental principle of any popular religion, that tenet is so conformable to sound reason, that philosophy is apt to incorporate itself with such a system of theology. And if the other dogmas of that system be contained in a sacred book, such as the Alcoran, or be determined by any visible authority, like that of the ROMAN pontiff, speculative reasoners naturally carry on their assent, and embrace a theory, which has been instilled into them by their earliest education, and which also possesses some degree of consistence and uniformity. But as these appearances are sure, all of them, to prove deceitful, philosophy will soon find herself very unequally yoked with her new associate: and instead of regulating each principle, as they advance together, she is at every turn perverted to serve the purposes of superstition. For besides the unavoidable incoherences, which must be reconciled and adjusted; one may safely affirm, that all popular theology, especially the scholastic, has a kind of appetite for absurdity and contradiction. If that theology went not beyond reason and common sense, her doctrines would appear too easy and familiar. Amazement must of necessity be raised: Mystery affected: Darkness and obscurity sought after: And a foundation of merit afforded to the devout votaries, who desire an opportunity of subduing their rebellious reason, by the belief of the most unintelligible sophisms.

Ecclesiastical history sufficiently confirms these reflections. When a controversy is started, some people always pretend with certainty to foretell the issue. Whichever opinion, say they, is most contrary to plain sense is sure to prevail; even where the general interest of the system requires not that decision. Though the reproach of heresy may, for some time, be bandied about among the disputants, it always rests at last on the side of reason. Any one, it is pretended, that has but learning enough of this kind to know the definition of ARIAN, PELAGIAN, ERASTIAN, SOCINIAN, SABELLIAN, EUTYCHIAN, NESTORIAN, MONOTHELITE, &c. not to mention PROTESTANT, whose fate is yet uncertain, will be convinced of the truth of this observation. It is thus a system becomes more absurd in the end, merely from its being reasonable and philosophical in the beginning.

To oppose the torrent of scholastic religion by such feeble maxims as these, that *it is impossible for the same thing to be and not to be*, that *the whole is greater than a part*, that *two and three make five;* is pretending to stop the ocean with a bullrush. Will you set up profane reason against sacred mystery? No punishment is great enough for your impiety. And the same fires, which were kindled for heretics, will serve also for the destruction of philosophers.

SECT. XII.—*With regard to Doubt or Conviction.*

We meet every day with people so sceptical with regard to history, that they assert it impossible for any nation ever to believe such absurd principles as those of GREEK and EGYPTIAN paganism; and at the same time so dogmatical with regard to religion, that they think the same absurdities are to be found in no other communion. CAMBYSES entertained like prejudices; and very impiously ridiculed, and even wounded, APIS, the great god of the EGYPTIANS, who appeared to his profane senses nothing but a large spotted bull. But HERODOTUS[1] judiciously ascribes this sally of passion to a real madness or disorder of the brain: Otherwise, says the historian, he never would have openly affronted any established worship. For on that head, continues he, every nation are best satisfied

[1] [Editions [...] Qug [...] the r [...] rerer, lib. iii. c. 38.]

with their own, and think they have the advantage over every other nation.

It must be allowed, that the ROMAN CATHOLICS are a very learned sect; and that no one communion, but that of the church of ENGLAND, can dispute their being the most learned of all the Christian churches: Yet AVERROES, the famous ARABIAN, who, no doubt, had heard of the EGYPTIAN superstitions, declares, that, of all religions, the most absurd and nonsensical is that, whose votaries eat, after having created, their deity.

I believe, indeed, that there is no tenet in all paganism, which would give so fair a scope to ridicule as this of the *real presence:* For it is so absurd, that it eludes the force of all argument. There are even some pleasant stories of that kind, which, though somewhat profane, are commonly told by the Catholics themselves. One day, a priest, it is said, gave inadvertently, instead of the sacrament, a counter, which had by accident fallen among the holy wafers. The communicant waited patiently for some time, expecting it would dissolve on his tongue: But finding that it still remained entire, he took it off. *I wish*, cried he to the priest, *you have not committed some mistake: I wish you have not given me God the Father: He is so hard and tough there is no swallowing him.*

A famous general, at that time in the MUSCOVITE service, having come to PARIS for the recovery of his wounds, brought along with him a young TURK, whom he had taken prisoner. Some of the doctors of the SORBONNE (who are altogether as positive as the dervises of CONSTANTINOPLE) thinking it a pity, that the poor TURK should be damned for want of instruction, solicited MUSTAPHA very hard to turn Christian, and promised him, for his encouragement, plenty of good wine in this world, and paradise in the next. These allurements were too powerful to be resisted; and therefore, having been well instructed and catechized, he at last agreed to receive the sacraments of baptism and the Lord's supper. The priest, however, to make every thing sure and solid, still continued his instructions and began the next day with the usual question, *How many Gods are there? None at all*, replies BENEDICT; for that was his new name. *How! None at all!* cries the priest. *To be sure*, said the honest proselyte. *You have told me all along that there is but one God: And yesterday I eat him.*

Such are the doctrines of our brethren the Catholics. But

to these doctrines we are so accustomed, that we never wonder at them : Though in a future age, it will probably become difficult to persuade some nations, that any human, two-legged creature could ever embrace such principles. And it is a thousand to one, but these nations themselves shall have something full as absurd in their own creed, to which they will give a most implicit and most religious assent.

I lodged[1] once at PARIS in the same *hotel* with an ambassador from TUNIS, who, having passed some years at LONDON, was returning home that way. One day I observed his MOORISH excellency diverting himself under the porch, with surveying the splendid equipages that drove along ; when there chanced to pass that way some *Capucin* friars, who had never seen a TURK ; as he, on his part, though accustomed to the EUROPEAN dresses, had never seen the grotesque figure of a *Capucin :* And there is no expressing the mutual admiration, with which they inspired each other. Had the chaplain of the embassy entered into a dispute with these FRANCISCANS, their reciprocal surprize had been of the same nature. Thus all mankind stand staring at one another ; and there is no beating it into their heads, that the turban of the AFRICAN is not just as good or as bad a fashion as the cowl of the EUROPEAN. *He is a very honest man,* said the prince of SALLEE, speaking of de RUYTER. *It is a pity he were a Christian.*

How can you worship leeks and onions ? we shall suppose a SORBONNIST to say to a priest of SAIS. If we worship them, replies the latter ; at least, we do not, at the same time, eat them. But what strange objects of adoration are cats and monkies ? says the learned doctor. They are at least as good as the relics or rotten bones of martyrs, answers his no less learned antagonist. Are you not mad, insists the Catholic, to cut one another's throat about the preference of a cabbage or a cucumber ? Yes, says the pagan ; I allow it, if you will confess, that those are still madder, who fight about the preference among volumes of sophistry, ten thousand of which are not equal in value to one cabbage or cucumber.[2]

Every by-stander will easily judge (but unfortunately the by-standers are few) that, if nothing were requisite to establish any popular system, but exposing the absurdities of

---

[1] [Probably in 1734. ED.]

[2] It is strange that the EGYPTIAN

religion, though so absurd, should yet have borne so great a resemblance to other systems, every voter of every superstition could give a sufficient reason for his blind and bigotted attachment to the principles in which he has been educated. But without so extensive a knowledge, on which to ground this assurance (and perhaps, better without it), there is not wanting a sufficient stock of religious zeal and faith among mankind. Diodorus Siculus[1] gives a remarkable instance to this purpose, of which he was himself an eye-witness. While Egypt lay under the greatest terror of the Roman name, a legionary soldier having inadvertently been guilty of the sacrilegious impiety of killing a cat, the whole people rose upon him with the utmost fury; and all the efforts of the prince were not able to save him. The senate and people of Rome, I am persuaded, would not, then, have been so delicate with regard to their national deities. They very frankly, a little after that time, voted Augustus a place in the celestial mansions; and would have dethroned every god in heaven, for his sake, had he seemed to desire it. *Presens divus habebitur* Augustus, says Horace. That is a very important point: And in other nations and other ages, the same circumstance has not been deemed altogether indifferent.[2]

Notwithstanding the sanctity of our holy religion, says Tully,[3] no crime is more common with us than sacrilege: But was it ever heard of, that an Egyptian violated the temple of a cat, an ibis, or a crocodile? There is no torture,

---

the Jewish, that ancient writers even of the greatest genius were not able to observe any difference between them. For it is very remarkable that both Tacitus and Suetonius, when they mention that decree of the senate, under Tiberius, by which the Egyptian and Jewish proselytes were banished from Rome, expressly treat these religions as the same; and it appears, that even the decree itself was founded on that supposition. 'Actum & de sacris Ægyptus Judaicisque pellendis: factumque patrum consultum, ut quatuor millia libertini generis *ea superstitione* infecta, quis idonea ætas, in insulam Sardiniam veherentur, coercendis illic latrociniis; & si ob gravitatem cœli interissent, *vile damnum*: Ceteri cederent Italia, nisi certam ante diem profanos ritus exuissent.' Tacit. ann. lib. ii. c. 85. Externas cæremonias, Ægyptios Judai-

cosque ritus compescuit; coactis qui *superstitione ea* tenebantur, religiosas vestes cum instrumento omni comburere, &c.' Sueton. Tiber. c. 36. These wise heathens, observing something in the general air, and genius, and spirit of the two religions to be the same, esteemed the differences of their dogmas too frivolous to deserve any attention.

[1] Lib. i. 83.

[2] When Louis the XIVth took on himself the protection of the Jesuit's College of Clermont, the society ordered the king's arms to be put up over the gate, and took down the cross in order to make way for it: Which gave occasion to the following epigram:

Sustulit hinc Christi, posuitque insignia Regis:

Impia gens, alium nescit habere Deum.

[3] De nat. Deor. i. 29.

an EGYPTIAN would not undergo, says the same author in another place,[1] rather than injure an ibis, an aspic, a cat, a dog, or a crocodile.   Thus it is strictly true, what DRYDEN observes,

> 'Of whatsoe'er descent their godhead be,
> 'Stock, stone, or other homely pedigree,
> 'In his defence his servants are as bold
> 'As if he had been born of beaten gold.'
>
> ABSALOM and ACHITOPHEL.

Nay, the baser the materials are, of which the divinity is composed, the greater devotion is he likely to excite in the breasts of his deluded votaries.   They exult in their shame, and make a merit with their deity, in braving, for his sake, all the ridicule and contumely of his enemies.   Ten thousand [2] Crusaders inlist themselves under the holy banners ; and even openly triumph in those parts of their religion, which their adversaries regard as the most reproachful.

There occurs, I own, a difficulty in the EGYPTIAN system of theology ; as indeed, few systems of that kind are entirely free from difficulties.   It is evident, from their method of propagation, that a couple of cats, in fifty years, would stock a whole kingdom ; and if that religious veneration were still paid them, it would, in twenty more, not only be easier in EGYPT to find a god than a man, which PETRONIUS says was the case in some parts of Italy ; but the gods must at last entirely starve the men, and leave themselves neither priests nor votaries remaining.   It is probable, therefore, that this wise nation, the most celebrated in antiquity for prudence and sound policy, foreseeing such dangerous consequences, reserved all their worship for the full-grown divinities, and used the freedom to drown the holy spawn or little sucking gods, without any scruple or remorse.   And thus the practice of warping the tenets of religion, in order to serve temporal interests, is not, by any means, to be regarded as an invention of these later ages.

The learned, philosophical VARRO, discoursing of religion, pretends not to deliver any thing beyond probabilities and appearances : Such was his good sense and moderation !   But the passionate, the zealous AUGUSTIN, insults the noble ROMAN on his scepticism and reserve, and professes the most thorough belief and assurance.[3]   A heathen poet, however,

---

[1] Tusc. Quaest. lib. v. 27.   [2] De civitate Dei, l. iii. c. 17.
[3] [Cross : Editions I. to O.]

contemporary with the saint, absurdly esteems the religious system of the latter so false, that even the credulity of children, he says, could not engage them to believe it.[1]

Is it strange, when mistakes are so common, to find every one positive and dogmatical? And that the zeal often rises in proportion to the error? *Movernut*, says SPARTIAN, *& ca tempestate, Judæi bellum quod vetabantur mutilare genitalia.*[2]

If ever there was a nation or a time, in which the public religion lost all authority over mankind, we might expect, that infidelity in ROME, during the CICERONIAN age, would openly have erected its throne, and that CICERO himself, in every speech and action, would have been its most declared abettor. But it appears, that, whatever sceptical liberties that great man might take, in his writings or in philosophical conversation; he yet avoided, in the common conduct of life, the imputation of deism and profaneness. Even in his own family, and to his wife TERENTIA, whom he highly trusted, he was willing to appear a devout religionist; and there remains a letter, addressed to her, in which he seriously desires her to offer sacrifice to APOLLO and ÆSCULAPIUS, in gratitude for the recovery of his health.[3]

POMPEY's devotion was much more sincere: In all his conduct, during the civil wars, he paid a great regard to auguries, dreams, and prophesies.[4] AUGUSTUS was tainted with superstition of every kind. As it is reported of MILTON, that his poetical genius never flowed with ease and abundance in the spring; so AUGUSTUS observed, that his own genius for dreaming never was so perfect during that season, nor was so much to be relied on, as during the rest of the year. That great and able emperor was also extremely uneasy, when he happened to change his shoes, and put the right foot shoe on the left foot.[5] In short it cannot be doubted, but the votaries of the established superstition of antiquity were as numerous in every state, as those of the modern religion are at present. Its influence was as universal; though it was not so great. As many people gave their assent to it; though that assent was not seemingly so strong, precise, and affirmative.

We may observe, that, notwithstanding the dogmatical,

[1] Claudii Rutilii Numitiani Iter. lib. i. l. 391.
[2] In vita Adriani. 14.
[3] Lib. xiv. epist. 7.
[4] Cicero de Divin. lib. ii. c. 21.
[5] Sueton Aug. c. 90, 91, 92. Plin. lib. ii. cap. 5.

imperious style of all superstition, the conviction of the religionists, in all ages, is more affected than real, and scarcely ever approaches, in any degree, to that solid belief and persuasion, which governs us in the common affairs of life. Men dare not avow, even to their own hearts, the doubts which they entertain on such subjects: They make a merit of implicit faith; and disguise to themselves their real infidelity, by the strongest asseverations and most positive bigotry. But nature is too hard for all their endeavours, and suffers not the obscure, glimmering light, afforded in those shadowy regions, to equal the strong impressions, made by common sense and by experience. The usual course of men's conduct belies their words, and shows, that their assent in these matters is some unaccountable operation of the mind between disbelief and conviction, but approaching much nearer to the former than to the latter.

Since, therefore, the mind of man appears of so loose and unsteady a texture, that, even at present, when so many persons find an interest in continually employing on it the chissel and the hammer, yet are they not able to engrave theological tenets with any lasting impression; how much more must this have been the case in ancient times, when the retainers to the holy function were so much fewer in comparison? No wonder, that the appearances were then very inconsistent, and that men, on some occasions, might seem determined infidels, and enemies to the established religion, without being so in reality; or at least, without knowing their own minds in that particular.

Another cause, which rendered the ancient religions much looser than the modern, is, that the former were *traditional* and the latter are *scriptural*; and the tradition in the former was complex, contradictory, and, on many occasions, doubtful; so that it could not possibly be reduced to any standard and canon, or afford any determinate articles of faith. The stories of the gods were numberless like the popish legends; and though every one, almost, believed a part of these stories, yet no one could believe or know the whole: While, at the same time, all must have acknowledged, that no one part stood on a better foundation than the rest. The traditions of different cities and nations were also, on many occasions, directly opposite; and no reason could be assigned for preferring one to the other. And as there was an infinite number of stories, with regard to which tradition was nowise positive; the gradation was insensible, from the most fundamental articles of faith, to those loose and precarious fictions. The pagan religion, therefore, seemed to vanish like a cloud, whenever one approached to it, and examined it piecemeal. It could never be ascertained by any fixed dogmas and principles. And though this did not convert the generality of mankind from so absurd a faith; for when will the people be reasonable? yet it made them faulter and hesitate more in maintaining their principles, and was even apt to produce, in certain dispositions of mind, some practices and opinions, which had the appearance of determined infidelity.

To which we may add, that the fables of the pagan religion were, of themselves, light, easy, and familiar; without devils, or seas of brimstone, or any object that could much terrify the imagination. Who could forbear smiling, when he thought of the loves of MARS and VENUS, or the amorous frolics of JUPITER and PAN? In this respect, it was a true poetical religion; if it had not rather too much levity for the graver kinds of poetry. We find that it has been adopted by modern bards; nor have these talked with greater freedom and irreverence of the gods, whom they regarded as fictions, than the ancients did of the real objects of their devotion.

The inference is by no means just, that, because a system of religion has made no deep impression on the minds of a people, it must therefore have been positively rejected by all men of common sense, and that opposite principles, in spite of the prejudices of education, were generally established by argument and reasoning. I know not, but a contrary inference may be more probable. The less importunate and assuming any species of superstition appears, the less will it provoke men's spleen and indignation, or engage them into enquiries concerning its foundation and origin. This in the mean time is obvious, that the empire of all religious faith over the understanding is wavering and uncertain, subject to every variety of humour, and dependent on the present incidents, which strike the imagination. The difference is only in the degrees. An ancient will place a stroke of impiety and one of superstition alternately, throughout a whole discourse:[1] A modern often thinks in the same way, though he may be more guarded in his expression.

LUCIAN tells us expressly,[2] that whoever believed not the most ridiculous fables of paganism was deemed by the people profane and impious. To what purpose, indeed, would that agreeable author have employed the whole force of his wit and satire against the national religion, had not that religion been generally believed by his countrymen and contemporaries?

LIVY[3] acknowledges as frankly, as any divine would at present, the common incredulity of his age; but then he condemns it as severely. And who can imagine, that a national superstition, which could delude so ingenious a man, would not also impose on the generality of the people?

The STOICS bestowed many magnificent and even impious epithets on their sage; that he alone was rich, free, a king, and equal to the immortal gods. They forgot to add, that he was not inferior in prudence and understanding to an old woman. For surely nothing can be more pitiful than the sentiments, which that sect entertain with regard to religious matters; while they seriously agree with the common augurs, that, when a raven croaks from the left, it is a good omen; but a bad one, when a rook makes a noise from the same quarter. PANÆTIUS was the only STOIC, among the GREEKS, who so much as doubted with regard to auguries and divination.[4] MARCUS ANTONINUS[5] tells us, that he himself had received many admonitions from the gods in his sleep. It is true, EPICTETUS[6] forbids us to regard the language of rooks and ravens; but it is not, that they do not speak truth: It is only, because they can fortel nothing but the breaking of our neck or the forfeiture of our estate; which are circumstances, says he, that nowise concern us.

[1] Witness this remarkable passage of TACITUS: 'Præter multiplices rerum humanarum casus cœlo terraque prodigia & fulminum monitus & futurorum præsagia, læta tristia, ambigua manifesta. Nec enim unquam atrocioribus populi Romani cladibus, magisve justis indiciis approbatum est, non esse curæ Diis securitatem nostram, esse ultionem.' Hist. lib. i. 3. AUGUSTUS's quarrel with NEPTUNE is an instance of the same kind. Had not the emperor believed NEPTUNE to be a real being, and to have

dominion over the sea, where had been the foundation of his anger? And if he believed it, what madness to provoke still farther that deity? The same observation may be made upon QUINTILIAN's exclamation, on account of the death of his children. lib. vi. Præf.

[2] Philopseudes. 3.
[3] Lib. x. cap. 40.
[4] Cicero de Divin. lib. i. cap. 3 & 7.
[5] Lib. i. § 17.
[6] Ench. § 17.

Thus the Stoics join a philosophical enthusiasm to a religious superstition. The force of their mind, being all turned to the side of morals, unbent itself in that of religion.[1]

Plato[2] introduces Socrates affirming, that the accusation of impiety raised against him was owing entirely to his rejecting such fables, as those of Saturn's castrating his father Uranus, and Jupiter's dethroning Saturn: Yet in a subsequent dialogue,[3] Socrates confesses, that the doctrine of the mortality of the soul was the received opinion of the people. Is there here any contradiction? Yes, surely: But the contradiction is not in Plato; it is in the people, whose religious principles in general are always composed of the most discordant parts; especially in an age, when superstition sate so easy and light upon them.[4]

The same Cicero, who affected, in his own family, to ap-

[1] The Stoics, I own, were not quite orthodox in the established religion; but one may see, from these instances, that they went a great way: And the people undoubtedly went every length.

[2] Euthyphro. 6.

[3] Phædo.

[4] Xenophon's conduct, as related by himself, is, at once, an incontestable proof of the general credulity of mankind in those ages, and the incoherencies, in all ages, of men's opinions in religious matters. That great captain and philosopher, the disciple of Socrates, and one who has delivered some of the most refined sentiments with regard to a deity, gave all the following marks of vulgar, pagan superstition. By Socrates's advice, he consulted the oracle of Delphi, before he would engage in the expedition of Cyrus. De exped. lib. iii. p. 294, ex edit. Leunel. Sees a dream the night after the generals were seized; which he pays great regard to, but thinks ambiguous. Id. p. 295. He and the whole army regard sneezing as a very lucky omen. Id. p. 300. Has another dream, when he comes to the river Centrites, which his fellow-general, Chirosophus, also pays great regard to. Id. lib. iv. p. 323. The Greeks, suffering from a cold north wind, sacrifice to it; and the historian observes, that it immediately abated. Id. p. 329. Xenophon consults the sacrifices in secret, before he would form any resolution with himself about settling a colony. Lib. v. p. 359. He was himself a very skilful augur. Id. p. 361. Is determined by the vic-

tims to refuse the sole command of the army which was offered him. Lib. vi. p. 273. Cleander, the Spartan, though very desirous of it, refuses for the same reason. Id. p. 392. Xenophon mentions an old dream with the interpretation given him, when he first joined Cyrus, p. 373. Mentions also the place of Hercules's descent into hell as believing it, and says the marks of it are still remaining. Id. p. 375. Had almost starved the army, rather than lead them to the field against the auspices. Id. p. 382, 383. His friend, Euclides, the augur, would not believe that he had brought no money from the expedition; till he (Euclides) sacrificed, and then he saw the matter clearly in the Exta. Lib. vii. p. 425. The same philosopher, proposing a project of mines for the encrease of the Athenian revenues, advises them first to consult the oracle. De rat. red. p. 392. That all this devotion was not a farce, in order to serve a political purpose, appears both from the facts themselves, and from the genius of that age, when little or nothing could be gained by hypocrisy. Besides, Xenophon, as appears from his Memorabilia, was a kind of heretic in those times, which no political devotee ever is. It is for the same reason, I maintain, that Newton, Locke, Clarke, &c. being Arians or Socinians, were very sincere in the creed they professed: And I always oppose this argument to some libertines, who will needs have it, that it was impossible but that these philosophers must have been hypocrites.

pear a devout religionist, makes no scruple, in a public court of judicature, of treating the doctrine of a future state as a ridiculous fable, to which no body could give any attention.[1] SALLUST[2] represents CÆSAR as speaking the same language in the open senate.[3]

But that all these freedoms implied not a total and universal infidelity and scepticism amongst the people, is too apparent to be denied. Though some parts of the national religion hung loose upon the minds of men, other parts adhered more closely to them : And it was the chief business of the sceptical philosophers to show, that there was no more foundation for one than for the other. This is the artifice of COTTA in the dialogues concerning the *nature of the gods.* He refutes the whole system of mythology by leading the orthodox gradually, from the more momentous stories, which were believed, to the more frivolous, which every one ridiculed : From the gods to the goddesses ; from the goddesses to the nymphs ; from the nymphs to the fawns and satyrs. His master, CARNEADES, had employed the same method of reasoning.[4]

Upon the whole, the greatest and most observable differences between a *traditional, mythological* religion, and a *systematical, scholastic* one are two : The former is often more reasonable, as consisting only of a multitude of stories, which, however groundless, imply no express absurdity and demonstrative contradiction ; and sits also so easy and light on men's minds, that, though it may be as universally received, it happily makes no such deep impression on the affections and understanding.

SECT. XIII. — *Impious conceptions of the divine nature[5] in popular religions of both kinds.*

The primary religion of mankind arises chiefly from an anxious fear of future events : and what ideas will naturally be en-

---

[1] PRO CLUENTIO, cap. 61.

[2] De bello CATILIN. 51.

[3] CICERO (Tusc. Quæst. lib. i. cap. 5, 6) and SENECA (Epist. 24.), as also JUVENAL (Satyr. 2. 149), maintain that there is no boy or old woman so ridiculous as to believe the poets in their accounts of a future state. Why then does LUCRETIUS so highly exalt his master for freeing us from these terrors? Perhaps the generality of mankind were then in the disposition of CEPHALUS in PLATO (de Rep. lib. i. 330 D.) who while he was young and healthful could ridicule these stories : but as soon as he became old and infirm, began to entertain apprehensions of their truth. This we may observe not to be unusual even at present.

[4] SEXT. EMPIR. advers. MATHEM. lib. ix. 429.

[5] [In most popular Editions L to Q.]

tertained of invisible, unknown powers, while men lie under dismal apprehensions of any kind, may easily be conceived. Every image of vengeance, severity, cruelty, and malice must occur, and must augment the ghastliness and horror, which oppresses the amazed religionist. A panic having once seized the mind, the active fancy still farther multiplies the objects of terror; while that profound darkness, or, what is worse, that glimmering light, with which we are environed, represents the spectres of divinity under the most dreadful appearances imaginable. And no idea of perverse wickedness can be framed, which those terrified devotees do not readily, without scruple, apply to their deity.

This appears the natural state of religion, when surveyed in one light. But if we consider, on the other hand, that spirit of praise and eulogy, which necessarily has place in all religions, and which is the consequence of these very terrors, we must expect a quite contrary system of theology to prevail. Every virtue, every excellence, must be ascribed to the divinity, and no exaggeration will be deemed sufficient to reach those perfections, with which he is endowed. Whatever strains of panegyric can be invented, are immediately embraced, without consulting any arguments or phænomena: It is esteemed a sufficient confirmation of them, that they give us more magnificent ideas of the divine objects of our worship and adoration.

Here therefore is a kind of contradiction between the different principles of human nature, which enter into religion. Our natural terrors present the notion of a devilish and malicious deity: Our propensity to adulation leads us to acknowledge an excellent and divine. And the influence of these opposite principles are various, according to the different situation of the human understanding.

In very barbarous and ignorant nations, such as the AFRICANS and INDIANS, nay even the JAPONESE, who can form no extensive ideas of power and knowledge, worship may be paid to a being, whom they confess to be wicked and detestable; though they may be cautious, perhaps, of pronouncing this judgment of him in public, or in his temple, where he may be supposed to hear their reproaches.

Such rude, imperfect ideas of the Divinity adhere long to all idolaters; and it may safely be affirmed, that the GREEKS themselves never got entirely rid of them. It is remarked by XENOPHON,[1] in praise of SOCRATES, that this philosopher assented not to the vulgar opinion, which supposed the gods to know some things, and be ignorant of others : He maintained, that they knew every thing ; what was done, said, or even thought.   But as this was a train of philosophy[2] much above the conception of his countrymen, we need not be surprised, if very frankly, in their books and conversation, they blamed the deities, whom they worshipped in their temples.   It is observable, that HERODOTUS in particular scruples not, in many passages, to ascribe *envy* to the gods ; a sentiment, of all others, the most suitable to a mean and devilish nature.   The pagan hymns, however, sung in public worship, contained nothing but epithets of praise ; even while the actions ascribed to the gods were the most barbarous and detestable.   When TIMOTHEUS, the poet, recited a hymn to DIANA, in which he enumerated, with the greatest eulogies, all the actions and attributes of that cruel, capricious goddess : *May your daughter*, said one present, *become such as the deity whom you celebrate.*[3]

But as men farther exalt their idea of their divinity ; it is their notion of his power and knowledge only, not of his goodness, which is improved.   On the contrary, in proportion to the supposed extent of his science and authority, their terrors naturally augment ; while they believe, that no secrecy can conceal them from his scrutiny, and that even the inmost recesses of their breast lie open before him.   They must then be careful not to form expressly any sentiment of blame and disapprobation.   All must be applause, ravishment, extacy.   And while their gloomy apprehensions make them ascribe to him measures of conduct, which, in human creatures, would be highly blamed, they must still affect to praise and admire that conduct in the object of their devotional addresses.   Thus it may safely be affirmed, that popular religions are really, in the conception of their more vulgar votaries, a species of dæmonism ; and the higher the deity is exalted in power and knowledge, the lower of course is he depressed in goodness and benevolence ; whatever epithets of praise may be bestowed on him by his amazed adorers.

---

[1] Mem. lib. i. 1, 19.
[2] It was considered among the ancients, as a very extraordinary, philosophical paradox, that the presence of the gods was not confined to the heavens, but was extended every where ; as we learn from LUCIAN. *Hermotimus sive De sectis*, 81.
[3] PLUTARCH, de Superstit. 10

Among idolaters, the words may be false, and belie the secret opinion: But among more exalted religionists, the opinion itself contracts a kind of falsehood, and belies the inward sentiment. The heart secretly detests such measures of cruel and implacable vengeance; but the judgment dares not but pronounce them perfect and adorable. And the additional misery of this inward struggle aggravates all the other terrors, by which these unhappy victims to superstition are for ever haunted.

LUCIAN [1] observes that a young man, who reads the history of the gods in HOMER or HESIOD, and finds their factions, wars, injustice, incest, adultery, and other immoralities so highly celebrated, is much surprised afterwards, when he comes into the world, to observe that punishments are by law inflicted on the same actions, which he had been taught to ascribe to superior beings. The contradiction is still perhaps stronger between the representations given us by some later religions and our natural ideas of generosity, lenity, impartiality, and justice; and in proportion to the multiplied terrors of these religions, the barbarous conceptions of the divinity are multiplied upon us. [2] Nothing can preserve untainted the genuine principles of

[1] Necyomantia, 3.

[2] Bacchus, a divine being, is represented by the heathen mythology as the inventor of dancing and the theatre. Plays were anciently even a part of public worship on the most solemn occasions, and often employed in times of pestilence, to appease the offended deities. But they have been zealously proscribed by the godly in later ages; and the playhouse, according to a learned divine, is the porch of hell.

But in order to show more evidently, that it is possible for a religion to represent the divinity in still a more immoral and unamiable light than he was pictured by the ancients, we shall cite a long passage from an author of taste and imagination, who was surely no enemy to Christianity. It is the Chevalier RAMSAY, a writer, who had so laudable an inclination to be orthodox, that his reason never found any difficulty, even in the doctrines which free-thinkers scruple the most, the trinity, incarnation, and satisfaction: His humanity alone, of which he seems to have had a great stock, rebelled against the doctrines of eternal reprobation and predestination. He expresses himself thus: 'What strange ideas,' says he, 'would an Indian or a Chinese philosopher have of our holy religion, if they judged by the schemes given of it by our modern free-thinkers, and pharisaical doctors of all sects? According to the odious and too *vulgar* system of these incredulous scoffers and credulous scriblers, "The God of the Jews is a most cruel, unjust, partial, and fantastical being. He created, about 6000 years ago, a man and a woman, and placed them in a fine garden of ASIA, of which there are no remains. This garden was furnished with all sorts of trees, fountains, and flowers. He allowed them the use of all the fruits of this beautiful garden, except one, that was plant ed in the midst thereof, and that had in it a secret virtue of preserving them in continual health and vigour of body and mind, of exciting their natural powers and making them wise. The devil entered into the body of a serpent, and solicited the first woman to eat of this forbidden fruit; she engaged her hus-

SECT.
XIII.

morals in our judgment of human conduct, but the absolute necessity of these principles to the existence of society. If common conception can indulge princes in a system of ethics, somewhat different from that which should regulate private persons; how much more those

tend to do the same. To punish this slight curiosity and natural desire of life and knowledge, God not only threw our first parents out of paradise, but he condemned all their posterity to temporal misery, and the greatest part of them to eternal pains, though the souls of these innocent children have no more relation to that of Adam than to those of Nero and Mahomet; since, according to the scholastic drivellers, fabulists, and mythologists, all souls are created pure, and infused immediately into mortal bodies, so soon as the fœtus is formed. To accomplish the barbarous, partial decree of predestination and reprobation, God abandoned all nations to darkness, idolatry, and superstition, without any saving knowledge or salutary graces; unless it was one particular nation, whom he chose as his peculiar people. This chosen nation was, however, the most stupid, ungrateful, rebellious and perfidious of all nations. After God had thus kept the far greater part of all the human species, during near 4000 years, in a reprobate state, he changed all of a sudden, and took a fancy for other nations beside the Jews. Then he sent his only begotten Son to the world, under a human form, to appease his wrath, satisfy his vindictive justice, and die for the pardon of sin. Very few nations, however, have heard of this gospel; and all the rest, though left in invincible ignorance, are damned without exception, or any possibility of remission. The greatest part of those who have heard of it, have changed only some speculative notions about God, and some external forms in worship: For, in other respects, the bulk of Christians have continued as corrupt as the rest of mankind in their morals; yea, so much the more perverse and criminal, that their lights were greater. Unless it be a very small select number, all other Christians, like the pagans, will be for ever damned; the great sacrifice offered up for them will become void and of no effect; God will take delight for ever, in their torments and blasphemies; and though he can, by one

fiat change their hearts, yet they will remain for ever unconverted and unconvertible, because he will be for ever unappeasable and irreconcileable. It is true, that all this makes God odious, a hater of souls, rather than a lover of them; a cruel, vindictive tyrant, an impotent or a wrathful dæmon, rather than an all-powerful, beneficent father of spirits: Yet all this is a mystery. He has secret reasons for his conduct, that are impenetrable; and though he appears unjust and barbarous, yet we must believe the contrary, because what is injustice, crime, cruelty, and the blackest malice in us, is in him justice, mercy, and sovereign goodness." Thus the incredulous free-thinkers, the judaizing Christians, and the fatalistic doctors have disfigured and dishonoured the sublime mysteries of our holy faith; thus they have confounded the nature of good and evil; transformed the most monstrous passions into divine attributes, and surpassed the pagans in blasphemy, by ascribing to the eternal nature, as perfections, what makes the most horrid crimes amongst men. The grosser pagans contented themselves with divinizing lust, incest, and adultery; but the predestinarian doctors have divinized cruelty, wrath, fury, vengeance, and all the blackest vices.' See the Chevalier Ramsay's philosophical principles of natural and revealed religion, Part ii. p. 401.

The same author asserts, in other places, that the *Arminian* and *Molinist* schemes serve very little to mend the matter: And having thus thrown himself out of all received sects of Christianity, he is obliged to advance a system of his own, which is a kind of *Origenism*, and supposes the pre-existence of the souls both of men and beasts, and the eternal salvation and conversion of all men, beasts, and devils. But this notion, being quite peculiar to himself, we need not treat of. I thought the opinions of this ingenious author very curious; but I pretend not to warrant the justness of them.

superior beings, whose attributes, views, and nature are so totally unknown to us? *Sunt superis sua jura.*[1] The gods have maxims of justice peculiar to themselves.

SECT. XIV.—*Bad influence*[2] *of popular religions on morality.*

Here I cannot forbear observing a fact, which may be worth the attention of such as make human nature the object of their enquiry. It is certain, that, in every religion, however sublime the verbal definition which it gives of its divinity, many of the votaries, perhaps the greatest number, will still seek the divine favour, not by virtue and good morals, which alone can be acceptable to a perfect being, but either by frivolous observances, by intemperate zeal, by rapturous extasies, or by the belief of mysterious and absurd opinions. The least part of the *Sadder*, as well as of the *Pentateuch*, consists in precepts of morality; and we may also be assured, that that part was always the least observed and regarded. When the old ROMANS were attacked with a pestilence, they never ascribed their sufferings to their vices, or dreamed of repentance and amendment. They never thought, that they were the general robbers of the world, whose ambition and avarice made desolate the earth, and reduced opulent nations to want and beggary. They only created a dictator,[3] in order to drive a nail into a door; and by that means, they thought that they had sufficiently appeased their incensed deity.

In ÆGINA, one faction forming a conspiracy, barbarously and treacherously assassinated seven hundred of their fellow-citizens; and carried their fury so far, that, one miserable fugitive having fled to the temple, they cut off his hands, by which he clung to the gates, and carrying him out of holy ground, immediately murdered him. *By this impiety*, says HERODOTUS,[4] (not by the other many cruel assassinations) *they offended the gods, and contracted an inexpiable guilt.*

Nay, if we should suppose, what never happens, that a popular religion were found, in which it was expressly declared, that nothing but morality could gain the divine favour; if an order of priests were instituted to inculcate this opinion, in

[1] Ovid. Metam. lib. ix. 499.
[2] [Most popular: Editions L to Q.]
[3] Called Dictator clavis figenda

causa. T. Livii, l. vii. c. 3.
[4] Lib. vi. 91.

daily sermons, and with all the arts of persuasion; yet so inveterate are the people's prejudices, that, for want of some other superstition, they would make the very attendance on these sermons the essentials of religion, rather than place them in virtue and good morals. The sublime prologue of ZALEUCUS's laws [1] inspired not the LOCRIANS, so far as we can learn, with any sounder notions of the measures of acceptance with the deity, than were familiar to the other GREEKS.

This observation, then, holds universally: But still one may be at some loss to account for it. It is not sufficient to observe, that the people, every where, degrade their deities into a similitude with themselves, and consider them merely as a species of human creatures, somewhat more potent and intelligent. This will not remove the difficulty. For there is no *man* so stupid, as that, judging by his natural reason, he would not esteem virtue and honesty the most valuable qualities, which any person could possess. Why not ascribe the same sentiment to his deity? Why not make all religion, or the chief part of it, to consist in these attainments?

Nor is it satisfactory to say, that the practice of morality is more difficult than that of superstition; and is therefore rejected. For, not to mention the excessive penances of the *Brachmans* and *Talapoins*; it is certain, that the *Rhamadan* of the TURKS, during which the poor wretches, for many days, often in the hottest months of the year, and in some of the hottest climates of the world, remain without eating or drinking from the rising to the setting sun; this *Rhamadan*, I say, must be more severe than the practice of any moral duty, even to the most vicious and depraved of mankind. The four lents of the MUSCOVITES, and the austerities of some *Roman Catholics*, appear more disagreeable than meekness and benevolence. In short, all virtue, when men are reconciled to it by ever so little practice, is agreeable: All superstition is for ever odious and burthensome.

Perhaps, the following account may be received as a true solution of the difficulty. The duties, which a man performs as a friend or parent, seem merely owing to his benefactor or children; nor can he be wanting to these duties, without breaking through all the ties of nature and morality. A

[1] To be found in Diod. Sic. lib. xii. 120.

strong inclination may prompt him to the performance : A sentiment of order and moral obligation joins its force to these natural ties : And the whole man, if truly virtuous, is drawn to his duty, without any effort or endeavour. Even with regard to the virtues, which are more austere, and more founded on reflection, such as public spirit, filial duty, temperance, or integrity ; the moral obligation, in our apprehension, removes all pretension to religious merit ; and the virtuous conduct is deemed no more than what we owe to society and to ourselves. In all this, a superstitious man finds nothing, which he has properly performed for the sake of his deity, or which can peculiarly recommend him to the divine favour and protection. He considers not, that the most genuine method of serving the divinity is by promoting the happiness of his creatures. He still looks out for some more immediate service of the supreme Being, in order to allay those terrors, with which he is haunted. And any practice, recommended to him, which either serves to no purpose in life, or offers the strongest violence to his natural inclinations ; that practice he will the more readily embrace, on account of those very circumstances, which should make him absolutely reject it. It seems the more purely religious, because it proceeds from no mixture of any other motive or consideration. And if, for its sake, he sacrifices much of his ease and quiet, his claim of merit appears still to rise upon him, in proportion to the zeal and devotion which he discovers. In restoring a loan, or paying a debt, his divinity is nowise beholden to him ; because these acts of justice are what he was bound to perform, and what many would have performed, were there no god in the universe. But if he fast a day, or give himself a sound whipping ; this has a direct reference, in his opinion, to the service of God. No other motive could engage him to such austerities. By these distinguished marks of devotion, he has now acquired the divine favour ; and may expect, in recompence, protection and safety in this world, and eternal happiness in the next.

Hence the greatest crimes have been found, in many instances, compatible with a superstitious piety and devotion : Hence, it is justly regarded as unsafe to draw any certain inference in favour of a man's morals, from the fervour or strictness of his religious exercises, even though he himself believe them sincere. Nay, it has been observed, that enormities of

the blackest dye have been rather apt to produce superstitious
terrors, and encrease the religious passion. BOMILCAR, having
formed a conspiracy for assassinating at once the whole senate
of CARTHAGE, and invading the liberties of his country, lost,
the opportunity, from a continual regard to omens and prophecies. *Those who undertake the most criminal and most dangerous
enterprizes are commonly the most superstitious*; as an ancient
historian[1] remarks on this occasion. Their devotion and spiritual faith rise with their fears. CATILINE was not contented
with the established deities and received rites of the national
religion : His anxious terrors made him seek new inventions
of this kind ;[2] which he never probably had dreamed of,
had he remained a good citizen, and obedient to the laws of
his country.

To which we may add, that, after the commission of crimes,
there arise remorses and secret horrors, which give no rest
to the mind, but make it have recourse to religious rites and
ceremonies, as expiations of its offences. Whatever weakens
or disorders the internal frame promotes the interests of
superstition : And nothing is more destructive to them than
a manly, steady virtue, which either preserves us from disastrous, melancholy accidents, or teaches us to bear them.
During such calm sunshine of the mind, these spectres of false
divinity never make their appearance. On the other hand,
while we abandon ourselves to the natural undisciplined
suggestions of our timid and anxious hearts, every kind of
barbarity is ascribed to the supreme Being, from the terrors
with which we are agitated ; and every kind of caprice, from
the methods which we embrace in order to appease him. *Barbarity, caprice ;* these qualities, however nominally disguised,
we may universally observe, form the ruling character of the
deity in popular religions. Even priests, instead of correcting
these depraved ideas of mankind, have often been found ready
to foster and encourage them. The more tremendous the
divinity is represented, the more tame and submissive do men
become to his ministers : And the more unaccountable the
measures of acceptance required by him, the more necessary
does it become to abandon our natural reason, and yield to
their ghostly guidance and direction. Thus it may be allowed,
that the artifices of men aggravate our natural infirmities and

[1] Diod. Sic. lib. xx. 43.
[2] Cic. Catil. i. 6, Sallust. de bello Catil. 22.

follies of this kind, but never originally beget them. Their root strikes deeper into the mind, and springs from the essential and universal properties of human nature.

SECT. XV. — General Corollary.

Though the stupidity of men, barbarous and uninstructed, be so great, that they may not see a sovereign author in the more obvious works of nature, to which they are so much familiarized; yet it scarcely seems possible, that any one of good understanding should reject that idea, when once it is suggested to him. A purpose, an intention, a design is evident in every thing; and when our comprehension is so far enlarged as to contemplate the first rise of this visible system, we must adopt, with the strongest conviction, the idea of some intelligent cause or author. The uniform maxims too, which prevail throughout the whole frame of the universe, naturally, if not necessarily, lead us to conceive this intelligence as single and undivided, where the prejudices of education oppose not so reasonable a theory. Even the contrarieties of nature, by discovering themselves every where, become proofs of some consistent plan, and establish one single purpose or intention, however inexplicable and incomprehensible.

Good and ill are universally intermingled and confounded; happiness and misery, wisdom and folly, virtue and vice. Nothing is pure and entirely of a piece. All advantages are attended with disadvantages. An universal compensation prevails in all conditions of being and existence. And it is not possible for us, by our most chimerical wishes, to form the idea of a station or situation altogether desirable. The draughts of life, according to the poet's fiction, are always mixed from the vessels on each hand of JUPITER: Or if any cup be presented altogether pure, it is drawn only, as the same poet tells us, from the left-handed vessel.

The more exquisite any good is, of which a small specimen is afforded us, the sharper is the evil, allied to it; and few exceptions are found to this uniform law of nature. The most sprightly wit borders on madness; the highest effusions of joy produce the deepest melancholy; the most ravishing pleasures are attended with the most cruel lassitude and disgust; the most flattering hopes make way for the severest disappointments. And, in general, no course of life has such safety (for happiness is not to be dreamed of) as the temperate and moderate, which maintains, as far as possible, a mediocrity, and a kind of insensibility, in every thing.

As the good, the great, the sublime, the ravishing are found eminently in the genuine principles of theism; it may be expected, from the analogy of nature, that the base, the absurd, the mean, the terrifying will be equally discovered in religious fictions and chimeras.

The universal propensity to believe in invisible, intelligent power, if not an original instinct, being at least a general attendant of human nature, may be considered as a kind of mark or stamp, which the divine workman has set upon his work; and nothing surely can more dignify mankind, than to be thus selected from all other parts of the creation, and to bear the image or impression of the universal Creator. But consult this image, as it appears in the popular religions of the world. How is the deity disfigured in our representations of him! What caprice, absurdity, and immorality are attributed to him! How much is he degraded even below the character, which we should naturally, in common life, ascribe to a man of sense and virtue!

What a noble privilege is it of human reason to attain the knowledge of the supreme Being; and, from the visible works of nature, be enabled to infer so sublime a principle as its supreme Creator? But turn the reverse of the medal. Survey most nations and most ages. Examine the religious principles, which have, in fact, prevailed in the world. You will scarcely be persuaded, that they are any thing but sick men's dreams: Or perhaps will regard them more as the playsome whimsies of monkies in human shape, than the serious, positive, dogmatical asseverations of a being, who dignifies himself with the name of rational.

Hear the verbal protestations of all men: Nothing so certain as their religious tenets. Examine their lives: You will scarcely think that they repose the smallest confidence in them.

The greatest and truest zeal gives us no security against hypocrisy: The most open impiety is attended with a secret dread and compunction.

No theological absurdities so glaring that they have not, sometimes, been embraced by men of the greatest and most cultivated understanding. No religious precepts so rigorous that they have not been adopted by the most voluptuous and most abandoned of men.

Ignorance is the mother of Devotion : A maxim that is proverbial, and confirmed by general experience. Look out for a people, entirely destitute of religion : If you find them at all, be assured, that they are but few degrees removed from brutes.

What so pure as some of the morals, included in some theological systems? What so corrupt as some of the practices, to which these systems give rise?

The comfortable views, exhibited by the belief of futurity, are ravishing and delightful. But how quickly vanish on the appearance of its terrors, which keep a more firm and durable possession of the human mind?

The whole is a riddle, an ænigma, an inexplicable mystery. Doubt, uncertainty, suspence of judgment appear the only result of our most accurate scrutiny, concerning this subject. But such is the frailty of human reason, and such the irresistible contagion of opinion, that even this deliberate doubt could scarcely be upheld; did we not enlarge our view, and opposing one species of superstition to another, set them a quarrelling; while we ourselves, during their fury and contention, happily make our escape into the calm, though obscure regions of philosophy.

ESSAYS

WITHDRAWN

ESSAYS WITHDRAWN.

Essay I.—*Of Essay Writing.*[1]

THE elegant Part of Mankind, who are not immers'd in the animal Life, but employ themselves in the Operations of the Mind, may be divided into the *learned* and *conversible*. The Learned are such as have chosen for their Portion the higher and more difficult Operations of the Mind, which require Leisure and Solitude, and cannot be brought to Perfection, without long Preparation and severe Labour. The conversible World join to a sociable Disposition, and a Taste of Pleasure, an Inclination to the easier and more gentle Exercises of the Understanding, to obvious Reflections on human Affairs, and the Duties of common Life, and to the Observation of the Blemishes or Perfections of the particular Objects, that surround them. Such Subjects of Thought furnish not sufficient Employment in Solitude, but require the Company and Conversation of our Fellow-Creatures, to render them a proper Exercise for the Mind : And this brings Mankind together in Society, where every one displays his Thoughts and Observations in the best Manner he is able, and mutually gives and receives Information, as well as Pleasure.

The Separation of the Learned from the conversible World seems to have been the great Defect of the last Age, and must have had a very bad Influence both on Books and Company : For what Possibility is there of finding Topics of Conversation fit for the Entertainment of rational Creatures, without having Recourse sometimes to History, Poetry, Politics, and the more obvious Principles, at least, of Philosophy? Must our whole Discourse be a continued Series of

[1] [This Essay appeared only in Edition C, 1742 : see ' History of the Editions,' Vol. iii. pp. 43-4. ED.]

gossipping Stories and idle Remarks? Must the Mind never rise higher, but be perpetually

> Stun'd and worn out with endless Chat
> Of WILL did this, and NAN said that?

This wou'd be to render the Time spent in Company the most unentertaining, as well as the most unprofitable Part of our Lives.

On the other Hand, Learning has been as great a Loser by being shut up in Colleges and Cells, and secluded from the World and good Company. By that Means, every Thing of what we call *Belles Lettres* became totally barbarous, being cultivated by Men without any Taste of Life or Manners, and without that Liberty and Facility of Thought and Expression, which can only be acquir'd by Conversation. Even Philosophy went to Wrack by this moaping recluse Method of Study, and became as chimerical in her Conclusions as she was unintelligible in her Stile and Manner of Delivery. And indeed, what cou'd be expected from Men who never consulted Experience in any of their Reasonings, or who never search'd for that Experience, where alone it is to be found, in common Life and Conversation?

'Tis with great Pleasure I observe, That Men of Letters, in this Age, have lost, in a great Measure, that Shyness and Bashfulness of Temper, which kept them at a Distance from Mankind; and, at the same Time, That Men of the World are proud of borrowing from Books their most agreeable Topics of Conversation. 'Tis to be hop'd, that this League betwixt the learned and conversible Worlds, which is so happily begun, will be still farther improv'd, to their mutual Advantage; and to that End, I know nothing more advantageous than such *Essays* as these with which I endeavour to entertain the Public. In this View, I cannot but consider myself as a Kind of Resident or Ambassador from the Dominions of Learning to those of Conversation; and shall think it my constant Duty to promote a good Correspondence betwixt these two States, which have so great a Dependence on each other. I shall give Intelligence to the Learned of whatever passes in Company, and shall endeavour to import into Company whatever Commodities I find in my native Country proper for their Use and Entertainment. The Balance of Trade we need not be jealous of, nor will there be any Difficulty to preserve it on both Sides. The Materials of this Commerce must chiefly be furnish'd by Conversation and common Life : The manufacturing of them alone belongs to Learning.

As 'twou'd be an unpardonable Negligence in an Ambassador not to pay his Respects to the Sovereign of the State where he is commission'd to reside ; so it wou'd be altogether inexcusable in me not to address myself, with a particular Respect, to the Fair Sex, who are the Sovereigns of the Empire of Conversation. I approach them with Reverence ; and were not my Countrymen, the Learned, a stubborn independent Race of Mortals, extremely jealous of their Liberty, and unaccustom'd to Subjection, I shou'd resign into their fair Hands the sovereign Authority over the Republic of Letters. As the Case stands, my Commission extends no farther, than to desire a League, offensive and defensive, against our common Enemies, against the Enemies of Reason and Beauty, People of dull Heads and cold Hearts. From this Moment let us pursue them with the severest Vengeance : Let no Quarter be given, but to those of sound Understandings and delicate Affections ; and these Characters, 'tis to be presum'd, we shall always find inseparable.

To be serious, and to quit the Allusion before it be worn thread-bare, I am of Opinion, that Women, that is, Women of Sense and Education (for to such alone I address myself) are much better Judges of all polite Writing than Men of the same Degree of Understanding ; and that 'tis a vain Pannic, if they be so far terrify'd with the common Ridicule that is levell'd against learned Ladies, as utterly to abandon every Kind of Books and Study to our Sex. Let the Dread of that Ridicule have no other Effect, than to make them conceal their knowledge before Fools, who are not worthy of it, nor of them. Such will still presume upon the vain Title of the Male Sex to affect a Superiority above them : But my fair Readers may be assur'd, that all Men of Sense, who know the World, have a great Deference for their Judgment of such Books as ly within the Compass of their Knowledge, and repose more Confidence in the Delicacy of their Taste, tho' unguided by Rules, than in all the dull Labours of Pedants and Commentators. In a neighbouring Nation, equally famous for good Taste, and for Gallantry, the Ladies are, in a Manner, the Sovereigns of the *learned* World, as well as of the *conversible*; and no polite Writer pretends to venture upon the Public, without the Approbation of some celebrated Judges of that Sex. Their Verdict is, indeed, sometimes complain'd of; and, in particular, I find, that the Admirers of *Corneille*, to save that great Poet's Honour upon the Ascendant that *Racine* began to take over him, always said, That it was not to be expected, that so old a Man could dispute the Prize, before such Judges, with so young a Man as his Rival. But this Observation has been found unjust, since Posterity seems to have ratify'd the Verdict of that Tribunal: And *Racine*, tho' dead, is still the Favourite of the Fair Sex, as well as of the best Judges among the Men.

There is only one Subject, on which I am apt to distrust the Judgment of Females, and that is, concerning Books of Gallantry and Devotion, which they commonly affect as high flown as possible; and most of them seem more delighted with the Warmth, than with the justness of the Passion. I mention Gallantry and Devotion as the same Subject, because, in Reality, they become the same when treated in this Manner; and we may observe, that they both depend upon the very same Complexion. As the Fair Sex have a great Share of the tender and amorous Disposition, it perverts their Judgment on this Occasion, and makes them be easily affected, even by what has no Propriety in the Expression nor Nature in the Sentiment. Mr. *Addison's* elegant Discourses of Religion have no Relish with them, in Comparison of Books of mystic Devotion: And *Otway's* Tragedies are rejected for the Rants of Mr. *Dryden*.

Wou'd the Ladies correct their false Taste in this Particular; Let them accustom themselves a little more to Books of all Kinds: Let them give Encouragement to Men of Sense and Knowledge to frequent their Company: And finally, let them concur heartily in that Union I have projected betwixt the learned and conversible Worlds. They may, perhaps, meet with more Complaisance from their usual Followers than from Men of Learning; but they cannot reasonably expect so sincere an Affection: And, I hope, they will never be guilty of so wrong a Choice, as to sacrifice the Substance to the Shadow.

ESSAY II.—*Of Moral Prejudices.*[1]

THERE is a Set of Men lately sprung up amongst us, who endeavour to distinguish themselves by ridiculing every Thing, that has hitherto appear'd sacred and venerable in the Eyes of Mankind. Reason, Sobriety, Honour, Friendship, Marriage, are the perpetual Subjects of their insipid Raillery: And even public Spirit, and a Regard to our Country, are treated as chimerical and romantic. Were the Schemes of these Anti-reformers to take Place, all the Bonds of Society must be broke, to make Way for the Indulgence of a licentious Mirth and Gaiety: The Companion of our drunken Frollies must be prefer'd to a Friend or Brother: Dissolute Prodigality must be supply'd at the Expence of every Thing valuable, either in public or private: And Men shall have so little Regard to any Thing beyond themselves, that, at last, a free Constitution of Government must become a Scheme perfectly impracticable among Mankind, and must degenerate into one universal System of Fraud and Corruption.

There is another Humour, which may be observ'd in some Pretenders to Wisdom, and which, if not so pernicious as the idle petulant Humour above-mention'd, must, however, have a very bad Effect on those, who indulge it. I mean that grave philosophic Endeavour after Perfection, which, under Pretext of reforming Prejudices and Errors, strikes at all the most endearing Sentiments of the Heart, and all the most useful Byasses and Instincts, which can govern a human Creature. The *Stoics* were remarkable for this Folly among the Antients; and I wish some of more venerable Characters in latter Times had not copy'd them too faithfully in this Particular. The virtuous and tender Sentiments, or Prejudices, if you will, have suffer'd mightily by these Reflections; while a certain sullen Pride or Contempt of Mankind has prevail'd in their Stead, and has been esteem'd the greatest Wisdom; tho', in Reality, it be the most egregious Folly of all others. *Statilius* being sollicited by *Brutus* to make one of that noble Band, who struck the God-like Stroke for the Liberty of *Rome*, refus'd to accom-

---

[1] [This Essay appeared only in Edition C, 1742: see 'History of the Editions,' Vol. III. p. 44.—ED.]

pany them, saying, *That all Men were Fools or Mad, and did not deserve that a wise Man should trouble his Head about them.*

My learned Reader will here easily recollect the Reason, which an antient Philosopher gave, why he wou'd not be reconcil'd to his Brother, who sollicited his Friendship. He was too much a Philosopher to think, that the Connexion of having sprung from the same Parent, ought to have any Influence on a reasonable Mind, and exprest his Sentiment after such a Manner as I think not proper to repeat. When your Friend is in Affliction, says *Epictetus*, you may counterfeit a Sympathy with him, if it give him Relief; but take Care not to allow any Compassion to sink into your Heart, or disturb that Tranquillity, which is the Perfection of Wisdom. *Diogenes* being ask'd by his Friends in his Sickness, What should be done with him after his Death? *Why,* says he, *throw me out into the Fields.* 'What! reply'd they, to the Birds or Beasts?' *No: Place a Cudgel by me, to defend myself withal.* 'To what Purpose, say they, you will not have any Sense, nor any Power of making Use of it.' *Then if the Beasts shou'd devour me,* cries he, *shall I be any more sensible of it?* I know none of the Sayings of that Philosopher, which shews more evidently both the Liveliness and Ferocity of his Temper.

How different from these are the Maxims by which *Eugenius* conducts himself! In his Youth he apply'd himself, with the most unwearied Labour, to the Study of Philosophy; and nothing was ever able to draw him from it, except when an Opportunity offer'd of serving his Friends, or doing a Pleasure to some Man of Merit. When he was about thirty Years of Age, he was determin'd to quit the free Life of a Batchelor (in which otherwise he wou'd have been inclin'd to remain), by considering, that he was the last Branch of an antient Family, which must have been extinguish'd had he died without Children. He made Choice of the virtuous and beautiful *Emira* for his Consort, who, after being the Solace of his Life for many Years, and having made him the Father of several Children, paid at last the general Debt to Nature. Nothing cou'd have supported him under so severe an Affliction, but the Consolation he receiv'd from his young Family, who were now become dearer to him on account of their deceast Mother. One Daughter in particular is his Darling, and the secret Joy of his Soul; because her Features, her Air, her Voice recal every Moment the tender Memory of his Spouse, and fill his Eyes with Tears. He conceals this Partiality as much as possible; and none but his intimate Friends are acquainted with it. To them he reveals all his Tenderness; nor is he so affectedly philosophical, as even to call it by the Name of *Weakness*. They know, that he still keeps the Birth-day of *Emira* with Tears, and a more fond and tender Recollection of past Pleasures; in like manner as it was celebrated in her Lifetime with Joy and Festivity. They know, that he preserves her Picture with the utmost Care, and has one Picture in Minature, which he always wears next to his Bosom: That he has left Orders in his last Will, that, in whatever Part of the World he shall happen to die, his Body shall be transported, and laid in the same Grave with her's: And that a Monument shall be erected over them, and their mutual Love and Happiness celebrated in an Epitaph, which he himself has compos'd for that Purpose.

A few Years ago I receiv'd a Letter from a Friend, who was abroad on his Travels, and shall here communicate it to the Public. It contains such an Instance of a Philosophic Spirit, as I think pretty extraordinary, and may serve as an Example, not to depart too far from the receiv'd Maxims of Conduct and Behaviour, by a refin'd Search after Happiness or Perfection. The Story I have been since assur'd of as Matter of Fact.

Paris. Aug. 2, 1737.

SIR,—I know you are more curious of Accounts of Men than of Buildings, and are more desirous of being inform'd of private History than of public Transactions: for which Reason, I thought the following Story, which is the common Topic of Conversation in this City, wou'd be no unacceptable Entertainment to you.

A young Lady of Birth and Fortune, being left intirely at her own Disposal, persisted long in a Resolution of leading a single Life, notwithstanding several advantageous Offers that had been made to her. She had been determin'd to embrace this Resolution, by observing the many unhappy Marriages among her Acquaintance, and by hearing the Complaints, which her Female Friends made of the Tyranny,

Inconstancy, Jealousy or Indifference of their Husbands. Being a Woman of strong Spirit and an uncommon Way of thinking, she found no Difficulty either in forming or maintaining this Resolution, and cou'd not suspect herself of such Weakness, as ever to be induc'd, by any Temptation, to depart from it. She had, however, entertain'd a strong Desire of having a Son, whose Education she was resolv'd to make the principal Concern of her Life, and by that Means supply the Place of those other Passions, which she was resolv'd for ever to renounce. She push'd her Philosophy to such an uncommon Length, as to find no Contradiction betwixt such a Desire and her former Resolution; and accordingly look'd about, with great Deliberation, to find, among all her Male-Acquaintance, one whose Character and Person were agreeable to her, without being able to satisfy herself on that Head. At Length, being in the Play-house one Evening, she sees in the *Parterre*, a young Man of a most engaging Countenance and modest Deportment; and feels such a Pre-possession in his Favour, that she had Hopes this must be the Person she had long sought for in vain. She immediately dispatches a Servant to him; desiring his Company, at her Lodgings, next Morning. The young Man was over-joy'd at the Message, and cou'd not command his Satisfaction, upon receiving such an Advance from a Lady of so great Beauty, Reputation and Quality. He was, therefore, much disappointed, when he found a Woman, who wou'd allow him no Freedoms; and amidst all her obliging Behaviour, confin'd and over-aw'd him to the Bounds of rational Discourse and Conversation. She seem'd, however, willing to commence a Friendship with him; and told him, that his Company wou'd always be acceptable to her, whenever he had a leisure Hour to bestow. He needed not much Entreaty to renew his Visits, being so struck with her Wit and Beauty, that he must have been unhappy, had he been debarr'd her Company. Every Conversation serv'd only the more to inflame his Passion, and gave him more Occasion to admire her Person and Understanding, as well as to rejoice in his own Good-fortune. He was not, however, without Anxiety, when he consider'd the Disproportion of their Birth and Fortune; nor was his Uneasiness allay'd even when he reflected on the extraordinary Manner in which their Acquaintance had commenc'd. Our Philosophical Heroine,

in the mean Time, discover'd, that her Lover's personal
Qualities did not belye his Phisiognomy; so that, judging
there was no Occasion for any farther Trial, she takes a
proper Opportunity of communicating to him her whole
Intention. Their Intercourse continu'd for some-time, till
at last her Wishes were crown'd, and she was now Mother
of a Boy, who was to be the Object of her future Care and
Concern. Gladly wou'd she have continu'd her Friendship
with the Father; but finding him too passionate a Lover to
remain within the Bounds of Friendship, she was oblig'd to
put a Violence upon herself. She sends him a Letter, in
which she had inclos'd a Bond of Annuity for a Thousand
Crowns; desiring him, at the same Time, never to see her
more, and to forget, if possible, all past Favours and Familiarities. He was Thunder-struck at receiving this Message;
and, having tried, in vain, all the Arts that might win upon
the Resolution of a Woman, resolv'd at last to attack her
by her *Foible*. He commences a Law-suit against her before
the Parliament of *Paris*; and claims his Son, whom he pretends a Right to educate as he pleas'd, according to the
usual Maxims of the Law in such Cases. She pleads, on
the other Hand, their express Agreement before their Commerce, and pretends, that he had renounc'd all Claim to any
Offspring that might arise from their Embraces. It is not
yet known, how the Parliament will determine in this extraordinary Case, which puzzles all the Lawyers, as much as
it does the Philosophers. As soon as they come to any
Issue, I shall inform you of it, and shall embrace any Opportunity of subscribing myself, as I do at present,

Sir,

Your most humble Servant.

Essay III.—*Of the Middle Station of Life.*[1]

THE Moral of the following Fable will easily discover itself,
without my explaining it. One Rivulet meeting another,
with whom he had been long united in strictest Amity, with
noisy Haughtiness and Disdain thus bespoke him, " What,
Brother! Still in the same State! Still low and creeping!

---

[1] [This Essay appeared only in Edition C, 1742: see 'History of the Editions.' Vol. III. p. 44. ED.]

Are you not asham'd, when you behold me, who, tho' lately in a like Condition with you, am now become a great River, and shall shortly be able to rival the *Danube* or the *Rhine*, provided those friendly Rains continue, which have favour'd my Banks, but neglected yours." Very true, replies the humble Rivulet: "You are now, indeed, swoln to a great Size: But methinks you are become, withal, somewhat turbulent and muddy. I am contented with my low Condition and my Purity."

Instead of commenting upon this Fable, I shall take Occasion, from it, to compare the different Stations of Life, and to perswade such of my Readers as are plac'd in the Middle Station to be satisfy'd with it, as the most eligible of all others. These form the most numerous Rank of Men, that can be suppos'd susceptible of Philosophy; and therefore, all Discourses of Morality ought principally to be address'd to them. The Great are too much immers'd in Pleasure; and the Poor too much occupy'd in providing for the Necessities of Life, to hearken to the calm Voice of Reason. The Middle Station, as it is most happy in many Respects, so particularly in this, that a Man, plac'd in it, can, with the greatest Leisure, consider his own Happiness, and reap a new Enjoyment, from comparing his Situation with that of persons above or below him.

Agur's prayer is sufficiently noted. *Two Things have I requir'd of thee, deny me them not before I die, Remove far from me Vanity and Lies; Give me neither Poverty nor Riches, Feed me with Food convenient for me: Lest I be full and deny thee, and say, Who is the Lord? Or lest I be poor, and steal, and take the Name of my GOD in vain.* The middle Station is here justly recommended, as affording the fullest *Security* for Virtue; and I may also add, that it gives Opportunity for the most ample *Exercise* of it, and furnishes Employment for every good Quality which we can possibly be possest of. Those, who are plac'd among the lower Ranks of Men, have little Opportunity of exerting any other Virtue, besides those of Patience, Resignation, Industry and Integrity. Those, who are advanc'd into the higher Stations, have full employment for their Generosity, Humanity, Affability and Charity. When a Man lyes betwixt these two Extremes, he can exert the former Virtues towards his *Superiors*, and the latter towards his *Inferiors*. Every moral Quality, which the human Soul is susceptible of, may have its Turn, and be called up to Action: And a Man may, after this Manner, be much more certain of his Progress in Virtue, than where his good Qualities lye dormant, and without Employment.

But there is another Virtue, that seems principally to lye among *Equals*, and is, for that Reason, chiefly calculated for the middle Station of Life. This Virtue is FRIENDSHIP. I believe most Men of generous Tempers are apt to envy the Great, when they consider the large Opportunities such Persons have of doing Good to their Fellow-creatures, and of acquiring the Friendship and Esteem of Men of Merit. They make no Advances in vain, and are not oblig'd to associate with those whom they have little Kindness for; like People of inferior Stations, who are subject to have their Proffers of Friendship rejected, even where they wou'd be most fond of placing their Affections. But tho' the Great have more Facility in acquiring Friendships, they cannot be so certain of the Sincerity of them, as Men of a lower Rank; since the Favours, they bestow, may acquire them Flattery, instead of Good-will and Kindness. It has been very judiciously remark'd, that we attach ourselves more by the Services we perform than by those we receive, and that a Man is in Danger of losing his Friends by obliging them too far. I shou'd, therefore, chuse to lye in the middle Way, and to have my Commerce with my Friend varied both by Obligations given and receiv'd. I have too much Pride to be willing that all the Obligations should ly on my Side; and shou'd be afraid, that, if they all lay on his, he wou'd also have too much Pride to be entirely easy under them, or have a perfect Complacency in my Company.

We may also remark of the middle Station of Life, that it is more favourable to the acquiring of *Wisdom* and *Ability*, as well as of *Virtue*, and that a man so situate has a better Chance for attaining a Knowledge both of Men and Things, than those of a more elevated Station. He enters, with more Familiarity, into human Life: Every Thing appears in its natural Colours before him: He has more Leisure to form Observations; and has, beside, the Motive of Ambition to push him on in his Attainments: being certain, that he can never rise to any Distinction or Eminence in the World, without his own industry. And here I cannot forbear communicating a Remark, which may appear somewhat extraordinary, *viz.*

That 'tis wisely ordain'd by Providence, that the middle Station shou'd be the most favourable to the improving our natural Abilities, since there is really more Capacity requisite to perform the Duties of that Station, than is requisite to act in the higher Spheres of Life. There are more natural Parts, and a stronger Genius requisite to make a good Lawyer or Physician, than to make a great Monarch. For let us take any Race or Succession of Kings, where Birth alone gives a Title to the Crown : The *English* Kings, for Instance; who have not been esteemed the most shining in History. From the Conquest to the Succession of his present Majesty, we may reckon twenty eight Sovereigns, omitting those who died Minors. Of these, eight are esteem'd Princes of great Capacity, viz. the *Conqueror, Harry* II. *Edward* I. *Edward* III. *Harry* V. and VII. *Elisabeth,* and the late King *William.* Now, I believe every one will allow, that, in the common Run of Mankind, there are not eight out of twenty-eight, who are fitted, by Nature, to make a Figure either on the Bench or at the Bar. Since *Charles* VII. ten Monarchs have reign'd in *France,* omitting *Francis* II. Five of those have been esteem'd Princes of Capacity, viz. *Loüis* XI. XII. and XIV. *Francis* I. and *Harry* IV. In short, the governing of Mankind well, requires a great deal of Virtue, Justice, and Humanity, but not a surprising Capacity. A certain Pope, whose Name I have forgot, us'd to say, *Let us divert ourselves, my Friends, the World governs itself.* There are, indeed, some critical Times, such as those in which *Harry* IV. liv'd, that call for the utmost Vigour; and a less Courage and Capacity, than what appear'd in that great Monarch, must have sunk under the Weight. But such Circumstances are rare; and even then, Fortune does, at least, one Half of the Business.

Since the common Professions, such as Law or Physic, require equal, if not superior Capacity, to what are exerted in the higher Spheres of Life, 'tis evident, that the Soul must be made of still a finer Mold, to shine in Philosophy or Poetry, or in any of the higher Parts of Learning. Courage and Resolution are chiefly requisite in a Commander: Justice and Humanity in a Statesman: But Genius and Capacity in a Scholar. Great Generals and great Politicians, are found in all Ages and Countries of the World, and frequently start up, at once, even amongst the greatest Barbarians. *Sweden* was sunk in Ignorance, when it produc'd *Gustavus*

Ericson, and *Gustavus Adolphus*: *Muscovy*, when the *Czar* appear'd: and, perhaps, *Carthage*, when it gave Birth to *Hannibal*. But *England* must pass thro' a long Gradation of its *Spencers*, *Johnsons*, *Wallers*, *Drydens*, before it arrive at an *Addison* or a *Pope*. A happy Talent for the liberal Arts and Sciences, is a Kind of Prodigy among Men. Nature must afford the richest Genius that comes from her hands; Education and Example must cultivate it from the earliest Infancy; And Industry must concur to carry it to any Degree of Perfection. No Man needs be surprised to see *Kouli-Kan* among the *Persians*: but *Homer*, in so early an Age, among the *Greeks*, is certainly Matter of the highest Wonder.

A man cannot show a Genius for War, who is not so fortunate as to be trusted with Command; and it seldom happens, in any State or Kingdom, that several, at once, are plac'd in that Situation. How many *Marlboroughs* were there in the confederate Army, who never rose so much as to the Command of a Regiment? But I am perswaded there has been but one *Milton* in *England* within these hundred Years; because every one may exert the Talents for Poetry who is possest of them; and no one cou'd exert them under greater Disadvantages than that divine Poet. If no Man were allow'd to write Verses, but who was, before-hand, named to be *laureat*, cou'd we expect a Poet in ten thousand Years?

Were we to distinguish the Ranks of Men by their Genius and Capacity more than by their Virtue and Usefulness to the Public, great Philosophers wou'd certainly challenge the first Rank, and must be plac'd at the Top of human Kind. So rare is this Character, that, perhaps, there has not, as yet, been above two in the World, who can lay a just Claim to it. At least, *Galileo* and *Newton* seem to me so far to excel all the rest, that I cannot admit any other into the same Class with them.

Great Poets may challenge the second Place: and this Species of Genius, tho' rare, is yet much more frequent than the former. Of the *Greek* Poets that remain, *Homer* alone seems to merit this Character: Of the *Romans*, *Virgil*, *Horace* and *Lucretius*: Of the *English*, *Milton* and *Pope*: *Corneille*, *Racine*, *Boileau* and *Voltaire* of the *French*: And *Tasso* and *Ariosto* of the *Italians*.

Great Orators and Historians are, perhaps, more rare than

great Poets: But as the Opportunities for exerting the Talents requisite for Eloquence, or acquiring the Knowledge requisite for writing History, depend, in some Measure, upon Fortune, we cannot pronounce these Productions of Genius to be more extraordinary than the former.

I should now return from this Digression, and show, that the middle Station of Life is more favourable to *Happiness*, as well as to *Virtue* and *Wisdom* : But as the Arguments, that prove this, seem pretty obvious, I shall here forbear insisting on them.

Essay IV.[1]—*Of Impudence and Modesty.*

I AM of opinion, That the common complaints against Providence are ill-grounded, and that the good or bad qualities of men are the causes of their good or bad fortune, more than what is generally imagined. There are, no doubt, instances to the contrary, and these too pretty numerous; but few, in comparison of the instances we have of a right distribution of prosperity and adversity: nor indeed could it be otherwise from the common course of human affairs. To be endowed with a benevolent disposition, and to love others, will almost infallibly procure love and esteem; which is the chief circumstance in life, and facilitates every enterprize and undertaking; besides the satisfaction, which immediately results from it. The case is much the same with the other virtues. Prosperity is naturally, though not necessarily, attached to virtue and merit; and adversity, in like manner, to vice and folly.

I must, however, confess, that this rule admits of an exception, with regard to one moral quality; and that *modesty* has a natural tendency to conceal a man's talents, as *impudence* displays them to the utmost, and has been the only cause why many have risen in the world, under all the disadvantages of low birth and little merit. Such indolence and incapacity is there in the generality of mankind, that they are apt to receive a man for whatever he has a mind to put himself off for: and admit his overbearing airs as proofs of that merit which he assumes to himself. A decent assurance seems to be the natural attendant of virtue; and few

[1] [This Essay appeared in Editions A to N. 1741-60. See 'History of the Editions.' Vol. III. p. 41.—Ed.]

men can distinguish impudence from it: As, on the other hand, diffidence, being the natural result of vice and folly, has drawn disgrace upon modesty, which in outward appearance so nearly resembles it.[1]

As impudence, though really a vice, has the same effects upon a man's fortune, as if it were a virtue; so we may observe, that it is almost as difficult to be attained, and is, in that respect, distinguished from all the other vices, which are acquired with little pains, and continually encrease upon indulgence. Many a man, being sensible that modesty is extremely prejudicial to him in making his fortune, has resolved to be impudent, and to put a bold face upon the matter; But, it is observable, that such people have seldom succeeded in the attempt, but have been obliged to relapse into their primitive modesty. Nothing carries a man through the world like a true genuine natural impudence. Its counterfeit is good for nothing, nor can ever support itself. In any other attempt, whatever faults a man commits and is sensible of, he is so much the nearer his end. But when he endeavours at impudence, if he ever failed in the attempt, the remembrance of that failure will make him blush, and will infallibly disconcert him: After which every blush is a cause for new blushes, till he be found out to be an arrant cheat, and a vain pretender to impudence.

If any thing can give a modest man more assurance, it must be some advantages of fortune, which chance procures to him. Riches naturally gain a man a favourable reception in the world, and give merit a double lustre, when a person is endowed with it; and supply its place, in a great measure, when it is absent. It is wonderful to observe what airs of superiority fools and knaves, with large possessions, give themselves above men of the greatest merit in poverty. Nor do the men of merit make any strong opposition to these usurpations; or rather seem to favour them by the modesty of their behaviour. Their good sense and experience make them diffident of their judgment, and cause them to examine every thing with the greatest accuracy: As, on the other

---

[1] [Editions A and B, 1741 2, insert the following paragraph: I was lately lamenting to a Friend of mine, who loves a Conceit, That popular Applause should be bestowed with so little Judgment, and that so many empty forward Coxcombs should rise up to a Figure in the World: Upon which he said there was nothing surprising in the Case. *Popular Fame*, says he, *is nothing but Breath or Air; and Air very naturally presses into a Vacuum.*]

hand, the delicacy of their sentiments makes them timorous lest they commit faults, and lose in the practice of the world that integrity of virtue, so to speak, of which they are so jealous. To make wisdom agree with confidence, is as difficult as to reconcile vice and modesty.

These are the reflections which have occurred upon this subject of impudence and modesty: and I hope the reader will not be displeased to see them wrought into the following allegory.

JUPITER, in the beginning, joined VIRTUE, WISDOM, and CONFIDENCE together; and VICE, FOLLY, and DIFFIDENCE: And thus connected, sent them into the world. But though he thought he had matched them with great judgment, and said that *Confidence* was the natural companion of *Virtue*, and that *Vice* deserved to be attended with *Diffidence*, they had not gone far before dissension arose among them. *Wisdom*, who was the guide of the one company, was always accustomed before she ventured upon any road, however beaten, to examine it carefully; to enquire whither it led; what dangers, difficulties and hindrances might possibly or probably occur in it. In these deliberations she usually consumed some time; which delay was very displeasing to *Confidence*, who was always inclined to hurry on, without much forethought or deliberation, in the first road he met. *Wisdom* and *Virtue* were inseparable: But *Confidence* one day, following his impetuous nature, advanced a considerable way before his guides and companions; and not feeling any want of their company, he never enquired after them, nor ever met with them more. In like manner, the other society, though joined by JUPITER, disagreed and separated. As *Folly* saw very little way before her, she had nothing to determine concerning the goodness of roads, nor could give the preference to one above another; and this want of resolution was encreased by *Diffidence*, who, with her doubts and scruples, always retarded the journey. This was a great annoyance to *Vice*, who loved not to hear of difficulties and delays, and was never satisfied without his full career, in whatever his inclinations led him to. *Folly*, he knew, though she harkened to *Diffidence*, would be easily managed when alone; and therefore, as a vicious horse throws his rider, he openly beat away his controller of all his pleasures, and proceeded in his journey with *Folly*, from whom he is inseparable.

Confidence and *Diffidence* being, after this manner, both thrown loose from their respective companies, wandered for some time; till at last chance led them at the same time to one village. *Confidence* went directly up to the great house, which belonged to WEALTH, the lord of the village; and without staying for a porter, intruded himself immediately into the innermost apartments, where he found *Vice* and *Folly* well received before him. He joined the train; recommended himself very quickly to his landlord; and entered into such familiarity with *Vice*, that he was enlisted in the same company with *Folly*. They were frequent guests of *Wealth*, and from that moment inseparable. *Diffidence*, in the mean time, not daring to approach the great house, accepted of an invitation from POVERTY, one of the tenants; and entering the cottage, found *Wisdom* and *Virtue*, who being repulsed by the landlord, had retired thither. *Virtue* took compassion of her, and *Wisdom* found, from her temper, that she would easily improve: So they admitted her into their society. Accordingly, by their means, she altered in a little time somewhat of her manner, and becoming much more amiable and engaging, was now known by the name of *Modesty*. As ill company has a greater effect than good, *Confidence*, though more refractory to counsel and example, degenerated so far by the society of *Vice* and *Folly*, as to pass by the name of IMPUDENCE. Mankind, who saw these societies as JUPITER first joined them, and know nothing of these mutual desertions, are thereby led into strange mistakes; and wherever they see *Impudence*, make account of finding *Virtue* and *Wisdom*; and wherever they observe *Modesty*, call her attendants *Vice* and *Folly*.

ESSAY V.[1]—*Of Love and Marriage.*

I KNOW not whence it proceeds, that women are so apt to take amiss every thing which is said in disparagement of the married state; and always consider a satyr upon matrimony as a satyr upon themselves. Do they mean, that they are the parties principally concerned, and that if a backwardness to enter into that state should prevail in the world, they would be the greatest sufferers? Or, are they sensible, that

[1] [This Essay appeared in Editions A to N. 1741 60. See 'History of the Editions,' Vol. iii., p. 44. ED.]

misfortunes and miscarriages of the married state are owing more to their sex than to ours? I hope they do not intend to confess either of these two particulars, or to give such an advantage to their adversaries, the men, as even to allow them to suspect it.

I have often had thoughts of complying with this humour of the fair sex, and of writing a panegyric upon marriage: But, in looking around for materials, they seemed to be of so mixed a nature, that at the conclusion of my reflections, I found that I was as much disposed to write a satyr, which might be placed on the opposite pages of the panegyric: And I am afraid, that as satyr is, on most occasions, thought to contain more truth than panegyric, I should have done their cause more harm than good by this expedient. To misrepresent facts is what, I know, they will not require of me. I must be more a friend to truth, than even to them, where their interests are opposite.

I shall tell the women what it is our sex complains of most in the married state; and if they be disposed to satisfy us in this particular, all the other differences will easily be accommodated. If I be not mistaken, 'tis their love of dominion, which is the ground of the quarrel; tho' 'tis very likely, that they will think it an unreasonable love of it in us, which makes us insist so much upon that point. However this may be, no passion seems to have more influence on female minds, than this for power; and there is a remarkable instance in history of its prevailing above another passion, which is the only one that can be supposed a proper counterpoise for it. We are told, that all the women in SCYTHIA once conspired against the men, and kept the secret so well, that they executed their design before they were suspected. They surprised the men in drink, or asleep; bound them all fast in chains; and having called a solemn council of the whole sex, it was debated what expedient should be used to improve the present advantage, and prevent their falling again into slavery. To kill all the men did not seem to be the relish of any part of the assembly, notwithstanding the injuries formerly received: and they were afterwards pleased to make a great merit of this lenity of theirs. It was, therefore, agreed to put out the eyes of the whole male sex, and thereby resign in all future time the vanity which they could draw from their beauty, in order to secure their authority. We must no longer pretend to dress and show, said they; but then we shall be free from slavery. We shall hear no more tender sighs; but in return we shall hear no more imperious commands. Love must for ever leave us; but he will carry subjection along with him.

'Tis regarded by some as an unlucky circumstance, since the women were resolved to maim the men, and deprive them of some of their senses, in order to render them humble and dependent, that the sense of hearing could not serve their purpose, since 'tis probable the females would rather have attacked that than the sight: And I think it is agreed among the learned, that, in a married state, 'tis not near so great an inconvenience to lose the former sense as the latter. However this may be, we are told by modern anecdotes, that some of the SCYTHIAN women did secretly spare their husbands' eyes; presuming, I suppose, that they could govern them as well by means of that sense as without it. But so incorrigible and untractable were these men, that their wives were all obliged, in a few years, as their youth and beauty decayed, to imitate the example of their sisters; which it was no difficult matter to do in a state where the female sex had once got the superiority.

I know not if our SCOTTISH ladies derive any thing of this humour from their SCYTHIAN ancestors; but, I must confess that I have often been surprized to see a woman very well pleased to take a fool for her mate, that she might govern with the less controul; and could not but think her sentiments, in this respect, still more barbarous than those of the SCYTHIAN women above-mentioned; as much as the eyes of the understanding are more valuable than those of the body.

But to be just, and to lay the blame more equally, I am afraid it is the fault of our sex, if the women be so fond of rule, and that if we did not abuse our authority, they would never think it worth while to dispute it. Tyrants, we know, produce rebels; and all history informs us, that rebels, when they prevail, are apt to become tyrants in their turn. For this reason, I could wish there were no pretensions to authority on either side; but that every thing was carried on with perfect equality, as between two equal members of the same body. And to induce both parties to embrace those amicable sentiments, I shall deliver to them PLATO's account of the origin of love and marriage.

Mankind, according to that fanciful philosopher, were not,

ESSAY
V.

in their original, divided into male and female, as at present ; but each individual person was a compound of both sexes, and was in himself both husband and wife, melted down into one living creature. This union, no doubt, was very intire, and the parts very well adjusted together, since there resulted a perfect harmony betwixt the male and female, altho' they were obliged to be inseparable companions. And so great were the harmony and happiness flowing from it, that the ANDROGYNES (for so PLATO calls them) or MEN-WOMEN, became insolent upon their prosperity, and rebelled against the Gods. To punish them for this temerity, JUPITER could contrive no better expedient, than to divorce the male-part from the female, and make two imperfect beings of the compound, which was before so perfect. Hence the origin of men and women, as distinct creatures. But notwithstanding this division, so lively is our remembrance of the happiness which we enjoyed in our primæval state, that we are never at rest in this situation ; but each of these halves is continually searching thro' the whole species to find the other half, which was broken from it: And when they meet, they join again with the greatest fondness and sympathy. But it often happens, that they are mistaken in this particular ; that they take for their half what no way corresponds to them ; and that the parts do not meet nor join in with each other, as is usual in fractures. In this case the union was soon dissolved, and each part is set loose again to hunt for its lost half, joining itself to every one whom it meets, by way of trial, and enjoying no rest till its perfect sympathy with its partner shews that it has at last been successful in its endeavours.

Were I disposed to carry on this fiction of PLATO, which accounts for the mutual love betwixt the sexes in so agreeable a manner, I would do it by the following allegory.

When JUPITER had separated the male from the female, and had quelled their pride and ambition by so severe an operation, he could not but repent him of the cruelty of his vengeance, and take compassion on poor mortals, who were now become incapable of any repose or tranquillity. Such cravings, such anxieties, such necessities arose, as made them curse their creation, and think existence itself a punishment. In vain had they recourse to every other occupation and amusement. In vain did they seek after every pleasure of sense, and every refinement of reason. Nothing could fill that void, which they felt in their hearts, or supply the loss of their partner, who was so fatally separated from them. To remedy this disorder, and to bestow some comfort, at least, on the human race in their forlorn situation, JUPITER sent down LOVE and HYMEN, to collect the broken halves of human kind, and piece them together in the best manner possible. These two deities found such a prompt disposition in mankind to unite again in their primæval state, that they proceeded on their work with wonderful success for some time; till at last, from many unlucky accidents, dissension arose betwixt them. The chief counsellor and favourite of HYMEN was CARE, who was continually filling his patron's head with prospects of futurity; a settlement, family, children, servants; so that little else was regarded in all the matches *they* made. On the other hand, *Love* had chosen PLEASURE for his favourite, who was as pernicious a counsellor as the other, and would never allow *Love* to look beyond the present momentary gratification, or the satisfying of the prevailing inclination. These two favourites became, in a little time, irreconcileable enemies, and made it their chief business to undermine each other in all their undertakings. No sooner had *Love* fixed upon two halves, which he was cementing together, and forming to a close union, but *Care* insinuates himself, and bringing HYMEN along with him, dissolves the union produced by love, and joins each half to some other half, which he had provided for it. To be revenged of this, *Pleasure* creeps in upon a pair already joined by HYMEN; and calling *Love* to his assistance, they under hand contrive to join each half by secret links, to halves, which HYMEN was wholly unacquainted with. It was not long before this quarrel was felt in its pernicious consequences; and such complaints arose before the throne of JUPITER, that he was obliged to summon the offending parties to appear before him, in order to give an account of their proceedings. After hearing the pleadings on both sides, he ordered an immediate reconcilement betwixt LOVE and HYMEN, as the only expedient for giving happiness to mankind: And that he might be sure this reconcilement should be durable, he laid his strict injunctions on them never to join any halves without consulting their favourites *Care* and *Pleasure*, and obtaining the consent of both to the conjunction. Where this order is strictly observed, the *Androgyne* is perfectly restored, and the human race enjoy the same happiness as in their primæval state.   The seam is scarce perceived that joins the two beings; but both of them combine to form one perfect and happy creature.

Essay VI.[1]—*Of the Study of History.*

THERE is nothing which I would recommend more earnestly to my female readers than the study of history, as an occupation, of all others, the best suited both to their sex and education, much more instructive than their ordinary books of amusement, and more entertaining than those serious compositions, which are usually to be found in their closets. Among other important truths, which they may learn from history, they may be informed of two particulars, the knowledge of which may contribute very much to their quiet and repose; *That* our sex, as well as theirs, are far from being such perfect creatures as they are apt to imagine, and, *That* Love is not the only passion, which governs the male-world, but is often overcome by avarice, ambition, vanity, and a thousand other passions.   Whether they be the false representations of mankind in those two particulars, which endear romances and novels so much to the fair sex, I know not; but must confess that I am sorry to see them have such an aversion to matter of fact, and such an appetite for falshood. I remember I was once desired by a young beauty, for whom I had some passion, to send her some novels and romances for her amusement in the country; but was not so ungenerous as to take the advantage, which such a course of reading might have given me, being resolved not to make use of poisoned arms against her.   I therefore sent her PLUTARCH'S Lives, assuring her, at the same time, that there was not a word of truth in them from beginning to end.   She perused them very attentively, 'till she came to the lives of ALEXANDER and CÆSAR, whose names she had heard of by accident; and then returned me the book, with many reproaches for deceiving her.

I may indeed be told that the fair sex have no such aversion to history, as I have represented, provided it be *secret* history, and contain some memorable transaction proper to excite their curiosity.   But as I do not find that truth, which

---

[1] [This Essay appeared in Editions A to N, 1741-60.   See 'History of the Editions,' Vol. III. p. 41.   ED.]

is the basis of history, is at all regarded in those anecdotes, I cannot admit of this as a proof of their passion for that study. However this may be, I see not why the same curiosity might not receive a more proper direction, and lead them to desire accounts of those who lived in past ages, as well as of their cotemporaries. What is it to CLEORA, whether FULVIA entertains a secret commerce of *Love* with PHILANDER or not? Has she not equal reason to be pleased, when she is informed (what is whispered about among historians) that CATO's sister had an intrigue with CÆSAR, and palmed her son, MARCUS BRUTUS, upon her husband for his own, tho' in reality he was her gallant's? And are not the loves of MESSALINA or JULIA as proper subjects of discourse as any intrigue that this city has produced of late years?

But I know not whence it comes, that I have been thus seduced into a kind of raillery against the ladies: Unless, perhaps, it proceed from the same cause, which makes the person, who is the favourite of the company, be often the object of their good-natured jests and pleasantries. We are pleased to address ourselves after any manner, to one who is agreeable to us; and, at the same time, presume that nothing will be taken amiss by a person, who is secure of the good opinion and affections of every one present. I shall now proceed to handle my subject more seriously, and shall point out the many advantages which flow from the study of history, and show how well suited it is to every one, but particularly to those who are debarred the severer studies, by the tenderness of their complexion, and the weakness of their education. The advantages found in history seem to be of three kinds, as it amuses the fancy, as it improves the understanding, and as it strengthens virtue.

In reality, what more agreeable entertainment to the mind, than to be transported into the remotest ages of the world, and to observe human society, in its infancy, making the first faint essays towards the arts and sciences: To see the policy of government, and the civility of conversation refining by degrees, and every thing which is ornamental to human life advancing towards its perfection. To remark the rise, progress, declension, and final extinction of the most flourishing empires: The virtues, which contributed to their greatness, and the vices, which drew on their ruin. In short, to see all human race, from the beginning of time, pass, as it were, in review before us; appearing in their true colours, without any of those disguises, which, during their life-time, so much perplexed the judgment of the beholders. What spectacle can be imagined, so magnificent, so various, so interesting? What amusement, either of the senses or imagination, can be compared with it? Shall those trifling pastimes, which engross so much of our time, be preferred as more satisfactory, and more fit to engage our attention? How perverse must that taste be, which is capable of so wrong a choice of pleasures?

But history is a most improving part of knowledge, as well as an agreeable amusement; and a great part of what we commonly call *Erudition*, and value so highly, is nothing but an acquaintance with historical facts. An extensive knowledge of this kind belongs to men of letters; but I must think it an unpardonable ignorance in persons of whatever sex or condition, not to be acquainted with the history of their own country, together with the histories of ancient GREECE and ROME. A woman may behave herself with good manners, and have even some vivacity in her turn of wit; but where her mind is so unfurnished, 'tis impossible her conversation can afford any entertainment to men of sense and reflection.

I must add, that history is not only a valuable part of knowledge, but opens the door to many other parts, and affords materials to most of the sciences. And indeed, if we consider the shortness of human life, and our limited knowledge, even of what passes in our own time, we must be sensible that we should be for ever children in understanding, were it not for this invention, which extends our experience to all past ages, and to the most distant nations; making them contribute as much to our improvement in wisdom, as if they had actually lain under our observation. A man acquainted with history may, in some respect, be said to have lived from the beginning of the world, and to have been making continual additions to his stock of knowledge in every century.

There is also an advantage in that experience which is acquired by history, above what is learned by the practice of the world, that it brings us acquainted with human affairs, without diminishing in the least from the most delicate sentiments of virtue. And, to tell the truth, I know not any study or occupation so unexceptionable as history in this particular. Poets can paint virtue in the most charming colours; but, as they address themselves entirely to the passions, they often become advocates for vice. Even philosophers are apt to bewilder themselves in the subtility of their speculations; and we have seen some go as far as to deny the reality of all moral distinctions. But I think it a remark worthy the attention of the speculative, that the historians have been, almost without exception, the true friends of virtue, and have always represented it in its proper colours, however they may have erred in their judgments of particular persons. MACHIAVEL himself discovers a true sentiment of virtue in his history of FLORENCE. When he talks as a *Politician*, in his general reasonings, he considers poisoning, assassination and perjury, as lawful arts of power; but when he speaks as an *Historian*, in his particular narrations, he shows so keen an indignation against vice, and so warm an approbation of virtue, in many passages, that I could not forbear applying to him that remark of HORACE, That if you chace away nature, tho' with ever so great indignity, she will always return upon you. Nor is this combination of historians in favour of virtue at all difficult to be accounted for. When a man of business enters into life and action, he is more apt to consider the characters of men, as they have relation to his interest, than as they stand in themselves; and has his judgment warped on every occasion by the violence of his passion. When a philosopher contemplates characters and manners in his closet, the general abstract view of the objects leaves the mind so cold and unmoved, that the sentiments of nature have no room to play, and he scarce feels the difference between vice and virtue. History keeps in a just medium betwixt these extremes, and places the objects in their true point of view. The writers of history, as well as the readers, are sufficiently interested in the characters and events, to have a lively sentiment of blame or praise; and, at the same time, have no particular interest or concern to pervert their judgment.

Vera voces tum demum pectore ab imo
Eliciuntur. LUCRET.[1]

---

[1] [Lucret. iii. 57. The reference was added in the Edition K.]

Essay VII

Of Avarice.[1]

'Tis easy to observe, that comic writers exaggerate every character, and draw their fop, or coward with stronger features than are any where to be met with in nature. This moral kind of painting for the stage has been often compared to the painting for cupolas and ceilings, where the colours are over-charged, and every part is drawn excessively large, and beyond nature. The figures seem monstrous and disproportioned, when seen too nigh; but become natural and regular, when seen at a distance, and placed in that point of view, in which they are intended to be surveyed. For a like reason, when characters are exhibited in theatrical representations, the want of reality removes, in a manner, the personages; and rendering them more cold and unentertaining, makes it necessary to compensate, by the force of colouring, what they want in substance. Thus we find in common life, that when a man once allows himself to depart from truth in his narrations, he never can keep within the bounds of probability; but adds still some new circumstance to render his stories more marvellous, and to satisfy his imagination. Two men in buckram suits became eleven to Sir John Falstaff before the end of the story.

There is only one vice, which may be found in life with as strong features, and as high a colouring as needs be employed by any satyrist or comic poet; and that is Avarice. Every day we meet with men of immense fortunes, without heirs, and on the very brink of the grave, who refuse themselves the most common necessaries of life, and go on heaping possessions on possessions, under all the real pressures of the severest poverty. An old usurer, says the story, lying in his last agonies, was presented by the priest with the crucifix to worship. He opens his eyes a moment before he expires, considers the crucifix, and cries, *These jewels are not true; I can only lend ten pistoles upon such a pledge.* This was probably the invention of some epigrammatist; and yet every one, from his own experience, may be able to recollect

¹ [This Essay appeared in Editions A to P, 1741-68. See History of the Editions, Vol. III, p. 41. Ed.]

almost as strong instances of perseverance in avarice. 'Tis commonly reported of a famous miser in this city, that finding himself near death, he sent for some of the magistrates, and gave them a bill of an hundred pounds, payable after his decease; which sum he intended should be disposed of in charitable uses; but scarce were they gone, when he orders them to be called back, and offers them ready money, if they would abate five pounds of the sum. Another noted miser in the north, intending to defraud his heirs, and leave his fortune to the building of an hospital, protracted the drawing of his will from day to day; and 'tis thought, that if those interested in it had not paid for the drawing it, he had died intestate. In short, none of the most furious excesses of love and ambition are in any respect to be compared to the extremes of avarice.

The best excuse that can be made for avarice is, that it generally prevails in old men, or in men of cold tempers, where all the other affections are extinct; and the mind being incapable of remaining without some passion or pursuit, at last finds out this monstrously absurd one, which suits the coldness and inactivity of its temper. At the same time, it seems very extraordinary, that so frosty, spiritless a passion should be able to carry us farther than all the warmth of youth and pleasure: but if we look more narrowly into the matter, we shall find, that this very circumstance renders the explication of the case more easy. When the temper is warm and full of vigour, it naturally shoots out more ways than one, and produces inferior passions to counter-balance, in some degree, its predominant inclination. 'Tis impossible for a person of that temper, however bent on any pursuit, to be deprived of all sense of shame, or all regard to the sentiments of mankind. His friends must have some influence over him: And other considerations are apt to have their weight. All this serves to restrain him within some bounds. But 'tis no wonder that the avaritious man, being, from the coldness of his temper, without regard to reputation, to friendship, or to pleasure, should be carried so far by his prevailing inclination, and should display his passion in such surprising instances.

Accordingly we find no vice so irreclaimable as avarice: And though there scarcely has been a moralist or philosopher, from the beginning of the world to this day, who has not levelled a stroke at it, we hardly find a single instance of any person's being cured of it. For this reason, I am more apt to approve of those, who attack it with wit and humour, than of those who treat it in a serious manner. There being so little hopes of doing good to the people infected with this vice, I would have the rest of mankind, at least, diverted by our manner of exposing it: As indeed there is no kind of diversion, of which they seem so willing to partake.

Among the fables of *Monsieur de la* MOTTE, there is one levelled against avarice, which seems to me more natural and easy, than most of the fables of that ingenious author. A miser, says he, being dead, and fairly interred, came to the banks of the STYX, desiring to be ferried over along with the other ghosts. CHARON demands his fare, and is surprized to see the miser, rather than pay it, throw himself into the river, and swim over to the other side, notwithstanding all the clamour and opposition that could be made to him. All hell was in an uproar; and each of the judges was meditating some punishment, suitable to a crime of such dangerous consequence to the infernal revenues. Shall he be chained to the rock with PROMETHEUS? Or tremble below the precipice in company with the DANAIDES? Or assist SISYPHUS in rolling his stone? No, says MINOS, none of these. We must invent some severer punishment. Let him be sent back to the earth, to see the use his heirs are making of his riches.

I hope it will not be interpreted as a design of setting myself in opposition to this celebrated author, if I proceed to deliver a fable of my own, which is intended to expose the same vice of avarice. The hint of it was taken from these lines of Mr. POPE.

> *Damn'd to the mines, an equal fate betides*
> *The slave that digs it, and the slave that hides.*

Our old mother Earth once lodged an indictment against AVARICE before the courts of heaven, for her wicked and malicious council and advice, in tempting, inducing, persuading, and traiterously seducing the children of the plaintiff to commit the detestable crime of parricide upon her, and, mangling her body, ransack her very bowels for hidden treasure. The indictment was very long and verbose;

but we must omit a great part of the repetitions and synony-
mous terms, not to tire our readers too much with our tale.
AVARICE, being called before JUPITER to answer to this
charge, had not much to say in her own defence. The injustice was clearly proved upon her. The fact, indeed, was
notorious, and the injury had been frequently repeated.
When therefore the plaintiff demanded justice, JUPITER
very readily gave sentence in her favour; and his decree
was to this purpose, That since dame *Avarice*, the defendant,
had thus grievously injured dame *Earth*, the plaintiff, she
was hereby ordered to take that treasure, of which she had
feloniously robbed the said plaintiff, by ransacking her
bosom, and in the same manner, as before, opening her
bosom, restore it back to her, without diminution or reten-
tion. From this sentence, it shall follow, says JUPITER to
the by-standers, That, in all future ages, the retainers of
Avarice shall bury and conceal their riches, and thereby
restore to the earth what they took from her.

ESSAY VIII.—*A Character of Sir Robert Walpole.*[1]

THERE never was a man, whose actions and character have
been more earnestly and openly canvassed, than those of the
present minister, who, having governed a learned and free
nation for so long a time, amidst such mighty opposition,
may make a large library of what has been wrote for and
against him, and is the subject of above half the paper that
has been blotted in the nation within these twenty years.
I wish for the honour of our country, that any one character
of him had been drawn with such *judgment* and *impartiality*,
as to have credit with posterity, and to shew, that our liberty
has, once at least, been employed to good purpose. I am
only afraid, of failing in the former quality of judgment:
But if it should be so, 'tis but one page more thrown away,
after an hundred thousand, upon the same subject, that have
perished, and become useless. In the mean time, I shall
flatter myself with the pleasing imagination, that the following character will be adopted by future historians.

[1] [This Essay first appeared in Edition C, 1742; in Editions D to P, 1748-
68, it was printed in a foot-note at the
end of the Essay, 'That Politics may
be reduced to a Science'; in Edition Q,
1770, it was dropt. See 'History of
the Editions,' Vol. III. p. 45.—ED.]

Sir *ROBERT WALPOLE*, prime minister of GREAT BRITAIN, is a man of ability, not a genius; good-natured, not virtuous; constant, not magnanimous; moderate, not equitable; [1] His virtues, in some instances, are free from the allay of those vices, which usually accompany such virtues: He is a generous friend, without being a bitter enemy. His vices, in other instances, are not compensated by those virtues which are nearly allyed to them; His want of enterprise is not attended with frugality. The private character of the man is better than the public: His virtues more than his vices: His fortune greater than his fame. With many good qualities he has incurred the public hatred: With good capacity he has not escaped ridicule. He would have been esteemed more worthy of his high station had he never possessed it; and is better qualified for the second than for the first place in any government. His ministry has been more advantageous to his family than to the public, better for this age than for posterity, and more pernicious by bad precedents than by real grievances. During his time trade has flourished, liberty declined, and learning gone to ruin. As I am a man, I love him; as I am a scholar, I hate him; as I am a BRITON, I calmly wish his fall. And were I a member of either house, I would give my vote for removing him from ST. JAMES'S; but should be glad to see him retire to HOUGHTON-HALL, to pass the remainder of his days in case and pleasure.

[1] *Moderate in the exercise of power, not equitable in engrossing it.*

UNPUBLISHED

ESSAYS.

UNPUBLISHED ESSAYS.

ESSAY I.[1]—*Of the Immortality of the Soul.*

By the mere light of reason it seems difficult to prove the Immortality of the Soul. The arguments for it are commonly derived either from *metaphysical* topics, or *moral, or physical.* But in reality, it is the gospel, and the gospel alone, that has brought life and immortality to light.

I. Metaphysical topics suppose that the soul is immaterial, and that it is impossible for thought to belong to a material substance.

But just metaphysics teach us, that the notion of substance is wholly confused and imperfect, and that we have no other idea of any substance, than as an aggregate of particular qualities inhering in an unknown something. Matter, therefore, and spirit, are at bottom equally unknown; and we cannot determine what qualities inhere in the one or in the other.

They likewise teach us, that nothing can be decided *à priori* concerning any cause or effect; and that experience, being the only source of our judgments of this nature, we cannot know from any other principle, whether matter, by its structure or arrangement, may not be the cause of thought. Abstract reasonings cannot decide any question of fact or existence.

But admitting a spiritual substance to be dispersed throughout the universe, like the ethereal fire of the *Stoics*, and to be the only inherent subject of thought, we have reason to conclude from *analogy*, that nature uses it after the manner she does the other substance, matter. She em-

---

[1] [Printed from the Proof Sheets in the Advocates' Library, Edinburgh. See History of the Editions,' Vol. iii. p. 71   Ed.]

plays it as a kind of paste or clay; modifies it into a variety of forms and existences; dissolves after a time each modification, and from its substance erects a new form. As the same material substance may successively compose the bodies of all animals, the same spiritual substance may compose their minds: their consciousness, or that system of thought, which they formed during life, may be continually dissolved by death; and nothing interests them in the new modification. The most positive assertors of the mortality of the soul, never denied the immortality of its substance. And that an immaterial substance, as well as a material, may lose its memory or consciousness, appears, in part, from experience, if the soul be immaterial.

Reasoning from the common course of nature, and without supposing any new interposition of the Supreme Cause, which ought always to be excluded from philosophy; what is incorruptible must also be ingenerable. The soul, therefore, if immortal, existed before our birth: And if the former existence noways concerned us, neither will the latter.

Animals undoubtedly feel, think, love, hate, will, and even reason, though in a more imperfect manner than man. Are their souls also immaterial and immortal?

II. Let us now consider the *moral* arguments, chiefly those derived from the justice of God, which is supposed to be further interested in the further punishment of the vicious and reward of the virtuous.

But these arguments are grounded on the supposition, that God has attributes beyond what he has exerted in this universe, with which alone we are acquainted. Whence do we infer the existence of these attributes?

'Tis very safe for us to affirm, that, whatever we know the Deity to have actually done, is best; but it is very dangerous to affirm, that he must always do what to us seems best. In how many instances would this reasoning fail us with regard to the present world.

But if any purpose of nature be clear, we may affirm, that the whole scope and intention of man's creation, so far as we can judge by natural reason, is limited to the present life. With how weak a concern, from the original, inherent structure of the mind and passions, does he ever look further? What comparison either for steadiness or efficacy, betwixt so floating an idea, and the most doubtful persuasion of any matter of fact, that occurs in common life?

There arise, indeed, in some minds, some unaccountable terrors with regard to futurity: But these would quickly vanish, were they not artificially fostered by precept and education. And those, who foster them: what is their motive? Only to gain a livelihood, and to acquire power and riches in this world. Their very zeal and industry, therefore, are an argument against them.

What cruelty, what iniquity, what injustice in nature, to confine thus all our concern, as well as all our knowledge, to the present life, if there be another scene still waiting us, of infinitely greater consequence? Ought this barbarous deceit to be ascribed to a beneficent and wise Being?

Observe with what exact proportion the task to be performed, and the performing powers, are adjusted throughout all nature. If the reason of man gives him a great superiority above other animals, his necessities are proportionably multiplied upon him. His whole time, his whole capacity, activity, courage, passion, find sufficient employment, in fencing against the miseries of his present condition. And frequently, nay almost always, are too slender for the business assigned them.

A pair of shoes, perhaps, was never yet wrought to the highest degree of perfection, which that commodity is capable of attaining. Yet it is necessary, at least very useful, that there should be some politicians and moralists, even some geometers, poets, and philosophers among mankind.

The powers of men are no more superior to their wants, considered merely in this life, than those of foxes and hares are, compared to *their* wants and to *their* period of existence. The inference from parity of reason is therefore obvious.

On the theory of the soul's mortality, the inferiority of women's capacity is easily accounted for: Their domestic life requires no higher faculties either of mind or body. This circumstance vanishes and becomes absolutely insignificant, on the religious theory: The one sex has an equal task to perform as the other: Their powers of reason and resolution ought also to have been equal, and both of them infinitely greater than at present.

As every effect implies a cause, and that another, till we reach the first cause of all, which is the *Deity*; every thing that happens, is ordained by him; and nothing can be the object of his punishment or vengeance.

By what rule are punishments and rewards distributed? What is the Divine standard of merit and demerit? Shall we Suppose, that human sentiments have place in the Deity? However bold that hypothesis, We have no conception of any other sentiments.[1]

According to human sentiments, sense, courage, good manners, industry, prudence, genius, &c. are essential parts of personal merits. Shall we therefore erect an elysium for poets and heroes, like that of the ancient mythology? Why confine all rewards to one species of virtue?

Punishment, without any proper end or purpose, is inconsistent with *our* ideas of goodness and justice; and no end can be served by it after the whole scene is closed.

Punishment, according to *our* conception, should bear some proportion to the offence. Why then eternal punishment for the temporary offences of so frail a creature as man? Can any one approve of *Alexander's* rage, who intended to exterminate a whole nation, because they had seized his favourite horse, Bucephalus?[2]

Heaven and hell suppose two distinct species of men, the good and the bad. But the greatest part of mankind float betwixt vice and virtue.

Were one to go round the world with an intention of giving a good supper to the righteous and a sound drubbing to the wicked, he would frequently be embarrassed in his choice, and would find, that the merits and demerits of most men and women scarcely amount to the value of either.

To suppose measures of approbation and blame, different from the human, confounds every thing. Whence do we learn, that there is such a thing as moral distinctions, but from our own sentiments?

What man, who has not met with personal provocation (or what good-natur'd man who has), could inflict on crimes, from the sense of blame alone, even the common, legal, frivolous punishments? And does any thing steel the breast of judges and juries against the sentiments of humanity but reflections on necessity and public interest?

By the Roman law, those who had been guilty of parri-

[1] [How bold that hypothesis! We ... have no conception of any other senti- ... ments. Editions of 1777 and 1783.]
[2] Quint. Curtis. lib. vi. cap. 5.

cide, and confessed their crime, were put into a sack, along with an ape, a dog, and a serpent; and thrown into the river: Death alone was the punishment of those, who denied their guilt, however fully proved. A criminal was tried before *Augustus*, and condemned after a full conviction : but the humane emperor, when he put the last interrogatory, gave it such a turn as to lead the wretch into a denial of his guilt. " *You surely*, said the prince, *did not kill your father?*"[1] This lenity suits our natural ideas of RIGHT, even towards the greatest of all criminals, and even though it prevents so inconsiderable a sufferance. Nay, even the most bigoted priest would naturally, without reflection, approve of it; provided the crime was not heresy or infidelity. For as these crimes hurt himself in his *temporal* interest and advantages : perhaps he may not be altogether so indulgent to them.

The chief source of moral ideas is the reflection on the interests of human society. Ought these interests, so short, so frivolous, to be guarded by punishments, eternal and infinite? The damnation of one man is an infinitely greater evil in the universe, than the subversion of a thousand millions of kingdoms.

Nature has rendered human infancy peculiarly frail and mortal; as it were on purpose to refute the notion of a probationary state. The half of mankind die before they are rational creatures.

III. The *physical* arguments from the analogy of nature are strong for the mortality of the soul : and these are really the only philosophical arguments, which ought to be admitted with regard to this question, or indeed any question of fact.

Where any two objects are so closely connected, that all alterations, which we have ever seen in the one, are attended with proportionable alterations in the other : we ought to conclude, by all rules of analogy, that, when there are still greater alterations produced in the former, and it is totally dissolved, there follows a total dissolution of the latter.

Sleep, a very small effect on the body, is attended with a temporary extinction : at least, a great confusion in the soul.

The weakness of the body and that of the mind in infancy

are exactly proportioned; their vigour in manhood, their sympathetic disorder in sickness, their common gradual decay in old age. The step further seems unavoidable; their common dissolution in death.

The last symptoms, which the mind discovers, are disorder, weakness, insensibility, and stupidity; the forerunners of its annihilation. The further progress of the same causes, encreasing the same effects, totally extinguish it.[1]

Judging by the usual analogy of nature, no form can continue, when transferred to a condition of life very different from the original one, in which it was placed. Trees perish in the water; fishes in the air; animals in the earth. Even so small a difference as that of climate is often fatal. What reason then to imagine, that an immense alteration, such as is made on the soul by the dissolution of its body, and all its organs of thought and sensation, can be effected without the dissolution of the whole?

Every thing is in common betwixt soul and body. The organs of the one are all of them the organs of the other. The existence therefore of the one must be dependent on the other.

The souls of animals are allowed to be mortal: and these bear so near a resemblance to the souls of men, that the analogy from one to the other forms a very strong argument. Their bodies are not more resembling: yet no one rejects the argument drawn from comparative anatomy. The *Metempsychosis* is therefore the only system of this kind, that philosophy can hearken to.

Nothing in this world is perpetual; Every thing, however seemingly firm, is in continual flux and change: The world itself gives symptoms of frailty and dissolution: How contrary to analogy, therefore, to imagine, that one single form, seeming the frailest of any, and subject to the greatest disorders, is immortal and indissoluble? What a daring theory is that![2] How lightly, not to say how rashly, entertained!

How to dispose of the infinite number of posthumous existences ought also to embarrass the religious theory. Every planet, in every solar system, we are at liberty to imagine peopled with intelligent, mortal beings: At least we can fix

---

[1] [The further progress of the same causes increasing the same effects totally extinguish it : Editions of 1777 and 1783.]

[2] [What theory is that! Editions of 1777 and 1783.]

on no other supposition. For these, then, a new universe must, every generation, be created beyond the bounds of the present universe : or one must have been created at first so prodigiously wide as to admit of this continual influx of beings. Ought such bold suppositions to be received by any philosophy : and that merely on the pretext of a bare possibility ?

When it is asked, whether *Agamemnon, Thersites, Hannibal, Nero,*[1] and every stupid clown, that ever existed in *Italy, Scythia, Bactria, or Guinea,* are now alive; can any man think, that a scrutiny of nature will furnish arguments strong enough to answer so strange a question in the affirmative ? The want of argument, without revelation, sufficiently establishes the negative. *Quanto facilius,* says Pliny,[2] *certiusque sibi quemque credere, ac specimen securitatis antegenitali sumere experimento.* Our insensibility, before the composition of the body, seems to natural reason a proof of a like state after dissolution.

Were our horrors of annihilation an original passion, not the effect of our general love of happiness, it would rather prove the mortality of the soul : For as nature does nothing in vain, she would never give us a horror against an impossible event. She may give us a horror against an unavoidable event, provided our endeavours, as in the present case, may often remove it to some distance. Death is in the end unavoidable ; yet the human species could not be preserved, had not nature inspired us with an aversion towards it. All doctrines are to be suspected which are favoured by our passions. And the hopes and fears which give rise to this[3] doctrine, are very obvious.

'Tis an infinite advantage in every controversy, to defend the negative. If the question be out of the common experienced course of nature, this circumstance is almost, if not altogether, decisive. By what arguments or analogies can we prove any state of existence, which no one ever saw, and which no way resembles any that ever was seen ? Who will repose such trust in any pretended philosophy, as to admit upon its testimony the reality of so marvellous a scene ?

---

[1] [*Verro*: Editions of 1777 and 1783.]
[2] Lib. 7 cap. 56.
[3] [The 'First proof' had *th* in the ... Text, and *this* as a correction in the Margin. The Editions of 1777 and 1783 read ...]

Some new species of logic is requisite for that purpose; and some new faculties of the mind, that they may enable us to comprehend that logic.

Nothing could set in a fuller light the infinite obligations which mankind have to Divine revelation; since we find, that no other medium could ascertain this great and important truth.

Essay II.[1]—*Of Suicide.*

ONE considerable advantage that arises from Philosophy, consists in the sovereign antidote which it affords to superstition and false religion. All other remedies against that pestilent distemper are vain, or at least uncertain. Plain good sense and the practice of the world, which alone serve most purposes of life, are here found ineffectual: History as well as daily experience furnish instances of men endowed with the strongest capacity for business and affairs, who have all their lives crouched under slavery to the grossest superstition. Even gaiety and sweetness of temper, which infuse a balm into every other wound, afford no remedy to so virulent a poison; as we may particularly observe of the fair Sex, who, tho' commonly possest of these rich presents of nature, feel many of their joys blasted by this importunate intruder. But when sound Philosophy has once gained possession of the mind, superstition is effectually excluded; and one may fairly affirm, that her triumph over this enemy is more complete than over most of the vices and imperfections incident to human nature. Love or anger, ambition or avarice, have their root in the temper and affections, which the soundest reason is scarce ever able fully to correct; but superstition being founded on false opinion, must immediately vanish when true philosophy has inspired juster sentiments of superior powers. The contest is here more equal between the distemper and the medicine, and nothing can hinder the latter from proving effectual, but its being false and sophisticated.

It will here be superfluous to magnify the merits of philosophy, by displaying the pernicious tendency of that vice of which it cures the human mind. The superstitious man, says

---

[1] [Printed from the Edition of 1777, with a few changes of punctuation. See 'History of the Editions,' vol. iii. p. 79. ED.]

TULLY,[1] is miserable in every scene, in every incident of life; even sleep itself, which banishes all other cares of unhappy mortals, affords to him matter of new terror; while he examines his dreams, and finds in those visions of the night prognostications of future calamities. I may add, that tho' death alone can put a full period to his misery, he dares not fly to this refuge, but still prolongs a miserable existence from a vain fear lest he offend his maker, by using the power, with which that beneficent being has endowed him. The presents of God and nature are ravished from us by this cruel enemy; and notwithstanding that one step would remove us from the regions of pain and sorrow, her menaces still chain us down to a hated being, which she herself chiefly contributes to render miserable.

'Tis observed by such as have been reduced by the calamities of life to the necessity of employing this fatal remedy, that if the unseasonable care of their friends deprive them of that species of Death, which they proposed to themselves, they seldom venture upon any other, or can summon up so much resolution a second time, as to execute their purpose. So great is our horror of death, that when it presents itself, under any form, besides that to which a man has endeavoured to reconcile his imagination, it acquires new terrors and overcomes his feeble courage: But when the menaces of superstition are joined to this natural timidity, no wonder it quite deprives men of all power over their lives, since even many pleasures and enjoyments, to which we are carried by a strong propensity, are torn from us by this inhuman tyrant. Let us here endeavour to restore men to their native liberty by examining all the common arguments against Suicide, and shewing that that action may be free from every imputation of guilt or blame, according to the sentiments of all the antient philosophers.

If Suicide be criminal, it must be a transgression of our duty either to God, our neighbour, or ourselves.—To prove that suicide is no transgression of our duty to God, the following considerations may perhaps suffice. In order to govern the material world, the almighty Creator has established general and immutable laws by which all bodies, from the greatest planet to the smallest particle of matter, are maintained in their proper sphere and function. To govern

---

[1] De Divin. lib. ii. 72. 150.

the animal world, he has endowed all living creatures with bodily and mental powers; with senses, passions, appetites, memory and judgment, by which they are impelled or regulated in that course of life to which they are destined. These two distinct principles of the material and animal world, continually encroach upon each other, and mutually retard or forward each others operations. The powers of men and of all other animals are restrained and directed by the nature and qualities of the surrounding bodies; and the modifications and actions of these bodies are incessantly altered by the operation of all animals. Man is stopt by rivers in his passage over the surface of the earth; and rivers, when properly directed, lend their force to the motion of machines, which serve to the use of man. But tho' the provinces of the material and animal powers are not kept entirely separate, there results from thence no discord or disorder in the creation; on the contrary, from the mixture, union and contrast of all the various powers of inanimate bodies and living creatures, arises that surprizing harmony and proportion which affords the surest argument of supreme wisdom. The providence of the Deity appears not immediately in any operation, but governs everything by those general and immutable laws, which have been established from the beginning of time. All events, in one sense, may be pronounced the action of the Almighty; they all proceed from those powers with which he has endowed his creatures. A house which falls by its own weight is not brought to ruin by his providence more than one destroyed by the hands of men; nor are the human faculties less his workmanship, than the laws of motion and gravitation. When the passions play, when the judgment dictates, when the limbs obey; this is all the operation of God, and upon these animate principles, as well as upon the inanimate, has he established the government of the universe. Every event is alike important in the eyes of that infinite being, who takes in at one glance the most distant regions of space and remotest periods of time. There is no event, however important to us, which he has exempted from the general laws that govern the universe, or which he has peculiarly reserved for his own immediate action and operation. The revolution of states and empires depends upon the smallest caprice or passion of single men; and the lives of men are shortened or extended by the smallest accident of air or diet, sunshine or tempest. Nature still continues her progress and operation; and if general laws be ever broke by particular volitions of the Deity, 'tis after a manner which entirely escapes human observation. As, on the one hand, the elements and other inanimate parts of the creation carry on their action without regard to the particular interest and situation of men; so men are entrusted to their own judgment and discretion, in the various shocks of matter, and may employ every faculty with which they are endowed, in order to provide for their ease, happiness, or preservation. What is the meaning then of that principle, that a man who, tired of life, and hunted by pain and misery, bravely overcomes all the natural terrors of death and makes his escape from this cruel scene; that such a man, I say, has incurred the indignation of his Creator by encroaching on the office of divine providence, and disturbing the order of the universe? shall we assert that the Almighty has reserved to himself in any peculiar manner the disposal of the lives of men, and has not submitted that event, in common with others, to the general laws by which the universe is governed? This is plainly false; the lives of men depend upon the same laws as the lives of all other animals; and these are subjected to the general laws of matter and motion. The fall of a tower, or the infusion of a poison, will destroy a man equally with the meanest creature; an inundation sweeps away every thing without distinction that comes within the reach of its fury. Since therefore the lives of men are for ever dependant on the general laws of matter and motion, is a man's disposing of his life criminal, because in every case it is criminal to encroach upon these laws, or disturb their operation? But this seems absurd; all animals are entrusted to their own prudence and skill for their conduct in the world, and have full authority, as far as their power extends, to alter all the operations of nature. Without the exercise of this authority they could not subsist a moment; every action, every motion of a man, innovates on the order of some parts of matter, and diverts from their ordinary course the general laws of motion. Putting together, therefore, these conclusions, we find that human life depends upon the general laws of matter and motion, and that it is no encroachment on the office of providence to disturb or alter these general laws: Has not every one, of consequence, the free disposal of his own life? And may he not lawfully employ that power with which nature has endowed him? In order to destroy the evidence of this conclusion, we must shew a reason, why this particular case is excepted; is it because human life is of so great importance, that 'tis a presumption for human prudence to dispose of it? But the life of a man is of no greater importance to the universe than that of an oyster. And were it of ever so great importance, the order of nature has actually submitted it to human prudence, and reduced us to a necessity in every incident of determining concerning it. Were the disposal of human life so much reserved as the peculiar province of the Almighty that it were an encroachment on his right, for men to dispose of their own lives; it would be equally criminal to act for the preservation of life as for its destruction. If I turn aside a stone which is falling upon my head, I disturb the course of nature, and I invade the peculiar province of the Almighty by lengthening out my life beyond the period which by the general laws of matter and motion he had assigned it.

A hair, a fly, an insect is able to destroy this mighty being whose life is of such importance. Is it an absurdity to suppose that human prudence may lawfully dispose of what depends on such insignificant causes? It would be no crime in me to divert the *Nile* or *Danube* from its course, were I able to effect such purposes. Where then is the crime of turning a few ounces of blood from their natural channel?— Do you imagine that I repine at providence or curse my creation, because I go out of life, and put a period to a being, which, were it to continue, would render me miserable? Far be such sentiments from me; I am only convinced of a matter of fact, which you yourself acknowledge possible, that human life may be unhappy, and that my existence, if further prolonged, would become ineligible: but I thank providence, both for the good which I have already enjoyed, and for the power with which I am endowed of escaping the ill that threatens me.[1] To you it belongs to repine at providence, who foolishly imagine that you have no such power, and who must still prolong a hated life, tho' loaded with pain and sickness, with shame and poverty.—Do you not teach, that when any ill befalls me, tho' by the malice of

[1] Agamus Deo gratias, quod nemo in vita teneri potest. SEN. Epist. 12.

my enemies, I ought to be resigned to providence, and that the actions of men are the operations of the Almighty as much as the actions of inanimate beings? When I fall upon my own sword, therefore, I receive my death equally from the hands of the Deity as if it had proceeded from a lion, a precipice, or a fever. The submission which you require to providence, in every calamity that befalls me, excludes not human skill and industry, if possibly by their means I can avoid or escape the calamity: And why may I not employ one remedy as well as another?—If my life be not my own, it were criminal for me to put it in danger, as well as to dispose of it; nor could one man deserve the appellation of *hero* whom glory or friendship transports into the greatest dangers, and another merit the reproach of *wretch* or *miscreant* who puts a period to his life from the same or like motives.—There is no being, which possesses any power or faculty, that it receives not from its Creator, nor is there any one, which by ever so irregular an action can encroach upon the plan of his providence, or disorder the universe. Its operations are his works equally with that chain of events, which it invades, and which ever principle prevails, we may for that very reason conclude it to be most favoured by him. Be it animate, or inanimate, rational, or irrational; 'tis all a case: Its power is still derived from the supreme creator, and is alike comprehended in the order of his providence. When the horror of pain prevails over the love of life; when a voluntary action anticipates the effects of blind causes; 'tis only in consequence of those powers and principles, which he has implanted in his creatures. Divine providence is still inviolate and placed far beyond the reach of human injuries.[1] 'Tis impious, says the old Roman superstition, to divert rivers from their course, or invade the prerogatives of nature. 'Tis impious, says the French superstition, to inoculate for the small-pox, or usurp the business of providence, by voluntarily producing distempers and maladies. 'Tis impious, says the modern *European* superstition, to put a period to our own life, and thereby rebel against our creator; and why not impious, say I, to build houses, cultivate the ground, or sail upon the ocean? In all these actions we employ our powers of mind and body, to produce some innovation in the course of nature; and in

[1] TACIT. Ann. lib. i. 79.

none of them do we any more. They are all of them therefore equally innocent, or equally criminal.—*But you are
placed by providence, like a centinel in a particular station,
and when you desert it without being recalled, you are equally
guilty of rebellion against your almighty sovereign, and have
incurred his displeasure.*—I ask, why do you conclude that
providence has placed me in this station? For my part I
find that I owe my birth to a long chain of causes, of which
many depended upon voluntary actions of men. *But Providence guided all these Causes, and nothing happens in the
universe without its consent and Co-operation.* If so, then
neither does my death, however voluntary, happen without
its consent ; and whenever pain or sorrow so far overcome
my patience, as to make me tired of life, I may conclude
that I am recalled from my station in the clearest and most
express terms. 'Tis Providence surely that has placed me
at this present moment in this chamber : But may I not
leave it when I think proper, without being liable to the imputation of having deserted my post or station? When I
shall be dead, the principles of which I am composed will
still perform their part in the universe, and will be equally
useful in the grand fabric, as when they composed this individual creature. The difference to the whole will be no
greater than betwixt my being in a chamber and in the open
air. The one change is of more importance to me than the
other ; but not more so to the universe.

'Tis a kind of blasphemy to imagine that any created
being can disturb the order of the world or invade the
business of providence ! It supposes, that that Being possesses powers and faculties, which it received not from its
creator, and which are not subordinate to his government
and authority. A man may disturb society no doubt, and
thereby incur the displeasure of the Almighty : But the
government of the world is placed far beyond his reach and
violence. And how does it appear that the Almighty is displeased with those actions that disturb society? By the
principles which he has implanted in human nature, and
which inspire us with a sentiment of remorse if we ourselves
have been guilty of such actions, and with that of blame and
disapprobation, if we ever observe them in others.—Let us
now examine, according to the method proposed, whether

Suicide be of this kind of actions, and be a breach of our duty to our *neighbour* and to *society*.

A man, who retires from life, does no harm to society: He only ceases to do good; which, if it is an injury, is of the lowest kind. All our obligations to do good to society seem to imply something reciprocal. I receive the benefits of society and therefore ought to promote its interests, but when I withdraw myself altogether from society, can I be bound any longer? But, allowing that our obligations to do good were perpetual, they have certainly some bounds; I am not obliged to do a small good to society at the expence of a great harm to myself; why then should I prolong a miserable existence, because of some frivolous advantage which the public may perhaps receive from me? If upon account of age and infirmities I may lawfully resign any office, and employ my time altogether in fencing against these calamities, and alleviating as much as possible the miseries of my future life: Why may I not cut short these miseries at once by an action which is no more prejudicial to society?—But suppose that it is no longer in my power to promote the interest of society; suppose that I am a burthen to it; suppose that my life hinders some person from being much more useful to society. In such cases my resignation of life must not only be innocent but laudable. And most people who lie under any temptation to abandon existence, are in some such situation; those, who have health, or power, or authority, have commonly better reason to be in humour with the world.

A man is engaged in a conspiracy for the public interest; is seized upon suspicion; is threatened with the rack; and knows from his own weakness that the secret will be extorted from him: Could such a one consult the public interest better than by putting a quick period to a miserable life? This was the case of the famous and brave *Strozi* of *Florence*. —Again, suppose a malefactor is justly condemned to a shameful death; can any reason be imagined, why he may not anticipate his punishment, and save himself all the anguish of thinking on its dreadful approaches? He invades the business of providence no more than the magistrate did, who ordered his execution: and his voluntary death is equally advantageous to society by ridding it of a pernicious member.

That suicide may often be consistent with interest and with our duty to ourselves, no one can question, who allows that age, sickness, or misfortune may render life a burthen, and make it worse even than annihilation. I believe that no man ever threw away life, while it was worth keeping. For such is our natural horror of death, that small motives will never be able to reconcile us to it; and though perhaps the situation of a man's health or fortune did not seem to require this remedy, we may at least be assured, that any one who, without apparent reason, has had recourse to it, was curst with such an incurable depravity or gloominess of temper as must poison all enjoyment, and render him equally miserable as if he had been loaded with the most grievous misfortunes. — If suicide be supposed a crime, 'tis only cowardice can impel us to it. If it be no crime, both prudence and courage should engage us to rid ourselves at once of existence, when it becomes a burthen. 'Tis the only way that we can then be useful to society, by setting an example, which, if imitated, would preserve to every one his chance for happiness in life and would effectually free him from all danger or misery.[1]

[1] It would be easy to prove that Suicide is as lawful under the Christian dispensation as it was to the Heathens. There is not a single text of Scripture which prohibits it. That great and infallible rule of faith and practice which must controul all philosophy and human reasoning, has left us in this particular to our natural liberty. Resignation to Providence is indeed recommended in Scripture; but that implies only submission to ills that are unavoidable, not to such as may be remedied by prudence or courage. *Thou shalt not kill*, is evidently meant to exclude only the killing of others over whose life we have no authority. That this precept, like most of the Scripture precepts, must be modified by reason and common sense, is plain from the practice of magistrates, who punish criminals capitally, notwithstanding the letter of the law. But were this commandment ever so express against suicide, it would now have no authority, for all the law of *Moses* is abolished, except so far as it is established by the law of Nature. And we have already endeavoured to prove, that suicide is not prohibited by that law. In all cases Christians and Heathens are precisely upon the same footing; *Cato* and *Brutus*, *Arria* and *Portia* acted heroically; those who now imitate their example ought to receive the same praises from posterity. The power of committing suicide is regarded by *Pliny* as an advantage which men possess even above the Deity himself. 'Deus non sibi potest *mortem* consciscere si velit, quod homini dedit optimum in tantis vitae *poenis.*'— Lib. ii. cap. 5.

Essay III.—*Of the Authenticity of Ossian's Poems.*[1]

I think the fate of this production the most curious effect of prejudice, where superstition had no share, that ever was in the world. A tiresome, insipid performance; which, if it had been presented in its real form, as the work of a contemporary, an obscure Highlander, no man could ever have had the patience to have once perused, has, by passing for the poetry of a royal bard, who flourished fifteen centuries ago, been universally read, has been pretty generally admired, and has been translated, in prose and verse, into several languages of Europe. Even the style of the supposed English translation has been admired, though harsh and absurd in the highest degree; jumping perpetually from verse to prose, and from prose to verse; and running, most of it, in the light cadence and measure of Molly Mog. Such is the Erse epic, which has been puffed with a zeal and enthusiasm that has drawn a ridicule on my countrymen.

But, to cut off at once the whole source of its reputation, I shall collect a few very obvious arguments against the notion of its great antiquity, with which so many people have been intoxicated, and which alone made it worthy of any attention.

(1.) The very manner in which it was presented to the public forms a strong presumption against its authenticity. The pretended translator goes on a mission to the Highlands to recover and collect a work, which, he affirmed, was dispersed, in fragments, among the natives. He returns, and gives a quarto volume, and then another quarto, with the same unsupported assurance as if it were a translation of the Orlando Furioso, or Louisade, or any poem the best known in Europe. It might have been expected, at least, that he would have told the public, and the subscribers to his mission, and the purchasers of his book, *This part I got from such a person, in such a place; that other part, from such another person. I was enabled to correct my first copy of such a passage by the recital of such another person; a fourth supplied such a defect in my first copy.* By such a history of his gradual discoveries he would have given some face of probability to them. Any man of common sense, who was in earnest, must, in this case,

[1] [Mr. Burton supposes that this Essay, found among Hume's papers, was withheld from publication out of a kindly feeling towards Dr. Blair. See Burton's *Life of Hume*, Vol. ii. p. 85, and seq. Ed.]

have seen the peculiar necessity of that precaution: any man that had regard to his own character, would have anxiously followed that obvious and easy method. All the friends of the pretended translator exhorted and entreated him to give them and the public that satisfaction. No! those who could doubt his veracity were fools, whom it was not worth while to satisfy. The most incredible of all facts was to be taken on his word, whom nobody knew; and an experiment was to be made, I suppose in jest, how far the credulity of the public would give way to assurance and dogmatical affirmation.

(2.) But, to show the utter incredibility of the fact, let these following considerations be weighed, or, rather, simply reflected on; for it seems ridiculous to weigh them. Consider the size of these poems. What is given us is asserted to be only a part of a much greater collection; yet even these pieces amount to two quartos. And they were composed, you say, in the Highlands, about fifteen centuries ago; and have been faithfully transmitted, ever since, by oral tradition, through ages totally ignorant of letters, by the rudest, perhaps, of all the European nations; the most necessitous, the most turbulent, the most ferocious, and the most unsettled. Did ever any event happen that approached within a hundred degrees of this mighty wonder, even to the nations the most fortunate in their climate and situation? Can a ballad be shown that has passed, uncorrupted, by oral tradition, through three generations, among the Greeks, or Italians, or Phœnicians, or Egyptians, or even among the natives of such countries as Otaheite or Molucca, who seem exempted by nature from all attention but to amusement, to poetry, and music?

But the Celtic nations, it is said, had peculiar advantages for preserving their traditional poetry. The Irish, the Welsh, the Bretons, are all Celtic nations, much better entitled than the Highlanders, from their soil, and climate, and situation, to have leisure for these amusements. They, accordingly, present us not with complete epic and historical poems, (for they never had the assurance to go that length,) but with very copious and circumstantial traditions, which are allowed, by all men of sense, to be scandalous and ridiculous impostures.

(3.) The style and genius of these pretended poems are another sufficient proof of the imposition. The Lapland and Runic odes, conveyed to us, besides their small compass, have a savage rudeness, and sometimes grandeur, suited to those ages. But this Erse poetry has an insipid correctness, and regularity, and uniformity, which betrays a man without genius, that has been acquainted with the productions of civilized nations, and had his imagination so limited to that tract, that it was impossible for him even to mimic the character which he pretended to assume.

The manners are still a more striking proof of their want of authenticity. We see nothing but the affected generosity and gallantry of chivalry, which are quite unknown, not only to all savage people, but to every nation not trained in these artificial modes of thinking. In Homer, for instance, and Virgil, and Ariosto, the heroes are represented as making a nocturnal incursion into the camp of the enemy. Homer and Virgil, who certainly were educated in much more civilized ages than those of Ossian, make no scruple of representing their heroes as committing undistinguished slaughter on the sleeping foe. But Orlando walks quietly through the camp of the Saracens, and scorns to kill even an infidel who cannot defend himself. Gaul and Oscar are knight-errants, still more romantic: they make a noise in the midst of the enemy's camp, that they may waken them, and thereby have a right to fight with them and to kill them. Nay, Fingal carries his ideas of chivalry still farther; much beyond what was ever dreamt of by Amadis de Gaul or Lancelot de Lake. When his territory is invaded, he scorns to repel the enemy with his whole force: he sends only an equal number against them, under an inferior captain: when these are repulsed, he sends a second detachment; and it is not till after a double defeat, that he deigns himself to descend from the hill, where he had remained, all the while, an idle spectator, and to attack the enemy. Fingal and Swaran combat each other all day, with the greatest fury. When darkness suspends the fight, they feast together with the greatest amity, and then renew the combat with the return of light. Are these the manners of barbarous nations, or even of people that have common sense? We may remark, that all this narrative is supposed to be given us by a contemporary poet. The facts, therefore, must be supposed entirely, or nearly, conformable to truth. The gallantry and extreme delicacy towards the women, which is found in these productions, is, if possible, still more contrary to the manners of barbarians. Among all rude nations, force and courage are the predominant virtues; and the inferiority of the females, in these particulars, renders them an object of contempt, not of deference and regard.

(4.) But I derive a new argument against the antiquity of these poems, from the general tenor of the narrative. Where manners are represented in them, probability, or even possibility, are totally disregarded: but in all other respects, the events are within the course of nature; no giants, no monsters, no magic, no incredible feats of strength or activity. Every transaction is conformable to familiar experience, and scarcely even deserves the name of wonderful. Did this ever happen in ancient and barbarous poetry? Why is this characteristic wanting, so essential to rude and ignorant ages? Ossian, you say, was singing the exploits of his contemporaries, and therefore could not falsify them in any great degree. But if this had been a restraint, your pretended Ossian had never sung the exploits of his contemporaries; he had gone back a generation or two, which would have been sufficient to throw an entire obscurity on the events; and he would thereby have attained the marvellous, which is alone striking to barbarians. I desire it may be observed, that manners are the only circumstances which a rude people cannot falsify; because they have no notion of any manners beside their own: but it is easy for them to let loose their imagination, and violate the course of nature, in every other particular; and indeed they take no pleasure in any other kind of narrative. In Ossian, nature is violated, where alone she ought to have been preserved; is preserved where alone she ought to have been violated.

(5.) But there is another species of the marvellous, wanting in Ossian, which is inseparable from all nations, civilized as well as barbarous, but still more, if possible, from the barbarous, and that is religion; no religious sentiment in this Erse poetry. All those Celtic heroes are more complete atheists than ever were bred in the school of Epicurus. To account for this singularity, we are told that a few generations before Ossian, the people quarrelled with their Druidical priests, and having expelled them, never afterwards adopted any other species of religion. It is not quite unnatural, I own, for the people to quarrel with their priests,—as we did with ours at the Reformation; but we attached ourselves with fresh zeal to our new preachers and new system; and this passion increased in proportion to our hatred of the old. But I suppose the reason of this strange absurdity in our new Erse poetry, is, that the author, finding by the assumed age of his heroes, that he must have given them the Druidical religion, and not trusting to his literature, (which seems indeed to be very slender) for making the representations consistent with antiquity, thought it safest to give them no religion at all; a circumstance so wonderfully unnatural, that it is sufficient alone, if men had eyes, to detect the imposition.

(6.) The state of the arts, as represented in those poems, is totally incompatible with the age assigned to them. We know, that the houses even of the Southern Britons, till conquered by the Romans, were nothing but huts erected in the woods; but a stately stone building is mentioned by Ossian, of which the walls remain, after it is consumed with fire. The melancholy circumstance of a fox is described, who looks out at the windows; an image, if I be not mistaken, borrowed from the Scriptures. The Caledonians, as well as the Irish, had no shipping but currachs, or wicker boats covered with hides: yet are they represented as passing, in great military expeditions, from the Hebrides to Denmark, Norway, and Sweden; a most glaring absurdity. They live entirely by hunting, yet muster armies, which make incursions to these countries as well as to Ireland: though it is certain from the experience of America, that the whole Highlands would scarce subsist a hundred persons by hunting. They are totally unacquainted with fishing; though that occupation first tempts all rude nations to venture on the sea. Ossian alludes to a wind or water-mill, a machine then unknown to the Greeks and Romans, according to the opinion of the best antiquaries. His barbarians, though ignorant of tillage, are well acquainted with the method of working all kinds of metals. The harp is the musical instrument of Ossian: but the bagpipe, from time immemorial, has been the instrument of the Highlanders. If ever the harp had been known among them, it never had given place to the other barbarous discord.

Stridenti miserum stipula disperdere carmen.

(7.) All the historical facts of this poem are opposed by traditions, which, if all these tales be not equally contempt-

ible, seem to merit much more attention. The Irish Scoti
are the undoubted ancestors of the present Highlanders, who
are but a small colony of that ancient people. But the Irish
traditions make Fingal, Ossian, Oscar, all Irishmen, and
place them some centuries distant from the Erse heroes.
They represent them as giants, and monsters, and enchanters,
a sure mark of a considerable antiquity of these traditions.
I ask the partisans of Erse poetry, since the names of these
heroes have crept over to Ireland, and have become quite
familiar to the natives of that country, how it happens, that
not a line of this poetry, in which they are all celebrated,
which, it is pretended, alone preserves their memory with
our Highlanders, and which is composed by one of these
heroes themselves in the Irish language, ever found its way
thither? The songs and traditions of the Senachies, the
genuine poetry of the Irish, carry in their rudeness and
absurdity the inseparable attendants of barbarism, a very
different aspect from the insipid correctness of Ossian;
where the incidents, if you will pardon the antithesis, are
the most unnatural, merely because they are natural. The
same observation extends to the Welsh, another Celtic
nation.

(8.) The fiction of these poems is, if possible, still more
palpably detected, by the great numbers of other traditions,
which, the author pretends, are still fresh in the Highlands,
with regard to all the personages. The poems, composed in
the age of Truthil and Cormac, ancestors of Ossian, are, he
says, full of complaints against the roguery and tyranny of
the Druids. He talks as familiarly of the poetry of that
period as Lucian or Longinus would of the Greek poetry of
the Socratic age. I suppose here is a new rich mine of
poetry ready to break out upon us, if the author thinks it
can turn to account. For probably he does not mind the
danger of detection, which he has little reason to apprehend
from his experience of the public credulity. But I shall
venture to assert, without any reserve or further inquiry,
that there is no Highlander who is not, in some degree, a
man of letters, that ever so much as heard there was a Druid
in the world. The margin of every page almost of this wonderful production is supported, as he pretends, by minute
oral traditions with regard to the personages. To the poem
of Dar-thula, there is prefixed a long account of the pedi-

gree, marriages, and adventures of three brothers, Nathos, Althos, and Ardan, heroes that lived fifteen hundred years ago in Argyleshire, and whose memory, it seems, is still celebrated there, and in every part of the Highlands. How ridiculous to advance such a pretension to the learned, who know that there is no tradition of Alexander the great all over the East; that the Turks, who have heard of him from their communication with the Greeks, believe him to have been the captain of Solomon's guard; that the Greek and Roman story, the moment it departs from the historical ages, becomes a heap of fiction and absurdity; that Cyrus himself, the conqueror of the East, became so much unknown, even in little more than half a century, that Herodotus himself, born and bred in Asia, within the limits of the Persian empire, could tell nothing of him, more than of Croesus, the contemporary of Cyrus, and who reigned in the neighbourhood of the historian, but the most ridiculous fables; and that the grandfather of Hengist and Horsa, the first Saxon conquerors, was conceived to be a divinity. I suppose it is sufficiently evident, that without the help of books and history, the very name of Julius Caesar would at present be totally unknown in Europe. A gentleman, who travelled into Italy, told me, that in visiting Frescati or Tusculum, his cicerone showed him the foundation and ruins of Cicero's country house. He asked the fellow who this Cicero might be, 'Un grandissimo gigante,' said he.

(9.) I ask, since the memory of Fingal and his ancestors and descendants is still so fresh in the Highlands, how it happens, that none of the compilers of the Scotch fabulous history ever laid hold of them, and inserted them in the list of our ancient monarchs, but we were obliged to have recourse to direct fiction and lying to make out their genealogies? It is to be remarked, that the Highlanders, who are now but an inferior part of the nation, anciently composed the whole; so that no tradition of theirs could be unknown to the court, the nobility, and the whole kingdom. Where, then, have these wonderful traditions skulked during so many centuries, that they have never come to light till yesterday? And the very names of our ancient kings are unknown: though it is pretended, that a very particular narrative of their transactions was still preserved, and universally diffused among a numerous tribe, who are the original stem of the nation. Father Innes, the only judicious writer that ever touched our ancient history, finds in monastic records the names, and little more than the names, of kings from Fergus, whom we call Fergus the Second, who lived long after the supposed Fingal : and he thence begins the true history of the nation. He had too good sense to give any attention to pretended traditions even of kings, much less would he have believed that the memory and adventures of every leader of banditti in every valley of the Highlands, could be circumstantially preserved by oral tradition through more than fifteen centuries.

(10.) I shall observe, that the character of the author, from all his publications, (for I shall mention nothing else,) gives us the greatest reason to suspect him of such a ludicrous imposition on the public. For to be sure it is only ludicrous ; or at most a trial of wit, like that of the sophist, who gave us Phalaris' Epistles, or of him that counterfeited Cicero's Consolation, or supplied the fragments of Petronius. These literary amusements have been very common ; and unless supported by too violent asseverations, or persisted in too long, never drew the opprobrious appellation of impostor on the author.

He writes an ancient history of Britain, which is plainly ludicrous. He gives us a long circumstantial history of the emigrations of the Belgae, Cimbri, and Sarmatae, so unsupported by any author of antiquity that nothing but a particular revelation could warrant it ; and yet it is delivered with such seeming confidence, (for we must not think he was in earnest,) that the history of the Punic wars is not related with greater seriousness by Livy. He has even left palpable contradictions in his narrative, in order to try the faith of his reader. He tells us, for instance, that the present inhabitants of Germany have no more connexion with the Germans mentioned by Tacitus, than with the ancient inhabitants of Peloponnesus : the Saxons and Angles, in particular, were all Sarmatians, a quite different tribe from the Germans, in manners, laws, language, and customs. Yet a few pages after, when he pretends to deliver the origin of the Anglo-Saxon constitution, he professedly derives the whole account from Tacitus. All this was only an experiment to see how far the force of affirmation could impose on the credulity of the public : but it did not succeed ; he was here in the open daylight of Greek and Roman erudition, not in the obscurity of his Erse poetry and traditions. Finding the style of his Ossian admired by some, he attempts a translation of Homer in the very same style. He begins and finishes, in six weeks, a work that was for ever to eclipse the translation of Pope, whom he does not even deign to mention in his preface; but this joke was still more unsuccessful: he made a shift, however, to bring the work to a second edition, where he says, that, notwithstanding all the envy of his malignant opponents, his name alone will preserve the work to a more equitable posterity!

In short, let him now take off the mask, and fairly and openly laugh at the credulity of the public, who could believe that long Erse epics had been secretly preserved in the Highlands of Scotland, from the age of Severus till his time.

The imposition is so gross, that he may well ask the world how they could ever possibly believe him to be in earnest?

But it may reasonably be expected that I should mention the external positive evidence, which is brought by Dr. Blair to support the authenticity of these poems. I own, that this evidence, considered in itself, is very respectable, and sufficient to support any fact, that both lies within the bounds of credibility, and has not become a matter of party. But will any man pretend to bring human testimony to prove, that above twenty thousand verses have been transmitted, by tradition and memory, during more than fifteen hundred years; that is, above fifty generations, according to the ordinary course of nature? verses, too, which have not, in their subject, any thing alluring or inviting to the people, no miracle, no wonders, no superstitions, no useful instruction; a people, too, who, during twelve centuries, at least, of that period, had no writing, no alphabet; and who, even in the other three centuries, made very little use of that imperfect alphabet for any purpose; a people who, from the miserable disadvantages of their soil and climate, were perpetually struggling with the greatest necessities of nature; who, from the imperfections of government, lived in a continual state of internal hostility; ever harassed with the incursions of neighbouring tribes, or meditating revenge and retaliation on their neighbours. Have such a people leisure to think of any poetry, except, perhaps, a miserable song or ballad, in praise of their own chieftain, or to the disparagement of his rivals?

I should be sorry to be suspected of saying any thing against the manners of the present Highlanders. I really believe that, besides their signal bravery, there is not any people in Europe, not even excepting the Swiss, who have more plain honesty and fidelity, are more capable of gratitude and attachment, than that race of men. Yet it was, no doubt, a great surprise to them to hear that, over and above their known good qualities, they were also possessed of an excellence which they never dreamt of, an elegant taste in poetry, and inherited from the most remote antiquity the finest compositions of that kind, far surpassing the popular traditional poems of any other language; no wonder they crowded to give testimony in favour of their authenticity. Most of them, no doubt, were sincere in the delusion; the same names that were to be found in their popular ballads were carefully preserved in the new publication; some incidents, too, were perhaps transferred from the one to the other; some sentiments also might be copied; and, on the whole, they were willing to believe, and still more willing to persuade others, that the whole was genuine. On such occasions, the greatest cloud of witnesses makes no manner of evidence. What Jansenist was there in Paris, which contains several thousands, that would not have given evidence for the miracles of Abbé Paris? The miracle is greater, but not the evidence, with regard to the authenticity of Ossian.

The late President Forbes was a great believer in the second sight; and I make no question but he could, on a month's warning, have overpowered you with evidence in its favour. But as finite added to finite never approaches a hair's breadth nearer to infinite: so a fact, incredible in itself, acquires not the smallest accession of probability by the accumulation of testimony.

The only real wonder in the whole affair is, that a person of so fine a taste as Dr. Blair, should be so great an admirer of these productions; and one of so clear and cool a judgment collect evidence of their authenticity.

LETTER TO THE AUTHORS OF THE CRITICAL REVIEW CONCERNING THE EPIGONIAD OF WILKIE.[1]

To the Authors of the Critical Review.

April, 1759.

GENTLEMEN, The great advantages which result from literary journals have recommended the use of them all over Europe; but as nothing is free from abuse, it must be confessed that some inconveniences have also attended these undertakings. The works of the learned multiply in such a surprising manner, that a journalist, in order to give an account to the public of all new performances, is obliged to peruse a small library every month, and as it is impossible for him to bestow equal attention on every piece which he criticises, he may readily be surprised into mistakes, and give to a book such a character as, on a more careful perusal, he would willingly retract. Even performances of the greatest merit are not secure against this injury; and, perhaps, are sometimes the most exposed to it. An author of genius scorns the vulgar arts of catching applause: he pays no court to the great: gives no adulation to those celebrated for learning: takes no care to provide himself of partisans, or *proneurs*, as the French call them: and by that means his work steals unobserved into the world: and it is some time before the public, and even men of penetration, are sensible of its merit. We take up the book with prepossession, peruse it carelessly, are feebly affected by its beauties, and lay it down with neglect, perhaps with disapprobation.

The public has done so much justice to the gentlemen engaged in the Critical Review, as to acknowledge that no literary journal was ever carried on in this country with

[1] [This letter was never republished by the Author. ED.]

equal spirit and impartiality : yet, I must confess that an article published in your Review of 1757, gave me great surprise, and not a little uneasiness. It regarded a book called the Epigoniad, a poem of the epic kind, which was at that time published with great applause at Edinburgh, and of which a few copies had been sent up to London. The author of that article had surely been lying under strong prepossessions, when he spoke so negligently of a work which abounds in such sublime beauties, and could endeavour to discredit a poem, consisting of near six thousand lines, on account of a few mistakes in expression and prosody, proceeding entirely from the author's being a Scotchman, who had never been out of his own country. As there is a new edition published of this poem, wherein all or most of these trivial mistakes are corrected, I flatter myself that you will gladly lay hold of this opportunity of retracting your oversight, and doing justice to a performance, which may, perhaps, be regarded as one of the ornaments of our language. I appeal from your sentence, as an old woman did from a sentence pronounced by Philip of Macedon :—I appeal from Philip, ill-counselled and in a hurry, to Philip, well-advised, and judging with deliberation. The authority which you possess with the public makes your censure fall with weight : and I question not but you will be the more ready, on that account, to redress any injury into which either negligence, prejudice, or mistake, may have betrayed you. As I profess myself to be an admirer of this performance, it will afford me pleasure to give you a short analysis of it, and to collect a few specimens of those great beauties in which it abounds.

The author, who appears throughout his whole work to be a great admirer and imitator of Homer, drew the subject of this poem from the fourth Iliad, where Sthenelus gives Agamemnon a short account of the sacking of Thebes. After the fall of those heroes, celebrated by Statius, their sons, and among the rest Diomede, undertook the siege of that city, and were so fortunate as to succeed in their enterprize, and to revenge on the Thebans and the tyrant Creon the death of their fathers. These young heroes were known to the Greeks under the title of the Epigoni, or the descendants ; and for this reason the author has given to his poem the title of Epigoniad, a name, it must be confessed somewhat unfortunately chosen, for as this particular was known only to a very few of the learned, the public were not able to conjecture what could be the subject of the poem, and were apt to neglect what it was impossible for them to understand.

There remained a tradition among the Greeks, that Homer had taken the siege of Thebes for the subject of a poem, which is lost ; and our author seems to have pleased himself with the thought of reviving the work, as well as of treading in the footsteps of his favourite author. The actors are mostly the same with those of the Iliad : Diomede is the hero : Ulysses, Agamemnon, Menelaus, Nestor, Idomeneus, Merion, even Thersites, all appear in different passages of the poem, and act parts suitable to the lively characters drawn of them by that great master. The whole turn of this new poem would almost lead us to imagine that the Scottish bard had found the lost manuscript of that father of poetry, and had made a faithful translation of it into English. Longinus imagines that the Odyssey was executed by Homer in his old age ; we shall allow the Iliad to be the work of his middle age : and we shall suppose that the Epigoniad was the essay of his youth, where his noble and sublime genius breaks forth by frequent intervals, and gives strong symptoms of that constant flame which distinguished its meridian.

The poem consists of nine books. We shall open the subject of it in the author's own words :

Ye pow'rs of song ! with whose immortal fire
Your bard enraptur'd sung Pelides' ire,
To Greece so fatal, when in evil hour,
He brav'd, in stern debate, the sov'reign pow'r,
By like example teach me now to show
From love, no less, what dire disasters flow.
For when the youth of Greece, by Theseus led,
Return'd to conquer where their fathers bled,
And punish guilty Thebes, by Heav'n ordain'd
For perfidy to fall, and oaths profan'd ;
Venus, still partial to the Theban arms,
Tydeus' son seduc'd by female charms ;
Who, from his plighted faith by passion sway'd,
The chiefs, the army, and himself betray'd.
This theme did once your favourite bard employ,
Whose verse immortaliz'd the fall of Troy :
But time's oblivious gulf, whose circle draws
All mortal things by fate's eternal laws,

In whose wide vortex worlds themselves are tost,
And rounding swift successively are lost,
This song hath snatch'd.   I now resume the strain,
Not from proud hope and emulation vain,
By this attempt to merit equal praise
With worth heroic, born in happier days.
Sooner the weed, that with the Spring appears,
And in the Summer's heat its blossom bears,
But, shriv'ling at the touch of Winter hoar,
Sinks to its native earth, and is no more ;
Might match the lofty oak, which long hath stood,
From age to age, the monarch of the wood.
But love excites me, and desire to trace
His glorious steps, tho' with unequal pace.
Before me still I see his awful shade,
With garlands crown'd of leaves which never fade ;
He points the path to fame, and bids me scale
Parnassus' slipp'ry height, where thousands fail :
I follow trembling ; for the cliffs are high,
And hov'ring round them watchful harpies fly,
To snatch the poet's wreath with envious claws,
And hiss contempt for merited applause.

The poet supposes that Cassandra, the daughter of the
King of Pelignium in Italy, was pursued by the love of
Ectretus, a barbarous tyrant in the neighbourhood ; and as
her father rejected his addresses, he drew on himself the resentment of the tyrant, who made war upon him, and forced
him to retire into Etolia, where Diomede gave him protection.   This hero falls himself in love with Cassandra, and
is so fortunate as to make equal impression on her heart ; but
before the completion of his marriage, he is called to the
siege of Thebes, and leaves, as he supposes, Cassandra in
Etolia with her father.   But Cassandra, anxious for her
lover's safety, and unwilling to part from the object of her
affections, had secretly put on a man's habit, had attended
him in the camp, and had fought by his side in all his
battles.   Meanwhile the siege of Thebes is drawn out to some
length, and Venus, who favours that city, in opposition to
Juno and Pallas, who seek its destruction, deliberates concerning the proper method of raising the siege.   The fittest
expedient seems to be the exciting in Diomede a jealousy of
Cassandra, and persuading him that her affections were
secretly engaged to Ectretus, and that the tyrant had invaded

Etolia in pursuit of his mistress. For this purpose Venus sends down Jealousy, whom the author personifies under the name of Zelotypé. Her person and flight are painted in the most splendid colours that poetry affords:

First to her feet the winged shoes she binds,
Which tread the air, and mount the rapid winds:
Aloft they bear her thro' th' ethereal plain,
Above the solid earth and liquid main:
Her arrows next she takes of pointed steel,
For sight too small, but terrible to feel:
Rous'd by their smart the savage lion roars,
And mad to combat rush the tusky boars,
Of wounds secure; for where their venom lights,
What feels their power all other torments slights.
A figur'd zone, mysteriously design'd,
Around her waist her yellow robe confin'd:
There dark Suspicion lurk'd, of sable hue;
There hasty Rage his deadly dagger drew;
Pale Envy inly pin'd: and by her side
Stood Phrenzy, raging with his chains unty'd:
Affronted Pride with thirst of vengeance burn'd,
And Love's excess to deepest hatred turn'd.
All these the artist's curious hand express'd,
The work divine his matchless skill confess'd.
The virgin last, around her shoulders flung
The bow; and by her side the quiver hung;
Then, springing up, her airy course she bends,
For Thebes; and lightly o'er the tents descends.
The son of Tydeus, 'midst his bands, she found
In arms complete, reposing on the ground:
And, as he slept, the hero thus address'd,
Her form to fancy's waking eye express'd.

Diomede, moved by the instigations of jealousy, and eager to defend his mistress and his country, calls an assembly of the princes, and proposes to raise the siege of Thebes, on account of the difficulty of the enterprize, and dangers which surround the army. Theseus, the general, breaks out into a passion at this proposal: but is pacified by Nestor. Idomeneus rises, and reproaches Diomede for his dishonourable counsel, and among other topics, upbraids him with his degeneracy from his father's bravery.

Should now, from hence arriv'd, some warrior's ghost
Greet valiant Tydeus on the Stygian coast,

And tell, when danger or distress is near,
That Diomed persuades the rest to fear :
He'd shun the synod of the mighty dead,
And hide his anguish in the deepest shade :
Nature in all an equal course maintains :
The lion's whelp succeeds to awe the plains :
Pards gender pards : from tigers tigers spring,
Nor doves are hatch'd beneath a vultur's wing :
Each parent's image in his offspring lives :
But nought of Tydeus in his son survives.

The debate is closed by Ulysses, who informs the princes
that the Thebans are preparing to march out in order to
attack them ; and that it is vain for them to deliberate any
longer concerning the conclusion of the war.

We have next a description of a battle between the Thebans, under Creon, and the confederate Greeks, under
Theseus. The battle is full of the spirit of Homer. We shall
not trouble our reader with particulars, which would appear
insipid in prose, especially if compared to the lively poetry of
our author. We shall only transcribe one passage, as a
specimen of his happy choice of circumstances :

Next Arcas, Cleon, valiant Chromeus dy'd ;
With Dares, to the Spartan chiefs ally'd.
And Phœmius, whom the gods in early youth
Had form'd for virtue and the love of truth ;
His gen'rous soul to noble deeds they turn'd,
And love to mankind in his bosom burn'd :
Cold thro' his throat the hissing weapon glides,
And on his neck the waving locks divides.
His fate the Graces mourn'd. The gods above,
Who sit around the starry throne of Jove,
On high Olympus bending from the skies,
His fate beheld with sorrow-streaming eyes.
Pallas alone, unalter'd and serene,
With secret triumph saw the mournful scene.
Not hard of heart : for none of all the pow'rs,
In earth or ocean, or th' Olympian tow'rs,
Holds equal sympathy with human grief,
Or with a freer hand bestows relief :
But conscious that a mind by virtue steel'd
To no impression of distress will yield ;
That, still unconquer'd, in its awful hour
O'er death it triumphs with immortal pow'r.

The battle ends with advantage to the confederate Greeks : but the approach of night prevents their total victory.

Creon, king of Thebes, sends next an embassy to the confederate Greeks, desiring a truce of seven days, in order to bury the dead. Diomede, impatient to return home, and stimulated by jealousy, violently opposes this overture, but it is over-ruled by the other princes, and the truce is concluded. The author, in imitation of Homer, and the other ancient poets, takes here an opportunity of describing games celebrated for honouring the dead. The games he has chosen are different from those which are to be found among the ancients, and the incidents are new and curious.

Diomede took no share in these games : his impatient spirit could not brook the delay which arose from the truce : he pretends that he consented not to it, and is not included in it : he therefore proposes to his troops to attack the Thebans while they are employed in performing the funeral rites of the dead ; but is opposed in this design by Deiphobus his tutor, who represents to him in the severest terms the rashness and iniquity of his proposal. After some altercation, Diomede, impatient of contradiction in his favourite object, and stung by the free reproaches of his tutor, breaks out into a violent passion, and throws his spear at Deiphobus, which pierced him to the heart.

This incident, which is apt to surprize us, seems to have been copied by our author, from that circumstance in the life of Alexander, where this heroic conqueror, moved by a sudden passion, stabs Clytus his ancient friend, by whom his life had been formerly saved in battle. The repentance of Diomede is equal to that of Alexander. No sooner had he struck the fatal blow than his eyes are opened : he is sensible of his guilt and shame ; he refuses all consolation ; abstains even from food : and shuts himself up alone in his tent. His followers, amazed at the violence of his passion, keep at a distance from him : all but Cassandra, who enters his tent with a potion, which she had prepared for him. While she stands before him alone, her timidity and passion betray her sex : and Diomede immediately perceives her to be Cassandra, who had followed him to the camp, under a warlike disguise. As his repentance for the murder of Deiphobus was now the ruling passion in his breast, he is not moved by tenderness for Cassandra : on the contrary, he considers her as the cause, however innocent, of the murder of his friend, and of his own guilt; and he treats her with such coldness that she retires in confusion. She even leaves the camp, and resolves to return to her father in Etolia ; but is taken on the road by a party of Thebans, who carry her to Creon. That tyrant determines to make the most political use of this incident : he sends privately a message to Diomede, threatening to put Cassandra to death, if that hero would not agree to a separate truce with Thebes. This proposal is at first rejected by Diomede, who threatens immediate destruction to Creon and all his race. Nothing can be more artfully managed by the poet than this incident. We shall hear him in his own words :

> Sternly the hero ended, and resign'd,
> To fierce disorder, all his mighty mind.
> Already in his thoughts, with vengeful hands,
> He dealt destruction 'midst the Theban bands,
> In fancy saw the tott'ring turrets fall,
> And led his warriors o'er the level'd wall.
> Rous'd with the thought, from his high seat he sprung,
> And grasp'd the sword, which on a column hung ;
> The shining blade he balanc'd thrice in air ;
> His lances next he view'd, and armour fair.
> When, hanging 'midst the costly panoply,
> A scarf embroider'd met the hero's eye,
> Which fair Cassandra's skilful hands had wrought,
> A present for her lord, in secret brought
> That day, when first he led his martial train
> In arms, to combat on the Theban plain.
> As some strong charm, which magic sounds compose,
> Suspends a downward torrent as it flows ;
> Checks in the precipice its headlong course,
> And calls it trembling upwards to its source :
> Such seem'd the robe, which, to the hero's eyes,
> Made the fair artist in her charms to rise.
> His rage, suspended in its full career,
> To love resigns, to grief and tender fear.
> Glad would he now his former words revoke,
> And change the purpose which in wrath he spoke ;
> From hostile hands his captive fair to gain,
> From fate to save her, or the servile chain :
> But pride, and shame, the fond design supprest ;
> Silent he stood, and lock'd it in his breast.

Yet had the wary Theban well divin'd,
By symptoms sure, each motion of his mind :
With joy he saw the heat of rage suppress'd ;
And thus again his artful words address'd.

The truce is concluded for twenty days ; but the perfidious Creon, hoping that Diomede would be overawed by the danger of his mistress, resolves to surprise the Greeks : and accordingly makes a sudden attack upon them, breaks into their camp, and carries everything before him. Diomede at first stands neuter ; but when Ulysses suggests to him, that after the defeat of the confederate Greeks, he has no security ; and that so treacherous a prince as Creon will not spare, much less restore Cassandra, he takes to arms, assaults the Thebans, and obliges them, to seek shelter within their walls. Creon, in revenge, puts Cassandra to death, and shews her head over the walls. This sight so inflames Diomede, that he attacks Thebes with double fury, takes the town by scalade, and gratifies his vengeance by the death of Creon.

This is a short abstract of the story on which this new poem is founded. The reader may perhaps conjecture (what I am not very anxious to conceal) that the execution of the Epigoniad is better than the design, the poetry superior to the fable, and the colouring of the particular parts more excellent than the general plan of the whole. Of all the great epic poems which have been the admiration of mankind, the Jerusalem of Tasso alone would make a tolerable novel, if reduced to prose, and related without that splendour of versification and imagery by which it is supported : yet in the opinion of many great judges, the Jerusalem is the least perfect of all these productions : chiefly, because it has least nature and simplicity in the sentiments, and is most liable to the objection of affectation and conceit. The story of a poem, whatever may be imagined, is the least essential part of it : the force of the versification, the vivacity of the images, the justness of the descriptions, the natural play of the passions, are the chief circumstances which distinguish the great poet from the prosaic novelist, and give him so high a rank among the heroes in literature ; and I will venture to affirm, that all these advantages, especially the three former, are to be found in an eminent degree in the Epigoniad. The author, inspired with the true genius of Greece,

and smit with the most profound veneration for Homer, dis-
dains all frivolous ornaments ; and relying entirely on his
sublime imagination, and his nervous and harmonious expression, has ventured to present to his reader the naked
beauties of nature, and challenges for his partizans all the
admirers of genuine antiquity.

There is one circumstance in which the poet has carried
his boldness of copying antiquity beyond the practice of
many, even judicious moderns.   He has drawn his personages, not only with all the simplicity of the Grecian
heroes, but also with some degree of their roughness, and
even of their ferocity.   This is a circumstance which a mere
modern is apt to find fault with in Homer, and which
perhaps he will not easily excuse in his imitator.   It is certain, that the ideas of manners are so much changed since
the age of Homer, that though the Iliad was always among
the ancients conceived to be a panegyric on the Greeks, yet the
reader is now almost always on the side of the Trojans, and is
much more interested for the humane and soft manners of
Priam, Hector, Andromache, Sarpedon, Æneas, Glaucus,
nay, even of Paris and Helen, than for the severe and cruel
bravery of Achilles, Agamemnon, and the other Grecian
heroes.   Sensible of this inconvenience, Fenelon, in his
elegant romance, has softened extremely the harsh manners of the heroic ages, and has contented himself with
retaining that amiable simplicity by which those ages were
distinguished.   If the reader be displeased, that the British
poet has not followed the example of the French writer, he
must, at least, allow that he has drawn a more exact and
faithful copy of antiquity, and has made fewer sacrifices of
truth to ornament.

There is another circumstance of our author's choice which
will be liable to dispute.   It may be thought that by introducing the heroes of Homer, he has lost all the charm of
novelty, and leads us into fictions which are somewhat stale
and thread-bare.   Boileau, the greatest critic of the French
nation, was of a very different opinion :

> La fable offre à l'esprit mille agréments divers
> Là tous les noms heureux semblent nez pour les vers :
> Ulysse, Agamemnon, Oreste, Idoménée,
> Hélène, Menelas, Paris, Hector, Enée.

It is certain that there is in that poetic ground a kind of enchantment which allures every person of a tender and lively imagination; nor is this impression diminished, but rather much increased, by our early introduction to the knowledge of it in our perusal of the Greek and Latin classics.

The same great French critic makes the apology of our poet in his use of the ancient mythology:

> Ainsi dans cet amas de nobles fictions,
> Le poet s'egeye en mille inventions,
> Orne, eleve, embellit, aggrandit toutes choses,
> Et trouve sous sa main des fleurs toujours ecloses.

It would seem, indeed, that if the machinery of the heathen gods be not admitted, epic poetry, at least all the marvellous part of it, must be entirely abandoned. The Christian religion, for many reasons, is unfit for the fabulous ornaments of poetry: the introduction of allegory, after the manner of Voltaire, is liable to many objections: and though a mere historical epic poem, like Leonidas, may have its beauties, it will always be inferior to the force and pathetic of tragedy, and must resign to that species of poetry the precedency which the former composition has always challenged among the productions of human genius. But with regard to these particulars, the author has himself made a sufficient apology in the judicious and spirited preface which accompanies his poem.

But though our poet has in general followed so successfully the footsteps of Homer, he has, in particular passages, chosen other ancient poets for his model. His seventh book contains an episode, very artfully inserted, concerning the death of Hercules: where he has plainly had Sophocles in his view, and has ventured to engage in a rivalship with that great master of the tragic scene. If the sublimity of our poet's imagination, and the energy of his style, appear any where conspicuous, it is in this episode, which we shall not scruple to compare with any poetry in the English language. Nothing can be more pathetic than the complaint of Hercules, when the poison of the centaur's robe begins first to prey upon him:

> Sov'reign of Heav'n and Earth! whose boundless sway
> The fates of men and mortal things obey,

If e'er delighted from the courts above,
In human form you sought Alcmene's love;
If fame's unchanging voice to all the Earth,
With truth, proclaims you author of my birth;
Whence, from a course of spotless glory run,
Successful toils and wreaths of triumph won,
Am I thus wretched? better that before
Some monster fierce had drank my streaming gore;
Or crush'd by Cacus, foe to gods and men,
My batter'd brains had strew'd his rocky den:
Than, from my glorious toils and triumphs past,
To fall subdu'd by female arts, at last.
O cool my boiling blood, ye winds, that blow
From mountains loaded with eternal snow,
And crack the icy cliffs; in vain! in vain!
Your rigour cannot quench my raging pain!
For round this heart the furies wave their brands,
And wring my entrails with their burning hands.
Now bending from the skies, O wife of Jove!
Enjoy the vengeance of thy injur'd love:
For fate, by me, the Thund'rer's guilt atones;
And, punish'd in her son, Alcmene groans:
The object of your hate shall soon expire,
Fix'd on my shoulders preys a net of fire;
Whom nor the toils nor dangers could subdue,
By false Eurystheus dictated from you:
Nor tyrants lawless, nor the monstrous brood
Which haunts the desert or infests the flood,
Nor Greece, nor all the barb'rous climes that lie
Where Phœbus ever points his golden eye;
A woman hath o'erthrown! ye gods! I yield
To female arts, unconquer'd in the field.
My arms—alas! are these the same that bow'd
Anteus, and his giant force subdu'd?
That dragg'd Nemea's monster from his den?
And slew the dragon in his native fen?
Alas! alas! their mighty muscles fail,
While pains infernal ev'ry nerve assail:
Alas, alas! I feel in streams of woe
These eyes dissolve, before untaught to flow.
Awake my virtue, oft in dangers try'd,
Patient in toils, in deaths unterrify'd,
Rouse to my aid; nor let my labours past,
With fame achiev'd, be blotted by the last:
Firm and unmov'd, the present shock endure;
Once triumph, and for ever rest secure.

CONCERNING WILKIE'S EPIGONIAD.

Our poet, though his genius be in many respects very original, has not disdained to imitate even modern poets. He has added to his heroic poem a dream, in the manner of Spenser, where the poet supposes himself to be introduced to Homer, who censures his poem in some particulars, and excuses it in others. This poem is indeed a species of apology for the Epigoniad, wrote in a very lively and elegant manner: it may be compared to a well-polished gem, of the purest water, and cut into the most beautiful form. Those who would judge of our author's talents for poetry, without perusing his larger work, may satisfy their curiosity, by running over this short poem. They will see the same force of imagination and harmony of numbers, which distinguish his longer performance: and may thence, with small application, receive a favourable impression of our author's genius.

D. H.

DEDICATION OF THE 'FOUR DISSERTATIONS,' 1757.[1]

To the Reverend Mr. Hume,[2] *Author of ' Douglas,' a Tragedy.*

My Dear Sir,—It was the practice of the antients to address their compositions only to friends and equals, and to render their dedications monuments of regard and affection, not of servility and flattery. In those days of ingenuous and candid liberty, a dedication did honour to the person to whom it was addressed, without degrading the author. If any partiality appeared towards the patron, it was at least the partiality of friendship and affection.

Another instance of true liberty, of which antient times can alone afford us an example, is the liberty of thought, which engaged men of letters, however different in their abstract opinions, to maintain a mutual friendship and regard ; and never to quarrel about principles, while they agreed in inclinations and manners. Science was often the subject of disputation, never of animosity. *Cicero*, an academic, addressed his philosophical treatises, sometimes to *Brutus*, a stoic ; sometimes to *Atticus*, an epicurean.

I have been seized with a strong desire of renewing these laudable practices of antiquity, by addressing the following dissertations to you, my good friend : For such I will ever call and esteem you, notwithstanding the opposition, which prevails between us, with regard to many of our speculative tenets. These differences of opinion I have only found to

[1] [The circumstances attending the publication of this 'Dedication' are given in the 'History of the Editions.' Vol. III. p. 65, where it has already been printed. It is repeated here, in order that Hume's eulogy of *Douglas* may stand by the side of his sanction of the *Epigoniad* and of his condemnation of the *Poems of Ossian*.—Ed.]

[2] [So Hume chose to spell the name : Burton's Life of Hume, Vol. II. p. 506. —Ed.]

enliven our conversation; while our common passion for science and letters served as a cement to our friendship. I still admired your genius, even when I imagined, that you lay under the influence of prejudice; and you sometimes told me, that you excused my errors, on account of the candor and sincerity, which, you thought, accompanied them.

But to tell truth, it is less my admiration of your fine genius, which has engaged me to make this address to you, than my esteem of your character and my affection to your person. That generosity of mind which ever accompanies you; that cordiality of friendship, that spirited honour and integrity, have long interested me strongly in your behalf, and have made me desirous, that a monument of our mutual amity should be publicly erected, and, if possible, be preserved to posterity.

I own too, that I have the ambition to be the first who shall in public express his admiration of your noble tragedy of DOUGLAS; one of the most interesting and pathetic pieces, that was ever exhibited on any theatre. Should I give it the preference to the *Merope* of *Maffei*, and to that of *Voltaire*, which it resembles in its subject; should I affirm, that it contained more fire and spirit than the former, more tenderness and simplicity than the latter; I might be accused of partiality; And how could I entirely acquit myself, after the professions of friendship, which I have made you? But the unfeigned tears which flowed from every eye, in the numerous representations which were made of it on this theatre; the unparalleled command, which you appeared to have over every affection of the human breast: These are incontestible proofs, that you possess the true theatric genius of *Shakespear* and *Otway*, refined from the unhappy barbarism of the one, and licentiousness of the other.

My enemies, you know, and, I own, even sometimes my friends, have reproached me with the love of paradoxes and singular opinions; and I expect to be exposed to the same imputation, on account of the character which I have here given of your DOUGLAS. I shall be told, no doubt, that I had artfully chosen the only time, when this high esteem of that piece could be regarded as a paradox, to wit, before its publication; and that not being able to contradict in this particular the sentiments of the public, I have, at least, resolved to go before them. But I shall be amply compensated for all these pleasantries, if you accept this testimony of my regard, and believe me to be, with the greatest sincerity,

Dear Sir,

Your most affectionate Friend,

and humble Servant,

DAVID HUME.

EDINBURGH: 3 *January*, 1757.'

FRAGMENTS OF A PAPER IN HUME'S HAND-WRITING, DESCRIBING THE DESCENT ON THE COAST OF BRITTANY, IN 1746, AND THE CAUSES OF ITS FAILURE.[1]

THE forces under Lieutenant General St. Clair consisted of five battalions, viz. the first battalion of the 1st Royal, the 5th Highlanders, 3rd Brag's, 4th Richbell's, 2d Harrison's, together with part of Frampton's, and some companies of Marines, making in all about 4500 men. The fleet consisted of   . Though this army and fleet had been at first fitted out for entering upon action in summer 1746, and making conquest of Canada, it was found, after several vain efforts to get out of the Channel, first under Commodore Cotes, then under Admiral Listock, that so much time had been unavoidably lost, from contrary winds and contrary orders, as to render it dangerous for so large a body of ships to proceed thither. The middle of May was the last day of rendezvous appointed at Spithead; and in the latter end of August, the fleet had yet got no farther than St. Helen's, about a league below it. It is an observation, that in the latter end of autumn, or beginning of winter, the north-west winds blow so furiously on the coast of North America, as to render it always difficult, and often impossible, for ships that set out late to reach any harbour in those parts. Instances have been found of vessels that have been obliged to take shelter from these storms, even in the Leeward Islands. It was therefore become necessary to abandon all thoughts of proceeding to America that season; and as the transports were fitted out and fleet equipped at great expense, an attempt was hastily made to turn them to some account in Europe, during the small remainder of the sum-

[1 This narrative, published as Appendix A to the 'Life of Hume,' Vol. I. p. 441, is supposed by Mr. Burton to have been 'drawn up as a vindication of the conduct of General St. Clair,' who took Hume with him as Secretary and Judge Advocate of all the Forces under his command. See 'Life of Hume,' Vol. I. pp. 208 and seq.—ED.]

mer. The distress of the allies in Flanders demanded the more immediate attention of the English nation and ministry, and required, if possible, some speedy remedy. 'Twas too late to think of sending the six battalions under General St. Clair, to reinforce Prince Charles of Lorraine, who commanded the armies of the allies; and their number was, besides, too inconsiderable to hope for any great advantages from that expedient. 'Twas more to be expected, that falling on the parts of France, supposed to be defenceless and disarmed, they might make a diversion, and occasion the sending a considerable detachment from the enemy's army in Flanders. But as time pressed, and allowed not leisure to concert and prepare this measure, the Duke of Newcastle, Secretary of State, hoped to find that General St. Clair had already planned and projected some enterprise of this nature. He formed this presumption on a hint which had been started very casually, and which had been immediately dropped by the General.

In the spring, when the obstructions and delays thrown in the way of the American enterprise were partly felt and partly foreseen, the Secretary, lamenting the great and, he feared, useless expense to which the nation had been put by that undertaking, gave occasion to the General to throw out a thought, which would naturally occur in such a situation. He said, ' Why may you not send the squadron and troops to some part of the coast of France, and at least frighten and alarm them as they have done us ; and, as all their troops are on the Flanders and German frontiers, 'tis most probable that such an alarm may make them recall some of them?' The subject was then no farther prosecuted; but the King, being informed of this casual hint of the General's, asked him if he had formed any plan or project by which the service above-mentioned might be effectuated. He assured his majesty that he had never so much as thought of it ; but that, if it was his pleasure, he would confer with Sir John Ligonier, and endeavour to find other people in London who could let him into some knowledge of the coast of France. To this the King replied, ' No, no: you need not give yourself any trouble about it.' And accordingly the General never more thought of it, farther than to inform the Duke of Newcastle of this conference with his majesty. However, the Duke being willing that the person who was to execute the undertaking should also be the projector of it, by which means both greater success might be hoped from it, and every body else be screened from reflection in case of its miscarriage, desired, in his letter of the 22d of August, that both the Admiral and General should give their opinion of such an invasion; and particularly the General, who, having, he said, formed some time ago a project of this nature, might be the better prepared to give his thoughts with regard to it. They both jointly replied, that their utter ignorance made them incapable of delivering their sentiments on so delicate a subject; and the General, in a separate letter, recalled to the Duke's memory the circumstances of the story, as above related.

Though they declined proposing a project, they both cheerfully offered, that if his majesty would honour them with any plan of operation for a descent, they would do their best to carry it into execution. They hoped that the Secretary of State, who, by his office, is led to turn his eyes every where, and who lives at London, the centre of commerce and intelligence, could better form and digest such a plan, than they who were cooped up in their ships, in a remote sea-port town, without any former acquaintance with the coast of France, and without any possibility of acquiring new knowledge. They at least hoped, that so difficult a task would not be required of them as either to give their sentiments without any materials afforded them to judge upon, or to collect materials, while the most inviolable secrecy was strictly enjoined on them. It is remarkable, that the Duke of Newcastle, among other advantages proposed by this expedition, mentions the giving assistance to such Protestants as are already in arms, or may be disposed to rise on the appearance of the English, as if we were living in the time of the League, or during the confusion of Francis the Second's minority.

Full of these reflections, they sailed from St. Helen's on the 23d of August, and arrived at Plymouth on the 29th, in obedience to their orders, which required them to put into that harbour for farther instructions. They there found positive orders to sail immediately, with the first fair wind, to the coast of France, and make an attempt on L'Orient, or Rochefort, or Rochelle, or sail up the river of Bourdeaux; or, if they judged any of these enterprises impracticable, to

sail to whatever other place on the western coast they should
think proper. Such unbounded discretionary powers could
not but be agreeable to the commanders, had it been accompanied with better, or indeed with any intelligence. As
the wind was then contrary, they had leisure to reply in
their letters of the 29th and 30th. They jointly represented
the difficulties, or rather impossibilities, of any attempt on
L'Orient, Rochefort, and Rochelle, by reason of the real
strength of these places, so far as their imperfect information could reach; or, if that were erroneous, by reason of
their own absolute want of intelligence, guides, and pilots,
which are the soul of all military operations.

The General, in a separate letter, enforced the same topics,
and added many other reflections of moment. He said, that
of all the places mentioned in his orders, Bourdeaux, if ac-
cessible, appeared to him the properest to be attempted;
both as it is one of the towns of greatest commerce and riches
in France, and as it is the farthest situated from their
Flanders' army, and on these accounts an attack on it would
most probably produce the wished-for alarm and diversion.
He added, that he himself knew the town to be of no
strength, and that the only place there capable of making
any defence, is Chateau Trompette, which serves it as a
citadel, and was intended, as almost all citadels are, more as
a curb, than a defence, on the inhabitants. But though
these circumstances promised some success, he observed that
there were many other difficulties to struggle with, which
threw a mighty damp on these promising expectations. In the
first place, he much questioned if there was in the fleet any one
person who had been ashore on the western coast of France,
except himself, who was once at Bourdeaux; and he, too, was
a stranger to all the country betwixt the town and the sea.
He had no single map of any part of France on board with
him; and what intelligence he may be able to force from
the people of the country can be but little to be depended
on, as it must be their interest to mislead him. And if
money prove necessary, either for obtaining intelligence,
carrying on of works, or even subsisting the officers, he
must raise it in the country; for, except a few chests of
Mexican dollars, consigned to other uses, he carried no
money with him. If he advanced any where into the country,
he must be at a very great loss for want of horses to draw
the artillery; as the inhabitants will undoubtedly carry off

as many of them as they could, and he had neither hussars nor dragoons to force them back again. And as to the preserving any conquests he might make, (of which the Duke had dropped some hints,) he observed that every place which was not impregnable to him, with such small force, must be untenable by him. On the whole, he engaged for nothing but obedience; he promised no success; he professed absolute ignorance with regard to every circumstance of the undertaking; he even could not fix on any particular undertaking; and yet he lay under positive orders to sail with the first fair wind, to approach the unknown coast, march through the unknown country, and attack the unknown cities of the most potent nation of the universe.

Meanwhile, Admiral Anson, who had put into Plymouth, and had been detained there by the same contrary winds, which still prevailed, had a conversation with the General and Admiral on the subject of their enterprise. He told them, that he remembered to have once casually heard from Mr. Hume, member for Southwark, that he had been at L'Orient, and that, though it be very strong by sea, it is not so by land. Though Mr. Hume, the gentleman mentioned, be bred to a mercantile profession, not to war, and though the intelligence received from him was only casual, imperfect, and by second-hand, yet it gave pleasure to the Admiral and General, as it afforded them a faint glimmering ray in their present obscurity and ignorance; and they accordingly resolved to follow it. They wrote to the Duke of Newcastle, September the 3d, that 'twas to L'Orient they intended to bend their course, as soon as the wind offered. To remedy the ignorance of the coast and want of pilots, as far as possible, Commodore Cotes in the Ruby, together with Captain Steward in the Hastings, and a sloop and tender, was immediately despatched by the Admiral to view Port L'Orient and all the places near it, so far as might regard the safe approach and anchorage of the ships. The ignorance of the country, and want of guides, was a desperate evil, for which the General could provide no remedy. But as the wind still continued contrary to the fleet and transports, though single ships of war might work their way against it, the General had occasion to see farther alterations made by the ministry in their project of an invasion.

The Duke of Newcastle, who had before informed the General that, if he could establish himself on any part of the

coast of France, two battalions of the Guards, and General
Huske's regiment, should be despatched after him, now says,
(Sept. 3), that these three battalions have got immediate
orders to follow him. He farther adds, that if the General
finds it impracticable to make any descent on the coast of
Brittany, or higher up in the Bay of Biscay, he would probably
find, on his return, some intelligence sent him, by the rein-
forcement, with regard to the coast of Normandy. Next day
the Duke changes his mind, and sends immediately this intelligence with regard to the coast of Normandy, and a plan
for annoying the French on that quarter, proposed by Major
Macdonald; and to this plan he seems entirely to give the
preference to the other, of making an attempt on the western
coast of France, to which he had before confined the Admiral
and General. They considered the plan, and conversed with
Major Macdonald, who came down to Plymouth a few days
after. They found that this plan had been given in some
years before, and was not in the least calculated for the present expedition, but required a body of cavalry as an essential
point towards its execution; an advantage of which the
General was entirely destitute. They found that Major Macdonald had had so few opportunities of improving himself in
the art of war, that it would be dangerous, without farther
information, to follow his plan in any military operations.
They found that he pretended only to know the strength of
the town, and nature of the country, in that province, but
had never acquainted himself with the sea-coast, or pitched
upon any proper place for disembarkation. They considered
that a very considerable step had been already taken towards
the execution of the other project on the coast of Brittany,
viz. the sending Commodore Cotes to inspect and sound the
coast; and that the same step must now be taken anew, in so
late a season, with regard to the coast of Normandy. They
thought that, if their whole operations were to begin, an attempt on the western coast was preferable, chiefly because
of its remoteness from the Flanders' army, which must increase and spread the alarm, if the country were really so
defenceless as was believed. They represented all those
reasons to the Secretary; but at the same time expressed
their intentions of remaining at Plymouth till they should
receive his majesty's positive orders with regard to the enterprise on which they were to engage.

The Duke immediately despatched a messenger, with full powers to them to go whithersoever they pleased. During this interval, the General was obliged, to his great regret, to remain in a manner wholly inactive. Plymouth was so remote a place, that it was not to be expected he could there get any proper intelligence. He was bound up by his orders to such inviolable secrecy, that he could not make any inquiries for it, or scarce receive it, if offered. The Secretary had sent Major Macdonald, and one Cooke, captain of a privateer, who, 'twas found, could be of no manner of service in this undertaking. These, he said, were the only persons he could find in London that pretended to know any thing of the coast of France, as if the question had been with regard to the coast of Japan or of California. The General desired to have maps of France, chiefly of Gascony and Brittany. He receives only a map of Gascony, together with one of Normandy. No map of Brittany; none of France; he is obliged to set out on so important an enterprise without intelligence, without pilots, without guides, without any map of the country to which he was bound, except a common map, on a small scale, of the kingdom of France, which his Aid-de-camp had been able to pick up in a shop at Plymouth. He represented all these difficulties to the ministry; he begged them not to flatter themselves with any success from a General who had such obstacles to surmount, and who must leave his conduct to the government of chance more than prudence. He was answered, that nothing was expected of him, but to land any where he pleased in France, to produce an alarm, and to return safe, with the fleet and transports, to the British dominions. Though he was sensible that more would be expected by the people, yet he cheerfully despised their rash judgments, while he acted in obedience to orders, and in the prosecution of his duty. The fleet sailed from Plymouth on the 15th of September, and, after a short voyage of three days, arrived, in the evening of the 18th, off the island of Groa, where they found Commodore Cotes and Captain Stuart, who gave them an account of the success which they had met with in the survey of the coast near L'Orient. The place they had pitched on for landing, was ten miles from that town, at the mouth of the river of Quimperlay. They represented it as a flat open shore, with deep water: on these accounts a good landing-place for the troops, but a dangerous place for the ships to ride in, on account of the rocks with which it was every where surrounded, and the high swell which was thrown in, from the Bay of Biscay, by the west and south-west winds.

It was then about eight in the evening, a full moon and a clear sky, with a gentle breeze blowing in shore. The question was, whether to sail directly to the landing-place, or hold off till morning. The two officers who had surveyed the coast were divided in opinion : one recommended the former measure, the other suggested some scruples, by representing the dangerous rocks that lay on every side of them, and the ignorance of all the pilots with regard to their number and situation. The Admiral was determined, by these reasons, to agree to this opinion. The question seemed little important, as it regarded only a short delay ; but really was of the utmost consequence, and was, indeed, the spring whence all the ill success in this expedition flowed.

The great age of Admiral Listock, as it increased his experience, should make us cautious of censuring his opinion in sea affairs, where he was allowed to have such consummate knowledge. But at the same time, it may beget a suspicion, that being now in the decline of life, he was thence naturally inclined rather to the prudent counsels which suit a concerted enterprise, than to the bold temerity which belongs to such hasty and blind undertakings. The unhappy consequences of this over-cautious measure immediately appeared. The Admiral had laid his account, that by a delay, which procured a greater safety to the fleet and transports, only four or five hours would be lost ; but the wind changing in the morning, and blowing fresh off shore, all next day, and part of next night, was spent before the ships could reach the landing-place. Some of them were not able to reach it till two days after.

During this time, the fleet lay full in view of the coast, and preparations were making in Port Louis, L'Orient, and over the whole country, for the reception of an enemy, who threatened them with so unexpected an invasion.

The force of France, either for offence or defence, consists chiefly in three different bodies of men : first, in a numerous veteran army, which was then entirely employed in Italy and on their frontiers, except some shattered regiments, which were dispersed about the country, for the advantage of re-

cruiting, and of which there were two regiments of dragoons
at that time in Brittany; secondly, in a regular and disciplined militia, with which all the fortified cities along the
sea-coast were garrisoned, and many of the frontier-towns,
that seemed not to be threatened with any immediate attack.
Some bodies of this militia had also been employed in the
field with the regular troops, and had acquired honour, which
gave spirits and courage to the rest: thirdly, in a numerous
body of coast militia, or gardes-du-cote, amounting to near
200,000, ill armed and ill disciplined, formidable alone by
their numbers; and in Brittany, by the ferocity of the inhabitants, esteemed of old and at present, the most warlike
and least civilized of all the French peasants. Regular
signals were concerted for the assembling of these forces by
alarm guns, flags, and fires; and in the morning of the 20th
of September, by break of day, a considerable body of all
these different kinds of troops, but chiefly of the last, amounting to above 3,000 men, were seen upon the sea-shore to
oppose the disembarkation of the British forces. A disposition,
therefore, of ships and boats must be made for the regular
landing of the army; and as the weather was then very
blustering, and the wind blew almost off shore, this could
not be effected till afternoon.

There appeared, in view of the fleet, three places which
seemed proper for a disembarkation, and which were separated
from each other either by a rising ground, or by a small arm of
the sea. The French militia had posted themselves in the two
places which lay nearest to L'Orient; and finding that they
were not numerous enough to cover the whole, they left the
third, which lay to the windward, almost wholly defenceless.
The General ordered the boats to rendezvous opposite to this
beach; and he saw the French troops march off from the
next contiguous landing-place, and take post opposite to him.
They placed themselves behind some sand-banks in such a
manner as to be entirely sheltered from the cannon of those
English ships which covered the landing, while at the same
time they could rush in upon the troops, as soon as their
approach to the shore had obliged the ships to leave off
firing.

The General remarked their plan of defence, and was determined to disappoint them. He observed, that the next
landing-place to the leeward was now empty; and that,

though the troops which had been posted on the more distant beach had quitted their station, and were making a circuit round an arm of the sea, in order to occupy the place deserted by the others, they had not as yet reached it. He immediately seized the opportunity. He ordered his boats to row directly forward, as if he intended to land on the beach opposite to him; but while the enemy were expecting him to advance, he ordered the boats to turn, at a signal; and, making all the speed that both oars and sails could give them, to steer directly to the place deserted by the enemy. In order to render the disembarkation more safe, he had previously ordered two tenders to attack a battery, which had been placed on a mount towards the right, and which was well situated for annoying the boats on their approach. The tenders succeeded in chasing the French from their guns; the boats reached the shore before any of the French could be opposite to them. The soldiers landed, to the number of about six hundred men, and formed in an instant; immediately upon which the whole militia dispersed and fled up into the country. The English followed them regularly and in good order; prognosticating success to the enterprise from such a fortunate beginning.

There was a creek, or arm of the sea, dry at low water, which lay on the right hand of the landing-place, and through which ran the nearest road to L'Orient, and the only one fit for the march of troops, or the draught of cannon and heavy carriages. As it was then high water, the French runaways were obliged, by this creek, to make a circuit of some miles; and they thereby misled the general, who, justly concluding they would take shelter in that town, and having no other guides to conduct him, thought that, by following their foot-steps, he would be led the readiest and shortest way to L'Orient. He detached, therefore, in pursuit of the flying militia, about a thousand men, under the command of Brigadier O'Farrel; who, after being harassed by some firing from the hedges, (by which Lieut.-Col. Erskine, Quarter-Master General, was dangerously wounded,) arrived that evening at Guidel, a village about a league distant from the landing-place. The general himself lay near the sea-shore, to wait for the landing of the rest of the forces. By break of day he led them up to join the brigadier at Guidel. He there learned from some peasants, taken prisoners, and who spoke the French language, (which few of the common people in Brittany are able to do,) that the road into which he had been led, by the reasons above specified, was the longest by four or five miles. He was also informed, what he had partly seen, that the road was very dangerous and difficult, running through narrow lanes and defiles, betwixt high hedges, faced with stone walls, and bordered in many places with thick woods and brushes, where a very few disciplined and brave troops might stop a whole army; and where even a few, without discipline or bravery, might, by firing suddenly upon the forces, throw them into confusion.

In order to acquire a more thorough knowledge of the country, of which he and the whole army were utterly ignorant, he here divided the troops into two equal bodies, and marched them up to L'Orient, by two different roads, which were pointed out to him. The one part, which he himself conducted, passed without much molestation. The other, under Brigadier O'Farrel, was not so fortunate. Two battalions of that detachment, Richbell's and Frampton's, partly from their want of experience, and partly from the terror naturally inspired into soldiers by finding themselves in a difficult country unknown both to themselves and leaders, and partly, perhaps, from accident, to which the courage of men is extremely liable, fell into confusion, before a handful of French peasants who fired at them from behind the hedges. Notwithstanding all the endeavours of the Brigadier, many of them threw down their arms and ran away; others fired in confusion, and wounded each other; and if any regular forces had been present to take advantage of this disorder, the most fatal consequences might have ensued. And though they were at last led on, and joined the general that evening before L'Orient, the panic still remained in these two battalions afterwards, and communicated itself to others; kept the whole army in anxiety, even when they were not in danger, and threw a mighty damp on the expectations of success, conceived from this undertaking. L'Orient, lately a small village, now a considerable town, on the coast of Brittany, lies in the extremity of a fine bay, the mouth of which is very narrow, and guarded by the strong citadel of Port Louis. This town has become the centre of the French East India trade, the seat of the company established for that commerce, and the magazine whence they distribute the East India commodities.

The great prizes made upon them by the English, during the course of the war, had given a check to this growing commerce; yet still the town was esteemed a valuable acquisition, were it only on account of the wealth it contained, and the store-houses of the company, a range of stately buildings, erected at public charge, both for use and ornament. The town itself is far from being strong. Two sides of it, which are not protected with water, are defended only with a plain wall, near thirty feet high, of no great thickness, and without any fosse or parapet. But the water which covers the other two sides, rendered it impossible to be invested, and gave an opportunity for multitudes of people to throw themselves into it from every corner of that populous country. And though these, for want of discipline, could not be trusted in the field against regular forces, yet became they of great use in a defence behind walls, by throwing up works, erecting batteries, and digging trenches, to secure (what was sufficient) for a few days, a weak town against a small and ill-provided army. The East India Company had numbers of cannon in their magazines, and had there erected a school of engineers, for the service of their ships and settlements; the vessels in the harbour supplied them with more cannon, and with seamen accustomed to their management and use; and whatever was wanting, either in artillery or warlike stores, could easily be brought by water from Port Louis, with which the town of L'Orient kept always an open communication.

But as these advantages, though great, require both a sufficient presence of mind, and some time, to be employed against an enemy, 'tis not improbable, that if the admiral had been supplied with proper pilots, and the general with proper guides, which could have led the English immediately upon the coast, and to the town, the very terror of so unexpected an invasion would have rendered the inhabitants incapable of resistance, and made them surrender at discretion. The want of these advantages had already lost two days; and more time must yet be consumed, before they could so much as make the appearance of an attack. Cannon was wanting, and the road by which the army had marched, was absolutely unfit for the conveyance of them. The general, therefore, having first despatched an officer and a party to reconnoitre the country, and find a nearer and better road, September 22d, went himself next day to the sea-shore, for the same purpose, and also in order to concert with the admiral the proper method of bringing up cannon ; as almost all the horses in the country, which are extremely weak and of a diminutive size, had been driven away by the peasants. Accordingly, a road was found, much nearer, though still ten miles of length ; and much better, though easily rendered impassable by rainy weather, as was afterwards experienced.

A council of war was held on board the Princessa, consisting of the admiral and general, Brigadier O'Farrel and Commodore Cotes. The engineers, Director-General Armstrong, and Captain Watson, who had surveyed the town of L'Orient, being called in, were asked their opinion with regard to the practicability of an attempt on it, together with the time, and artillery, and ammunition, requisite for that purpose. Their answer was, that with two twelve pounders and a ten inch mortar, planted on the spot which they had pitched on for erecting a battery, they engaged either to make a practicable breach in the walls, or with cartridges, bombs, and red-hot balls, destroy the town, by laying it in ashes in twenty-four hours. Captain Chalmers, the captain of the artillery, who had not then seen the town, was of the same opinion, from their description of it, provided the battery was within the proper distance. Had the king's orders been less positive for making an attempt on some part of the coast of France, yet such flattering views offered by men who promised what lay within the sphere of their own profession, must have engaged the attention of the admiral and general, and induced them to venture on a much more hazardous and difficult undertaking. 'Twas accordingly agreed that four twelve pounders, and a ten inch mortar, together with three field-pieces, should be drawn up to the camp by sailors, in order to make, with still greater assurance, the attempt, whose success seemed so certain to the engineers. These pieces of artillery, with the stores demanded, notwithstanding all difficulties, were drawn to the camp in two days, except two twelve pounders, which arrived not till the day afterwards. A third part of the sailors of the whole fleet, together with all the marines, were employed in this drudgery ; the admiral gave all assistance in his power to the general: and the public, in one instance, saw that it was not impossible for land and sea officers to live in harmony together, and concur in promoting the success of an enterprise.

The general, on his arrival in the camp, found the officer returned whom he had sent to summon the town of L'Orient. By his information, it appeared that the inhabitants were so much alarmed by the suddenness of this incursion, and the terror of a force which their fears magnified, as to think of surrendering, though upon conditions, which would have rendered the conquest of no avail to their enemies. The inhabitants insisted upon an absolute security to their houses and goods; the East India Company to their magazines and store-houses; and the garrison, consisting of about seven hundred regular militia and troops, besides a great number of irregulars, demanded a liberty of marching out with all the honours of war. A weak town that opened its gates on such conditions was not worth the entering; since it must immediately be abandoned, leaving only to its conquerors the shame of their own folly, and perhaps the reproach of treachery. The general, therefore, partly trusting to the promise of the engineers, and partly desirous of improving the advantages gained by the present danger, when the deputies arrived next day, September 23d, from the governor, from the town, and from the East India Company, refused to receive any articles but those from the governor, who commanded in the name of his most Christian majesty. He even refused liberty to the garrison to march out; well knowing that, as the town was not invested, they could take that liberty whenever they pleased.

Meanwhile, every accident concurred to render the enterprise of the English abortive. Some deserters got into the town, who informed the garrison of the true force of the English, which, conjecturing from the greatness and number of the ships, they had much magnified. Even this small body diminished daily, from the fatigue of excessive duty, and from the great rains that began to fall. Scarce three thousand were left to do duty, which still augmented the fatigue to the few that remained; especially when joined to the frequent alarms, that the unaccountable panic they were struck with made but too frequent. Rains had so spoilt the roads as to render it impracticable to bring up any heavier cannon, or more of the same calibre, so long a way, by the mere force of seamen. But what, above all things, made the enterprise appear desperate, was the discovery of the ignorance of the engineers, chiefly of the director-general, who in the

whole course of his proceedings appeared neither to have
skill in contrivance, nor order and diligence in execution.
His own want of capacity and experience, made his projects
of no use; his blind obstinacy rendered him incapable of
making use of the capacity of others. Though the general
offered to place and support the battery wherever the en-
gineer thought proper, he chose to set it above six hundred
yards from the wall, where such small cannon could do no
manner of execution. He planted it at so oblique an angle
to the wall that the ball thrown from the largest cannon
must have recoiled, without making any impression. He
trusted much to the red-hot balls, with which he promised
to lay the town in ashes in twenty-four hours; yet, by his
negligence, or that of others, the furnace with which these
balls were to be heated, was forgot. After the furnace was
brought, he found that the bellows, and other implements
necessary for the execution of that work, were also left on
board the store-ships. With great difficulty, and infinite
pains, ammunition and artillery stores were drawn up from
the sea-shore in tumbrels. He was totally ignorant, till some
days after, that he had along with him ammunition wagons,
which would have much facilitated this labour. His orders
to the officers of the train were so confused, or so ill obeyed,
that no ammunition came regularly up to the camp, to serve
the few cannon and the mortars that played upon the town.
Not only fascines, piquets, and every thing necessary for the
battery, were supplied him beyond his demand; but even
workmen, notwithstanding the great fatigue and small numbers of the army. These workmen found no addition to their
fatigue in obeying his orders. He left them often unem-
ployed, for want of knowing in what business he should
occupy them.

Meanwhile the French garrison, being so weakly attacked,
had leisure to prepare for a defence, and make proper use of
their great number of workmen, if not of soldiers, and the
nearness and plenty of their military stores. By throwing
up earth in the inside of the wall, they had planted a great
many cannon, some of a large calibre, and opened six batteries against one that played upon them from the English.
The distance alone of the besiegers' battery, made these
cannon of the enemy do less execution; but that same distance rendered the attack absolutely ineffectual. Were the

battery brought nearer, to a hundred paces for instance, 'twould be requisite to make it communicate with the camp by trenches and a covered way, to dig which was the work of some days for so small an army. During this time, the besieged, foreseeing the place to which the attack must be directed, could easily fortify it by retrenchments in the inside of the wall; and planting ten cannon to one, could silence the besiegers' feeble battery in a few hours. They would not even have had leisure to make a breach in the thin wall, which first discovered itself; and that breach, if made, could not possibly serve to any purpose. Above fifteen thousand men, completely armed by the East India Company, and brave while protected by cannon and ramparts, still stood in opposition to three thousand, discouraged with fatigue, with sickness, and with despair of ever succeeding in so unequal a contest.

A certain foreign writer, more anxious to tell his stories in an entertaining manner than to assure himself of their reality, has endeavoured to put this expedition in a ridiculous light; but as there is not one circumstance of his narration, which has truth in it, or even the least appearance of truth, it would be needless to lose time in refuting it.[1] With regard to the prejudices of the public, a few questions may suffice.

Was the attempt altogether impracticable from the beginning? The general neither proposed it, nor planned it, nor approved it, nor answered for its success. Did the disappointment proceed from want of expedition? He had no pilots, guides, nor intelligence, afforded him; and could not possibly provide himself in any of these advantages, so necessary to all military operations. Were the engineers blamable? This has always been considered as a branch of military knowledge, distinct from that of a commander, and which is altogether intrusted to those to whose profession it peculiarly belongs. By his vigour in combating the vain terrors spread amongst the troops, and by his prudence in timely desisting from a fruitless enterprise, the misfortune was confined merely to a disappointment, without any loss or any dishonour to the British arms. Commanders, from

---

[1] [Mr. Burton proves from a passage in Hume's Correspondence that the reference is to Voltaire, although no such narration is found among Voltaire's acknowledged works. Life: vol. ii. p. 219. Ed.]

the situation of affairs, have had opportunities of acquiring
more honour; yet there is no one whose conduct, in every
circumstance, could be more free from reproach. On the
first of October, the fleet sailed out of Quimperlay Road,
from one of the most dangerous situations that so large a
fleet had ever lain in, at so late a season, and in so stormy
a sea as the Bay of Biscay. The reflection on this danger
had been no inconsiderable cause of hastening the re-em-
barkation of the troops. And the more so, that the secretary had given express orders to the admiral not to bring the
fleet into any hazard. The prudence of the hasty departure
appeared the more visibly the very day the fleet sailed, when
a violent storm arising from the south west, it was concluded,
that if the ships had been lying at anchor on the coast, many
of them must have necessarily been driven ashore, and
wrecked on the rocks that surrounded them. The fleet was
dispersed, and six transports being separated from the rest,
went immediately for England, carrying with them about
eight hundred of the forces. The rest put into Quiberon
Bay, and the general landed his small body on the peninsula
of that name. By erecting a battery of some guns on the
narrow neck of land, which joins the peninsula to the continent, he rendered his situation almost impregnable, while
he saw the fleet riding secure in his neighbourhood, in one
of the finest bays in the world.

The industry and spirit of the general supported both
himself and the army against all these disadvantages, while
there was the smallest prospect of success. But his prudence determined him to abandon it, when it appeared
altogether desperate.

The engineers, seeing no manner of effect from their shells
and red-hot balls, and sensible that 'twas impossible either
to make a breach from a battery, erected at so great a distance, or to place the battery nearer, under such a superiority
of French cannon, at last unanimously brought a report to
the general, that they had no longer any hope of success;
and that even all the ammunition, which, with infinite
labour, had been brought, was expended: no prospect remained of being farther supplied, on account of the broken
roads, which lay between them and the fleet. The council
of war held in consequence of this report, balanced the
reasons for continuing or abandoning the enterprise, if men

can be said to balance where they find nothing on the one
side but an extreme desire to serve their king and country,
and on the other every maxim of war and prudence.   They
unanimously agreed to abandon the attempt, and return on
board the transports.   The whole troops were accordingly
re-embarked by the 28th of September, with the loss of near
twenty men killed and wounded, on the whole enterprise.

SCOTTICISMS.[1]

Will, in the first person, as *I will walk, we will walk*, expresses the intention or resolution of the person, along with the future event : In the second and third person, as, *you will, he will, they will*, it expresses the future action or event, without comprehending or excluding the volition.

Shall, in the first person, whether singular or plural, expresses the future action or event, without excluding or comprehending the intention or resolution : But in the *second* or *third* person, it marks a necessity, and commonly a necessity proceeding from the person who speaks; as, *he shall walk, you shall repent it*.

These variations seem to have proceeded from a politeness in the *English*, who, in speaking to others, or of others, made use of the term *will*, which implies volition, even where the event may be the subject of necessity and constraint. And in speaking of themselves, made use of the term *shall*, which implies constraint, even though the event may be the object of choice.

Wou'd and *shou'd* are conjunctive moods, subject to the same rule ; only, we may observe, that in a sentence, where there is a condition exprest, and a consequence of that condition, the former always requires *shou'd*, and the latter *wou'd*, in the second and third persons ; as, *if he shou'd fall, he wou'd break his leg*, etc.

These is the plural of *this ; those* of *that*. The former,

---

[1] [This *List of Scotticisms*, printed from the Edinburgh Edition of 1826, is said to occur in some copies of the 'Political Discourses.' Edition II. The present Editor has not found it in any Edition publ'shed during Hume's lifetime,—"I told him that David Hume had made a short collection of Scotticisms. 'I wonder (said *Johnson*) that he should find them.'"—BOSWELL.]

therefore, expresses what is near: the latter what is more remote. As, in these lines of the Duke of Buckingham,

> " Philosophers and poets vainly strove,
>   In every age, the lumpish mass to move.
>   But THOSE were pedants if compared with THESE
>   Who know not only to instruct, but please."

Where a relative is to follow, and the subject has not been mentioned immediately before, *those* is always required. *Those observations which he made. Those kingdoms which Alexander conquered.*

In the verbs, which end in *t*, or *te*, we frequently omit *ed* in the preterperfect and in the participle; as, *he operate, it was cultivate. Milton* says, *in thought more elevate*: but he is the only author who uses that expression.

Notice should not be used as a verb. The proper phrase is *take notice.* Yet I find Lord Shaftesbury uses *notic'd*, the participle: And *unnotic'd* is very common.

Hinder to do, is Scotch. The *English* phrase is, *hinder from doing.* Yet Milton says, *Hindered not Satan to pervert the mind.* Book IX.

SCOTCH.	ENGLISH.
Conform to	Conformable to
Friends and acquaintances	Friends and acquaintance
Maltreat	Abuse
Advert to	Attend to
Proven, improven, approver.	Prov'd, improv'd, approv'd
Pled	Pleaded
Incarcerate	Imprison
Tear to pieces	Tear in pieces
Drunk, run	Drank, ran
Fresh weather	Open weather
Tender	Sickly
In the long run	At long run
Notwithstanding of that	Notwithstanding that
Contented himself to do	Contented himself with doing
'Tis a question if	'Tis a question whether
Discretion	Civility
With child to a man	With child by a man
Out of hand	Presently
Simply impossible	Absolutely impossible
A park	An enclosure
In time coming	In time to come

SCOTCH.	ENGLISH.
Nothing else	No other thing
Mind it	Remember it
Denuded	Divested
Severals	Several
Some better	Something better
Anent	With regard to
Allenarly	Solely
Alongst. Yet the *English* say both amid, amidst, among, and amongst	Along
Evenly	Even
As I shall answer	I protest or declare
Cause him do it. Yet 'tis good *English* to say, make him do it	Cause him to do it
Marry upon	Marry to
Learn	Teach
There, where	Thither, whither
Effectuate. This word in *English* means to effect with pains and difficulty	Effect
A wright. Yet 'tis good *English* to say a wheelwright	A Carpenter
Defunct	Deceast
Evite	Avoid
Part with child	Miscarry
Notour	Notorious
To want it	To be without a thing, even though it be not desirable
To be difficulted	To be puzzled
Rebuted	Discouraged by repulses
For ordinary	Usually
Think shame	Asham'd
In favours of	In favour of
Dubiety	Doubtfulness
Prejudge	Hurt
Compete	Enter into competition
Heritable	Hereditary
To remeed	To remedy
Bankier	Banker
Adduce a proof	Produce a proof
Superplus	Surplus
Forfaulture	Forfeiture
In no event	In no case
Common soldiers	Private men
Big with a man	Great with a man

SCOTCH.	ENGLISH.
Bygone	Past
Debitor	Debtor
Exeemed	Exempted
Yesternight	Last night
Big coat	Great coat
A chimney	A grate
Annualrent	Interest
Tenible argument	Good argument
Amissing	Missing
To condescend upon	To specify
To discharge	To forbid
To extinguish an obligation	To cancel an obligation
To depone	To depose
A compliment	A present
To inquire at a man	To inquire of a man
To be angry at a man	To be angry with a man
To send an errand	To send off an errand
To furnish goods to him	To furnish him with goods
To open up	To open, or lay open
Thucydide, Herodot, Sueton	*Thucydides, Herodotus, Suetonius*
Butter and bread	Bread and butter
Pepper and vinegar	Vinegar and pepper
Paper, pen, and ink	Pen, ink, and paper
Readily	Probably
On a sudden	Of a sudden
As ever I saw	As I ever saw
For my share	For my part
Misgive	Fail
Rather chuse to buy as sell	Rather chuse to buy than sell
Deduce	Deduct
Look't over the window	Look't out at the window
A pretty enough girl	A pretty girl enough
'Tis a week since he left this	'Tis a week since he left this place
Come in to the fire	Come near the fire
To take off a new coat	To make up a new suit
Alwise	Always
Cut out his hair	Cut off his hair
Cry him	Call him
To crave	To dun, to ask payment
To get a stomach	To get an appetite
Vacance	Vacation

INDEX

TO

THE FOURTH VOLUME.

f. means 'and following pages.'

THE

PHILOSOPHICAL WORKS

OF

DAVID HUME

VOL. IV.

THE

PHILOSOPHICAL WORKS

OF

DAVID HUME

EDITED BY

T. H. GREEN AND T. H. GROSE

LATE FELLOW AND TUTOR OF BALLIOL
COLLEGE, OXFORD

FELLOW AND TUTOR OF QUEEN'S
COLLEGE, OXFORD

IN FOUR VOLUMES
VOL. IV.

NEW IMPRESSION

LONGMANS, GREEN, AND CO.
39 PATERNOSTER ROW, LONDON
NEW YORK AND BOMBAY
1898

www.ingramcontent.com/pod-product-compliance
Lightning Source LLC
Chambersburg PA
CBHW052343110726
47901CB00005B/1336